.

Education for
DEMOCRACY

Education for
DEMOCRACY

Renewing the Wisconsin Idea

Edited by Chad Alan Goldberg

THE UNIVERSITY OF WISCONSIN PRESS

Publication of this book has been made possible, in part,
through support from the Anonymous Fund of the College of Letters and
Science at the University of Wisconsin–Madison.

The University of Wisconsin Press
728 State Street, Suite 443
Madison, Wisconsin 53706
uwpress.wisc.edu

Gray's Inn House, 127 Clerkenwell Road
London ECIR 5DB, United Kingdom
eurospanbookstore.com

Printed in the United States of America
This book may be available in a digital edition.

Library of Congress Cataloging-in-Publication Data
Names: Goldberg, Chad Alan, editor.
Title: Education for democracy : renewing the Wisconsin Idea /
edited by Chad Alan Goldberg.
Description: Madison, Wisconsin : The University of Wisconsin Press, [2020] |
Includes bibliographical references and index.
Identifiers: LCCN 2020013484 | ISBN 9780299328900 (cloth)
Subjects: LCSH: University of Wisconsin--History. | University of Wisconsin—
Madison—History. | University of Wisconsin System—History. |
Democracy and education—Wisconsin. | State universities and colleges—
Wisconsin. | Community and college—Wisconsin.
Classification: LCC LA388.5 .E38 2020 | DDC 370.9775/83—dc23
LC record available at https://lccn.loc.gov/2020013484

The prophetic spirit does not succeed in giving the
reality of its hour what it wills to give it. But it instils the vision
in the people for all time to come.

—MARTIN BUBER

Contents

Acknowledgments

I owe a special thanks to Gwen Walker, former executive editor at the University of Wisconsin Press, who invited me in October 2017 to undertake a new book on the Wisconsin Idea. I am grateful to her successor, Nathan MacBrien, for shepherding the project to its completion. I am also grateful to the manuscript's reviewers for their constructive comments and helpful suggestions. Anna Muenchrath, Jacqulyn Teoh, Jennifer Conn, Scott Mueller, Adam Mehring, and Twin Oaks Indexing helped to turn the manuscript into the book that is now before you. Support for this scholarship was generously provided by the University of Wisconsin–Madison Office of the Provost and the Office of the Vice Chancellor for Research and Graduate Education with funding from the Wisconsin Alumni Research Foundation.

The book is based upon a highly successful outreach course on the Wisconsin Idea that was inaugurated at the University of Wisconsin–Madison in 2016. More than anyone else, Patrick J. Brenzel is responsible for conceiving, developing, and implementing that course. Therefore he also deserves special thanks. Patrick first floated the idea for the course at a strategic planning meeting of the university's sociology department in 2015. The Wisconsin Idea, he pointed out, was at risk. Why not address the issues fearlessly, he asked, and open the conversation to everyone? As Patrick himself put it in a memorandum he circulated soon after the meeting, "A course of this type would boost the public perception of all departments involved and of the entire University community," it would boost the morale of the university's staff and faculty after political developments had severely undercut it, and it would deepen the pride of alumni in their alma mater. It has been a personal and professional pleasure to work with him and others in the development of the course. While many colleagues were involved, I would especially like to thank Eric Sandgren, Thomas O'Guinn, and Cora Bagley Marrett, who each taught and led the course from 2017 to 2019. A key component of the course was a public lecture series, free and open to the community, in which leading scholars and community leaders who exemplify the Wisconsin Idea were invited to participate. All the contributors to this volume took part in that public lecture series between 2016 and 2018, and I am grateful for their contributions. I am grateful as well to the students and auditors who participated in the course, whose contributions also stimulated my thinking about the Wisconsin Idea and its significance.

Emily Auerbach's chapter, "The Power to Change Lives: The UW Odyssey Project," includes material originally published in *Mapping the Field of Adult and Continuing Education: An International Compendium*, vol. 1, *Adult Learners*, edited by Alan B. Knox, Simone C. O. Conceição, and Larry G. Martin (Sterling, VA: Stylus, 2017). I thank Stylus Publishing, LLC, for permission to reproduce this material here.

Katherine J. Cramer's chapter, "The Turn Away from Government and the Need to Revive the Civic Purpose of Higher Education," was previously published in *Perspectives on Politics* 14, no. 2 (June 2016). I thank Cambridge University Press for permission to reproduce this material here.

I thank the staff of University Archives and Records Management at the University of Wisconsin–Madison, particularly digital and media archivist Catherine H. Phan; Jack Berndt, manager of the Tripp Heritage Museum / Sauk Prairie Area Historical Society; and Cassie Mordini, communications and marketing coordinator of the Aldo Leopold Foundation, for their assistance in tracking down historical sources. The Aldo Leopold Foundation kindly provided permission to include the images in Curt Meine's chapter, "The Crucible of Conservation."

I am grateful to my colleague Alfonso Morales for his helpful advice about how to produce an edited volume.

My spouse and colleague, Dr. Anna Paretskaya, took the time to carefully read and helpfully comment on my introductory chapter. I am grateful for her encouragement and advice.

I deeply appreciate the friends and colleagues throughout the University of Wisconsin System, many of them fellow members of the American Association of University Professors and/or union brothers and sisters in the American Federation of Teachers, who continue to defend the Wisconsin Idea in the face of powerful forces bent on undermining it. They understand how deeply consonant the Wisconsin Idea is with the old motto of the American Federation of Teachers: education for democracy, and democracy in education. It is an honor to fight alongside them.

Preface

In February 2015, former Wisconsin governor Scott Walker released a state budget that struck the Wisconsin Idea from the mission of the University of Wisconsin. I doubt that this was Walker's doing. I doubt that Walker even knew
what the Wisconsin Idea was but rather acted as a pawn to financial supporters
in attempting to strip the ideas of public service, the fearless search for truth,
and the creation of a learned citizenship that is equipped to self-govern. And
in all honesty, I forgive the citizens themselves for having forgotten what the
Wisconsin Idea was and how Wisconsin was considered groundbreaking in
its efforts to bring cutting-edge knowledge to the people of the state in every
field. History is so easily forgotten. Fortunately, a critical number of educators
and alumni remembered, and the references to the Wisconsin Idea were returned to the budget. It is OK if *you* don't know what the Wisconsin Idea is.
Hopefully the stories contained here will help you.

It bothers me to see knowledge and truth politicized. For years, the University
of Wisconsin has been flogged by the state legislature and the former governor
to undermine the public perception of higher education, those who attend it,
and any knowledge it produces—at least the knowledge that can't be monetized
by corporations. Budgets have been slashed, tenure stripped, and the academic
freedom to pursue a once noble research agenda has been threatened.

I attended the University of Wisconsin starting in 1982 and graduated with
a degree in mechanical engineering. My time at the university was life-changing.
While the University of Wisconsin has no monopoly on a great higher education experience, please count me among those alums who are eternally grateful
for the experience of having been here. I have always had food on my table,
clothes on my back, and a roof over my head. But something on this campus,
the spirit of this place, is transcendent. And my feeling of obligation and
honor in giving back has been a guiding force for me as it was for my father
who attended the university in the 1950s. This place is responsible.

Distressed by the shift in public perception toward education and the University of Wisconsin, I talked my department, the Department of Sociology at the University of Wisconsin–Madison, into teaching a new course on the Wisconsin Idea and coupling this with a public lecture series. With guest speakers from across the campus and the community, this is an opportunity to discuss what the Wisconsin Idea has been in the past, how it survives today, and what we hope it will be. Yes, that's correct—I am a mechanical engineer who works in a sociology department for far less than I would make in the private sector because working for a university is a noble thing to do.

The mindset known as the Wisconsin Idea grew from a seed planted by John Bascom's short tenure as president of the University of Wisconsin from 1874 to 1887; it would become the foundation for Social Security, public broadcasting, workmen's compensation insurance, and a host of other labor laws, environmental regulations, and so many other great things. Among those great things was a Wisconsin legislative session in 1911 during which a thousand laws were passed—good laws, transparent laws, laws that benefited the common citizen and gave them the tools to self-govern. And the University of Wisconsin played a critical role. This book tells some of those unique and inspiring stories.

On the heels of that record-breaking legislative session over a hundred years ago, inquiries came in from around the country to one Charles McCarthy, head of Wisconsin's innovative Legislative Reference Library. They were the ones who made it all happen. "How did you do it?" "What's your secret?" As there was no easy way to answer all of the inquiries, McCarthy wrote a book, published in 1912, called *The Wisconsin Idea*.

When I was an undergraduate, I was taught all of the pithy one-liners that defined the Wisconsin Idea: "the boundaries of the university are the boundaries of the state"; "that continual and fearless sifting and winnowing by which alone the truth can be found"; "I will not be content until the beneficent influence of the University of Wisconsin touches every family in the state." But the legacy of the Wisconsin Idea is far richer and more complex than what we can tease out of a simple comment. This was made obvious when I spoke in 2018 to a room full of academic advisors and student peer advisors on the University of Wisconsin–Madison campus in an effort to promote an undergraduate course on the Wisconsin Idea that I had envisioned two years earlier. As I write this, we are going into our fourth year of teaching this class coupled with a public lecture series. The ongoing need to recover the legacy of the Wisconsin Idea is clear. In a room of two hundred people, only one person was aware that a book was written bearing the phrase that would henceforth express the way in which we do business. To say that Wisconsin was known nationally for transparent and egalitarian government is an understatement. That its public university could serve as a partner in making that happen was unheard of. From where I stood in the university's Science Hall speaking to campus advisors and student peer advisors, I could see its historic Radio Hall. That handsome little sandstone building marks the birthplace of the first public radio broadcast. On any warm day, crowds of prospective students and their parents pass Radio Hall with a campus tour guide clad in a red polo shirt, who shares with them the story of that first radio broadcast and explains that the University of Wisconsin campus houses the longest continually running radio station in the world. Impressive, no doubt, is the technological feat that allowed this to take place: engineering students building those earliest vacuum tubes from scratch over and over until they got it right. But what gets lost in their story is the *vision* that gripped those earliest University of Wisconsin faculty—the vision to democratize information that sits in the hands of the "experts" and put it in the hands of citizens.

This movement of information from teacher to student is the primary goal of any college or university. But at Wisconsin, John Bascom's earliest expression of the Wisconsin Idea was almost sacramental. The honor bestowed upon any of us as college graduates obligates us to share our expertise with the world not for personal enrichment but for the sake of making the world a better place. And the role of experts is not to talk constantly—they must also listen. Fixing what might be wrong with the world around us means listening to those who are closest to the problems in order to truly understand them. Wisconsin's partnership among citizens, state government, and its public university was groundbreaking. Make no mistake: What happened in Wisconsin was special and quickly became a source of inspiration throughout the United States.

As you read the chapters that follow, I hope you focus less on the fact that Wisconsin was "first" in so many things. As we are naturally competitive, we approach too many things as if they are a race or a contest. I hope you focus instead on the *vision* of those earliest torchbearers of the Wisconsin Idea and their successors today. Victory is found *not* in being first to reach definitive conclusions from research but in envisioning how to apply knowledge for the sake of the people in ways that are innovative, collaborative, and broadly beneficial.

I am disheartened by contemporary efforts to dismantle the Wisconsin Idea. While public outcry prevented the effort in 2015 to strike the Wisconsin Idea from the mission statement of the University of Wisconsin System, efforts are now underway to create a "New Wisconsin Idea." With claims that universities are no longer the sole holders of knowledge, and with no mention of empowering citizens so that they may work co-operatively and self-govern, the "New Wisconsin Idea" hardly resembles the old one. I suggest you not fall for it. This wolf in sheep's clothing is merely another attempt to undermine both the efforts of those who have committed their lives to developing expertise and the pathways that allow that expertise to be shared, debated publicly, and discussed in open forums. There are real attacks on the Wisconsin Idea, and the attacks bear a strong resemblance to the attacks we underwent as a state over a hundred years ago. We enjoyed decades of prosperity following the creation of the Wisconsin Idea, but the jury is out on our future.

When things are broken, there are certainly many ways we can go about repairing them. Reigniting the Wisconsin Idea in a way that addresses our twenty-first-century problems is only one approach, and you will likely have your own ideas about how that might be accomplished. But as you read the chapters in this book, I urge you to keep these thoughts in mind: Always be open to learning new things and refining your idea of "truth." Reach across the table and shake the hand of someone who is not exactly like you. And recognize your own true value—it is found not so much in your bank accounts as in your ability to empower others to elevate themselves above hard times. John Bascom would be proud of you.

Education for

DEMOCRACY

Introduction

The University's Service to Democracy

CHAD ALAN GOLDBERG

What is the role of the public university in a democratic society? Even those who work and study at public universities rarely pause to reflect on this question. We are too busy, and many of us assume we know the answer already. Faculty and research staff may say that the role of the public university is to support systematic inquiry that will advance the frontiers of knowledge. Students and instructional staff may say it is to educate students. But what kind of knowledge, what kind of education, and why should the public pay for and support either of these activities? This book is about one conception of the public university's role in a democratic society. This conception, which came to be known as the Wisconsin Idea, emerged in a particular time and place but has more general relevance because the problems it addressed are confined neither to Wisconsin nor to the past; it is a conception that has changed and developed since its beginning but has remained tied to the core principle of service to democracy; and it is a conception that has been severely undermined in the twenty-first century by forces hostile to it but for that very reason is more timely than ever.

WHAT IS THE WISCONSIN IDEA?

Jack Stark, an English professor at the University of Wisconsin–Eau Claire who later became a lawyer in the Wisconsin Legislative Reference Bureau, usefully distinguished two ways of defining the Wisconsin Idea: a narrow definition that emphasizes "the University's service to the state" and a broader definition that emphasizes the Wisconsin Idea's "political dimension."[1] In an article written in the mid-1990s for the *Wisconsin Blue Book*, an almanac published biennially by the Legislative Reference Bureau, Stark opted for the narrower definition. My own elucidation of the Wisconsin Idea begins with this narrow definition, but as I will argue below, it cannot be so easily and neatly separated from the Wisconsin Idea's broader political dimension.

As a preliminary definition, the Wisconsin Idea refers to the responsibility of the University of Wisconsin to serve the needs of the state and its people.[2] This is the meaning of the slogan that the boundaries of the university are the boundaries of the state. Public service is the reason for the state university's existence, which makes it a "universal institution" in the sense that it has a responsibility to promote the general or public interest.[3] Historian J. David Hoeveler has traced the core of this idea to John Bascom, president of the University of Wisconsin from 1874 to 1887, who emphasized that public education created a reciprocal obligation of public service. "Bascom urged from the graduates of the state university a large loyalty to the state and a life of service to the state by those who had benefited from the state's sponsorship of their education. . . . The state university graduates, as he foresaw their role, would function almost like a new force, a fourth estate in the state's public life."[4] Moreover, for Bascom, it was the *kind* of education that university graduates received that prepared them to play this role as an "intellectual elite" or "intellectual vanguard": not narrowly utilitarian training to "fuel the engines of industrial growth," but "free and full" education in the humanities and social sciences (including sociology, which Bascom taught) to provide the "wide, inclusive vision of life and society" that "the social organism needs for its means of adaptation and survival." Envisioning a leading role for these "educational men" in public affairs, Bascom stressed that they must dedicate themselves to more than their own advancement. "You have no right to seek your own weal," he insisted in an 1877 baccalaureate sermon, "if your own weal does not include the public weal."[5]

From this early notion of the university as a preparatory school for a new, educated service elite, a more complex conception of the university's public-service role eventually developed. This conception came to include three main elements. The first element is the contribution that the university's faculty have made to the state government by serving on administrative commissions or in other public offices or by providing knowledge, expertise, and policy advice to elected officials.[6] This aspect of the university's service was exemplified by the Saturday lunches at which Robert M. "Fighting Bob" La Follette Sr., the reformist governor of Wisconsin from 1901 to 1906, discussed the issues of the day with university professors.[7] Adlai Stevenson, the Democratic Party's nominee for US president in 1952, later summarized this element in a speech delivered in Madison, Wisconsin, during his election campaign. "The Wisconsin tradition," Stevenson declared, "meant more than a simple belief in the people. It also meant a faith in the application of intelligence and reason to the problems of society. It meant a deep conviction that the role of government was not to stumble along like a drunkard in the dark, but to light its way by the best torches of knowledge and understanding it could find."[8]

The second element of the university's public service is the contributions it has made directly to the people of Wisconsin by helping to solve problems that are important to them or by conducting outreach activities.[9] Along these lines, Hoeveler refers to "the value to the state that would come from the research of the university's faculty," such as the application of the new knowledge they produced to agriculture and industry.[10] This application, it is important to note, had broader social ends than facilitating private profit. As University of Wisconsin president (1887–92) Thomas Chamberlin put it, agricultural research aimed not only to benefit the farmer but to "furnish better and safer food to every citizen." Professor Stephen Babcock's famous butterfat test was a case in point; it discouraged dairy farmers from diluting their milk with water and instead incentivized them to improve its quality.[11] This aspect of the university's public service implicitly rejects the notion of knowledge for its own sake. Knowledge must instead be socially useful in some way; it is ultimately produced to benefit the public. Alongside its socially useful research, the university's outreach activities were exemplified by the work of its Extension Division (also called General Extension) and Cooperative Extension service, which were established respectively in 1907 and 1914.[12] These outreach activities imply an expansive vision of the university's mission: rather than limit itself to professional training for Bascom's intellectual vanguard, a public university must also provide continuing education for adult citizens. As Charles R. Van Hise, president of the University of Wisconsin from 1903 to 1918, put it in a report to the university's regents, "A very large fraction of the work of the University is done not for the students who are here, but for the two and one-half millions of people of the state."[13] The University of Wisconsin has accomplished this outreach work in a variety of ways, from correspondence classes and public lectures to pioneering use of radio and later television for educational purposes.[14] In these ways, the university promotes the formation of an educated democratic public and the active participation of its members in cooperative problem solving.

The third element of the university's public service is a strong commitment to academic freedom and the pursuit of truth, which is essential for effective social inquiry into common problems.[15] The Board of Regents famously affirmed this commitment in 1894 after University of Wisconsin economics professor Richard T. Ely came under attack for promoting socialism and trade unionism. "Whatever may be the limitations which trammel inquiry elsewhere," the regents declared, "we believe the great state University of Wisconsin should ever encourage that continual and fearless sifting and winnowing by which alone the truth can be found."[16] It is worth recalling that two other key figures in the development of the Wisconsin Idea, economist John R. Commons and sociologist Edward A. Ross, had "lost their academic positions in celebrated academic freedom cases between 1894 and 1900," and Ely himself later served on the committee that produced the landmark Declaration of Principles on Academic Freedom and Academic Tenure issued by the newly formed American Association of University Professors in 1915.[17] Academic freedom and the closely related notions of tenure and faculty self-governance developed in the early twentieth century in conjunction with the increasing professionalization of American faculty, their growing orientation to research and involvement in public policy debates, and their claims to expertise. Tenure and an increased role for faculty in university governance gave faculty the freedom they needed to challenge conventional wisdom, test controversial ideas, and question university administrators on issues of curriculum and quality without fear of reprisal.[18] Academic freedom, in turn, was not a privilege but a necessary prerequisite for faculty to carry out their professional responsibilities.[19] Hence, the Wisconsin Idea and the notion of academic freedom did not merely develop in tandem; the university's commitment to academic freedom is an essential component of the Wisconsin Idea because faculty cannot fulfill their service mission without it.

Of course, as noted by Gwen Drury, a scholar who has written and spoken extensively about the Wisconsin Idea, "the University of Wisconsin shared a similar [public-service] mission with other state universities."[20] What distinguished the University of Wisconsin, she argues, is not so much its publicservice mission as the manner in which this mission was understood and practiced. Drury emphasizes in particular the democratic conception of this mission: "'Service' was often a reflection of 'noblesse oblige' at many private universities, while at Wisconsin it was expressly egalitarian and democratic."[21] This is an important point. As historian Frederick Jackson Turner put it, public service at the University of Wisconsin was understood to mean "service to democracy," and all of the university's work fell under this ideal.[22] The architects of the Wisconsin Idea, Drury explains, wanted to "make sure that conditions in the state . . . did not allow a shift of power away from the broadest number of citizens and toward a limited group of powerful, monied people." Instead, they sought to create conditions in which "all citizens would be prepared, and feel confident in their ability, to fully participate in a true democracy and a prosperous economy."[23] They sought to realize this aspiration in two ways: first, by furnishing citizens with knowledge, information, and education, which they "could use to make their own decisions and govern themselves most effectively"; and second, by fostering "broad and deep social connections" among the citizenry.[24] A notable example of the latter effort was the Civic and Social Center Bureau, an extension program founded in 1910 and directed by political activist Edward Ward (described by one of his contemporaries as an "enthusiastic apostle of democracy") to "help develop the civic, social and recreational resources of municipalities."[25]

We thus arrive at a fuller definition of the Wisconsin Idea: it refers to the historic mission of the University of Wisconsin to serve democracy, in part by sharing expert knowledge with state government to inform and improve public policy, and in part by research and outreach activities to enrich the lives and promote the well-being of the people, all of which requires a robust commitment to academic freedom. While this is an improvement on our preliminary definition, an emphasis on the university's role as public servant is ultimately too circumscribed. To begin with, ideas must have influential social carriers to become efficacious, and university professors and administrators were only one of several groups that provided the impetus for the Wisconsin Idea in the early twentieth century. They formed part of a broader "reformist coalition" that also included "dedicated and innovative civil servants" led by University of Wisconsin graduate and political reformer Charles McCarthy, who established the state's Legislative Reference Library (later Bureau) in 1901; political advocates of a cooperative commonwealth, most notably urban socialists in Milwaukee and militant farm organizations like the Wisconsin Society of Equity; and a group of progressive Republican politicians, headed by La Follette (governor of Wisconsin from 1901 to 1906) and Francis E. McGovern (governor of Wisconsin from 1911 to 1915).[26] Moreover, the university was only one of three institutional "pillars" of the Wisconsin Idea. As historian John Buenker points out, the other two pillars on which the Wisconsin Idea rested were McCarthy's Legislative Reference Library, which political conservatives assailed as a "progressive bill factory," and several quasi-independent administrative commissions created between 1899 and 1914, which were supposed to provide nonpartisan, scientific, expert regulation.[27] Together with the University of Wisconsin, these were the structural positions from which the advocates of the Wisconsin Idea sought to realize their vision. Finally, an emphasis on the university's role as public servant is too limited because that role presupposed and implied a broader set of philosophical and ideological tenets.

To clarify the tacit assumptions and implications of the Wisconsin Idea, it is necessary to situate it in the historical context in which it was originally produced, and especially in relation to the social forces and ideas against which it was directed. Buenker places the Wisconsin Idea in the context of American progressivism, a congeries of reform movements that arose in the first two decades of the twentieth century in response to the problems created by rapid industrialization and urbanization after the US Civil War. Prominent among these problems was an unprecedented concentration of economic wealth and power in American society. In Wisconsin and elsewhere, progressive reformers opposed the growth of large, monopolistic corporations they called "trusts," which they blamed for most of the nation's social problems, as well as the corruption of politics by business interests. To combat these threats, reformers adopted two related strategies: "The first was to expand the size, scope, and authority of government at all levels, so that it might intervene in the socio-economic order on behalf of those who were demanding protection against corporate excesses." The second strategy was "the reconstruction and purification of politics and government, in order to curb the pernicious influence of 'special interests' by granting 'power to the people' and promoting honest, cost-effective government by apolitical experts."[28] These strategies were articulated in several related though not entirely coherent idioms: a language of antimonopolism, which in Wisconsin was directed against "'the special interests,' meaning railroads, lumber barons, public utilities, and manufacturers"; a language of social bonds, which explicitly rejected "classical economics, limited government, and rugged individualism"; and a language of social efficiency, which joined "social science expertise to industrial scientific management."[29] All three of these idioms were present in the Wisconsin Idea as it was formulated in the early twentieth century.

From this perspective, it is possible to outline the broader, political dimension of the Wisconsin Idea. Most importantly, the Wisconsin Idea presupposes and implies what Buenker calls a commonwealth model of society. Drawing on the language of social bonds, this model posits a definable public interest or collective good that is "greater than the sum of individual or private interests, that transcends all of these particular concerns, and that can best be achieved through enlightened cooperation fostered by public institutions." In this model, politics is a "public activity animated by a shared commitment to advance the common good." Buenker's summation of this model is a cogent statement of the Wisconsin Idea's underlying credo, which is by no means universally shared. Standing in sharp contrast to it is what Buenker calls a marketplace model in which society and polity are conceived as arenas of competition for power, wealth, and status; the public interest is reducible to the "sum of competing interests"; "government exists solely to facilitate the private pursuit of particularistic goals, and to enhance the opportunities available to competitors"; and the role of politicians is to "mediate disputes among warring competitors and distribute benefits according to the power of the contestants."[30]

The Wisconsin Idea also valorized social investment, professional expertise, social efficiency, and a democratic and practical form of public education.

Social investment referred to the investment of money and effort by society as a whole into activities like education and research that initially benefit individuals or private groups but eventually "redound to the public welfare" and "ultimately enhance the general quality of life."[31] The aim of such investment was not to replace individual initiative but rather—in keeping with what Ely and McCarthy called the new individualism—to "help individuals realize their own potential, thus ultimately benefiting the commonwealth."[32] Social investment required a partnership between the state university, which furnished "the necessary technical and theoretical knowledge," and an increasingly professionalized government.[33] As Commons put it, expert administration was the "instrument which society must gradually forge and improve for using social knowledge in the interest of valid social purposes."[34] The progressive reformers who championed the Wisconsin Idea in the early twentieth century believed that these purposes included social efficiency, meaning the achievement of a more harmonious and equitable social order and cost-effective government through competent leadership. Proponents of the Wisconsin Idea also believed that public education should be widely accessible and that educators should seek to overcome entrenched divisions between theory and academic instruction, on the one hand, and applied research and practical training of a vocational or technical kind, on the other hand.[35] If public education was reconstructed along these lines, the Wisconsin Idea's advocates were confident that professional and expert administrators would be "answerable to a well-educated citizenry."[36] "Woven together, the commonwealth model and the concepts of social investment, the new individualism, professional expertise, humanistic efficiency, fiscal economy, and practical, democratic public education constituted the intellectual framework on which to erect Wisconsin's service state."[37]

The Wisconsin Idea was a historically specific response to a set of problems that confronted citizens of the state in the early twentieth century, but these problems were by no means confined to Wisconsin. Both the general nature of the problems that the Wisconsin Idea addressed and the ties that its leading proponents had to "national and international circles of progressive thought and organization" account for the wider significance it acquired outside the state.[38] Firmly connected to these circles, they "functioned as major links and conduits in the symbiotic relationship between state and nation."[39] From "the country's most renowned public university, one that achieved national celebrity as 'the university that runs a state,'" Van Hise and Commons were recruited to serve on national commissions, and Commons helped write labor laws in several states.[40] The civil servant McCarthy served on the US Commission on Industrial Relations, advised progressive governors in other states as well as national statesmen like Theodore Roosevelt and Woodrow Wilson, helped establish

legislative reference libraries in other states and the Philippine Islands, prepared plans for a similar service for the US Congress, and helped write the
platforms of the national and Illinois Progressive parties in 1912.[41] As a US
senator from 1906 to 1925, La Follette advocated for "Wisconsin-style measures on the national stage."[42] As a result of these connections, "Wisconsin
enjoyed a synergistic relationship" with developments in other states, at the
national level, and even in other nations during the Progressive Era.[43] Although
Wisconsin undoubtedly "borrowed as much as it contributed," the Wisconsin
Idea was widely hailed as a progressive model for others to follow.[44] "All
through the Union," Theodore Roosevelt wrote in 1912, "we need to learn the
Wisconsin lesson of scientific popular self-help"; newspapers and periodicals
across the United States published articles on Wisconsin's achievements; and
in a striking fulfillment of Bascom's vision, hundreds of students educated at
the University of Wisconsin "occupied important positions in government,
public service, and education" where they "carried the essentials of the Wisconsin Idea to other locales."[45] As late as the 1950s, long after the Progressive
Era had ended, University of Wisconsin history professor Vernon Carstensen
could praise the Wisconsin Idea as "a term that has had and still has both
national and international currency."[46]

The Development and Internal Tensions
of the Wisconsin Idea

The Wisconsin Idea has exercised an enduring influence within and beyond
the state that gave birth to it, but it would be a mistake to think that it has
remained static since it first took shape in the early twentieth century. Like all
living traditions, it has changed and developed over time. A comprehensive
discussion of its development since the Progressive Era is beyond the scope of
this introduction, and there is no need to duplicate the detailed history of its
evolution that Stark has already provided, but a few general points are worth
underscoring. The first point is that the development of the Wisconsin Idea
must be understood in relation to structural changes in the organization of the
university and state government. There was significant expansion and reorganization of the university after the Second World War, driven by the postwar
baby boom, increased public and private funding, and the "educational revolution" that dramatically expanded access to higher education in the United
States.[47] These changes included the creation of the University of Wisconsin–
Extension in 1965, which consolidated the university's extension work while
separating it from the research and instruction conducted on campus, and the
merger of the University of Wisconsin with the Wisconsin State Universities

system to create the University of Wisconsin System in 1971.[48] (A different set of structural changes driven by very different causes, which I discuss below, occurred in the twenty-first century.) Wisconsin's state government also underwent significant structural changes. Perhaps the most consequential of these changes for the development of the Wisconsin Idea was the state government's growing reliance on in-house staff rather than university experts. Partly as a result of these institutional changes in the university and state government in the twentieth century, Stark concluded that "the relative amounts of energy expended" on different components of the university's service to the state shifted. From 1900 to 1915, "when many of the innovations credited to Wisconsin were developed, policy advice [to state government] was the most impressive component." But in the last half of the twentieth century, outreach activities became the most important component.[49]

A second point is that the genuine development of the Wisconsin Idea, through which it is more fully realized and elaborated, must be distinguished from efforts to narrow its definition or divert it to new purposes that distort its original meaning. A good example of the latter comes from the Blue Ribbon Commission on Twenty-First Century Jobs established by Republican governor Tommy G. Thompson in 1996. The commission proposed a "New Wisconsin Idea" for the twenty-first century: "Innovative learning opportunities should be available to all Wisconsin citizens in a seamless manner throughout their lives, delivered wherever they may be."[50] On the face of it, this formulation appears innocuous and entirely in keeping with the old Wisconsin Idea, particularly its emphasis on expanding access to public education and integrating practical training into the university curriculum.[51] The problem with the "New Wisconsin Idea," however, is that the commission severely diminished the scope of the Wisconsin Idea in order to instrumentalize it for the purpose of economic growth. Since the commission's charge was to study and propose "private and public sector initiatives to strengthen Wisconsin's long term economic future," it only considered "the role the University of Wisconsin System . . . can play in job development."[52] "The biggest impediment to the growth of the Wisconsin economy," the commission posited, was "a shortage of skilled labor."[53] The commission then proposed that the university help fill this need through a variety of "workforce development strategies."[54] Thus, when the commission extolled "innovative learning opportunities," it meant first and foremost opportunities to learn the skills that would attract private capital to the state. As the commission (fetishizing the market) put it, "the imperatives for the jobs of the future require that the Wisconsin Idea be rewritten for the 21st Century."[55] Certainly, there is nothing objectionable in the notion that the state university should prepare students for their future careers in "emerging jobs."[56] What *is* objectionable is limiting the mission of the university exclusively to workforce training, thereby ignoring and devaluing other ways that the university can serve the public. Such an approach turns the university away from its broader public responsibilities. For their part, university professors were encouraged to "be involved with the private sector as consultants, board members and entrepreneurs."[57] By seeking out "industry consortia to promote and exploit research," faculty would ensure that "the benefits of research coming from Wisconsin universities are increasingly available to and used by Wisconsin businesses."[58] In this respect, the New Wisconsin Idea was a remarkable turnabout: it redirected the university's service from state government, the public, and democracy to private capital—the very trusts and special interests whose power the old Wisconsin Idea had sought to curb.

A third point is that the development of the Wisconsin Idea has been shaped not only by institutional reorganization and efforts at redefinition but also by social conflict. From the beginning, the university's role in the Wisconsin Idea and in efforts to make education more democratic and practical was "the subject of serious dispute, even among its own faculty. . . . Within the university, arguments raged over the relative importance of research, over teaching and governmental service, over pure versus applied research, over liberal arts versus professional training, and, above all, over the legitimacy of extension work and public service."[59] These arguments have continued to flare up periodically. "Nor did the university's activist orientation always find favor with the Board of Regents, the legislature, or other public officials."[60] Hostile "political counterforces" came to power as early as Wisconsin's 1914 gubernatorial election and have reemerged periodically since then.[61] The critics of the Wisconsin Idea have typically seized upon its internal tensions in order to discredit it, and therefore their criticism (much like the effort to redefine the Wisconsin Idea in the 1990s) has often taken the form of a one-sided or exaggerated development of elements that the original architects of the Wisconsin Idea tried to reconcile and synthesize. Criticism, in turn, has compelled later proponents of the Wisconsin Idea to clarify, elaborate, or rework its elements as they seek to give it more coherence, internal consistency, and expansiveness of scope. In these ways, social conflict has been a potential impetus to the creative development of the Wisconsin Idea.

I will not attempt to catalogue here all of the internal tensions that the Wisconsin Idea contains but merely draw attention to three examples that are especially relevant to this book's central concern with education and democracy. One set of tensions pertains to the university's service to the state. As the German sociologist Max Weber pointed out, the ideal of the cultivated gentleman rather than the specialist was the end that higher education traditionally sought. "Behind all present discussions of the foundations of the educational system," Weber wrote, "the struggle of the 'specialist type of man' against the older type of 'cultivated man' is hidden at some decisive point." As we have seen, the advocates of the Wisconsin Idea refused to take sides in this struggle; they instead sought to integrate academic education (the "free and full" education in the humanities and social sciences that Bascom advocated) with vocational-technical training ("specialized training for expertness," as Weber called it).[62] However, since these two types of education have different ends, they have remained in tension. The question of the end of education is also related to the tension within the Wisconsin Idea between professional education for full-time students (to create Bascom's intellectual vanguard) and continuing adult education for the general public. Turning from education to the university's service more generally, we have seen that the Wisconsin Idea directed it simultaneously to governing elites and to ordinary citizens. Since the needs of these groups differed, these orientations were also in tension. Finally, the role of the University of Wisconsin as public servant immersed it in politics, which "undermined its claim to being a universal institution above the *Sturm und Drang* of politics," and its close association with progressivism made it vulnerable to political backlash when conservatives came to power in 1914. "Once the university proclaimed public service as its reason for existence, then justified its ever-growing budget requests on those grounds, and boasted of its economic value to the state, it could not escape retaliation by those who had different agendas or different accounting methods."[63] As I suggest below, these issues remain timely.

A second major tension contained within the Wisconsin Idea was "the universal progressive conundrum between efficiency, expertise, and economy on the one hand, and 'power to the people' on the other."[64] The notion of social efficiency had a potentially "darker side as social control or coercion," and when defined in terms of productivity and profit it was at odds with the communitarian language of social bonds and Bascom's organic "idea of society . . . as a unity of parts and not as a collection of autonomous pieces."[65] Likewise, democratic self-government stood in tension with the increased role of professional expertise in public affairs. "It is just as ridiculous," McCarthy wrote in 1912, "to elect a railroad commission as it would be to elect, on a state-wide ballot, a professor of comparative philology at the university."[66] Progressive reformers like McCarthy recognized that experts perform indispensable functions in a complex society, but they were less clear about how to incorporate professional expertise into democratic decision-making in a way that did not subordinate democratic publics to expert administration. McCarthy argued that popularly elected legislators would determine policy while experts would carry it out.[67]

But as Weber pointed out, the dependence of the public and their elected representatives on the expertise of bureaucrats gives those bureaucrats potentially enormous power. This is especially the case in situations of uncertainty, when the need for expert advice is greatest. Furthermore, how can a democratic society foster and benefit from the expertise and skills of a university-trained, professional class while mitigating new forms of social stratification based on educational credentials? And how can a democratic society ensure that Bascom's intellectual vanguard of "educational men" will not pursue self-interested goals while pretending to represent the general interest?[68] While the architects of the Wisconsin Idea tried to reconcile or at least balance the tensions between democratic self-government and expert administration, they remain an inherent feature of the Wisconsin Idea.

A third major tension within the Wisconsin Idea pertains to the people whom the state's university and government are supposed to serve. As we have seen, these institutions were supposed to serve the state of Wisconsin in a democratic and egalitarian fashion, advance the common good, and enable everyone to realize their individual potential and participate fully in the state's polity and economy. However, the Wisconsin Idea ignored several groups in the state that lacked "effective organization or political significance" in the early twentieth century, including "women, African Americans and Native Americans, immigrants of southern and eastern European stock, and the lower socioeconomic orders in general." Buenker suggests that in this time period "the tenets of the Wisconsin Idea were almost exclusively of, by, and for white males of northwestern European ancestry."[69] This criticism, taken up in the twenty-first century by right-wing detractors of the Wisconsin Idea like Thomas C. Leonard (discussed below), raises important questions for the Wisconsin Idea's proponents: Who are the people whom the state's university and government are supposed to serve, and where do the social boundaries of the state lie?[70] The original architects of the Wisconsin Idea answered these questions far too exclusively. However, these exclusions were evidently not inherent in the Wisconsin Idea because its subsequent development involved more expansive conceptions of the people and the social boundaries of the state. The university's changing relationship to the state's Native Americans is a case in point. In a public lecture on Native Americans and the Wisconsin Idea given in 2016, Aaron Bird Bear, an assistant dean for student diversity at the University of Wisconsin–Madison, pointed out that the university was established on land taken from Native Americans, Progressive Era policies toward Native Americans were deeply injurious, and McCarthy and other early architects of the Wisconsin Idea ignored Native Americans and their history. Yet Bird Bear applauded recent developments as evidence of a new era of partnership between the university and the state's Native American nations. These developments included the expertise that the university's law school shared with the Ho-Chunk Nation to help it draft a new tribal constitution in the 1990s, effective outreach by the University of Wisconsin–Extension, and a 2015 summit between the University of Wisconsin–Madison and the state's Native American nations on environment and health. Praising these initiatives as "honest and sincere partnerships," Bird Bear concluded that the Wisconsin Idea was "alive and well."[71]

THE WISCONSIN IDEA AND ITS DISCONTENTS

Just as our understanding of the Wisconsin Idea is deepened by a grasp of the social forces and ideas against which it was directed, so too does it become clearer in relation to the criticisms directed against it. The Wisconsin Idea can be criticized from the political left or from the political right. From the left, it can be condemned for promoting social engineering or providing a fig leaf for the university's "real" functions of producing workers and reproducing social inequality. From the right, it is denounced for advancing the interests of the highly educated and promoting social engineering at the expense of individual rights and liberties. Interestingly, the two types of criticism converge in certain respects. Both leftist and rightist critics must caricature the Wisconsin Idea in order to equate it unequivocally with social engineering, and they share similar assumptions about the functions of higher education, even if the right openly advocates some of the functions (producing workers) that the left finds politically suspect. This book is predominantly concerned with the Wisconsin Idea's discontents on the right because in the twenty-first century it is the political right that has been setting the agenda and reshaping higher education in Wisconsin and elsewhere.[72]

One prominent critic of the Wisconsin Idea was Michael S. Joyce, a protégé of Irving Kristol (one of the intellectual founders and leaders of the neoconservative movement in the United States) and later a key figure and patron in an influential network of right-wing research and civic organizations. These organizations included the Milwaukee-based Lynde and Harry Bradley Foundation, which Joyce led from 1985 to 2001.[73] In 1994, three years before the publication of the Blue Ribbon Commission's report on the New Wisconsin Idea, Joyce wrote a broadside against the Wisconsin Idea that appeared in *Wisconsin Interest*, published by the conservative Wisconsin Policy Research Institute (WPRI). The WPRI (renamed the Badger Institute in 2017) was funded by the Bradley Foundation and would later publish a report in 2016 attacking tenure at the University of Wisconsin.[74]

Joyce's main thesis was that the Wisconsin Idea legitimized the modern state and modern science as instruments for "the perfection of the community" while denigrating individualism and the "private, voluntary associations of civil society."[75] In this respect, he saw the Wisconsin Idea as different in degree but not in kind from Marxist totalitarianism.[76] He acknowledged that the progressive advocates of the Wisconsin Idea sought to challenge the corrupting influence of special interests in public affairs and especially public education; their "key solution," he suggested, was "to shield education from crass political influence by establishing separate, non-partisan bodies for finance and personnel selection." However, he insisted, "our historical experience with progressivism teaches us that you cannot protect 'the people' from the interests by turning over decisions to supposedly apolitical bureaucrats and experts— by 'depoliticizing' education." The reason, Joyce argued, was twofold. First, progressive reformers merely replaced one set of special interests with another: government bureaucrats and academic experts. Second, while these bureaucrats and experts claim to be above politics, there is no such thing as depoliticized education: "For the fact of the matter is that setting educational policy is always and everywhere a profoundly political matter. . . . In the highest sense, education policy allows a self-governing people to determine what skills, moral values, and political commitments it will pass on to the next generation. It's our way of defining just what kind of people we are or would like to be, as we strive to live up to our most cherished political ideals."[77] In his view, progressive reform had empowered "teacher unions" and "education bureaucrats" to propagate radical political ideals (among which Joyce apparently included environmentalism and feminism) while rendering these new special interests unaccountable to the demands of citizens and parents in civil society.

The Wisconsin Idea was important, Joyce suggested, insofar as it "became the centerpiece of the progressive liberal reform movement, which went on to reshape America's political landscape for the rest of [the twentieth] century."[78] By the mid-1990s, he argued, this movement was already "exhausted" as a "political, social, and economic doctrine," but its ultimate demise and the corresponding revitalization of civil society could be hastened in several ways. First, he argued, Americans must be treated not as the "passive clients" of professional experts but as "genuinely self-governing citizens" able to "reassume control over their daily lives" and "make critical choices for themselves." Second, "common sense" and "traditional folk wisdom" must be legitimized. This means, he explained, confronting "the radical skepticism about such 'unscientific' approaches propagated by professional pseudo-scientists eager to preserve their intellectual hegemony." Third, the "traditional, local institutions" of civil society must be reinvigorated and re-empowered. Fourth, power and authority must be devolved from political, intellectual, and cultural elites in the nation's capital, the universities, and the media to "states, localities, and revitalized 'mediating structures.'" Fifth, he wrote, "the political hegemony of the 'helping' and 'caring' professionals and bureaucrats" who "profit . . . from the Nanny state" must be forcefully challenged.[79] Invoking the nineteenth-century French historian and political writer Alexis de Tocqueville and "the civil movements that cut the ground from beneath Soviet Marxism" more than a century after Tocqueville's death, Joyce concluded his article with the prediction that a powerful "parents' resistance movement" would soon emerge to demand constitutional protection for the "right of parents to direct the up-bringing and education of their children"—in other words, to make education a private rather than a public matter.

Joyce's article invites deeper consideration about several issues, which ultimately helps to sharpen our understanding of the Wisconsin Idea. First, what does civil society mean, and do civil society and the state stand in a zero-sum relationship, as Joyce implied? Civil society is an ambiguous term that means different things to different people, and Joyce exploited this ambiguity to rhetorical effect. Joyce himself identified civil society with "private, voluntary associations." But for others, civil society is synonymous with or includes the capitalist market, about which Joyce said very little.[80] Furthermore, Joyce treated civil society and the state as antithetical, as though each can only grow stronger at the expense of the other. But is this assumption warranted? Sociologist Theda Skocpol has shown that "throughout most of American history, active democratic government and a vibrant civil society centered in federated associations went hand in hand."[81] Comparative studies also challenge Joyce's assumption. Sociologist Robert Wuthnow found that "voluntary associations continue to flourish" in all advanced industrial societies "despite the massive expansion of the state that [Tocqueville] so much feared and warned against. . . . If anything, the growth of government welfare services appears to have stimulated, rather than eroded voluntary activity."[82]

Second, who are the special interests? As we have seen, Bascom hoped that university graduates would serve as a force for promoting the public good. This view has roots in the German idealist philosophy that shaped his outlook. The German philosopher Georg Wilhelm Friedrich Hegel, for instance, described university-educated civil servants as a kind of universal class, which is to say, a class who, more than any other, represent the general interest.[83] In contrast, Joyce argued that "bureaucrats and experts"—the very people produced by Bascom's university—"inevitably become the special interests." Special interests are a longstanding concern in American political thought. James Madison, one of America's founding fathers and later its fourth president

(1809–17), famously defined a faction in Federalist Paper No. 10 as a group of citizens who pursue a common interest that is harmful to the rights of others or to the interests of the community.[84] Madison warned about the dangers that such factions pose to a republic, but his warning left important questions unanswered. Is every organized pressure group a faction? If not, how do we know when a group is a faction? Often it is a matter of political controversy whether a group's special interests are harmful to or coincide with the interests of the community.

When conservatives like Joyce describe teachers and "academic experts" as special interests, university professors are apt to discount the criticism as unfair. We don't recognize ourselves in this characterization. However, it is an idea that finds support among a surprising range of thinkers, not all of them right wing. There is in fact a long line of theorizing that identifies the highly educated as a "new class" pursuing their own power and privilege while pretending to represent universal interests.[85] These theories were developed in three major waves. From 1870 to 1917—precisely when the Wisconsin Idea first took shape—European revolutionary anarchists like Mikhail Bakunin and Jan Machajski warned about the dangers of a new form of domination based on monopoly of knowledge.[86] Shortly before Bascom became president of the University of Wisconsin, and well before the university was described as "ruling the state," Bakunin darkly predicted that a "new class, a new hierarchy of real and pretended scientists and scholars," would dominate "the immense ignorant majority" in "the name of knowledge," thus establishing the "reign of scientific intelligence, the most aristocratic, despotic, arrogant and contemptuous of all regimes." The "organization and the government of the new society by Socialistic scientists and professors," he declared, would be "the worst of all despotic government!"[87] Elaborating these ideas, Machajski distinguished two sources of social inequality: ownership of private property, on the one hand, and educational credentials and control of state offices, on the other hand. Machajski argued that if revolutionaries abolished private property without also eliminating inequities created by educational credentials and control of state offices, they would succeed only in creating a new form of class domination.[88] From the late 1930s onward, a second wave of theorizing identified bureaucrats in the Soviet Union and managers in the capitalist West as the new class.[89] It was only during the third wave of theorizing in the 1970s that "the political right (the neoconservatives) began to develop their own New Class theories" for the first time, but this third wave was not limited to the political right.[90] Third-wave theorizing about the new class of the highly educated was bound up with critical analyses of the knowledge that they produce, which according to some accounts was not the benign instrument that Commons imagined in the Progressive Era. The French philosopher and historian Michel Foucault tried to show, for instance, how knowledge and power are always entangled with, reinforce, and legitimize each other, and the anthropologist James Scott criticized "high modernism" for privileging the expertise of scientists, engineers, and bureaucrats over local, practical knowledge.[91] These theories of the new class, articulated from the political left as well as the right, rest on the suspicion that intellectuals and knowledge producers hide their self-interested ambitions and will to power under the cloak of universalistic ideals.

When Joyce denounced the Wisconsin Idea as the self-serving ideology of university-educated bureaucrats and experts, he built upon an extensive foundation laid by generations of new class theorists.[92] The critique is therefore not easy to dismiss. One obvious though inadequate response is to point out that even if civil servants and university professors are not as universal as they present themselves, it does not mean that the political right or business interests are the universal class. Going further, it is also possible to maintain that the highly educated are indeed a universal class, albeit a "flawed" or "morally ambiguous" one, as sociologist Alvin Gouldner put it. "The New Class," Gouldner frankly admitted, "is elitist and self-seeking and uses its special knowledge to advance its own interests and power, and to control its own work situation." Nevertheless, he added, this new class may be "the best card that history has presently given us to play" because it also embodies, however "partially and transiently," the "collective interest."[93] This response, too, is inadequate because even if the claim is correct, it is hard to convince people outside of the new class. Indeed, it is not always easy to know who is a special interest and who represents the general interest. Perhaps, however, that is the wrong question to ask. The best response to Joyce's criticism begins with the acknowledgment that bureaucrats and experts are not exceptionally virtuous people who somehow manage to put the general interest above their own. But, as sociologist Pierre Bourdieu has argued, under the right social conditions, the only way they can satisfy their particular interests is to contribute to producing the universal.[94] The question we should therefore ask instead is, What social conditions are necessary for people to develop an interest in the universal? What institutional arrangements encourage people to harness their self-interest to serve the common good? The Wisconsin Idea is, at bottom, precisely the effort to identify and construct these arrangements.

Joyce's criticism of the Wisconsin Idea also provokes reflection on a third issue: the relationship between education and politics. Joyce argued that the attempt to "shield education" from "political influence" is a form of mystification because "educational policy is always and everywhere a profoundly political matter."[95] And indeed the University of Wisconsin has historically been dogged

by conservative criticisms that it involved itself in politics. In the early twentieth century, Van Hise denied this charge. However, he added, if "it is meant
that the University is attempting to lead in the advancement of the people; if
it is meant that problems which relate to water powers, to forests, to marketing, to the public utilities, to labor, are legitimate fields of university inquiry
and teaching, then the university is in politics, and will remain there so long
as it is a virile institution worthy of the support of the people of this state."[96]
As Van Hise understood, a great deal depends on what is meant by politics.

For Aristotle, the polis was a partnership that citizens formed for the sake
of a good life, and politics was thus the search for those social arrangements
that best enable citizens to achieve that end. The university's service to the
public may be understood as political in this sense to the extent that it aims to
facilitate human development or flourishing. However, in a modern, pluralistic society where there are diverse substantive conceptions of the good life, the
university can only be guided by what the German philosopher Axel Honneth
calls a *formal* conception of ethical life. This conception is formal in the sense
that "it only normatively emphasizes the social preconditions of human self-
realization, and not the goals served by those conditions."[97] In other words,
rather than endorsing one particular form of individual self-realization for
everyone, the university can promote through its public service "the *general
social conditions* required for the realization of any number of different substantive ways life."[98] When Joyce argued that educational policy is a political
matter, he seemed to mean that it is political in something like the Aristotelian
sense: it involves the transmission of "moral values" and "political ideals," not
just skills.[99] This point is a useful corrective to the depoliticized New Wisconsin Idea and its narrow focus on workforce development. But Joyce lacked
Honneth's formal conception of ethical life, and therefore he could only imagine educational policy as championing substantive values or ways of living
(preferably, he thought, his own conservative values).

Whether it relies on a formal or substantive conception of ethical life, politics in the Aristotelian sense must be distinguished from the narrow and re-
ductionist understanding of politics as the struggle for partisan power and
advantage. If education is conceived as merely another means to gain or maintain power, the search for truth will be sacrificed to political expediency. When,
for example, an economics professor with a joint appointment at the University of Wisconsin–Madison and the University of Wisconsin–Extension published research in 2015 that challenged the purported benefits of anti-union
"right-to-work" laws, a Republican state senator publicly castigated him for
"hiding behind academic freedom to issue partisan, garbage research."[100] The

troubling implication of this political attack was that research is only valuable and legitimate insofar as it supports the aims and ideas of the governing party or politically dominant groups.

Fourth, Joyce's article invites further reflection on previously noted tensions in the Wisconsin Idea concerning expertise and service to the people. Joyce wished to "restore the intellectual and cultural legitimacy of citizenly common sense" and to "re-establish the dignity of traditional folk wisdom," in contrast to modern science (or rather, as he was careful to say, "pseudo-scientists eager to preserve their intellectual hegemony"). Some of the chapters in this volume—all written by authors who are committed or at least sympathetic to the Wisconsin Idea—share this concern. They advocate a two-way flow of information between experts and ordinary people that requires respect for common sense. This is a salutary corrective to overconfidence in professional and scientific expertise. However, just as the subordination of democracy to expertise distorts the Wisconsin Idea, so too does the subordination of expertise to folk wisdom. After all, the "continual and fearless sifting and winnowing by which alone the truth can be found" sometimes requires scholars and researchers to challenge lay knowledge. And as sociologist Jeffrey C. Goldfarb has pointed out, one (though not the only) function of intellectuals in a democratic society is to subvert common sense when it becomes restrictive.[101] Recent controversies over vaccination and climate change also raise questions about whether folk wisdom always deserves the legitimacy that Joyce wished to confer upon it and what such legitimation might mean practically. Finally, we might return to a question raised earlier: In a pluralistic and diverse society, who are the folk? If in the early twentieth century the architects of the Wisconsin Idea were insufficiently reflective about the people whom the university was supposed to serve, Joyce's critique of the Wisconsin Idea at the end of the century was equally vague about which people he wished to empower.

Thomas C. Leonard, a researcher and lecturer at Princeton University, took up and extended earlier criticisms of the Wisconsin Idea in his 2016 book *Illiberal Reformers*. Like Buenker, Leonard situated the Wisconsin Idea in the context of American progressivism. And like Joyce, he emphasized progressive reformers' aversion to laissez-faire economics and their embrace of social science and the administrative state as instruments of social and economic reform. According to Leonard, these were the principles at the core of progressivism: "First, modern government should be guided by science and not politics; and second, an industrialized economy should be supervised, investigated, and regulated by the visible hand of a modern administrative state."[102] Leonard rightly linked the ascendance of progressive reform in Wisconsin and elsewhere in the early twentieth century to the professionalization of the social sciences, the use of social-scientific authority to challenge laissez-faire economics, and the building of a modern administrative and regulatory state "guided by expert social scientists."[103] The emergence of "the professor of social science, the scholar-activist, the social worker, the muckraking journalist, and the economic expert advising or serving in government," confident in "their own expertise as a reliable, even necessary, guide to the public good," thus went hand in hand with "an epoch-making change in the relationship of government to American economic life."[104] In Leonard's account, Wisconsin pioneered these developments in the Progressive Era. Governor La Follette "empowered the University of Wisconsin faculty and unleashed them on the state," and together—inspired by political and social developments in Germany—they built "the first prototype of American administrative government."[105] This model was then replicated at the national level during the presidency of Woodrow Wilson from 1913 to 1921.

What Leonard added to this otherwise well-trodden ground was an attempt to link progressive reformers' rejection of laissez-faire economics to repugnant expressions of elitism, sexism, nativism, and racism—in short, what Buenker called the "darker side" of social efficiency as "social control or coercion." Apparent in the writings of several prominent figures associated with the Wisconsin Idea, including Van Hise, Ely, Commons, Ross, and Turner, this darker side manifested itself in support for eugenics, the restriction of immigration, and measures to protect native-born white workingmen from the competition of cheaper labor provided by immigrants, women, and racial minorities.[106] Leonard argued that such views were inseparable from progressives' rejection of laissez-faire economics because they stemmed from the same underlying assumptions about and orientations to the social world. Eugenics, for instance, was considered scientific, required expertise, promised efficiency, and stemmed from "the belief that racial health," like the market, "was too important to be left unregulated. . . . The social organism subordinated its constituent individuals, and its health, welfare, and morals trumped the individual's rights and liberties."[107] Hence, Leonard maintained, progressivism was doubly illiberal, and necessarily so: it not only "discarded economic liberties" but "assaulted political and civil liberties, too, trampling on individual rights to person, to free movement, to free expression, to marriage and to reproduction," all of which reformers regarded as impediments to "necessary improvements to society's health, welfare, and morals."[108]

A full assessment of Leonard's scholarship is beyond the scope of this introduction and is available elsewhere.[109] The pertinent question here is whether

Leonard has succeeded in discrediting progressivism and, by extension, the Wisconsin Idea. The implication of Leonard's thesis is that the only way to avoid the elitism, sexism, nativism, and racism that he finds among early twentieth-century progressives (including prominent architects of the Wisconsin Idea) is to embrace the economic libertarianism and utilitarian individualism that they rejected. This is a dubious suggestion. As we have seen, there is a real tension within the Wisconsin Idea between expertise and democracy, but the democratic elements are no less genuine and significant than its potential for elitism, and the development of the Wisconsin Idea has made those democratic elements more rather than less pronounced.[110] Moreover, the progressives who advocated the Wisconsin Idea in the early twentieth century were not uniquely or especially prone to the social exclusion of women, immigrants, and racial minorities. Laissez-faire ideology of that time also took sexist, nativist, and racist forms; its proponents welcomed the cheap labor that immigrants supplied, but they became alarmed when immigrants demanded unemployment relief or gained political power, and they blamed enduring social inequalities on "innate group characteristics" rather than "exclusionary social, political, or economic structures."[111]

This does not mean that the Wisconsin Idea and laissez-faire economics were equally bad for women, immigrants, and racial minorities. If the Wisconsin Idea contained potentially problematic elements like the notion of social efficiency that made exclusionary views and practices possible, it also contained within itself potential solutions. Gains in equality for women and minorities have been achieved through the very instruments of social reform that the Wisconsin Idea emphasized: social science and the administrative and regulatory state. The civil rights movement is a case in point. Research by social scientists Kenneth B. Clark and Mamie Phipps Clark played an important role in the 1954 US Supreme Court decision that found segregated schools to be unconstitutional, and the Supreme Court's expansive reinterpretation of Congress's power to regulate interstate commerce during the New Deal made possible the 1964 Civil Rights Act.[112] The Wisconsin Idea was thus capable of developing in a more inclusive direction, which explains why no contemporary proponent of the Wisconsin Idea would condone the elitism, sexism, nativism, and racism that its early architects sometimes expressed. In contrast, the tendency to blame inequality on innate group characteristics remains "a persistent legacy of an ideology that sees 'the market' as inherently egalitarian."[113] In sum, the best way to avoid elitism, sexism, nativism, and racism is not to return to unregulated markets, but rather to deepen and extend the democratic ideals at the heart of the Wisconsin Idea.

Why Is a Book about the
Wisconsin Idea Needed Now?

Already in the early 1970s and again in the early 1990s, as changing demands on faculty discouraged their involvement in public service and as state government turned less often to the university for assistance, administrators and faculty members in the University of Wisconsin System lamented the fading or outright demise of the Wisconsin Idea. Writing in the mid-1990s, Stark concluded that these assessments were too harsh in light of the continued flourishing of the university's extension work and the numbers of faculty still serving state government.[114] However, political developments during the administration of Republican governor Scott Walker (2011–19) brought what may be the most radical challenge to the Wisconsin Idea yet. This challenge was grave enough that faculty across the University of Wisconsin System, beginning with the flagship campus in Madison, voted no confidence in the regents (mostly appointed by the governor) and system president (appointed by the regents) in a historically unprecedented protest wave in 2016.[115] Following Walker's failed bid for the Republican nomination in the 2016 US presidential election, he was narrowly defeated in Wisconsin's 2018 gubernatorial election by Tony Evers, a longtime champion of public education. As the state's Superintendent of Public Instruction and an ex officio member of the University of Wisconsin System Board of Regents since 2009, Evers was often the only independent and critical voice on a board that was increasingly filled with Walker appointees. But a single election is not sufficient to undo the serious and sustained damage that has been done to the Wisconsin Idea. Walker was a transformative governor, and like-minded members of his party who continue to control the state legislature (and who diminished the governor's powers after Walker was defeated) are committed to preserving his legacies.

In 2015, Governor Walker tried to change the university's historic mission by eliminating its commitment to "search for truth" and "improve the human condition." He sought to substitute instead the narrower, economistic goal of "meet[ing] the state's workforce needs."[116] This was essentially a reaffirmation and attempt to codify the New Wisconsin Idea of the 1990s and its circumscribed focus on workforce development, but in a more heavy-handed way and without the earlier emphasis on social investment to create "high-quality jobs" instead of "'hit and run' development that imposes environmental and infrastructure costs."[117] A public outcry soon forced the governor to back down, but the effort to reshape the university's guiding principles did not end there. Walker, the regents he appointed, and the state's Republican-controlled legislature pursued the same end by different means: massive budget cuts and the dismantling of tenure and shared governance. Moreover, these changes were made with little public discussion or debate about their larger import.

First, deep budget cuts deprived the University of Wisconsin of crucial resources needed to carry out its historic mission. The legislature cut $250 million from the University of Wisconsin System in the 2011–13 state budget, cut more than $100 million in the 2013–15 budget, and cut another $250 million in the 2015–17 state budget.[118] Although state budget cuts to higher education after the Great Recession of 2008 were not unique to Wisconsin, the Badger State did not increase spending between 2013 and 2018 as most other states did; instead, it experienced the fourth-largest decline in per-student spending in those years.[119] By 2015–16, state support for the University of Wisconsin System, adjusted for inflation, was "in a historic decline" and "hit an all-time low."[120] The legislature also imposed a tuition freeze in 2013, thereby choking off an alternative source of funding for the university, while failing to compensate with increased public spending. (As a result, the university budget grew more dependent on federal grants and private gifts, with the increasing importance of the latter contributing to a kind of creeping privatization.) The legislature increased state funding for the University of Wisconsin System by $36 million in the 2017–19 state budget—the first such increase since Republicans gained control of the state government in 2011—but this modest increase, likely intended to improve Walker's chances of reelection in 2018, failed to compensate for previous cuts.[121] The defunding of the university resulted in reduced class offerings, increased class sizes, and lengthened time to complete a degree, thereby diminishing the quality of education, and it created a rationale to give chancellors of the System's individual campuses more "flexibility" and to close programs in the humanities and social sciences.[122]

Second, the weakening of tenure also undercut the Wisconsin Idea. As we have seen, the institution of tenure was closely associated with academic freedom, a key element of the Wisconsin Idea, and developed together with it in the early twentieth century. When the Wisconsin legislature removed tenure from state law in 2015—a century after the American Association of University Professors issued its landmark Declaration of Principles on Academic Freedom and Academic Tenure—the Board of Regents developed new tenure policies that failed to meet the standards set by the American Association of University Professors. The new policies permitted the dismissal of faculty for something less than "just cause," which refers to an inability or unwillingness to fulfill professional and institutional responsibilities; they made it easier to lay off faculty; and they diminished the due process rights of faculty facing discipline or dismissal.[123] The regents, appointed by Walker, defended these changes on the grounds that the university must operate like a business and thus have more flexibility to fire faculty.[124] This was, of course, precisely the view that the American Association of University Professors forcefully rejected in its 1915 statement. "The declaration proclaimed that the 'conception of a university as an ordinary business venture, and of academic teaching as a purely private employment,' demonstrated 'a radical failure to apprehend the nature of the social function discharged by the professional scholar.' . . . In carrying out their critical service to society, faculty . . . were not 'in any proper sense the employees' of [university] trustees, because 'once appointed, the scholar has professional functions to perform in which the appointing authorities have neither competency nor moral right to intervene.'"[125]

Third, political counterforces hostile to the Wisconsin Idea vitiated the sharing of university governance with students, academic staff, and faculty. The state legislature stripped graduate student workers, academic staff, and faculty of collective bargaining rights in 2011; defunded United Council for UW Students (the University of Wisconsin System student government organization) in the 2013–15 budget; and rescinded faculty's responsibility for academic and educational activities and faculty personnel matters in 2015. (Faculty are now merely responsible for advising chancellors about these matters.) For good measure, the legislature also explicitly declared that the specific responsibilities of students, academic staff, and faculty are subordinate to the responsibilities and powers of the Board of Regents, the president of the University of Wisconsin System, and the chancellors of their respective campuses.[126] This was a significant change because it negated an earlier definition of shared governance enshrined in the 1994 *Spoto v. Board of Regents* court case. In that case, which concerned a dispute over merit pay for faculty, a Dane County circuit court ruled that university governance was in fact really shared: none of the partners could unilaterally make decisions in areas of joint responsibility but instead had to reach a consensus together.[127] Emboldened by these legislative attacks, the regents and system president showed a similar disdain for shared governance. For instance, the regents' new tenure policies allow academic programs to be discontinued for financial reasons determined by campus chancellors and no longer exclusively on the basis of educational considerations determined primarily by the faculty.[128] Likewise, in "the UW System's biggest shift since its inception by the Legislature in 1971," the regents and system president decided in 2017 to merge its thirteen two-year campuses with seven of its four-year colleges, dissolve the University of Wisconsin–Extension as a separate unit, and transfer its functions to the University of Wisconsin–Madison and the central System office—all without consulting faculty, staff, or students.[129] Two years later, when the Board of Regents formed a search committee to select a new president of the University of Wisconsin System, the search committee included no faculty, staff, or students (except for the board's student regent).[130] Without a meaningful voice in university governance, faculty and staff cannot effectively fulfill their professional mission. Conversely, politically appointed regents and university administrators are empowered to replace the university's historic mission with new goals like Walker's restrictive focus on workforce training.

At the beginning of this introduction, I noted that a narrow definition of the Wisconsin Idea focused on the university's service to the public cannot be easily and neatly separated from the Wisconsin Idea's broader, political dimension. The defunding of the university and the dismantling of tenure and shared governance must accordingly be seen as part of a larger political project by the radical right to dismantle the historic achievements of progressivism and to substitute a marketplace model for the commonwealth model of society that underpinned them.[131] All of the major policy areas that McCarthy discussed in his 1912 book on the Wisconsin Idea were affected. As we have seen, the architects of the Wisconsin Idea sought to use government power to protect citizens from what McCarthy called "predatory wealth" and to free state government from its corrupting influence. Walker, in contrast, declared Wisconsin "open for business," signed into law regressive tax cuts that favored the state's wealthiest citizens, and generally rejected social investment except in the form of tax breaks and public subsidies to private capital.[132] Good government also suffered under the Walker administration: corporations were permitted to donate directly to political parties; the state's century-old civil service system was weakened; the state's nonpartisan Government Accountability Board that oversaw elections and enforced ethics codes was replaced with new bodies made up of partisan appointees; and the Republican-controlled legislature entrenched the grip of Walker's party on power by means of extensive gerrymandering and restrictive voter identification laws, which depressed voter turnout and skewed the electorate.[133] In the area of labor, health, and public welfare, the Walker era saw the drastic curtailment of collective bargaining for public employees (a practice that Wisconsin had pioneered in 1959); the enactment of anti-union, so-called right-to-work legislation; and a raft of legislation retrenching the state's social welfare programs. In the area of conservation, Walker "moved to reduce the role of science in environmental policymaking and to silence discussion of controversial subjects, including climate change, by state employees," and he signed into law a series of "controversial rollbacks in environmental protection . . . to help specific companies avoid regulatory roadblocks."[134] In sum, "Wisconsin's century-old progressive legacy has been dismantled in virtually every area: labor rights, environmental protection, voting rights, government transparency."[135]

Just as a full understanding of the Wisconsin Idea required attention to its social carriers and institutional pillars in the early twentieth century, a similar analysis can be made of the assault on the Wisconsin Idea in the twenty-first century. The social base of this assault includes right-wing critics of the Wisconsin Idea like Joyce and Leonard, Republican politicians on the radical right who have implemented their ideas, and extremely wealthy and reactionary magnates who have provided financial support. These groups are linked through a network of personal and organizational ties. For instance, the Bradley Foundation, which Joyce led from 1985 to 2001, later promoted Walker and his political agenda, and Walker appointed the son of Michael W. Grebe, who succeeded Joyce as president of the foundation from 2002 through 2016, to the University of Wisconsin System Board of Regents. Other institutional pillars include conservative think tanks and nonprofits, such as the Wisconsin Policy Research Institute that published Joyce's criticism; funders such as the Koch Industries Political Action Committee, Americans for Prosperity (funded by the billionaire Charles and David Koch brothers), and the Wisconsin Club for Growth; and the American Legislative Exchange Council, which serves as a radical right-wing bill factory for the entire nation.[136] Lastly, the dismantling of the Wisconsin Idea was made possible by the forging of a new electoral coalition quite different from the reformist coalition that supported the Wisconsin Idea a century ago. The same theories of the new class that Joyce used to criticize the Wisconsin Idea can also help to illuminate this development. If the Wisconsin Idea at the beginning of the twentieth century reflected a political alliance of the emerging new class of highly educated professionals with workers and farmers against "predatory wealth," then the dismantling of the Wisconsin Idea a hundred years later arguably reflects a top-bottom alliance between economic capital and those classes with little capital of any kind against the new class, the bearers of cultural capital, who have always been the main social carriers of the Wisconsin Idea.[137] Enabled and supported by this alliance, politicians on the radical right set out to dismantle the structural positions from which the new class exercised political influence and to put it firmly in its place: subordinated to the interests and needs of economic capital.[138] While this top-bottom coalition no doubt accommodated some immediate or short-term interests of the state's non-college-educated citizens, it has not served the fundamental or long-term interest of the public well. Instead, Wisconsin has experienced its highest level of income inequality since the Great Depression, dramatically rising poverty rates, nonexistent wage growth, diminished resources for public education, worsening roads, and declining water quality. By 2016, "the University of Wisconsin–Madison had fallen, for the first time, out of the rankings of the country's top five research schools," and the state's voter identification law, "one of the strictest in the nation," deterred an estimated 11 percent of the state's population from voting in the 2016 presidential election.[139]

Just as the significance of the Wisconsin Idea always extended beyond the state where it emerged, so too the dismantling of the Wisconsin Idea is relevant beyond the state's boundaries. Wisconsin is arguably at the forefront of aggressive efforts to reshape public universities in the United States, but it is hardly alone. As the 2016 film *Starving the Beast* documented, right-wing think tanks and politicians have promoted "disruptive innovation" on university campuses across the country.[140] What these efforts have in common is the attempt to redefine public higher education as a commodified private good rather than a socialized public good, the use of budget cuts to force reduction or elimination of politically disfavored programs or practices, an insistence that universities focus on job training rather than provide a broad liberal arts education, and (when it comes to the academic workforce) the aggressive substitution of managerial accountability for professional responsibility. The assault on the broader political dimension of the Wisconsin Idea is similarly germane outside of the state. As writer Dan Kaufman points out and Lewis A. Friedland underscores in his chapter for this volume, Wisconsin "went from a widely admired 'laboratory of democracy' to a testing ground" for "corporate interests and conservative activists" bent on remaking not merely state-level but national politics.[141] Indeed, it was precisely because of Wisconsin's historic progressive legacy that the state "became a target for national conservatives. As Scott Walker boasted in his memoir, if he could change Wisconsin, he and his allies could 'do it anywhere.'"[142] Hence, if this volume focuses on Wisconsin, it is not an indication of parochialism; rather, it is because Wisconsin is a paradigmatic case that reveals in an especially clear way a wider set of problems and challenges. To paraphrase a certain talented German philosopher: if readers outside of Wisconsin shrug their shoulders at political developments in the Badger State, or optimistically comfort themselves with the thought that things are not nearly so bad elsewhere, then they must plainly be told, *De te fabula narratur.*

The need for a new book about the Wisconsin Idea—a need that extends beyond the state of Wisconsin—should now be readily apparent. As powerful political forces seek to radically overhaul the public university and the broader social and political context that sustained it, a vigorous public discussion is needed about the university's purpose and role in a democratic society, the full range of ways it can and should serve the public, and the reasons it deserves robust public support. Furthermore, it is vital that these questions not be left to politicians, regents, and university administrators to answer behind closed doors; they must be openly and transparently addressed, with fearless sifting and winnowing, in democratic and informed public debate. An important aim of this edited volume is to foster such a discussion. After all, "if intellectuals do not provoke serious talk about the problems we face, no one will."[143] In addition, inspired by the conviction that the ideal of service to democracy is a compelling countervision to the utilitarian and business-centered notions of higher education that are aggressively promoted in Wisconsin and elsewhere today, this volume is meant to make a substantive contribution to the discussion it intends to provoke. While focused on the Wisconsin experience, it suggests important lessons for other embattled land-grant or public research universities. First, university leaders often think they must adopt the market model of university purpose as a protective ideology to legitimize their institutions to the tax-paying public. The Wisconsin experience shows that in the long run this stratagem has perverse consequences; it offers little real protection and instead emboldens more radical attacks on public higher education. Public universities are most defensible and most deserving of public support when they are genuinely committed to the ideal of service to democracy. Second, the university's public service, understood as service to democracy, cannot be neatly separated from politics in a broad sense. The university's commitment to the ideal of service to democracy must entail a political commitment to promoting the social conditions on which the ideal depends. Third, a well-rounded ideal of service to democracy contains a variety of internal tensions. These tensions probably cannot be resolved in any definitive way, and it is better to preserve them than to substitute more simplistic and one-sided alternatives. Fourth, the ideal of service to democracy develops as it is reinterpreted over time. Although it cannot be redefined to mean anything one wants, neither is its meaning completely fixed by the people who initially formulated it. This is why the ideal must be renewed and not merely conserved.

A LOOK AHEAD

The chapters that follow are on the whole sympathetic to the Wisconsin Idea though not unquestioning. Together, they seek to persuade the public of the value of the Wisconsin Idea while also acknowledging the need for its ongoing development to achieve more fully the goals it set for itself. The chapters are arranged in a roughly chronological order according to their subject matter, beginning with J. David Hoeveler's discussion of John Bascom in the late nineteenth century and concluding with Katherine J. Cramer's essay, first published in 2016, on the need to revive the civic purpose of higher education—a sentiment that Bascom would surely have endorsed. Linking the chapters together are four overarching themes. Although no chapter fully addresses all of these themes, each chapter engages deeply with one or more of them.

The first theme is the production of new knowledge and its role in good government. As Hoeveler's contribution points out, Bascom believed that the university served the state and the public in part "by the research and scholarship of its faculty in the production of new knowledge." However, Hoeveler argues, two forces threaten this aspect of the Wisconsin Idea today: a misguided insistence that the university serve only the immediate needs of the market, which ignores a broader range of socially useful knowledge, and a growing intolerance of controversial ideas on campus. He finds hope for a renewal of the Wisconsin Idea in the convergence of a handful of politically diverse thinkers on the communitarian values that imbued Bascom's thinking.[144] While Hoeveler underscores the value of knowledge production, Karen Bogenschneider investigates how new knowledge can inform and foster what Theodore Roosevelt called "wise experimental legislation" for "the social and political betterment of the people."[145] She compares the legendary partnership between the university and state government in 1911, described by McCarthy and praised by Roosevelt, to a more recent effort in which she has played a leading role: a series of Family Impact Seminars that have brought university researchers and state legislators together since 1992 to deliberate about family issues. Bogenschneider argues that these Family Impact Seminars have been effective in multiple ways: informing policy decisions with relevant research, facilitating trust and mutual appreciation between researchers and policymakers, and fostering more civil and respectful communication and collaboration across partisan and ideological divisions. Drawing on her experience with the Family Impact Seminars, her contribution identifies impediments to fruitful cooperation between university researchers and policymakers, and it suggests ways to mitigate them. While the Family Impact Seminars provide a valuable model for cooperation between university researchers and policymakers under normal politics, its effectiveness may prove to be limited in a new political context (described in Lewis A. Friedland's chapter) in which the governing party sets out to transform the university and change the rules and institutions for making political decisions.

A second theme in the essays that follow is the university's outreach to the people and assistance in solving problems that are important to them. Caitlin Cieslik-Miskimen's essay reexamines Willard G. Bleyer's role as a pioneer of journalism education at the University of Wisconsin in the early decades of the twentieth century. As she shows, Bleyer was motivated by the conviction that journalists had a responsibility to help ensure the success of democracy and the welfare of society. He believed that the university could prepare journalists to fulfill this responsibility by means of a broad education that did not merely impart professional skills but also exposed students to the liberal arts, public outreach, and community engagement. Bleyer's approach thus combined seemingly disparate forms of education. Maryo Gard Ewell's contribution describes the university's extension work in the arts throughout the twentieth century. She stresses the participatory and democratizing aspects of this work; rather than promoting arts consumption, it helped ordinary people to develop their artistic talents and encouraged them to make their own art. In this way, arts extension challenged assumptions that the arts are frivolous or the exclusive purview of cultural elites; it showed on the contrary that the arts have the power to uplift and enrich life and build community—for everyone. Finally, Curt Meine's chapter explores conservation as an application of knowledge to help solve public problems. As Meine shows, the unchecked exploitation of Wisconsin's natural assets posed a fundamental question to its citizens: "whether the mechanisms of democracy could be used in new ways to safeguard the long-term public interest in those natural assets." The answer to that question, he argues, depended on the evolving relationships among the Wisconsin Idea, conservation, and the state's political culture. He charts the university's role in Wisconsin's rise as a national leader in conservation; the tension within conservationism between expert-driven approaches and those that are collaborative and community-based; the transition from conservationism to modern environmentalism, which became a flashpoint for broader political-cultural conflicts in the 1990s; and the consequent undermining of Wisconsin's conservation tradition. "As goes our political culture," Meine suggests, "so goes the Wisconsin Idea. As goes the Wisconsin Idea, so goes conservation in Wisconsin." A "reinvigorated commitment to conservation under the Wisconsin Idea" thus requires a new, different, and more supportive political culture. These chapters remind us that public universities, at their best, do more than train workers for jobs; they also prepare citizens for society, facilitate cooperative problem solving, and help us to realize our full potential as human beings.

Some essays take up a third theme that has already been explored in this introduction: In a society that is diverse and pluralistic, increasingly unequal, and ever more globalized, where are the boundaries of the state, who are the people the university should serve, and to whom is it responsible? Both Emily Auerbach's and R. Richard Wagner's chapters suggest expansive answers to these questions. Auerbach's essay showcases the UW Odyssey Project, an award-winning program created in 2003 that offers University of Wisconsin–Madison humanities classes to adult students from socially and economically disadvantaged backgrounds. These students, most of whom are racial or ethnic minorities, bear little resemblance to the intellectual vanguard that Bascom wanted to create in the late nineteenth century; they are precisely the kind of people that the original architects of the Wisconsin Idea ignored or excluded in the early twentieth century; yet it is precisely their transformative experiences in the Odyssey Project that demonstrate how socially useful the humanities really are—for everyone. (In this way, Auerbach's chapter on the UW Odyssey Project dovetails with Gard Ewell's chapter on arts extension.) Auerbach's contribution illustrates how underrepresented minorities can be effectively engaged in a jumpstart college humanities course, and it offers valuable lessons to educators of adults seeking greater diversity in their programs. She urges readers to consider its implications for their own local programs and interests as they read her personal narrative of launching and directing the Odyssey Project for over a decade. Wagner's chapter focuses on a different marginalized group: the state's homosexual and gender-nonconforming citizens. Van Hise surely did not have them in mind when he extolled the university's far-reaching beneficence, the university's mission was not presumed to include the study of such persons when the Wisconsin Idea was first conceived, and some advocates of the Wisconsin Idea encouraged the criminalization and suppression of homosexuality in the early twentieth century. Nevertheless, Wagner shows, academics at the university played a significant role in Wisconsin's progress from criminalization and suppression of homosexuality toward recognition of gay rights. Their research, despite its flaws and limitations, helped to reveal the lives of LGBT individuals in the state, allowed their voices to come through, and suggested new ways to think about them outside of criminal and medical frameworks. As both of these chapters suggest, an important way in which the university can serve democracy is by fostering the creation of a broader, more expanded sort of community.

Several essays engage with a fourth theme, which this introduction has also already explored: recent challenges to the Wisconsin Idea and the changing social, economic, and political conditions that help to explain them. Jane L. Collins argues that a shared vision of the public sector and its role in society links the Wisconsin Idea to the state's massive protests against the evisceration of public-sector collective bargaining in 2011. Her chapter explicates this shared vision, provides a new interpretation of the 2011 protests as a defense of that vision, and shows that it has been a source of recurring controversy and conflict in Wisconsin for more than a century. Friedland's contribution situates the 2011 protests within a far-reaching transformation of Wisconsin from a widely hailed "laboratory of democracy" (jurist Louis Brandeis's famous phrase) in the early twentieth century to a laboratory of oligarchy in the twenty-first century. Oligarchy is what results when an ultra-wealthy stratum converts its wealth into political power, which it then uses to facilitate and defend the concentration of wealth in its hands. The defense of concentrated wealth involves crippling democratic opposition and changing the rules of elections and government. As Friedland shows, the transformation of Wisconsin along these lines can only be understood in relation to broader, long-term political developments that transcend the state. The hollowing out of democracy in Wisconsin and elsewhere makes it urgently necessary to revive higher education's civic mission—namely, "to ensure that democracy persists," as Cramer puts it. Her essay invokes the Wisconsin Idea to call for such a revival and points to a range of impediments that must be overcome for it to succeed, some of which are part of the university's political context and some of which are internal to the university itself. Among the impediments within the university, she emphasizes elitism in both a socioeconomic sense and in what academics consider valid knowledge. Academics can help reinvigorate the university's civic mission, she suggests, by changing "the manner in which we do our research, how we communicate our results, and with whom we share our knowledge." Thus, like Meine, Cramer explores difficult questions about the role of experts and expertise in a democratic society. While these chapters provide an account of the conditions that are undermining the Wisconsin Idea in the twenty-first century, they also help us to understand, by extension, what kinds of conditions may be necessary to renew and sustain it.

Perhaps it is fitting to conclude this introduction where it began: with Stark's essay on the Wisconsin Idea, written a quarter of a century ago. That essay emphasized the role of great men—exceptionally virtuous and "impressive persons" like Van Hise, Commons, La Follette, and McCarthy—to explain the success of the Wisconsin Idea, and it concluded that the Wisconsin Idea's future prospects likewise depended on the "desire" of government elites, university administrators, and faculty. "If they resolutely decide that the Idea will die, it will die. If they resolutely decide that the Idea will become stronger, it will become stronger."[146] As a political appeal to inspire support for the Wisconsin Idea, this emphasis on individual will and desire made sense; as historical and sociological analysis it was flawed by its neglect of interests, circumstances, and nonelites. Stark was right to reject the vulgar materialistic assumption, apparently adopted by some critics of the Wisconsin Idea, that ideas merely reflect the economic and political interests of the groups that carry them. The relationship between ideas and interests is more complicated. This introductory essay rests on the assumption that "ideas become effective forces in history" when particular groups become carriers for them and when those ideas determine the tracks along which group members' ideal and material interests push their actions.[147] Stark was right, too, that human beings make their own history. However, as a nineteenth-century revolutionary chastened by disappointment once put it, they do so under circumstances that are transmitted from the past, not chosen by themselves.[148] Lastly, Stark was not wrong about the important role of elites in history, but as social historians remind us, history is also made from below. Ultimately, then, the future prospects of the Wisconsin Idea depend on a broader range of factors than Stark acknowledged: both the persuasiveness of the ideas we promote in public debate and the interests that influence our conduct, our desires and the circumstances that enable and constrain their fulfillment, elites and the ordinary citizens who make up the public. Chastened by our own disappointments, we recognize that "it will likely prove more difficult to rebuild the state's progressive traditions than it was to destroy them."[149] We nevertheless continue to share Stark's hope that people within and beyond Wisconsin will take the path of renewing the Wisconsin Idea and its ideal of service to democracy.

Notes

1. John O. (Jack) Stark, *The Wisconsin Idea: The University's Service to the State* (Madison: Legislative Reference Bureau, 1995), 102. Reprinted from the *State of Wisconsin 1995–1996 Blue Book*, ed. Lawrence S. Barish (Madison: Wisconsin Legislative Reference Bureau, 1995), http://digital.library.wisc.edu/1711.dl/WI.WIBlueBk1995. The two meanings of the Wisconsin Idea reflect the term's history. Reformer and civil servant Charles McCarthy used the term in 1912 "to summarize the various ameliorative activities of the Wisconsin progressive movement, including those of the University," but it "increasingly referred more narrowly to University public service" after a conservative Republican was elected governor of Wisconsin in 1914. E. David Cronon and John W. Jenkins, *The University of Wisconsin: A History*, vol. 3, *1925–1945* (Madison: University of Wisconsin Press, 1994), 828.

2. The constitution of the state of Wisconsin established the University of Wisconsin in 1848, the year that Wisconsin was admitted to the Union. The university became a land-grant institution in 1866 by virtue of the Morrill Act, which the US Congress passed in 1862. The Morrill Act gave federal lands to Wisconsin and other states for the purpose of selling the land and using the proceeds to fund public colleges, which were obliged to include instruction in agriculture and the mechanic arts, though "without excluding other scientific and classical studies." Library of Congress, *A Century of Lawmaking for a New Nation: U.S. Congressional Documents and Debates, 1774–1875* (Washington, DC: Library of Congress, 1999), 503–5.

3. John D. Buenker, *The History of Wisconsin*, vol. 4, *The Progressive Era, 1893–1914* (Madison: State Historical Society of Wisconsin, 1998), 606. Of course, as state support for higher education diminishes, so too does the university's responsibility to serve the public. There is an old joke in Wisconsin about the declining proportion of the university's budget that comes from the state: the University of Wisconsin used to be the state university; it then became a state-subsidized university; now it is merely a university in the state of Wisconsin.

4. J. David Hoeveler, *John Bascom and the Origins of the Wisconsin Idea* (Madison: University of Wisconsin Press, 2016), 107–8.

5. Hoeveler, *John Bascom*, 107–9. Bascom, quoted on p. 108. Cf. Gwen Drury, "The Wisconsin Idea: The Vision That Made Wisconsin Famous," July 22, 2011, p. 5, http://ls.wisc.edu/assets/misc/documents/wi-idea-history-intro-summary-essay.pdf. Of course, as the costs of higher education are privatized and students incur mounting levels of debt, they do not feel the obligation of public service, nor can they afford to devote themselves to it.

6. Stark, *Wisconsin Idea*, 102, 163. University of Wisconsin president Charles Van Hise defined the university's service to the state in part "by having faculty members share their expert knowledge with government agencies of all kinds." Buenker, *History of Wisconsin*, 379. On the university's expert advice to state government, see also Charles McCarthy, *The Wisconsin Idea* (New York: Macmillan, 1912), 136–41; Drury, "Wisconsin Idea," 8; Hoeveler, *John Bascom*, 4.

7. Buenker, *History of Wisconsin*, 9, 519. Buenker notes that "[Charles] McCarthy and other progressive intellectuals ardently desired to replace the *ad hoc* brain trust and Saturday luncheon groups with a permanent system of trained, apolitical, civil-service experts, somewhat along German lines" (597).

8. Stevenson, quoted in Stark, *Wisconsin Idea*, 101.

9. Stark, *Wisconsin Idea*, 102, 163.

10. Hoeveler, *John Bascom*, 3–4. On the application of new knowledge to agriculture and industry, see also McCarthy, *Wisconsin Idea*, 127–31, 141–52.

11. Stark, *Wisconsin Idea*, 114, 135–37.

12. Van Hise defined the university's service to the state in part "by reinvigorating and expanding the Extension Division." Buenker, *History of Wisconsin*, 379, see also 384; McCarthy, *Wisconsin Idea*, 131–36. Merle Curti and Vernon Carstensen, *The University of Wisconsin: A History*, vol. 2, *1848–1925* (Madison: University of Wisconsin Press, 1949), 549–94; Cronon and Jenkins, *University of Wisconsin*, 3:757–828; Drury, "Wisconsin Idea," 8–9. "The university extension division," McCarthy wrote, "is the great, powerful link which connects every part of the university with the individual in the state. It must be remembered that this has a potent influence upon the public and the state and that the influence of the university reaches out into the homes of the state through this extension department by means of its correspondence classes, debates, etc., more completely than in any other state" (127). "The increasing spirit in Wisconsin demanded that the university should serve the state and all of its people and that it should be an institution for all the people within the state and not merely for the few who could send their sons and daughters to Madison; thus was brought about the establishment of the extension division" (132). As a result of the university's extension work, "the professor comes in contact with the needs of the citizen and tempers his theory to practice and the citizen learns to respect the professor—and demands more like him" (141).

13. Van Hise in a 1906 report, quoted in Stark, *Wisconsin Idea*, 114.

14. On correspondence classes and public lectures, see Buenker, *History of Wisconsin*, 383–86. On the university's use of radio and later television for educational purposes, see Cronon and Jenkins, *University of Wisconsin*, 3:815–28; Stark, *Wisconsin Idea*, 149–50, 156.

15. Hoeveler, *John Bascom*, 3–4. See also W. Lee Hansen, ed., *Academic Freedom on Trial: 100 Years of Sifting and Winnowing at the University of Wisconsin–Madison* (Madison: University of Wisconsin Publications, 1998). Academic freedom forms an important basis (though not the only one) for the autonomy of the cultural sphere or field, which is in turn "the fundamental ground on which the modern intellectual stands." Jeffrey C. Goldfarb, *Civility and Subversion: The Intellectual in Democratic Society* (New York: Cambridge University Press, 1998), 28. On the autonomy of the cultural field, see also pp. 375–80 in Chad Alan Goldberg, "Struggle and Solidarity: Civic Republican Elements in Pierre Bourdieu's Political Sociology," *Theory and Society* 42, no. 4 (July 2013): 369–94.

16. Stark, *Wisconsin Idea*, 103, 172n10. Hoeveler, *John Bascom*, 182.

17. Larry G. Gerber, *The Rise and Decline of Faculty Governance: Professionalization and the Modern American University* (Baltimore: Johns Hopkins University Press, 2014), 45, 51. The 1915 Declaration of Principles on Academic Freedom and Academic Tenure is available at https://www.aaup.org/NR/rdonlyres/A6520A9D-0A9A-47B3-B550-C006B5B224E7/0/1915Declaration.pdf.

18. National Education Association / American Federation of Teachers, "The Truth about Tenure in Higher Education," Diversity in Higher Education, https://diversityin highereducation.com/articles/The-Truth-About-Tenure-in-Higher-Education.

19. Gerber, *Rise and Decline*, 26, 32, 46. A profession may be defined as a high-status occupation characterized by (1) control of a body of abstract, specialized knowledge, (2) substantial autonomy from supervision, (3) authority over clients and subordinate occupational groups, and (4) a duty to use knowledge for the public good or for the benefit of clients. Professionalization is the process by which the members of an occupation claim the status of a profession by demonstrating its four hallmarks. Randy Hodson and Teresa A. Sullivan, *The Social Organization of Work*, 5th ed. (Belmont, CA: Wadsworth, 2012), 260–66.

20. Drury, "Wisconsin Idea," 4.

21. Drury, "Wisconsin Idea," 10.

22. Frederick Jackson Turner, *The Frontier in American History* (New York: Henry Holt, 1921), 283. See also McCarthy, *Wisconsin Idea*, 124, which quotes Turner extensively on this point.

23. Drury, "Wisconsin Idea," 7.

24. Drury, "Wisconsin Idea," 9.

25. Kevin Mattson, *Creating a Democratic Public: The Struggle for Urban Participatory Democracy during the Progressive Era* (University Park: Pennsylvania State University Press, 1998), 53. Mattson discusses the social centers movement in which Ward was involved; he notes that the Social Center Association of America was formed in 1911 "out of a conference held in Madison, Wisconsin" (66–67). Stark, *Wisconsin Idea*, 146. See also McCarthy, *Wisconsin Idea*, 134.

26. Buenker, *History of Wisconsin*, vii–viii, x. In 1897, Milwaukee socialists formed Branch One of the Social Democratic Party of America, a short-lived predecessor of the better-known Socialist Party of America, established in 1901 (21, 165). The Wisconsin Society of Equity was a "successor to the Grange, founded in 1902" (296). Buenker

identified a broader set of social carriers this way: "The fully evolved Wisconsin Idea
appealed most strongly to social scientists, public servants, labor unionists, Social
Democrats, urban dwellers, and proponents of Teddy Roosevelt's New Nationalism"
(603).

27. Buenker, *History of Wisconsin*, ix–x, 593–94. On the Legislative Reference
Library, see pp. 594–96. On the University of Wisconsin, see pp. 596–97. On the
expert commissions, see pp. 598–600. Examples include the state's Industrial Commission, Railroad Commission (which became the Public Service Commission in 1931),
and Tax Commission.

28. Buenker, *History of Wisconsin*, 578. See also McCarthy, *Wisconsin Idea*, 1–18.

29. Buenker, *History of Wisconsin*, 578–79. Buenker borrows the notion of these
three languages from historian Daniel T. Rodgers.

30. Buenker, *History of Wisconsin*, 585–86. The commonwealth model endured for
a long time in Wisconsin. As late as 1994, historian William Cronon extolled the state's
communitarian values. William Cronon, *Planning Another Century of Good Government: The Wisconsin Idea in the Twenty-First Century* (Madison: State of Wisconsin
Commission for the Study of Administrative Value and Efficiency, 1994). However, as
Jane L. Collins shows in her contribution to this volume, the commonwealth model
has been periodically challenged, and the ascendance of the radical right in state government after 2010 pushed Wisconsin in a far more divisive and polarizing direction.

31. Buenker, *History of Wisconsin*, 588–89.

32. Buenker, *History of Wisconsin*, 589.

33. Buenker, *History of Wisconsin*, 589; on professionalized government, see 590–91.
Bascom anticipated the commonwealth model of society and the closely related notion
of social investment. Arthur J. Altmeyer, a University of Wisconsin graduate who studied
with Commons and later became chairman of the US Social Security Board (1937–46)
and US Commissioner for Social Security (1946–53), wrote the following in 1958: "The
essence of Bascom's teaching and of the Wisconsin Idea was simply but emphatically
expressed in the belief that government had an affirmative obligation to promote the
well-being of its citizens, and that the University had an equally affirmative obligation to serve the state in helping to achieve that objective." Arthur J. Altmeyer, "The
Wisconsin Idea and Social Security," *Wisconsin Magazine of History* 42, no. 1 (Autumn
1958): 19. "The idea of society as organic, as a unity of parts and not as a collection of
autonomous pieces, gave Bascom a governing model. And it set his priority of the
social interest over the individual interest." Hoeveler, *John Bascom*, 39. Accordingly,
Bascom sought to imbue the University of Wisconsin with a "larger social, reformist
purpose" (103). In his view, "public education should enhance the public spirit," which
is necessary "to meet the designs of powerful, private interests that injure the social
organism" (105). For this reason, "Bascom . . . made sociology central to his teaching
program at Wisconsin. . . . In the social sciences, Bascom proclaimed, we find the
means of 'social redemption,' for these disciplines supply that enlarged view of the
whole that the social organism needs for its means of adaptation and survival, and its
moral progress" (107). Bascom was not, however, a socialist (166).

34. Commons, quoted in Buenker, *History of Wisconsin*, 590.

35. Buenker, *History of Wisconsin*, 591–93. See also McCarthy, *Wisconsin Idea*, 124–25, 141.

36. Buenker, *History of Wisconsin*, 590.

37. Buenker, *History of Wisconsin*, 593. Buenker adds that progressives viewed Wisconsin's service state, "at least potentially, as the embodiment of the public interest and guardian of the public trust. . . . This mutually held belief in the service state permeated the writings of Ely, Commons, Van Hise, McCarthy, and Ross. . . . The kernel of it appeared in La Follette's gubernatorial messages and speeches. . . . Most obviously, it was the foundation stone on which stood the three pillars of the Wisconsin Idea: the Legislative Reference Library, the University of Wisconsin, and the quasi-independent commissions of experts" (593–94). Buenker sums up this conception of Wisconsin's service state in several places. "[The Wisconsin Idea's] premise was a 'commonwealth' conception of society in which there was a definable 'public interest' that transcended particularistic concerns and that could best be achieved by enlightened cooperation among state government, the state university, and the private sector. Together, the government and the university were to provide the required social investment for a variety of endeavors whose immediate beneficiaries were private citizens or organizations, but which would ultimately redound to the general welfare" (viii). "In theory, the Wisconsin Idea involved the establishment of an efficient, economical, and honest general welfare state managed by apolitical experts who were subject to control by sophisticated voters who were sensitive to local governments" (603).

38. Buenker, *History of Wisconsin*, 583.

39. Buenker, *History of Wisconsin*, 580, 583. On the international networks that defined progressive thought, see Daniel T. Rodgers, *Atlantic Crossings: Social Politics in a Progressive Age* (Cambridge, MA: Harvard University Press, 1998).

40. Buenker, *History of Wisconsin*, ix; see also 582–83.

41. Buenker, *History of Wisconsin*, ix, 581–82.

42. Buenker, *History of Wisconsin*, ix.

43. Buenker, *History of Wisconsin*, 577, 583. "Many of Wisconsin's signature laws, programs, and agencies had analogs not only elsewhere in the United States, but also in Europe, Australia, New Zealand, and Japan. Paralleling the Wisconsin Idea, at least in some of its most important aspects, were the 'Iowa Idea' of [Iowa governor and later US senator] Albert B. Cummins, the 'New Idea' of New Jersey's [lawyer] George L. Record and [professor and later US president] Woodrow Wilson, the 'Oregon System' of [lawyer and state legislator] William S. U'Ren, and several others. The 1912 [US] presidential campaign also produced the 'New Freedom' of Woodrow Wilson and the 'New Nationalism' of Theodore Roosevelt" (577).

44. Buenker, *History of Wisconsin*, 584.

45. Theodore Roosevelt, introduction to McCarthy, *Wisconsin Idea*, x; Buenker, *History of Wisconsin*, ix, 582.

46. Vernon Carstensen, "The Origin and Early Development of the Wisconsin Idea," *Wisconsin Magazine of History* 39, no. 3 (Spring 1956): 181.

47. Talcott Parsons and Gerald M. Platt, *The American University* (Cambridge, MA: Harvard University Press, 1973), 3–6. At the University of Wisconsin, a considerable

amount of expansion and reorganization occurred under university president Fred
Harvey Harrington from 1962 to 1970. See E. David Cronon and John W. Jenkins,
The University of Wisconsin: A History, vol. 4, *1945–1971* (Madison: University of Wisconsin Press, 1999), especially 163–224. Harrington was a strong proponent of the
Wisconsin Idea: "Not since the visionary days of the great Van Hise had a UW leader
offered such a broad and optimistic affirmation of the Wisconsin Idea of a service
university. . . . Harrington believed deeply in the Wisconsin Idea of a service university
committed to helping the people of Wisconsin and their government solve problems
of immediate and longer range concern" (172, 174).

48. On the creation of the University of Wisconsin–Extension, see Cronon and
Jenkins, *University of Wisconsin*, 4:295–372. University of Wisconsin president Fred
Harvey Harrington believed the reorganization of extension work would enable the
university "once again to provide pioneering leadership in this field, as it had in the
glory days of its great President Van Hise. He was convinced the expanding domestic
agenda of the Kennedy and Johnson administrations in Washington and the parallel
interest of the great national foundations would bring vastly increased support for
urban extension activities." Unfortunately, the reorganization "did not bring the revitalization of UW outreach Harrington expected," the expected "increase in federal and
foundation support for new urban extension services" did not materialize, and Harrington did not "foresee the long-term consequences of severing ties between extension
and the Madison campus" (209–10). On the creation of the University of Wisconsin
System, see pp. 521–96. At the time of this writing, the University of Wisconsin System
is one of the largest systems of public higher education in the United States; it employs
about 39,000 faculty and staff statewide, educates approximately 170,000 students
each year, and serves more than one million citizens through statewide extension programs. The system comprises two doctoral research universities, eleven comprehensive
universities that grant baccalaureate and master's degrees, and thirteen two-year branch
campuses that grant associate degrees.

49. Stark, *Wisconsin Idea*, 163–64.

50. Governor's Blue Ribbon Commission on 21st Century Jobs, *The New Wisconsin
Idea: The Innovative Learning State* (Madison: Commission, 1997), 10. Thompson's commission was not the first individual or group to propose a new Wisconsin Idea. In 1928
University of Wisconsin president Glenn Frank "impressed a group of businessmen by
explaining his notion of a 'new Wisconsin Idea' that would link the state and University through the faculty's research." Cronon and Jenkins, *University of Wisconsin*, 3:86.
When Wisconsin governor Patrick J. Lucey met with University of Wisconsin faculty
members in 1971 to urge their support for his proposed merger that would create the
University of Wisconsin System, he called for a "'New Wisconsin Idea'" to "cope with
the new challenges of the 1970s." Cronon and Jenkins, *University of Wisconsin*, 4:582.

51. The commission proposed several laudable social investments, from improvement of the state's transportation infrastructure to encouragement of foreign-language
training (an implicit acknowledgment of the value of the humanities), and it explicitly
promoted "high-quality jobs" over "'hit and run' development that imposes environmental and infrastructure costs." Governor's Blue Ribbon Commission, *New Wisconsin*

Idea, 13, 15, 27, 35. The commission's recommendations were quite progressive in these respects, especially when compared to the policies that the state legislature would begin to adopt fifteen years later.

52. Governor's Blue Ribbon Commission, *New Wisconsin Idea*, 5.

53. Governor's Blue Ribbon Commission, *New Wisconsin Idea*, 11.

54. Governor's Blue Ribbon Commission, *New Wisconsin Idea*, 31–42.

55. Governor's Blue Ribbon Commission, *New Wisconsin Idea*, 10.

56. Governor's Blue Ribbon Commission, *New Wisconsin Idea*, 10.

57. Governor's Blue Ribbon Commission, *New Wisconsin Idea*, 40.

58. Governor's Blue Ribbon Commission, *New Wisconsin Idea*, 43.

59. Buenker, *History of Wisconsin*, 387.

60. Buenker, *History of Wisconsin*, 387.

61. Stark, *Wisconsin Idea*, 164–71. Another instance occurred after the conservative Milwaukee industrialist Julius Heil was elected governor of Wisconsin in 1938. Cronon and Jenkins, *University of Wisconsin*, 3:352, 364–84.

62. Max Weber, *From Max Weber: Essays in Sociology*, ed. H. H. Gerth and C. Wright Mills (New York: Oxford University Press, 1946), 242–43. These remarks were first published posthumously in German in 1922. Weber feared that the irresistible expansion of bureaucracy would ultimately lead to the prevalence of "specialists without spirit." Max Weber, *The Protestant Ethic and the Spirit of Capitalism*, trans. Talcott Parsons (New York: Routledge, 1930), 124. On the refusal to take sides, see Buenker, *History of Wisconsin*, 593. Weber's gendered language underscores the biases of higher education in his time, but see Theda Skocpol, *Protecting Soldiers and Mothers: The Political Origins of Social Policy in the United States* (Cambridge, MA: Harvard University Press, 1992), 340–43, on women in American higher education. She notes that "the United States led the world in offering higher education to women in its decentralized and fast-growing system of colleges and universities," in part because "educated women were badly needed to staff the public schools that became one of the bulwarks of American mass democracy" (340–41). Wisconsin was one of eight state universities open to women in 1870 (341). See Hoeveler, *John Bascom*, chap. 10, on Bascom's support for co-education. On the importance of the humanities for a democratic society, see Martha C. Nussbaum, *Not for Profit: Why Democracy Needs the Humanities* (Princeton, NJ: Princeton University Press, 2010).

63. Buenker, *History of Wisconsin*, 606.

64. Buenker, *History of Wisconsin*, 603. Cf. Thomas C. Leonard, *Illiberal Reformers: Race, Eugenics and American Economics in the Progressive Era* (Princeton, NJ: Princeton University Press, 2016), 49–54. For an argument that at least some American progressives in the early twentieth century were committed to deepening democratic self-government, see Mattson, *Creating a Democratic Public*.

65. Buenker, *History of Wisconsin*, 579, 604; Hoeveler, *John Bascom*, 39.

66. McCarthy, *Wisconsin Idea*, 46. The sociologist Jeffrey C. Goldfarb has framed the tension between expertise and democracy as the "paradox of the democratic intellectual"; see Goldfarb, *Civility and Subversion*, 6–8.

67. Buenker, *History of Wisconsin*, 598.

68. The problem of reconciling democracy with scientific or professional expertise was widely discussed among American intellectuals in the Progressive Era. For John Dewey's reflections, see Robert B. Westbrook, *John Dewey and American Democracy* (Ithaca, NY: Cornell University Press, 1991), 187–88, 193–94, 299, 306–18. For Weber's concerns about bureaucracy, tensions between democracy and bureaucracy, and the formation of a new privileged stratum based on educational certificates, see Weber, *From Max Weber*, 196–244. Weber and McCarthy were contemporaries, and Weber drew on his experience with the German model that inspired McCarthy. On the power of uncertainty, see Randall Collins, *Sociological Insight*, 2nd ed. (New York: Oxford University Press, 1992), 81–85. On monopoly of knowledge as a basis for claims to power and privilege by highly educated groups, see Lawrence Peter King and Iván Szelényi, *Theories of the New Class: Intellectuals and Power* (Minneapolis: University of Minnesota Press, 2004).

69. Buenker, *History of Wisconsin*, 606–9. He finds that the "architects of the Wisconsin Idea," with the exception of La Follette, expressed insufficient concern about the status and voting rights of women, or treated women as "a dependent class in need of protection" (607). He notes that in the early twentieth century, "Wisconsin's black population was very small and had little or no political clout, so it is not surprising that they were ignored" (608). "Nor did Wisconsin's progressives," again with the exception of La Follette, "take much notice of the state's Native Americans" (608). "As for southern and eastern European immigrants, several Wisconsin progressives, especially professors [Edward A.] Ross and [John R.] Commons, were among the nation's loudest advocates of immigration restriction" (608).

70. Leonard, *Illiberal Reformers*; Thomas C. Leonard, "Wisconsin Progressives Had Regressive Beliefs," *Wisconsin Interest* (Fall 2016): 16–23.

71. Aaron Bird Bear, "Notes from the Ethnic Cleansing Zone: The Wisconsin Idea, Imperialist Nostalgia, and the Remaking of a Shared Future" (lecture, University of Wisconsin–Madison, November 29, 2016), https://www.youtube.com/watch?v=o2gA y37Aa9Q.

72. There is relatively little published criticism from the radical left that is directed specifically at the Wisconsin Idea. However, it is possible to infer such criticisms from the wider scholarship on the social functions of education. On social engineering, see the criticism of McCarthy and Commons in Herman Schwendinger and Julia R. Schwendinger, *The Sociologists of the Chair: A Radical Analysis of the Formative Years of North American Sociology (1883–1922)* (New York: Basic Books, 1974), 229–32. For the classic Marxist argument that the function of education is to produce workers, see Samuel Bowles and Herbert Gintis, *Schooling in Capitalist America: Educational Reform and the Contradictions of Economic Life* (New York: Basic Books, 1976). On the role of the university in reproducing social inequality, see Pierre Bourdieu and Jean-Claude Passeron, *The Inheritors: French Students and Their Relations to Culture*, trans. Richard Nice (Chicago: University of Chicago Press, [1964] 1979); Pierre Bourdieu and Jean-Claude Passeron, *Reproduction in Education, Society and Culture*, trans. Richard Nice (London: Sage, [1970] 1977).

73. Wolfgang Saxon, "Michael S. Joyce, Research Patron, Dies at 63," *New York Times*, March 3, 2006, https://www.nytimes.com/2006/03/03/us/michael-s-joyce-re search-patron-dies-at-63.html.

74. Pat Schneider, "Conservative Think Tank Tells UW Regents to Make Campuses Prove They Need Tenure," *Capital Times*, March 2, 2016, https://madison.com/ct/news/local/education/university/conservative-think-tank-tells-uw-regents-to-make -campuses-prove/article_104a55fb-873e-531b-b57c-f26d1abc23bb.html. The WPRI was a member of the State Policy Network, the sister organization of the American Legislative Exchange Council (ALEC). On ALEC, see Lewis A. Friedland's chapter in this volume. One wonders whether the New Wisconsin Idea was, at least in part, a reaction to Joyce's criticism of the "old" Wisconsin Idea and an attempt to "rescue" it from such criticism.

75. Michael S. Joyce, "The Legacy of the 'Wisconsin Idea,'" *Wisconsin Interest* 3, no. 2 (Fall/Winter 1994), 9–10.

76. Joyce, "Legacy of the 'Wisconsin Idea,'" 13–14.

77. Joyce, "Legacy of the 'Wisconsin Idea,'" 12.

78. Joyce, "Legacy of the 'Wisconsin Idea,'" 9.

79. Joyce, "Legacy of the 'Wisconsin Idea,'" 12–13.

80. Jeffrey C. Alexander, *The Civil Sphere* (New York: Oxford University Press, 2006), 23–36.

81. Theda Skocpol, Marshall Ganz, Ziad Munson, Bayliss Camp, Michele Swers, and Jennifer Oser, "How Americans Became Civic," in *Civic Engagement in American Democracy*, ed. Theda Skocpol and Morris P. Fiorina (New York: Russell Sage Foundation, 1999), 33.

82. Robert Wuthnow, "Tocqueville's Question Reconsidered: Voluntarism and Public Discourse in Advanced Societies," in *Between States and Markets: The Voluntary Sector in Comparative Perspective*, ed. Robert Wuthnow (Princeton, NJ: Princeton University Press, 1991), 292.

83. Shlomo Avineri, *Hegel's Theory of the Modern State* (New York: Cambridge University Press, 1972), 105, 107–8, 155–61; King and Szelényi, *Theories of the New Class*, 3–5.

84. Alexander Hamilton, James Madison, and John Jay, *The Federalist Papers* (New York: Penguin, 1961), 78.

85. Alvin W. Gouldner, *The Future of Intellectuals and the Rise of the New Class* (New York: Oxford University Press, 1979), 94–101. Gouldner suggests that the "takeoff" period for the new class in the United States was about 1900 to 1930 (15). The notion in modern social thought of a new class can be traced back to Hegel, who identified civil servants as the carrier of the modern state's universalism; the French social reformer Henri de Saint-Simon, who envisioned the rule of modern society by scientists; and the German philosopher and revolutionary Karl Marx, who regarded the working class, not Hegel's civil servants, as the true universal class, but who nevertheless assigned to intellectuals the crucial role of developing the worker's emancipatory consciousness. King and Szelényi, *Theories of the New Class*, 1–18. "The three proto-theories foreshadow three New Class actors that will occupy the center stage of

various later New Class theories: the bureaucracy, the technocracy, and the critical intelligentsia" (3). However, in contrast to later theorists of the new class, Hegel, Saint-Simon, and Marx justified rather than criticized the social influence of these actors.

86. King and Szelényi, *Theories of the New Class*, 21–29. As anarchists warned about the domination of a new class in Europe, engineer Fredrick Taylor and social scientist Thorstein Veblen urged university-educated engineers to rationalize capitalist production in the United States (145–49). "In the West, . . . from the turn of the twentieth century onward, a group of highly educated, more specifically the technically skilled, came forward with a new claim for power. The Progressive Era in the United States, the ideology (and organizations) of the 'scientific management movements' among engineers in particular, signaled the beginning of this technocratic project" (xxv).

87. Bakunin, quoted in King and Szelényi, *Theories of the New Class*, xiii, 21. On claims that "Wisconsin was 'a university that rules a state,'" see McCarthy, *Wisconsin Idea*, 137; Buenker, *History of Wisconsin*, 386.

88. King and Szelényi, *Theories of the New Class*, 24–29. Machajski published his ideas in 1905. Similar ideas can be found in Max Weber's work: "The development of the diploma from universities, and business and engineering colleges, and the universal clamor for the creation of educational certificates in all fields make for the formation of a privileged stratum in bureaus and in offices. Such certificates support their holders' . . . claims to monopolize social and economically advantageous positions." Weber, *From Max Weber*, 241. Cf. sociologist Karl Mannheim: "The modern bourgeoisie had from the beginning a twofold social root—on the one hand the owners of capital, on the other those individuals whose only capital consisted in their education." Karl Mannheim, *Ideology and Utopia: An Introduction to the Sociology of Knowledge*, trans. Louis Wirth and Edward Shils (New York: Harcourt, Brace, 1936), 156. For a more recent version of this argument, see Randall Collins, *The Credential Society: An Historical Sociology of Education and Stratification* (New York: Academic Press, 1979).

89. King and Szelényi, *Theories of the New Class*, 45–65, 144–56.

90. King and Szelényi, *Theories of the New Class*, 156–73, quotation from p. xxi.

91. Michel Foucault, *Power/Knowledge: Selected Interviews and Other Writings, 1972–1977*, ed. Colin Gordon (New York: Pantheon, 1980); James C. Scott, *Seeing Like a State: How Certain Schemes to Improve the Human Condition Have Failed* (New Haven, CT: Yale University Press, 1998).

92. Cf. Gouldner, *Future of Intellectuals*, on academic freedom, "the drive to use 'brain trusts' and experts in public policy development," the "development of an 'independent' Civil Service," and "reform movements seeking 'honesty in government'" as arenas of contest between the new and old classes (16–17); professionalism as an ideology of the new class (19, 37–39); and the role of public education and the university in the reproduction of the new class (43–47). Gouldner was careful to say that professionalism is not "*only* an ideology," though "it is that, *too*. . . . The ideological dimension of professional claims . . . should not exclude recognition of the special skill and knowledge base of some occupations" (106n31). For a different view about intellectuals and ideology, see Goldfarb, *Civility and Subversion*; he argues that intellectuals can be publicly engaged without being ideologues (37–41).

93. Gouldner, *Future of Intellectuals*, 7–8, see also 83–85. What makes the new class universal, in Gouldner's view, is that it is the social carrier for what he called the culture of critical discourse (28–43).

94. For an elaboration of this point, see pp. 380–84 in Goldberg, "Struggle and Solidarity." "To ignore the role of values in shaping a group's behavior is vulgar materialism; to omit analysis of the conditions under which persons conform with or deviate from their values is vulgar idealism." Gouldner, *Future of Intellectuals*, 59.

95. Joyce, "Legacy of the 'Wisconsin Idea,'" 12.

96. Buenker, *History of Wisconsin*, 380.

97. Axel Honneth, "Pathologies of the Social: The Past and Present of Social Philosophy," in *Disrespect: The Normative Foundations of Critical Theory* (Malden, MA: Polity Press, 2007), 36.

98. Christopher F. Zurn, *Axel Honneth: A Critical Theory of the Social* (Malden, MA: Polity Press, 2015), 122, emphasis in original.

99. Joyce, "Legacy of the 'Wisconsin Idea,'" 12.

100. Shawn Johnson, "Legislator Rejects UW Economist's Report Disputing Benefits of Right-to-Work Laws," Wisconsin Public Radio, March 3, 2015, https://www.wpr.org/legislator-rejects-uw-economists-report-disputing-benefits-right-work-laws.

101. Goldfarb, *Civility and Subversion*.

102. Leonard, *Illiberal Reformers*, xi.

103. Leonard, *Illiberal Reformers*, ix–x.

104. Leonard, *Illiberal Reformers*, x–xi.

105. Leonard, *Illiberal Reformers*, 40–42.

106. See Leonard, *Illiberal Reformers*, 68–69, 110, on Van Hise's support of eugenics. Ely, Commons, and Ross are discussed extensively throughout Leonard's book. Turner's nativism is noted briefly on p. 137. See also Leonard, "Wisconsin Progressives Had Regressive Beliefs."

107. Leonard, *Illiberal Reformers*, 190–91.

108. Leonard, *Illiberal Reformers*, 191.

109. For a critical assessment and historiographical contextualization of Leonard's book, see Marshall I. Steinbaum and Bernard A. Weisberger, "The Intellectual Legacy of Progressive Economics: A Review Essay of Thomas C. Leonard's *Illiberal Reformers*," *Journal of Economic Literature* 55, no. 3 (2017): 1064–83. For a perspective that is attentive to the varieties of progressivism and disagreements among progressives in the early twentieth century, see Westbrook, *John Dewey and American Democracy*; Rogers M. Smith, *Civic Ideals: Conflicting Visions of Citizenship in U.S. History* (New Haven, CT: Yale University Press, 1997), 410–69.

110. Steinbaum and Weisberger point out that the Wisconsin Idea had broad public support in the early twentieth century: "Anathema as this might be to laissez-faire proponents, the citizens of Wisconsin liked [the Wisconsin Idea] enough to reelect [Robert M.] La Follette [as governor] three times [in 1900, 1902, and 1904] and then send him on to the [US] Senate for the rest of his life [1906–25]. . . . The brain trust of the Wisconsin Idea did not seize the reins of power. La Follette offered the voters a program, they voted to put it into effect, and the experts then worked out the details

which, in a modern economy, were complex. The people's will was not snatched away, but put into execution by appointed experts under the final authority of elected officials." They add: "La Follette, campaigning for reform in rural Wisconsin, would hold audiences of farmers spellbound for hours with the reading of public reports loaded with statistics to prove to them how they were being swindled by excessive railroad shipping charges—proof, if ever it was necessary, that expertise and empirical analysis need not be at odds with populist politics." Steinbaum and Weisberger, "Intellectual Legacy," 1074, 1076.

111. Steinbaum and Weisberger, "Intellectual Legacy," 1077–78.

112. Neither Kenneth B. Clark nor Mamie Phipps Clark were faculty at the University of Wisconsin, but their work nevertheless exemplified the spirit of the Wisconsin Idea. At the time, University of Wisconsin president Fred Harvey Harrington aligned the university with "the broad goals of the civil rights movement." Cronon and Jenkins, *University of Wisconsin*, 4:215. R. Richard Wagner's chapter in this volume provides another case in point; it shows in regard to nonnormative sexuality both the darker side of social efficiency and the potential within the Wisconsin Idea for solutions to social exclusion and coercion.

113. Steinbaum and Weisberger, "Intellectual Legacy," 1078.

114. Stark, *Wisconsin Idea*, 164.

115. "A nationally unprecedented series of votes of no confidence in UW System President Ray Cross and the Board of Regents, led by AFT-Wisconsin Higher Education Council and American Association of University Professors members, has spread rapidly across the UW System. The first such resolution was passed by the UW–Madison faculty senate . . . followed quickly by faculty senates at the River Falls, La Crosse, Green Bay, and Stout campuses; by the academic staff senate at UW–Milwaukee; and by a historic, unanimous vote of the full UW–Milwaukee faculty. . . . The votes are a response to the complicity of Cross and the Regents in undermining tenure, academic freedom, and shared governance, and their failure to advocate for the UW System." AFT-Wisconsin, "Higher Ed Council Members Lead Wave of No Confidence Votes," *Union Voice*, May 2016, p. 2, http://wi.aft.org/files/2016-05_aft-wisconsin_newsletter .pdf. See also Brock Read, "U. of Wisconsin at Madison Faculty Votes No Confidence in System's President and Regents," *Chronicle of Higher Education*, May 2, 2016, https:// www.chronicle.com/blogs/ticker/u-of-wisconsin-at-madison-faculty-votes-no-con fidence-in-systems-president-and-regents/110999; Scott Jaschik, "Vote of No Confidence in U Wisconsin Board, President," *Inside Higher Ed*, May 3, 2016, https://www .insidehighered.com/quicktakes/2016/05/03/vote-no-confidence-u-wisconsin-board -president; Chad Alan Goldberg, "Why I Wrote the No-Confidence Resolution at UW– Madison," *Wisconsin State Journal*, May 11, 2016, https://madison.com/wsj/opinion/ column/chad-alan-goldberg-why-i-wrote-the-no-confidence-resolution/article_ccea5fa4 -9295-56ed-99e7-482c5211b902.html.

116. Valerie Strauss, "How Gov. Walker Tried to Quietly Change the Mission of the University of Wisconsin," *Washington Post*, February 5, 2015, https://www.washington post.com/news/answer-sheet/wp/2015/02/05/how-gov-walker-tried-to-quietly-change -the-mission-of-the-university-of-wisconsin/?utm_term=.f69e5ac13d78; Alia Wong,

"The Governor Who (Maybe) Tried to Kill Liberal-Arts Education," *Atlantic*, February 11, 2015, https://www.theatlantic.com/education/archive/2015/02/the-governor -who-maybe-tried-to-kill-liberal-arts-education/385366/; Dan Kaufman, *The Fall of Wisconsin: The Conservative Conquest of a Progressive Bastion and the Future of American Politics* (New York: W. W. Norton, 2018), 235.

117. Governor's Blue Ribbon Commission, *New Wisconsin Idea*, 15.

118. Luke Schaetzel, "Just How Much Has the UW System Lost since 2011?" The Observatory, November 9, 2016, https://observatory.journalism.wisc.edu/2016/11/09/ just-how-much-has-the-uw-system-lost-since-2011/.

119. Rich Kremer, "Report: Wisconsin Saw Fourth-Largest Decline in Higher Ed Funding between 2013 and 2018," Wisconsin Public Radio, April 15, 2019, https://www .wpr.org/report-wisconsin-saw-fourth-largest-decline-higher-ed-funding-between -2013-and-2018.

120. Tom Kertscher, "Scott Walker, Who Cut Funds to Wisconsin University System, Says System Has Its Largest Budget Ever," Politifact Wisconsin, May 25, 2016, https://www.politifact.com/wisconsin/statements/2016/may/25/scott-walker/scott -walker-who-cut-funds-wisconsin-university-sy/.

121. Shawn Johnson, "GOP Lawmakers Reject Walker's Tuition Cut," Wisconsin Public Radio, May 25, 2017, https://www.wpr.org/gop-lawmakers-reject-walkers-tuition -cut.

122. Danielle Kaeding, "UW–Superior Suspends 25 Programs," Wisconsin Public Radio, October 31, 2017, https://www.wpr.org/uw-superior-suspends-25-programs; Hank Reichman, "No Longer Superior?" Academe Blog, November 4, 2017, https:// academeblog.org/2017/11/04/no-longer-superior/; Colleen Flaherty, "U Wisconsin– Stevens Point to Eliminate 13 Majors," *Inside Higher Ed*, March 6, 2018, https://www .insidehighered.com/quicktakes/2018/03/06/u-wisconsin-stevens-point-eliminate -13-majors; Mark Sommerhauser, "Controversy Follows UW–Stevens Point Decision to Cut Humanities Programs," *Wisconsin State Journal*, March 11, 2018, https://madi son.com/wsj/news/local/education/university/controversy-follows-uw-stevens-point -decision-to-cut-humanities-programs/article_e9f59317-6d91-545a-a95e-c64befb444 47.html; Glen Moberg, "UW–Stevens Point Students Hold Sit-In to Protest Cuts to Humanities," Wisconsin Public Radio, March 21, 2018, https://www.wpr.org/uw-stevens -point-students-hold-sit-protest-cuts-humanities; Nick Heynen, "Hundreds Protest Proposal to Eliminate Liberal Arts Majors at UW–Stevens Point," *Wisconsin State Journal*, March 23, 2018, https://madison.com/wsj/news/local/education/university/pho tos-hundreds-protest-proposal-to-eliminate-liberal-arts-majors-at/collection_2d7fc4 78-4b2a-5941-89c4-e3d26d3ea4a8.html; Karen Herzog, "UW–Stevens Point Rolls Out Transformation That Would Cut 6 Liberal Arts Degrees, Focus on Careers," *Milwaukee Journal Sentinel*, November 12, 2018, https://www.jsonline.com/story/news/educa tion/2018/11/12/uw-stevens-point-transformation-trims-humanities-focuses-careers/197 6108002/; Mitch Smith, "Students in Rural America Ask, 'What Is a University without a History Major?'" *New York Times*, January 12, 2019, https://www.nytimes.com/ 2019/01/12/us/rural-colleges-money-students-leaving.html. The opposition of students

and faculty ultimately prevented program closures at the University of Wisconsin–Stevens Point. Colleen Flaherty, "Cuts Reversed at Stevens Point," *Inside Higher Ed*, April 11, 2019, https://www.insidehighered.com/news/2019/04/11/stevens-point-abandons-controversial-plan-cut-liberal-arts-majors-including-history.

123. Colleen Flaherty, "Trying to Kill Tenure," *Inside Higher Ed*, June 1, 2015, https://www.insidehighered.com/news/2015/06/01/wisconsin-faculty-incensed-motion-eliminate-tenure-state-statute; Hank Reichman, "The End of Tenure in Wisconsin?" Academe Blog, June 2, 2015, https://academeblog.org/2015/06/02/the-end-of-tenure-in-wisconsin/; Karen Herzog, "National Focus on UW System Sharpening over Tenure, Governance," *Milwaukee Journal Sentinel*, June 4, 2015, http://archive.jsonline.com/news/national-focus-on-uw-sharpening-over-tenure-governance-b99511901z1-306017731.html; Colleen Flaherty, "Losing Hope in Wisconsin," *Inside Higher Ed*, June 5, 2015, https://www.insidehighered.com/news/2015/06/05/faculty-members-protest-tenure-shared-governance-changes-board-regents; John K. Wilson, "AAUP Resolution on Wisconsin Attacks on Academic Freedom and Shared Governance," Academe Blog, June 13, 2015, https://academeblog.org/2015/06/13/aaup-resolution-on-wisconsin-attacks-on-academic-freedom-and-shared-governance/; "AAUP/AFT-Wisconsin Joint Statement on the Proposed Regent Policies," AAUP, February 3, 2016, https://www.aaup.org/news/statement-wisconsin-policies#.XRVAjS3Mz9M; Chad Alan Goldberg and Elena Levy-Navarro (with James Oberly and Jon Shelton), "Search for Truth in Peril on UW System Campuses," *Wisconsin State Journal*, March 4, 2016, https://madison.com/wsj/opinion/column/search-for-truth-in-peril-on-uw-system-campuses-/article_ce51c3b9-390e-5f1e-8e2e-9e4c9debe371.html; Colleen Flaherty, "U of Wisconsin Regents Adopt New Tenure Policies," *Inside Higher Ed*, March 10, 2016, https://www.insidehighered.com/quicktakes/2016/03/10/breaking-u-wisconsin-regents-adopt-new-tenure-policies; Nico Savidge, "Regents Approve New Policies for UW Tenure over Professors' Objections," *Wisconsin State Journal*, March 11, 2016, https://madison.com/wsj/news/local/education/university/regents-approve-new-policies-for-uw-tenure-over-professors-objections/article_e0aa29b5-438b-5182-8870-5cd76fb80144.html; Colleen Flaherty, "'Fake' Tenure?" *Inside Higher Ed*, March 11, 2016, https://www.insidehighered.com/news/2016/03/11/u-wisconsin-board-regents-approves-new-tenure-policies-despite-faculty-concerns; Nico Savidge, "Changes to Tenure, Budget and Regents Show Extent of Scott Walker's Impact on UW," *Wisconsin State Journal*, March 27, 2016, https://madison.com/wsj/news/local/education/university/changes-to-tenure-budget-and-regents-show-extent-of-scott/article_90954155-df31-5fdb-bb93-dd93a0f81225.html; Colleen Flaherty, "What Remains of Tenure," *Inside Higher Ed*, December 7, 2016, https://www.insidehighered.com/news/2016/12/07/faculty-members-university-wisconsin-oppose-proposed-change-new-post-tenure-review; Chuck Rybak, *UW Struggle: When a State Attacks Its University* (Minneapolis: University of Minnesota Press, 2017).

124. The weakening of tenure extended to faculty the same logic of "flexibility" that had already been imposed on other university employees. Chad Alan Goldberg, "Regents Can't Have It Both Ways," *Milwaukee Journal-Sentinel*, December 29, 2015, http://archive.jsonline.com/news/opinion/letters-b99641738z1-363777671.html/.

125. Gerber, *Rise and Decline*, 52.

126. These changes in university governance are documented in many of the sources provided in note 123. See also Jeffrey J. Selingo, "U. of Wisconsin Faculty Would Lose Collective-Bargaining Rights under Governor's Proposal," *Chronicle of Higher Education,* February 13, 2011, https://www.chronicle.com/article/U-of-Wisconsin-Faculty -Would/126354. The legislation that drastically curtailed collective bargaining rights for public employees in 2011 (noted below) eliminated collective bargaining rights entirely for the university's faculty, academic staff, and graduate student workers. Sara Goldrick-Rab and Chad Alan Goldberg, "University of Wisconsin System Needs Accountability for Everyone," *Milwaukee Journal-Sentinel,* March 16, 2015, http://archive.jsonline.com/ news/opinion/university-of-wisconsin-system-needs-accountability-for-everyone-b99 46314221-296507081.html/; Timothy V. Kaufman-Osborn, "The Downfall of Shared Governance at Wisconsin," *Academe* 103, no. 1 (January–February 2017): n.p., https:// www.aaup.org/article/downfall-shared-governance-wisconsin#.XRpd5C3Mz9M; Rachel Ida Buff, "Disaster Capitalism Hits Higher Education in Wisconsin," *Nation,* February 23, 2018, https://www.thenation.com/article/disaster-capitalism-hits-higher-education -in-wisconsin/. My discussion of shared governance does not mention the university's support staff (previously known as classified staff and currently as university staff) because the Board of Regents did not extend shared governance to them until 2013, after the state legislature drastically curtailed their collective bargaining rights. See Regent Policy Document 20–20, https://www.wisconsin.edu/regents/policies/university-staff-gov ernance/. In contrast to students, faculty, and academic staff, whose governance rights are codified in state law (Chapter 36.09 of the Wisconsin Statutes), university staff enjoy governance rights as a matter of regent policy.

127. Ann H. Franke, "Legal Watch: Enforcing the Obligation to Consult with Faculty," *Academe* 81, no. 4 (July–August 1995): 80.

128. Goldberg and Levy-Navarro, "Search for Truth in Peril."

129. "Faculty Groups Slam UW System President Ray Cross for Secretly Planning Sweeping Restructuring," *Milwaukee Journal Sentinel,* February 6, 2018, https://www .jsonline.com/story/news/education/2018/02/06/uw-system-president-ray-cross-has-fur ther-damaged-already-damaged-relationship/312031002/. The system president's contempt for shared governance was made clear in an email message he sent to a regent. If the "'shared governance' leaders" had been "involved in the process," he wrote, "we wouldn't be doing anything."

130. Scott Jaschik, "In Break with Precedent, No Professors on Wisconsin Presidential Search," *Inside Higher Ed,* November 11, 2019, https://www.insidehighered.com/ quicktakes/2019/11/11/break-precedent-no-professors-wisconsin-presidential-search; "AAUP Wisconsin / AFT-Wisconsin Higher Education Council Joint Statement on UW System President Search," AAUP, November 12, 2019, https://aaupwi.wordpress .com/2019/11/12/aaup-wisconsin-aft-wisconsin-higher-education-council-joint-state ment-on-uw-system-president-search/; Devi Shastri, "Team Searching for UW System's Next President Has No Faculty, No Staff, Little Diversity," *Milwaukee Journal Senti- nel,* November 16, 2019, https://eu.jsonline.com/story/news/education/2019/11/15/team -seeking-next-uw-system-leader-has-no-faculty-little-diversity/2580460001/; "American

Association of University Professors, Statement on the University of Wisconsin's Presidential Search," AAUP, November 19, 2019, https://www.aaup.org/news/statement-university-wisconsin-presidential-search; Eric Kelderman, "Wisconsin's Search for a New President Has Just Begun, Faculty Already Fear the Worst," *Chronicle of Higher Education*, December 6, 2019, https://www.chronicle.com/article/Wisconsin-s-Search-for-a-New/247680.

131. Walker adopted the Wisconsin Idea's language of antimonopolism to present himself as an opponent of "special interests," even as he used this rhetoric to assail the Wisconsin Idea's legacies. "It is characteristic of conservative revolutions . . .," as sociologist Pierre Bourdieu noted, "that they present restorations as revolutions." Pierre Bourdieu, *Acts of Resistance: Against the Tyranny of the Market*, trans. Richard Nice (New York: New Press, 1998), 35. On the appropriation of populist language by American conservatives to identify and assail a new set of "special interests," see Michael Kazin, *The Populist Persuasion: An American History* (Ithaca, NY: Cornell University Press, 1995).

132. "Scott Walker Era of Wisconsin Government Ends," *Wisconsin State Journal*, November 10, 2018, https://madison.com/news/local/govt-and-politics/scott-walker-era-of-wisconsin-government-ends/article_4b4cddb8-eed6-57da-8799-5b428d26b595.html; Teodor Teofilov, "Which Taxpayers Saved the Most from Tax Cuts under Gov. Scott Walker?" The Observatory, March 20, 2018, https://observatory.journalism.wisc.edu/2018/03/19/which-taxpayers-saved-the-most-from-tax-cuts-under-gov-scott-walker/. Tax breaks and public subsidies for private capital were often ineffective; the Wisconsin Economic Development Corporation that Walker created in 2011 gave state tax credits to companies that failed to create the number of jobs they promised or which created jobs outside of the state. Shayndi Raice, "Wisconsin Group Negotiated Tax Credits for Jobs That Didn't Arrive," *Wall Street Journal*, June 12, 2019, https://www.wsj.com/articles/wisconsin-economic-development-group-paid-for-jobs-added-in-other-states-11560250801.

133. Dan Kaufman, "The Destruction of Progressive Wisconsin," *New York Times*, January 16, 2016, https://www.nytimes.com/2016/01/17/opinion/campaign-stops/the-destruction-of-progressive-wisconsin.html; "Corporate Political Spending Can Stay Secret in Wisconsin," *Wisconsin Law Journal*, January 26, 2016, https://wislawjournal.com/2016/01/26/corporate-political-spending-can-stay-secret-in-wisconsin/; Jason Stein and Patrick Marley, "Scott Walker Signs Civil Service Overhaul," *Milwaukee Journal Sentinel*, February 12, 2016, http://archive.jsonline.com/news/statepolitics/scott-walker-to-sign-civil-service-overhaul-friday-b99658717z1-368606201.html.

134. Siri Carpenter, "How Scott Walker Dismantled Wisconsin's Environmental Legacy," *Scientific American*, June 17, 2015, https://www.scientificamerican.com/article/how-scott-walker-dismantled-wisconsin-s-environmental-legacy/.

135. Kaufman, *Fall of Wisconsin*, 6. Kaufman's book documents Wisconsin's conservative revolution in detail. See also the chapters in this volume by Jane L. Collins and Lewis A. Friedland. For an earlier account at the beginning of Wisconsin's sharp turn to the right, see Mari Jo Buhle and Paul Buhle, eds., *It Started in Wisconsin* (New York: Verso, 2011).

136. In addition to Lewis A. Friedland's chapter in this volume, see William Cronon, "Who's Really behind Recent Republican Legislation in Wisconsin and Elsewhere? (Hint: It Didn't Start Here)," Scholar as Citizen (blog), March 15, 2011, http://scholar-citizen.williamcronon.net/tag/wpri; Jane Mayer, *Dark Money: The Hidden History of the Billionaires behind the Rise of the Radical Right* (New York: Doubleday, 2016), 307–12; Lisa Graves, "The Corruption of the Wisconsin Idea: ALEC and Other Developments" (lecture, University of Wisconsin–Madison, September 20, 2016), https://www.youtube.com/watch?v=kd_4phEYbRE; Daniel Bice, "Hacked Records Show Bradley Foundation Taking Its Conservative Wisconsin Model National," *Milwaukee Journal Sentinel*, May 5, 2017, https://projects.jsonline.com/news/2017/5/5/hacked-records-show-bradley-foundation-taking-wisconsin-model-national.html; Nancy MacLean, *Democracy in Chains: The Deep History of the Radical Right's Stealth Plan for America* (New York: Viking, 2017), especially xvi–xvii, 103, 220.

137. John McGowan has posited a similar top-bottom alliance at the national level; see pp. 119–20, 128 in McGowan, "The Future of the Intellectuals: Was Alvin Gouldner Right?" in *The New Public Intellectual: Politics, Theory, and the Public Sphere*, ed. Jeffrey R. Di Leo and Peter Hitchcock (New York: Palgrave Macmillan, 2016), 117–31. Exit polls for Wisconsin's 2012 gubernatorial recall election, 2014 gubernatorial election, and 2018 gubernatorial election provide some support for this interpretation. Voter support for Walker was correlated with income in all three elections. Furthermore, in all three elections, the majority of voters without college degrees supported Walker; voters with college degrees were evenly split in 2012 and 2014 but mostly opposed Walker in 2018; and the most educated voters (those with postgraduate study or advanced degrees) consistently opposed Walker by large majorities. For 2012 exit polls, see http://www.cnn.com/interactive/2012/06/politics/table.wisc.exitpolls/. For 2014 exit polls, see http://www.cnn.com/election/2014/results/state/WI/governor/. For 2018 exit polls, see https://www.cnn.com/election/2018/exit-polls/wisconsin.

138. The anarchist Machajski urged socialists to immediately follow a successful anticapitalist revolution with a new revolution against the educated elite who filled state offices and received state benefits. One is tempted to say that Wisconsin's radical right skipped the first revolution and proceeded immediately to the second.

139. Kaufman, *Fall of Wisconsin*, 6, 233. Danielle Kaeding, "Income Inequality in Wisconsin at Highest Level since Great Depression," Wisconsin Public Radio, August 30, 2017, https://www.wpr.org/income-inequality-wisconsin-highest-level-great-depression. The report documenting income inequality in Wisconsin, written by the Wisconsin Budget Project and the Center on Wisconsin Strategy, can be found at http://www.wisconsinbudgetproject.org/wp-content/uploads/2017/08/Pulling-Apart-2017.pdf.

140. The phrase "disruptive innovation" comes from Clayton M. Christensen, *The Innovator's Dilemma: The Revolutionary Book That Will Change the Way You Do Business* (New York: Harper Business, 2011). Christensen promoted disruptive innovation as a means to achieve competitive advantage. For *Starving the Beast*, see http://www.starvingthebeast.net/.

141. Kaufman, *Fall of Wisconsin*, 6–7, 265–66; Bice, "Hacked Records."

142. Kaufman, *Fall of Wisconsin*, 7.

143. Goldfarb, *Civility and Subversion*, 3.

144. Although Bascom was a strong proponent of academic freedom, some readers might worry that communitarianism could itself threaten the free exchange of ideas on university campuses. Interestingly, Bascom advocated women's suffrage on communitarian rather than individualistic grounds, and he apparently valued academic freedom for similar reasons. "The state . . . has an obligation to locate and remove restrictions on individuals; these restrictions impede society's progress. That state best fulfills its functions when it both helps to enlarge individual powers and integrates them into the social organism." Hoeveler, *John Bascom*, 145. Whether such grounds provide the best defense for academic freedom is, of course, a matter of debate.

145. Roosevelt, in McCarthy, *Wisconsin Idea*, vii.

146. Stark, *Wisconsin Idea*, 113–14, 171–72.

147. Weber, *Protestant Ethic*, 48. "Not ideas, but material and ideal interests, directly govern men's conduct. Yet very frequently the 'world images' that have been created by 'ideas' have, like switchmen, determined the tracks along which action has been pushed by the dynamic of interest." Weber, *From Max Weber*, 280.

148. Karl Marx, "The Eighteenth Brumaire of Louis Bonaparte," in *The Marx-Engels Reader*, 2nd ed., ed. Robert C. Tucker (New York: W. W. Norton, 1978), 595.

149. Kaufman, *Fall of Wisconsin*, 269.

John Bascom and the Wisconsin Idea

Legacy and Prospects

J. DAVID HOEVELER

The introductory chapter in this volume has already introduced readers to John Bascom, president of the University of Wisconsin from 1874 to 1887. He brought to Madison a formidable repertoire of books and essays he had written in philosophy, theology, and sociology, to which he added significantly during his tenure at the university. But Bascom also engaged the world about him; he wrote about politics, gender, education, economics, and other subjects. He taught courses on moral philosophy and sociology, and from his classroom came two individuals, also introduced in this volume's introductory chapter, who shaped the history of the state and of the university: Robert M. La Follette Sr. and Charles R. Van Hise. As governor of the state (1901–6) and president of its university (1903–18), respectively, they imagined and helped to implement the Wisconsin Idea. Belle Case, another graduate of the University of Wisconsin, married La Follette and became the first woman to receive a law degree in Wisconsin. She knew well the partnership of Robert and "Van" and their shared ambitions: "Two students of the class of 1879, Bob La Follette and Charles Van Hise, profoundly influenced in youth by a great teacher, were now, as mature men, collaborating to sustain former President Bascom's ideal of the relation of a state university to the State."[1]

When I began research for a book about John Bascom, I wanted to learn whether a study of his thinking might provide some intellectual depth and larger framework for the Wisconsin "Idea." After all, the name intimates some extended conceptual parameters, and the career of a deep thinker like Bascom might disclose a richer context from which grew the more familiar notions of the term in the Progressive Era—because, in fact, what became practice in Wisconsin was already being widely emulated by other universities. Extension courses were becoming commonplace, as were outreach efforts that connected universities to farms and industries. Officials at the University of Nebraska, for example, had set up Farmers' Institutes; attended rural Grange meetings and picnics; gave demonstrations on a variety of matters, from bee culture to sheep raising; and even had a train, "the alfalfa special," built into the state's railroad network. It had most of these activities in place before Wisconsin's programs.[2] Wisconsin, however, does stand out for its amazing intellectual activity—from Bascom to economists Richard T. Ely and John R. Commons, historian Frederick Jackson Turner, and sociologist Edward A. Ross. I intend to argue in this essay that if we lose sight of that ingredient, we are left with a dangerous over-focus on the service ideal that easily, and in fact today, is corrupting the Wisconsin Idea. In the mind of Bascom, we have all three components of the Wisconsin Idea—the university's special connection to the political structures and operations of the state government, its outreach to the state, and its commitment to academic freedom and the pursuit of truth—in full integration with each other, and a formidable grounding of all in his large edifice of liberal learning.

But first, let me expand on the introductory chapter's brief remarks about John Bascom.[3] He was born May 1, 1827, in Genoa, New York, the Finger Lakes region of that state. He came from a long line of Calvinists, going back even to the Huguenots in France and to the English Puritans. John's ancestors came to New England in the 1630s. A continuing line of Congregational ministers extended down to his father, John Bascom Sr. Likewise did the family of his maternal ancestry, the Woodbridges, have deep New England roots. But the father's death only a year after John's birth left his wife, Laura Woodbridge Bascom, to raise four children on a small farm in Ludlowville, New York. They lived in near poverty. His three sisters, all older than John, generously pooled their resources so that their brother could attend their father's alma mater, Williams College. There, John Bascom studied with the legendary school president and moral philosopher Mark Hopkins. After an interlude and some indecision, Bascom resumed his education at Auburn Theological Seminary, near the family farm, and then at Andover Theological Seminary in Massachusetts. In 1855 Hopkins appointed his prize student to a professorship at Williams, where he served for almost two decades before his summons to the University of Wisconsin presidency in 1874.

One of the pleasures of doing a study of John Bascom comes in engaging a powerful, speculative mind, one that ranged broadly over the many intellectual fields of his time. But a short summary will have to suffice. So we will begin by identifying three influences in Bascom's thinking. First, Bascom entered energetically into the contested domain of epistemology. From John Locke to George Berkeley to David Hume, philosophers addressed ancient questions about what the mind can know, the existence or nonexistence of external objects, and the mind's capacity to shape the reality of which we are cognizant. Then, in the late eighteenth century, Immanuel Kant threw philosophy into turmoil. At the same time that he attributed to mind the ability to shape empirical sense data into a meaningful structure through the "forms of intuition" (space, time, and causality among the twelve he identified), he also drew strictures on the mind's ability to know anything transcending these sense data—that is, to know "things-in-themselves" (noumena). The tradition of German idealism grew from Kant as philosophers like Johann Gottlieb Fichte, Friedrich Wilhelm Joseph von Schelling, and Georg Wilhelm Friedrich Hegel sought to breach Kant's rigid dualism, to break down the barriers between the earthly and transcendent, the natural and the supernatural. Bascom identified with this effort, and his earliest philosophical writings placed him with those intuitionists who gave the human mind the power to glimpse transcendent reality.

Second, Bascom embraced and heavily articulated a liberal Protestant theology. He painstakingly liberated himself from the Calvinism of his ancestral heritage. He wanted religious thinking to reject dogma and confessional formulations. These encumbrances serve only to impede new thinking and contain the ever-restless, inquiring human mind, he contended. His own priorities made Bascom antagonistic toward biblical fundamentalism. Scripture, he believed, expressed the efforts of the faithful, three thousand years ago, to understand God's revelation. Bascom opted for a "progressive revelation," in which the gains in human knowledge, especially in science, disclosed the fuller contents of the divine mind. Bascom's religious liberalism also governed his "social gospel." The church, he insisted, belongs in the world and finds its work in the moral and material improvement of society and in its quest for social justice in the world. Bascom stated these ideas in the baccalaureate address he gave in Madison in 1884, titled "The New Theology."

And a third influence in Bascom's thinking was evolution. The naturalist Charles Darwin published his epic work, *On the Origin of Species*, in 1859. Bascom called evolution "the great idea of the nineteenth century." Why did he say so? Because evolution signified to him a dynamic structure of life, where change was a governing reality, a universe of chance, flux, spontaneity, and openness, a reality that discredited all notions of fixity and permanence of truth. Also, it was because evolution showed the interconnection of all things; it depicted life as a whole, a vast integration of types and kinds (species). And finally, evolution demonstrated to Bascom the power of mind, mind as the survival instrument of *Homo sapiens* in the contested struggle for life and mastery.

More than any president of a major American university in his time, Bascom applied his grand philosophy to contemporary social and political issues.

What he depicted as universal reality, a holistic system of integrated parts, a dynamic interrelation of material and spiritual being, he envisioned also for society and for the state. In short, he idealized an organic model of society, a unity of many components in harmonial participation with each other. By use of this analogy, furthermore, Bascom warned against two bad tendencies. First, it too often happens, he said, that in the social process key elements—particular groups—get left out. They suffer in neglect or suppression, and the organism falls into dysfunction because of the resulting imbalance. By the other tendency, some groups or some segments become too powerful. They distort the social organism by another kind of imbalance and also produce disequilibrium. Both conditions deprive the system of maximum efficiency and of the fairness and social justice that should prevail in it.

In all the topics that Bascom addressed under this model, one priority stood out. He became a champion of the public interest, the right of the collective to protect itself against these bad tendencies. I discuss these subjects at length in *John Bascom and the Origins of the Wisconsin Idea*, but I will just note that Bascom illustrated these principles in his attention to some highly contested matters in his time: temperance, women's equality, and the cause of labor. Bascom knew only too well the challenge he took on in championing the case for public rights over individual rights. Our national political ethos, he attested, flourishes with the ideal of the free and unfettered individual, and our political rhetoric reverberates with dire warnings of government's tyranny and of state oppression.[4]

So Bascom sought to pose a counterideology at a time when the doctrine of laissez-faire economics also dominated academic teaching in this subject. For all its pretension, the free market, Bascom believed, did not assure equality of opportunity. We do not all begin the race at the same starting line. And always, wealth feeds on wealth. And wealth means power, power to influence and corrupt all our institutions, from the political system to the economic. Bascom wrote that "we are losing our idea of government" if we so eviscerate its powers that we cannot protect and promote the well-being of the whole. We need different priorities. The state, he averred, must be an agency of empowerment, to all individuals and to those disadvantaged, especially.[5]

Finally, Bascom made two extensions of these ideas that gave a new role to state universities and in turn rounded out his early formulation of the Wisconsin Idea. First, a university education, Bascom believed, should provide students with a large understanding of themselves as individuals and of the universe in which they lived. He meant this goal to include studies that give insight to spiritual and material reality. His whole intellectual system, as noted, led him so to assert. He once stated to the University of Wisconsin Board of

Regents that he hoped that every course taught at the university would have a philosophical foundation. He warned against educating for merely practical ends and utilitarian purposes, lest the university feed the "blind rush" of material forces that too much control our lives. His own publications in sociology grounded that subject in theology, to wit, what he called "the natural theology of the social sciences." He urged an expanded program of the natural sciences at the university for the same reason and took great pride in two new science buildings built during his presidency.[6]

As the introductory chapter of this volume emphasizes, Bascom believed that university graduates equipped with this special kind of education could make a valuable contribution to the state. They will help inaugurate "the new era of collective power." This is how Robert M. La Follette Sr. remembered it: Bascom "was forever telling us what the state was doing for us and urging our return obligation not to use our education wholly for our own selfish benefit, but to return some service to the state." For all of these ideals, La Follette believed, Bascom "may be said to have originated the Wisconsin idea in education."[7] Bascom, in addition, met often with students, and especially in his Sunday afternoon sessions with seniors he urged these ideas. One of his daughters, Florence, who became a nationally renowned geologist, remembered her undergraduate experience at the university. "Our student meetings . . . were addressed by the president on themes of ethical import with a vigor and potency. Our obligations to the state were made exceedingly plain, and the seed was sown which later fructified in the 'Wisconsin Idea.'"[8] Bascom's Wisconsin Idea was thus also an education for citizenship.

The university, Bascom believed, served the state and the larger public in another way—by the research and scholarship of its faculty in the production of new knowledge. In another of his reports to the University of Wisconsin Board of Regents, Bascom urged that faculty be free to pursue their areas of expertise and have more time available for that purpose. But he also insisted that new knowledge have a public extension. Because, as an organism, the state needed to adapt to the world as it changed, adjust to new social and economic realities. State officials, administrators, legislators, all need the intellectual tools that enhance the survival strategies needed for the social organism. For it, like the individual, must work by trial and error. The university must function as society's brain, the agent of its evolutionary progress. As Bascom wrote: "Intelligence, should be fruitful in collective as well as in individual effort."[9] What students owe to the state, Bascom asserted, is ideas. But the acquisition of this vital element, Bascom urged, can occur only under the condition of complete academic freedom. Any constraints simply will not yield the most useful intelligence for social progress. In fact, we have from

Bascom a statement worth pondering: "The freedom of instruction is worth more than any one thing taught."[10] This statement and what has preceded it here leads us to ask if we might neatly summarize Bascom's understanding of the university. I think so. It is first and foremost, and above all, a house of intellect.[11]

～

This essay seeks to take the measure of the Wisconsin Idea in its contemporary situation. It will look at politics and it will consider the battle of ideas in early twenty-first-century America. How might we better understand the Wisconsin Idea in these locales if we bring into the discussion the large intellectual outline John Bascom gave to this notion in its Ur-moment? Can we gain some critical advantage in creating a dialogue between Bascom and the array of individuals today who are weighing in about the contested domain of American higher education—governors and state legislators, scholars and university leaders, journalists and op-ed polemicists, pundits and bloggers everywhere? What in this contemporary record places the Wisconsin Idea under threat? What resources in this record might defenders of the Wisconsin Idea draw upon to give it new expression, new relevance, new vitality, renewal?

Certain changes and new trends will inform any discussion of higher education today. Observers note that for the last half century or so we have lived in an era of postindustrialism and neoliberalism. The latter references a new ascendancy of market economics, policies of privatization in national agendas, the diminution of the public sector, and downsizing of governments. Most importantly for our purposes, the record indicates a decline in state support for public universities, from the 1970s on and in the work of both Republican and Democratic state administrations. The trend has accelerated, and in the last twenty-five years state support has fallen by about 25 percent in real dollars. The public universities lost much ground to private institutions in these years, and more so with the Great Recession of 2008 and afterward.[12]

But in the later years this retrenchment became more polemical, more politically charged. Governors and state legislators protested that their state universities were not a good investment, that their research and academic programs did not fuel the economy, did not promote business growth and new hiring. Some like Rick Scott, governor of Florida from 2011 to 2019, insisted that state tax dollars should bolster science and high-tech studies, not "educate more people who can't get jobs in anthropology."[13] Pat McCrory, governor of North Carolina from 2013 to 2017, not only moved to dismiss the progressive president of the University of North Carolina but made it clear that the flagship campus in Chapel Hill had no business teaching courses in "gender studies or Swahili." Public schools, he said, should find their priority in skill-based education as presumably employers would find this training most appealing among graduates they wanted to hire.[14]

And then there was Wisconsin. The introductory chapter of this volume describes the political transformation of the state and its university system under Republican governor Scott Walker (2011–19), and there is no need to repeat the details here. Robin Vos, a Republican member of the Wisconsin State Assembly representing Racine County since 2005 and Assembly Speaker since 2013, summed up the changes to higher education this way: "We're going to have a more market-based approach where we're more responsive to the private sector."[15] In the 2019–20 University of Wisconsin System budget, Republicans consolidated their successes. It reverberated with "workforce development" and "operational efficiencies." It detailed large new expenditures for science, technology, engineering, and mathematics (STEM) programs and building projects to support those studies.[16]

These actions reflected a long-simmering, and often vocal resentment against the University of Wisconsin among state conservatives. In 2015 Walker appointed to the University of Wisconsin Board of Regents Michael M. Grebe, the son of Michael W. Grebe, who had served as the president and chief executive officer of the conservative Bradley Foundation from 2002 through 2016, and then as the chair of Walker's 2016 US presidential campaign. Michael M. Grebe wanted the University of Wisconsin to be run more like a business with each local chancellor exercising powers akin to those of chief executive officers. Vos endorsed this model. And US congressman from Wisconsin Paul Ryan, who served as Speaker of the US House of Representatives from October 2015 to January 2019, spoke the mind of many Republicans. This disciple of author Ayn Rand considered the whole progressive tradition in the state "a cancer." "This stuff came from these German intellectuals to Madison, University of Wisconsin," he said. He wanted "to indict the entire vision of progressivism."[17] Another wide attack had come earlier from conservative activist Michael S. Joyce, who preceded Michael W. Grebe as chairman of the Bradley Foundation from 1985 to 2001. As discussed in this volume's introductory chapter, Joyce charged the Wisconsin Idea with laying the roots of the long and corrupting legacy of progressivism in Wisconsin. Most responsible for it: that "intellectual giant" John Bascom.[18]

As state supported declined, universities turned increasingly to private business, including some of the nation's most powerful corporations, as new sources of revenue. That redirection also reflected conservatives' complaints about what colleges and universities taught. Too much of it was abstract and impractical, unconnected to the demands of the marketplace. We see here but one aspect of an ascending anti-intellectualism in American life today that troubles observers on both the left and the right. And certainly it threatens the Wisconsin Idea as Bascom conceived it. It honors only a distorted version of the "service" ideal and eviscerates the intellectual.[19]

Once again Robin Vos provides us an apt illustration. With his persistent demands that the University of Wisconsin System devote its instructional program to the material growth of the state, he scorned work that struck him as esoteric and frivolous—that is, useless knowledge. Lest anyone have no idea what he meant, he exemplified by citing "the ancient mating habits of whatever." That statement circulated widely and won the ridicule it deserved.[20] But what makes the matter all the more poignant is that Vos failed to note what was happening in his own state. At the University of Wisconsin–Milwaukee's School of Freshwater Sciences, professors Fred Binkowski and Osvaldo Villet were studying the mating habits of yellow perch. This species, once abundant in Lake Michigan, became decimated due to invasive species. The researchers were doing experiments in photothermal manipulation, effected by moderating water temperature and lighting to "trick" the perch into year-long mating. Said one observer: "This is a huge thing." The efforts could restore a multi-billion dollar industry.[21] And all this work was being done as "basic research," at a time when, many feared, the "capitalist university" was abandoning basic research for contracted projects with corporations. Biochemistry, for example, had moved heavily in that direction.[22] But any scientist will tell you, you just don't know where new knowledge, acquired through basic research, will lead.

~

Another hot-topic controversy focused on freedom of speech on the campuses. But had the American university ceased to be the locus for the battle of ideas? Many so charged as the public witnessed recurring efforts of vociferous and sometimes violent students to prevent certain speakers from having access to campus facilities or shouting them down if they did gain such access. These interventions gave conservatives especially a rallying cry in their intensifying campaign against higher education.[23] They charged hypocrisy, for earlier the issue of free speech, in the Cold War and McCarthyist climate in the United States, had seen many on the left seek to liberate the campuses from statutory prohibitions against Communists or other radical groups. Now conservative outcries intensified as campuses tried to protect students from harsh words or illiberal ideologies. We began to hear of "safe spaces" and "trigger warnings." Many of different political persuasions found these alleged protections and security against "microaggressions" a violation of the "open campus" ideal.[24] The Intercollegiate Institute, a conservative organization, kept vigilant and tallied leftist protests and campus shutdowns. In fact, however, it was not clear that conservatives were mostly victims of free-speech violations, but the right seemed to make the most political hay of these incidents.[25]

The University of Chicago led the way in bringing some reasonableness to free-speech policies, and other institutions followed Chicago. So did the University of Wisconsin. At the behest of the state legislature, the University of Wisconsin Board of Regents in 2017 gave a ringing endorsement to the ideals of academic freedom and its traditional place in the university's history. Thus it cited the 1894 "sifting and winnowing" phrase from the Ely trial of that year. And it also stated emphatically that "it is not the proper role of the university to shield individuals from ideas and opinions they, or others, find unwelcome, disagreeable, or even deeply offensive." The policy also specified punitive action to be taken against violators of this principle, particularly any who disrupt on-campus events. Essentially, it said, three strikes and you're out.[26] Some protested that these stringencies would create a climate of fear on the campus, discouraging legitimate protest. But altogether, I believe, the statement was fair-minded. Clearly, though, it had political motivations behind it. It was brought to us by the same people who wanted to strike the Wisconsin Idea from the state statutes, who made harmful changes in the tenure system, and who diminished faculty governance.

The standards pronounced by the University of Wisconsin Board of Regents did specify the need for order and constraint in certain circumstances but they did not answer the question much contested everywhere: Who has the legitimate right to speak on college campuses? Strict libertarians wanted no restraints; others made "sensitivity" a governing principle that would exclude extremists. But did a university not have a right to insist that campus speech meet its criteria of responsible discourse? Here John Bascom's model, the university as a house of intellect, offers helpful guidelines, I believe.

In the work of universities, scholars must submit their research to rigorous reviews and critical assessments. And we hold our students to precise standards as well. Certainly an institution need not restrict its invitees only to other scholars but nonetheless may insist that those who address its community have a record of experience that transcends mere opinion. Politicians, businesspeople, other professionals, and workers of all kinds can supplement and enhance the campus's intellectual life. I find occasional expressions of this Bascom derivative. For example, philosophy professor Jason N. Blum writes: "Colleges certainly should protect freedom of speech, but . . . must also endorse the value of worthy speech—that which seeks insight or to provide a reasoned defense of a position, rather than merely to titillate or provoke."[27] Certainly no university is obligated to provide space for the hateful harangues of far-right agitators Milo Yiannopolous or Ann Coulter. But to deny it to political scientist Charles Murray, or former US Secretary of State Madeleine Albright, or newspaper columnist George F. Will, or former US Attorney General Eric Holder, is pure anti-intellectualism. If bad science disturbs you, fight it with better science.

And in the matter of our dealing with ideas at odds with our own, as the regents stated, Bascom has an additional relevance. In 1877 he asked the editors of the student newspaper to place in its pages a statement from him. It was a short piece he titled "The Spirit of the University." That spirit, he said, is something that transcends the classroom and the other activities of campus life. Specifically, it is "an inspiration, a growing estimate of truth, an appetite for excellence. . . . The central spirit of our University," Bascom urged, "should be a large-minded love of knowledge, a thorough disposition candidly and completely to know the truth." He urged that the University of Wisconsin "escape the spirit that dare not inquire lest it break in on beliefs already entertained."[28]

That last point of emphasis has yet another application to the contemporary situation in the University of Wisconsin System. In September 2016 Wisconsin State Assembly Speaker Robin Vos issued a charge and a challenge. The charge: his investigation of money spent to invite outside speakers to the University of Wisconsin campuses showed a manifest favoritism to individuals of liberal political persuasion. The challenge: "I would like to challenge the [University of Wisconsin] System to practice what it preaches" and to live up to the regents' statement that the university does not fulfill its purposes in shielding students from ideas and opinions averse to those of their own. Vos now upheld the banner of "intellectual diversity." Then: "I challenge the [University of Wisconsin] System this year to find more ways . . . to ensure that all perspectives, including conservative ones, are present in the classroom."[29]

I received a follow-up inquiry from the *Milwaukee Journal Sentinel*, the largest newspaper in the state of Wisconsin, about my reaction to Vos's statement. And I conceded that Vos had a valid point. Liberal opinion does have the dominant voice on our campuses and that fact represents a negligence on our part. "I'll go even further," I said, "and repeat what I've said previously: The greater threat to academic freedom today comes from the radical left, less than from the radical right." I added: "That an accomplished public servant like former [US] Secretary of State Condoleezza Rice, invited to give the commencement address at Rutgers [University] in 2014, should receive such angry protests as to dissuade her from appearing, illustrates leftist intolerance on that campus."[30]

≈

I propose in this last section of the essay to bring the Wisconsin Idea into a further intellectual dialogue with thinkers, among the left and the right, who offer arguments and insights that can reinforce the Wisconsin Idea in its early conception by John Bascom, and give it a contemporary relevance. I wish to look particularly at voices of dissent from the strenuous ideologies briefly referenced above, again in both the liberal and conservative camps. I believe that the Wisconsin Idea can draw from both sides and give itself a renewal that will also moderate the polemics that so besiege it now. I believe we might even find some common ground.

With respect to conservatism, here are some preliminary thoughts. First, John Bascom, as noted, based his social criticism and his reform programs on a model of the organic society. This model, in fact, has its modern foundation in the British philosopher and statesman Edmund Burke, the great eighteenth-century conservative and thoroughgoing critic of the French Revolution. For Burke, like Bascom, the word "society" signifies something cohesive, a cooperative unity of different parts, and not a mere collection of individuals. Bascom furthermore insisted that this understanding gave high priority to the public interest, the commonweal. "The general good must override individual good," he wrote, "since the last is included in the first." For him, personal liberty, whether that of the drunkard or that of the billionaire, may not exercise veto power over the collective need. Bascom invoked Burke to reinforce his point. If we allow each individual to seek what he regards as his own liberty and without regard to the public measure, Bascom believed, we have a result Burke greatly feared. Bascom quoted Burke: "The commonwealth itself in a few generations crumbles away, is disconnected into the dust and powder of individuality, and is at length dispersed to all winds of heaven."[31]

Second, like Burke, Bascom wanted people to think of the state not merely as an ad hoc assemblage of functions put in place to address quotidian matters and make the needed improvements. Like Burke, Bascom wanted the state to have a certain hold on people's imagination, to convey ideas of a transcendent good, a higher ideal to which all, as a collective unity, may claim a connection.[32]

I have found that recently in the United States many conservative thinkers, overwhelmed and put off by the ascendancy of President Donald Trump and his reshaping of the Republican Party, have sought to recover a more authentic conservatism; they have looked for their own intellectual roots and given them renewed attention. Much of this effort, in fact, goes back to the era of former president Ronald Reagan, where some conservative writers found grounds of dissent in the emergence of neoliberalism. Their efforts, I believe, portend a healthier environment for the Wisconsin Idea as Bascom first outlined it.

Yuval Levin, editor of the conservative magazine *National Affairs* and frequent contributor to the conservative magazines *National Review* and the *Weekly Standard*, wrote *The Fractured Republic* in 2016. He has been called "the leading intellectual of reform conservatism."[33] Levin labeled himself "a cultural conservative." The book's subtitle registers a key theme of the new conservative revision: *Renewing America's Social Contract in the Age of Individualism*. He wrote at the outset: "In our cultural, economic, political, and social life [there] has been a trajectory of increasing individualism, diversity, dynamism, and liberalization. And it has come at the cost of dwindling solidarity, cohesion, stability, authority, and social order." Atomism describes the normative situation of most Americans now, Levin lamented. He described an America beset by declining social capital—"the common stock of rules and norms that enable people to live and work together." Increasingly, he observed, we sort ourselves into like-minded, homogeneous communities, from our neighborhood to the television shows we watch and the websites we seek out and the "virtual communities" that flourish there. Identity politics bespeaks the ethos of group rights and multiculturalism, a phenomenon that actually reinforces our individualism at the expense of our commonality. Especially important, said Levin, these fracturing effects have eroded our idea of society, leaving us one consisting "only of individuals and a state." Some people can cope with the loss of connectedness, but Levin fears that too many cannot. Levin, like Bascom before him, warns that too many people, especially the poorer and less educated, feel an "estrangement from America's core institutions."[34]

Conservative revision has had another powerful voice in newspaper columnist David Brooks, whose ever insightful essays for the *New York Times* recurringly recall *soi-disant* conservatives, so prominent in the Trump years, to their true history and vocation. For one thing, he reflects a fondness for an American conservatism, alive not so long ago, that displayed a rich intellectual content. He began his professional career in that era, the 1980s and 1990s, when, he tells us, he found conservative journalists and pundits who wrote about all kinds of things—history, literature, sociology, theology, and "life in general." But conservative writing, like too much of journalism in general, Brooks feared, succumbed to the constraints of a mass audience and now offers mostly "perpetual hysteria and simple-minded polemics."[35]

That lament has become a chorus. Wisconsin supplies another example. For more than two decades Charles J. Sykes had a morning conservative talk radio show in Milwaukee. But the Trump movement, he relates, with its anti-intellectual populism, white nationalists, and assorted amoral derelicts, drove him out of that conservative camp and into an effort to recover the years of conservative intellectual splendor, from the 1950s and through the Reagan ascendancy. In his book *How the Right Lost Its Mind,* Sykes shows how something in the name of conservatism has since emerged, but it "is not a form of conservatism that Edmund Burke, or even Barry Goldwater, would have recognized."[36] Also, Jonah Goldberg, a senior editor of *National Review,* vilified Donald Trump, who, he said, was "in no way whatsoever an intellectual," and who led him to rethink the true principles of conservatism, because Trump was destroying them.[37] Or consider Max Boot, a writer of longstanding conservative credentials. He titled his book *The Corrosion of Conservatism: Why I Left the Right.* He too embraced that recent period when Republicans rightly earned the label "the party of ideas." How quickly it became a lost era when populist anti-intellectualism took over the party. Never, writes Boot, have we had so thoroughly ignorant a president as Donald Trump, a president "who could not tell Edmund Burke from [former US Navy admiral] Arleigh Burke."[38]

Brooks has written at length on the need for a renewed public ethic in American politics. The priority of the individual interest over the public interest plagues us, he believes. We could get a better understanding of this matter, he has asserted, by recognizing a fact that Bascom stressed heavily: the unavoidable implication of all of us in a great human complex, the social organism. Our nation, Brooks avers, began with a sense of personal liberty, but one rooted in a shared community: "We the People" as the US Constitution specifies. But, Brooks fears, we have moved increasingly, and dangerously, into a radical subjectivism that reifies only the autonomous individual. This new ethic reads: "There is no we. We are all nomads who walk around with our own individual opinions about existence, meaning and the Universe. Each person is a self-created choosing individual, pursuing individual desires." And when we translate this notion into social practice, Brooks confirms, we have pure free-market capitalism. And this is where the Republican Party has moved, he warns, into an ideological stasis of "market fundamentalism." Here Brooks's conservatism meets Bascom's progressivism. "Market fundamentalism," Brooks attests, "is an inhumane philosophy that makes economic growth society's prime value and leaves people atomized and unattached." As such, the primary threat to conservatives and the "sacred order" they embrace is no longer the state. It is the "radical individualism" that erodes those nurturing, healthy attachments, revered by true conservatives, that grow society.[39]

Brooks joined with a large number of critics, not all self-identified as conservatives, who wanted to see conservatism recover its deeper, purer content. Often that means bringing Burke back into the picture. Newspaper columnist E. J. Dionne Jr., writing in 2013, saw a conservative reform movement underway. Its partisans invoked the Burkean notion that "society is an organism," he observed, and challenged prevailing conservatism's ideology of individual autonomy.[40] Brooks, too, endorses the countermodel of Burke, and accuses Republicans of making "ideological choices that offend conservatism's Burkean roots." The true conservative, he insists, "does not see a nation composed of individuals who should be given maximum liberty to make choices. Instead, the individual is part of a social organism and thrives only within attachments to family, community and nation that precede choice." Brooks, like, Dionne, detects a shifting tide in conservative opinion, a new generation of opinion leaders (he names ten of them) that dissents from the cult of individualism and looks to family, religion, and neighborhood to recover from the atomizing effects of modern capitalism. But the Republican Party, Brooks added, has instituted policies that betray this true conservative model.[41]

∾

Intellectual ferment on the left also yields some reflections about how the Wisconsin Idea, as Bascom fashioned it, can find a relevant contemporary habitat. Mark Lilla, professor of humanities at Columbia University and award-winning essayist for the *New York Review of Books*, gave much attention to the crisis in American higher education in his book *The Once and Future Liberal: After Identity Politics*. Like the conservatives we have observed, he perceives an ethic of individualism that has become destructive. So, he states, "I write as a frustrated American liberal." American higher education, he elaborates, has succumbed to this ethic and proliferated curricular programs that are "narrow and exclusionary." And he blames "the politics of identity," "the de facto creed of two generations of liberal politicians." In education and politics, the liberal vocabulary reverberates with terms like "personal choice," "individual rights," "self-definition."[42]

Liberalism's prospects, Lilla urges, "will depend in no small measure on what happens in our institutions of higher education." His book details in many examples how "identity" has distorted the curriculum, reinforcing the bad tendencies in an "increasingly individualistic and atomized nation." Liberalism, he affirms, once bore the ideals of a common citizenship, even through the civil rights movement, the early phase of the women's rights movement, and gay rights. But that ideal of commonality faded as liberals took recourse to political parties as means of identity priorities, or "elective affinities." Lilla asks, Where have these new directions landed us? He answers: in a complete ignoring of citizenship as the means of our individual self-fulfillment. Our colleges today do not teach about our traditional ties and obligations; they do not instill "an image of what our shared way of life ought to be." But in its great tradition, this is what liberalism is, says Lilla: "a tool for inclusion."[43]

William Egginton also looked at the great tradition of liberalism and spotted large cracks in the edifice. A professor in the humanities at the Johns Hopkins University, Egginton labels himself a disciple of the philosopher Richard Rorty's pragmatism and liberal politics. He defends multiculturalism and affirmative action and appreciates the contributions to American higher education made by scholarship on race and gender.[44] Egginton believes, however, that pre-occupation with racial and sexual identities has taken these liberalizing effects in an unhealthy direction. "Once," he writes, "it was a demand for equal treatment for all. Now, [the cult of identity] calls for cultures to be walled off and the boundaries to be policed." Hence the student protests and shutting down of campus facilities to prevent "unacceptable" speech. A new intolerance rises. At its extreme the radical left has sought to discredit the whole legacy of the Western cultural tradition (white and male), Egginton laments. But it fails to observe how indispensable is that tradition to the very freedoms the radicals pretend to uphold.[45]

Against the cult of individualism and the obsession with the immediate, Egginton calls for a recovery of the traditional purposes of higher education. It must transcend these limitations. Appealing to the theologian and poet John Henry Newman's *The Idea of the University* (1854), Egginton urges that we in-still in it an expansive vision. He quotes Newman: "The mind never views any part of the extended subject-matter of Knowledge without recollecting that it is but a part. . . . It makes everything in some sort lead to everything else." Bascom described this objective similarly. And like Bascom, Egginton wants to resupply higher education with a larger public ideal. We have fallen into a conviction, he writes, "that education is only or primarily a private resource and tool for economic self-improvement." But we have also the higher purpose of "cultivating the public mind," citing Newman again. Here, Egginton main-tains, the liberal arts have a special burden: They must elevate "those aspects of being human that are not reducible to today's dominant model of the in-dividual." We must rediscover "the universal community of humanity." Our civic culture, our very republic, depends on it.[46]

Bascom, too, made this link between an education that is broad in scope and interconnects the vast and different components of our common experience. In a baccalaureate address in Madison, he advocated that we must attend not so much to the individual but to those aspects of our lives that constitute our collective, social selves. We need to illuminate "the permanent life of the race, this pervasive life of the whole human family," he told his Madison audience.[47]

I turn for a final sampling to Marilynne Robinson. A novelist and essayist, she has won wide attention, including a Pulitzer Prize for her book *Gilead* in 2005. She brings to her reflections on society and culture a religious perspective, a modern-day Calvinism. In a 2015 address at Stanford University, she spoke on "The American Scholar Now," and then published the piece in *Harper's Magazine* with the title "Save Our Public Universities." Robinson decried the diminishing support by state governments of their universities and cited the situation in Wisconsin particularly. Our universities no longer make sense to the public officials entrusted to their support, she added, because intellect and love of learning for themselves no longer appeal. So the public institutions pay the price for what has transpired in the social culture, "a fundamental shift" in American consciousness. She summarizes that shift very neatly: The "Citizen," with all that word entails about loyalty and obligation to a larger public, "has become the taxpayer." "The Citizen," she adds, "had a country, a community, children and grandchildren, even—a word we no longer hear—posterity. The taxpayer has a 401(k)." So what we once considered public assets we now see as public burdens.[48]

Robinson's essay has inspiring words about the power and creativity of the human mind, the transforming effects of intellect, and their place in our Western civilization. Bascom's ideals resurface here. Historically, they made universities what they were. How, then, Robinson asks, not to lament that our colleges and universities have moved from the ideals of opening minds and preparing them for citizenship to honing some abilities so that the graduate might join "a docile though skilled working class." We are saying to this generation of students, Robinson regretted, that "they must give up the thought of shaping their own lives, of having even the moral or political right to stabilize them against the rigors and uncertainties of the markets, those great gods." We just do not convey to these students that they might bring to the world the gift of minds "stimulated by broad access to knowledge." We offer instead to give them "competitive adequacy" for the national and global market, in short, not an education but a training.[49]

≈

Robinson's essay, and the other commentary above, help us address a recent episode in the University of Wisconsin System. In March 2018 officials at the University of Wisconsin–Stevens Point announced that the school would eliminate thirteen (later reduced to six) liberal arts degrees, including English, French, German, history, political science, and sociology. It would expand other subjects into majors: computer information systems, conservation law, finance, fire science, graphic design, chemical engineering, management, and marketing. And it would create new majors, such as environmental engineering, ecosystem design and remediation, and captive wildlife. Observers noted that the change registered the first effect of the regents' new provisions for more easily getting rid of tenured faculty. Others recognized the clear political subtext at work here. "The push away from liberal arts and toward workplace skills," wrote journalist Valerie Strauss, "is championed by conservatives who see many four-year colleges and universities as politically correct institutions that graduate too many students without practical job skills—but with liberal political views."[50]

Wisconsin enjoyed such a large reputation for its historic achievements in higher education that all the changes we have noted in this essay got national attention and generated much response. This one did, too, almost all of it negative. University of Wisconsin–Stevens Point provost Greg Summers had the unhappy task of defending the new regime. He cited declining enrollments in the liberal arts programs and claimed that "too many general education programs have little purposeful cohesion and little relevance to the majority of students."[51] Many didn't buy it. Summers misjudged the students, one critic said. They are desperate for an education that "promotes meaning and value in their lives and one that transcends a career and occupation." Another felt outrage that the University of Wisconsin–Stevens Point and other universities must "genuflect before a crass tin-foil god of the bottom line." How sad, said another, to see the academy of today in a hostile takeover "by administrators with no academic credentials or love of scholarship" and responsive only to "business, plutocracy and profit." Some saw a dangerous shift in American higher education as represented by the University of Wisconsin–Stevens Point: from "a focus on making good citizens, not good taxpayers; good men and women, not good-wage earners."[52]

True enough, but much of this discussion missed another important point. The reformers in the name of "grow the economy" and the entrepreneurial university assume that the kind of curricular changes at the University of Wisconsin–Stevens Point answer the needs of businesspeople and give income advantages to graduates of these new curriculums. This is wrong on both counts. Charles Sykes, no friend to American universities, cites in his book *Fail U.: The False Promise of Higher Education* a 2013 survey of employers that asked what they look for in hiring college graduates. He summarizes the conclusion: "93 percent of employers say that a demonstrated capacity to think critically, communicate clearly, and solve complex problems is more important than a candidate's undergraduate major."[53]

Also, these reforms are really doing the students trapped in them no great favors. Christopher Newfield, professor of literature and American studies at the University of California, Santa Barbara, makes that clear in his remarkable book from 2016, *The Great Mistake: How We Wrecked Public Universities and How We Can Fix Them*. It's a book laden with empirical data and does not invoke liberal education in terms of "personal enrichment" or other sentimental nostrums that do not appeal to hard-nosed critics of the universities. A bad situation exists, says Newfield. We have an elite set of institutions that graduates students thoroughly trained in complex subjects—history, literature, philosophy, physics, and so on—students who have, in short, "learned to learn." They will do very well after college. There is another group who come out of college with "limited learning" and some mastery in a particular skill. They will do okay, as middle managers and sales people, jobs that mostly suit a twentieth-century economy; but they will not have prestige or job security or affordable health care in the twenty-first-century economy. But more and more, writes Newfield, a large number of students get the "fast-food version" of a college education, passing through with virtually no "knowledge work" and entering an economy of stagnant wages and a "winner-take-all society" that does not care much for preserving a solid working or middle class, as witness the stubborn wage stagnation of recent decades.[54]

And finally, on the University of Wisconsin–Stevens Point: Summers, pulling out all the stops to defend the reforms there, invoked the Wisconsin Idea. He envisioned the transformed University of Wisconsin–Stevens Point as the model for "a new kind of regional university," designed to address the changing world of professional work and solving local problems. These efforts, he avowed, will place the new model within "the best tradition of the Wisconsin Idea."[55] Imagine: an idea, the Wisconsin Idea, that began in the exciting intellectual explorations of an early president of the University of Wisconsin, one who wrote and taught about philosophy, history, art, literature, sociology, and economics, now finds itself invoked in a program that will no longer permit students to have majors in these subjects! But we allow this hijacking of the Wisconsin Idea only if we think of it as merely a program of service, as a device for utilitarian solutions to shifting quotidian challenges and the ad hoc demands of the prevailing marketplace. John Bascom strongly believed that the University of Wisconsin would have a critical role in advancing the material prosperity of the state of Wisconsin. But that process of growth always had these effects for him within an expansive understanding and application of the human intellect, of its place within the nexus of a larger public interest, and of the special role that graduates of the university would play in helping the state improve the moral and cultural lives of its citizens.

So Bascom at Madison oversaw an educational program suitable to those ends. But by no means must we try to duplicate the nineteenth-century intellectual cosmos in which Bascom thrived. The very effort would set itself against the whole spirit of his system—seeking new ideas and breaking from old ones. That effort, Bascom believed, required the most expansive vision one could bring to it. "Inquiry," the president told his audience in another baccalaureate sermon, "is a continuous, living, process. It is not the work of one man, or generation, or period." And so must the modern university approach its work. In philosophy, Bascom believed, we work to arrive at "the provisional opinion." And that standard applies to all fields of learning.[56] But that quest assigns to the university an obligation to its students as well: to provide for them the opportunity to exercise their own intellects and expand their visions as they do. In thinking how to renew the Wisconsin Idea, certainly we should honor these intentions as the legacy John Bascom bequeathed to us.

NOTES

1. Belle Case La Follette, *Robert M. La Follette, June 14, 1855–June 18, 1925*, vol. 1 (New York: Macmillan, 1953), 38.

2. Robert N. Manley, *Centennial History of the University of Nebraska*, vol. 1 (Lincoln: University of Nebraska Press, 1969), 36, 62, 184.

3. In what follows in this section I will summarize from the book I wrote about Bascom: J. David Hoeveler, *John Bascom and the Origins of the Wisconsin Idea* (Madison: University of Wisconsin Press, 2016). Here and there in the essay I will provide some references to original sources in the Bascom collection, offering the reader some flavor of a writer often challenging in his prose, but lively and piquant as well.

4. John Bascom, *Sociology* (New York: G. P. Putnam's Sons, 1887), 158, 160, 210.

5. John Bascom, *Sociology*, 44–45.

6. John Bascom, "What Do the Members of a State University Owe to the State?" *University Review* I (December 1884), 93.

7. Robert M. La Follette Sr., *La Follette's Autobiography: A Personal Narrative of Political Experiences* (Madison: University of Wisconsin Press, [1911] 1960), 12–13.

8. Florence Bascom, "The University in 1874–1887," *Wisconsin Magazine of History* 8, no. 3 (March 1925): 307.

9. John Bascom, "The Functions of the State," *Independent*, January 31, 1889.

10. John Bascom, *Ethics or Science of Duty* (New York: G. P. Putnam's Sons, 1879), 307.

11. For excellent historical overviews and assessments of the Wisconsin Idea, see David J. Weerts, "Covenant, Contract, and the Politics of the Wisconsin Idea," *Academe* 102, no. 5 (September–October 2016): 10–15, https://www.aaup.org/article/cove nant-contract-and-politics-wisconsin-idea; Gwen Drury, "The Wisconsin Idea: The Vision That Made Wisconsin Famous," July 22, 2011, http://ls.wisc.edu/assets/misc/documents/wi-idea-history-intro-summary-essay.pdf.

12. Christopher Newfield, *The Great Mistake: How We Wrecked Public Universities and How We Can Fix Them* (Baltimore, MD: Johns Hopkins University Press, 2016), 136–37.

13. Stephanie Reitz, "Colleges Defend Humanities amid Tight Budgets," *Boston Globe*, November 26, 2011, http://archive.boston.com/news/education/higher/articles/2011/11/26/colleges_defend_humanities_amid_tight_budgets_1322327983/.

14. Jason Stanley, "Fascism and the University," *Chronicle of Higher Education*, September 2, 2018, https://www.chronicle.com/article/Fascismthe-University/244382.

15. Dan Kaufman, *The Fall of Wisconsin: The Conservative Conquest of a Progressive Bastion and the Future of American Politics* (New York: W. W. Norton, 2018), 235; Nico Savidge, "Changes to Tenure, Budget and Regents Show Extent of Scott Walker's Impact on UW," *Wisconsin State Journal*, March 27, 2016, https://madison.com/wsj/news/local/education/university/changes-to-tenure-budget-and-regents-show-extent-of-scott/article_90954155-df31-5fdb-bb93-dd93a0f81225.html. Savidge is quoted in Martin Kich, "Walker's Wisconsin," Academe Blog, March 28, 2016, https://academeblog.org/2016/03/28/walkers-wisconsin/.

16. Karen Herzog, "UW System's Proposed Operating Budget Mirrors GOP State Lawmakers' Agenda," *Milwaukee Journal Sentinel*, August 20, 2018, https://www.json line.com/story/news/education/2018/08/20/uw-system-frames-budget-request-around -gop-driven-goals/1042500002/.

17. Kaufman, *Fall of Wisconsin*, 45.

18. David J. Vanness, "The Withering of a Once-Great State University," *Chronicle of Higher Education*, July 13, 2015, https://www.chronicle.com/article/The-Withering-of -a-Once-Great/231565; Michael S. Joyce, "The Legacy of the 'Wisconsin Idea': Hastening the Demise of an Exhausted Progressivism," *Wisconsin Interest* 3, no. 2 (Fall/Winter 1994), 9–14. For another conservative brief on the corruptions of liberalism and a plea for Lockean individualism and antistatism, see Jonah Goldberg, *Suicide of the West: How the Rebirth of Tribalism, Populism, Nationalism, and Identity Politics Is Destroying American Democracy* (New York: Crown Forum, 2018). Goldberg lays the intellectual corruptions of progressivism at the feet of Richard T. Ely and the "Wisconsin School." They sought to import German romantic ideas into the United States and embraced the "organic" model of society, one that Goldberg rejects (177–78, 179–81, 205).

19. For more complete discussions of this business model, see Sheila Slaughter and Larry L. Leslie, *Academic Capitalism: Politics, Policies, and the Entrepreneurial University* (Baltimore, MD: Johns Hopkins University Press, 1997), 14–15, 64–65, 179, 180–82, 204–5, and the relevant sections of Walter W. McMahon, *Higher Learning, Greater Good: The Private and Social Benefits of Higher Education* (Baltimore, MD: Johns Hopkins University Press, 2009).

20. Pat Schneider, "UW–Madison Researchers React to Robin Vos' 'Ancient Mating Habits of Whatever' Remark," *Capital Times*, November 8, 2014, https://madison .com/ct/news/local/writers/pat_schneider/uw-madison-researchers-react-to-robin-vos -ancient-mating-habits/article_3144b1da-66a7-11e4-93fc-e3c72cb3062d.html.

21. David D. Haynes, "Sex and the Single Perch," *Milwakee Journal Sentinel*, November 28, 2014, http://archive.jsonline.com/news/opinion/sex-and-the-single-perch -saving-a-species-b99397780z1-284155491.html.

22. Newfield, *Great Mistake*, 127–28; Greg Lukianoff and Jonathan Haidt, *The Coddling of the American Mind: How Good Intentions and Bad Ideas Are Setting Up a Generation for Failure* (New York: Penguin Press, 2018), 6–7.

23. Joan W. Scott, "How the Right Weaponized Free Speech," *Chronicle of Higher Education*, January 7, 2018, https://www.chronicle.com/article/How-the-Right-Weap onized-Free/242142.

24. See, for an example among many one could cite, A. Douglas Stone and Mary Schwab-Stone, "The Sheltering Campus: Why College Is Not Home," *New York Times*, February 5, 2016, https://www.nytimes.com/2016/02/07/education/edlife/adolescent-development-college-students.html.

25. Chris Quintana, "Fired Over Speech? You're Probably a Liberal," *Chronicle of Higher Education*, May 11, 2018. The online version of Quintana's article appears under a different title here: https://www.chronicle.com/article/The-Real-Free-Speech-Crisis-Is/243284. For descriptions of the most notorious of these campus battles—Middlebury College, Evergreen State College, Yale University, University of California, Berkeley—see Lukianoff and Haidt, *Coddling*.

26. Board of Regents of the University of Wisconsin System, "Friday Agenda and Materials," September 28, 2017, https://www.wisconsin.edu/regents/download/meeting_materials/2017/october/Board-of-Regents-Friday-Agenda-and-Materials-October-2017.pdf.

27. Jason N. Blum, "Don't Bow to Blowhards," *Chronicle of Higher Education*, September 3, 2017, https://www.chronicle.com/article/Don-t-Bow-to-Blowhards/241048.

28. John Bascom, "The Spirit of the University," *University Press*, March 10, 1877 (University of Wisconsin Archives, Steenbock Library, University of Wisconsin–Madison, microform, series 20/0/0/1 and 20/1/3/00/3 77A4).

29. Robin Vos, "A Free Speech Challenge to the UW System," Right Wisconsin, September 6, 2016, https://rightwisconsin.com. This op-ed has apparently been removed from the website.

30. Karen Herzog, "Vos Says Speakers at UW Campuses Too Liberal," *Milwaukee Journal Sentinel*, September 13, 2016, https://www.jsonline.com/story/news/education/2016/09/13/vos-says-speakers-at-uw-campuses-too-liberal/90121674/. If I may make a personal illustration of this point: A few years ago, I offered a graduate seminar titled "American Conservative Thinkers: The Classical Tradition." We studied thinkers like James Madison, John C. Calhoun, William Graham Sumner, Albert Jay Nock, H. L. Mencken, the Southern Agrarians, Irving Babbitt, Friedrich Hayek, Peter Viereck, Russell Kirk, Whittaker Chambers, William F. Buckley Jr., George Will, Irving Kristol, Michael Novak, Jeane Kirkpatrick, Gertrude Himmelfarb, and others. When I surveyed the students for their views of the course at semester's end, one comment in particular struck me: "Why have I not heard of these people before?"

31. John Bascom, *A Christian State: Baccalaureate Sermon, Preached in the Assembly Hall, University of Wisconsin, June 19th, 1887* (Milwaukee: Cramer, Aikens & Cramer, 1887), 25. Bascom was quoting from Edmund Burke's *Reflections on the Revolution in France*, first published in 1790.

32. Bascom, "State?," 98; John Bascom, *Education and the State: A Baccalaureate Sermon Delivered at the University of Wisconsin, June 17, 1877* (Madison: Democrat Co., 1877), 8.

33. Richard V. Reeves, *Dream Hoarders: How the American Upper Middle Class Is Leaving Everyone Else in the Dust, Why That Is a Problem, and What to Do about It* (Washington, DC: Brookings Institution, 2017), 76.

34. Yuval Levin, *The Fractured Republic: Renewing America's Social Contract in the Age of Individualism* (New York: Basic Books, 2016), 154, 7, 76, 77–78, 79, 89, 151, 126,

100, quotation from p. 2. Levin writes: "We have set loose a scourge of loneliness and isolation . . . as the distinct social dysfunction of our age of individualism" (98).

35. David Brooks, "The Conservative Intellectual Crisis," *New York Times*, October 28, 2016, https://www.nytimes.com/2016/10/28/opinion/the-conservative-intellectual-crisis.html; David Brooks, "The G.O.P. Is Rotting," *New York Times*, December 7, 2017, https://www.nytimes.com/2017/12/07/opinion/the-gop-is-rotting.html.

36. Charles J. Sykes, *How the Right Lost Its Mind* (New York: St. Martin's Press, 2017), 18.

37. Goldberg, *Suicide of the West*, 16, 287–88, 345.

38. Max Boot, *The Corrosion of Conservatism: Why I Left the Right* (New York: W. W. Norton, 2018), 175–77, 58. Other prominent conservatives who left the Republican Party for similar reasons include George F. Will and Steve Schmidt. I shared the appreciation of these writers for conservative thinking in the 1970s and 1980s and tried to capture it in the book I wrote titled *Watch on the Right: Conservative Intellectuals in the Reagan Era* (Madison: University of Wisconsin Press, 1992).

39. David Brooks, "Anthony Kennedy and the Privatization of Meaning," *New York Times*, June 28, 2018, https://www.nytimes.com/2018/06/28/opinion/anthony-kennedy-individualism.html; David Brooks, "Republican or Conservative, You Have to Choose," *New York Times*, June 25, 2018, https://www.nytimes.com/2018/06/25/opinion/trump-republican-party-conservative.html.

40. E. J. Dionne Jr., "Channeling Edmund Burke, the Original Conservative Reformer," *Seattle Times*, July 1, 2013, https://www.seattletimes.com/opinion/channeling-edmund-burke-the-original-conservative-reformer/.

41. David Brooks, "The Republican Collapse," *New York Times*, October 5, 2007, https://www.nytimes.com/2007/10/05/opinion/05brooks.html; David Brooks, "A Renaissance on the Right," *New York Times*, April 12, 2018, https://www.nytimes.com/2018/04/12/opinion/renaissance-right-gop.html.

42. Mark Lilla, *The Once and Future Liberal: After Identity Politics* (New York: Harper Collins, 2017), 6, 9–10, 29. Lilla also concedes that conservative thinkers in the 1970s and 1980s had "serious, fresh ideas about reforming, not abolishing government" (21).

43. Lilla, *Once and Future Liberal*, 59, 102, 14–15, 64–65.

44. William Egginton, *The Splintering of the American Mind: Identity Politics, Inequality, and Community on Today's College Campuses* (New York: Bloomsbury, 2018), 12, 43, 55, 81, 31–32, quotation from p. 55.

45. Egginton, *Splintering of the American Mind*, 12, 79, 88, 164, 89–90.

46. Egginton, *Splintering of the American Mind*, 209–10, 89–90, 193.

47. John Bascom, *The Seat of Sin: Baccalaureate Sermon, University of Wisconsin, June 18th, 1876* (University of Wisconsin Archives, microform, series 4/6/2 425–5B6), p. 14. Bascom, *Christian State*, 21.

48. Marilynne Robinson, "The American Scholar Now," in *What Are We Doing Here? Essays* (New York: Farrar, Straus and Giroux, 2018), 84–85, 88, quotation from p. 89.

49. Robinson, "American Scholar Now," 89, 86, quotation from pp. 94–95.

50. Pat Schneider, "Planned Liberal Arts Cuts at UW–Stevens Point Fan Right-Left Debate on Higher Education," *Capital Times*, April 7, 2018, https://madison.com/ct/news/local/education/university/planned-liberal-arts-cuts-at-uw-stevens-point-fan-right/article_7d3b3274-3c4a-573d-b2db-de2a27a0c906.html; Valerie Strauss, "A University of Wisconsin Campus Pushes Plan to Drop 13 Majors—Including English, History and Philosophy," *Washington Post*, March 21, 2018, https://www.washingtonpost.com/news/answer-sheet/wp/2018/03/21/university-of-wisconsin-campus-pushes-plan-to-drop-13-majors-including-english-history-and-philosophy/?utm_term=.b81ab3574f4a.

51. Greg Summers, "Why the University of Wisconsin Stevens Point Plans to Eliminate Certain Traditional Liberal Arts Majors," *Inside Higher Ed*, April 2, 2018, https://www.insidehighered.com/views/2018/04/02/why-university-wisconsin-stevens-point-plans-eliminate-certain-traditional-liberal.

52. Online comments on Summers, "Liberal Arts Majors."

53. Charles J. Sykes, *Fail U.: The False Promise of Higher Education* (New York: St. Martin's Press, 2016), 70.

54. Newfield, *Great Mistake*, 265–68, 298–99.

55. Greg Summers, "Back to the Future at Stevens Point," *Chronicle of Higher Education*, March 29, 2018, https://www.chronicle.com/article/Back-to-the-Future-at-Stevens/242978.

56. John Bascom, *Truth and Truthfulness: A Baccalaureate Sermon Delivered to the Graduating Class of the University of Wisconsin, June 19, 1881* (Milwaukee: Cramer, Aikens & Cramer, 1881), 20.

Accuracy Always

Willard Bleyer and the Push for Better Journalism

CAITLIN CIESLIK-MISKIMEN

In November 1924, a small group of high school students and teachers boarded the train at the Superior, Wisconsin, Union Depot and settled in for the long journey to the University of Wisconsin campus in Madison. The traveling party included two editors and the circulation manager of the city's largest high school publication, Superior Central's *The Devil's Pi*; the editor of the school's yearbook; their adviser and printing instructor, Mr. Harold L. Mahnke; and representatives from the student publications at Superior East High School. As delegates to the fifth annual Central Interscholastic Press Association (CIPA) conference, they planned to attend an intensive two-day event designed to help high school publications tackle the unique problems newspapers, yearbooks, and magazine staffs faced. Founded by professors in the University of Wisconsin's journalism department, CIPA was the largest organization of its kind in the United States.[1] With a goal of providing guidance and establishing standards for one of the most rapidly growing categories of publications in the first few decades of the twentieth century, CIPA had quickly grown since its founding in 1920 to become the most prolific organization of its kind in the United States. Its membership included high schools from practically every state as well as Canada, and attendance at its annual conference steadily increased from year to year.

In addition to its annual meeting, CIPA published the *Scholastic Editor*, a magazine "intended to be a bulletin of association news and helpful hints to editors of secondary school publications," both large and small.[2] It contained advice on running a yearbook or a newspaper, story ideas, layout ideas, dos and don'ts, tips on selling advertising, and tricks for boosting circulation, subscriptions, and overall student engagement. It offered upon request critiques of publications and ran an exceedingly popular national contest, which bestowed all-American, first- and second-class honors across multiple divisions upon those newspapers, annuals, and magazines judged to be the best in the country. Mr. Mahnke and his students in Superior were active in the organization. He contributed columns to the *Scholastic Editor*, spoke regularly at the conventions, and served as the lead organizer of the Central Printing Teachers' Association, a subgroup within CIPA designed to aid printing instructors and advocate for the recognition of printing as a course of study. The school's publications regularly won recognition from the organization; the *Echo*, its annual, received second-class honors, and critics "highly commended" the *Devil's Pi*.[3] The local newspaper, the *Superior Telegram*, frequently covered the students' trips to CIPA conventions and applauded the efforts of its student journalists when the city's publications won high honors.

The 1924 CIPA convention attracted more than one thousand high school students and teachers from across the United States and Canada and was reported to be the largest journalistic meeting in the world.[4] To accommodate the crowds, organizers moved the conference to the university's Stock Pavilion. (Originally built in 1909 for statewide livestock shows, the Stock Pavilion had more seating than any building in Madison until 1930.) Over the course of two days, delegates attended a variety of different sessions designed to address the issues of the day concerning the writing and production of student newspapers, magazines, and annuals. There were sections for newspapers' editors and staff; business, circulation, and advertising managers; advisers; printing instructors; and sessions of general interest, including a keynote speech from Lee White, an editorial writer of national renown for the *Detroit News*.[5] Throughout, professors from the University of Wisconsin's burgeoning journalism department were front and center, including Willard Grosvenor Bleyer, the university's first journalism professor and a pioneering voice in journalism education. The university's support of CIPA attracted accolades. The *Journalism Bulletin* called it a "good extension effort" that promised to "raise standards" and influence high school journalists to pursue university training.[6]

For Bleyer, CIPA represented an extension of the journalism department's mission to serve the citizens of the state (and, by extension, the country). It fit within his mission to develop a journalism program that would improve the quality of reporting and ensure the functioning of democracy—something that was especially needed at a time when significant economic and technological changes were transforming the publishing industry, as well as society as a whole.[7] Bleyer frequently worried that the "monopolistic tendency" that characterized the American economy had a detrimental effect on newspapers; it transformed newspapers into a mass-produced product focused on courting a mass audience with sensationalized news—not the accurate, level-headed style of reporting he believed journalists had an obligation to produce. Journalism, Bleyer believed, was the solution to the problems that plagued American society.[8] As a result, Bleyer was resolute in his conviction that newspaper work was equivalent to—if not more integral than—law and medicine in a modern society. "Universities have spent millions of dollars on establishing and maintaining medical and law schools," he wrote in 1931. "Are journalists less important to the welfare of society and to the success of democratic government?"[9]

If departments of journalism were up to the task of preparing journalists ready to protect democratic interests, they needed to be actively engaged with the world beyond the confines of campus. As a result, Bleyer and his colleagues spearheaded a number of programs and initiatives designed to improve training for journalists, increase the collaboration between journalists and the university, and connect the work done on campus with the broader community. These activities included hosting a variety of conferences for professional reporting and publishing groups, conducting surveys of newspapers, delivering speeches to journalism associations throughout the country, writing editorials and articles promoting journalism education, sponsoring summer sessions and shortcourses, and founding organizations and associations designed to advance the university-level study of journalism. Correspondence in Bleyer's papers included letters to the heads of various departments and schools of journalism, such as the University of Oregon and the University of Colorado; professors at Stanford University; journalism publications; government agencies; and citizens interested in, and concerned about, the future of journalism in the United States.

While the training of journalists was his primary goal, Bleyer also acted, to a certain extent, as a public relations practitioner, and he developed promotional strategies designed to boost the university's standing with the general public and build a strong national reputation for its research and academic programs. He oversaw the revival and led the expansion of the University of Wisconsin's *Press Bulletin*, a weekly promotional publication that circulated news from the campus to daily and weekly newspapers across the state, national newspapers and magazines, and agricultural and trade journalists. The *Bulletin* represented an important "first step" in establishing a distribution system of university information for newspapers. Bleyer also encouraged reporters and editors to visit the campus and see the work of the university firsthand; this practice, he believed, would be of "very great" benefit to the university and result in positive news coverage and better understanding of the work of its faculty.[10]

Often, examinations of Bleyer's legacy at the University of Wisconsin focus on his contributions to the university training of journalists and the intellectual development of journalism and, more broadly, mass communication as an academic field. Scholars generally recognize Bleyer as a "pioneer in journalism education,"[11] deserving of a place alongside Walter Williams, founder of the first school of journalism in the United States at the University of Missouri, and newspaper publisher Joseph Pulitzer, whose endowment—and not his academic vision—led to the creation of the Pulitzer School of Journalism at Columbia University. Bleyer's early attitudes formed the foundation for modern journalism education and influenced hundreds of undergraduate and graduate students trained at the University of Wisconsin in the first three decades of the twentieth century. Among these students were several who would go on to become prominent communication scholars and leading academics in the field, including the future director of the School of Journalism at the University of Wisconsin, Ralph O. Nafziger. The extent of Bleyer's network and their influence in journalism study earned him the nickname "Daddy Bleyer."[12] During a summer meeting in the early 1930s, leaders and directors of journalism schools from across the country met in Madison; at that time, all heads of journalism schools, with the exception of Williams of Missouri, had previously been Bleyer students.[13] In a field that has traditionally traced its roots to the late 1940s and early 1950s, there has been a push to recognize Bleyer as the heart of a network of scholars that rose to prominence after World War II and to establish academic journalism's true origins closer to the turn of the century.[14]

These scholarly examinations of Bleyer, however, lose sight of the public outreach component of his educational philosophy and the extensive work he did within the broader community not only to legitimize journalism as a field of study, but also to improve reporting and win continued support for the work of journalism itself. Bleyer's pioneering reputation as a journalism educator is well deserved; he did singlehandedly (at least until another professor, Grant Milnor Hyde, joined him on the faculty in 1912) build a program that quickly won national recognition as a leader in journalism education. Under his leadership, the journalism program at the University of Wisconsin grew from offering one class (Law and the Press) housed in the English department to a standalone department enrolling hundreds of students in its courses, and its eventual establishment as a School of Journalism in 1927 and one of the earliest journalism programs to grant doctoral degrees. But Bleyer's focus did not solely extend to the undergraduate, and later, graduate journalism curriculum. Inspired by the tenets of the Wisconsin Idea, he also pursued a variety of community-engagement strategies, rooted in the belief that the university's broader mission was to service the citizens and the state of Wisconsin. In this sense, the journalism department's support of CIPA, its annual convention, and *Scholastic Editor* reflected the department's broader mission not only to educate and train future journalists but also to communicate the importance of journalism within a modern, democratic society. By speaking in front of high school newspaper staffs and members of other high school press associations scattered across the country, Bleyer advocated for his view of what journalism education could and should be. When he participated in events such as CIPA's annual convention, wrote columns in the *Scholastic Editor* that detailed the history of American journalism, and spoke before high school press associations across the country, he described journalism as "the greatest of all the professions" and a worthy pursuit for a high school student, especially those looking for a career that answered a higher calling.[15]

Ultimately, the quiet, reserved Bleyer embraced an idealistic view of the journalist and championed the role of the press in society. This was a position he took within the classroom—although his rather dull lecture style often masked his passionate views to his students—and outside of it. The press, in Bleyer's view, was one of the most important professions, due to its direct influence on the functioning of democracy. "No other profession has a more vital relation to the welfare of society or to the success of democratic government," Bleyer wrote.[16] At a speech at the opening of the Medill School of Journalism at Northwestern University in 1921, Bleyer remarked that the "incompetent lawyer may lose the client's money, or even his freedom," but a poorly trained or incompetent journalist who gave "day after day inaccurate information, [or] colored information . . . unconsciously" poisoned public opinion and created "false impressions." The privileged position of the journalist—and the demands and challenges placed on reporting in the twentieth century—demanded professional training, similar to law schools and schools of medicine around the country. Nothing less than the "success of our democracy was at stake."[17] He peppered his writings and speeches with his personal motto, "Accuracy Always," and a favorite quote of his from Woodrow Wilson, "The food of opinion is the news of the day."[18] As a "strong voice for responsibility and respectability," Bleyer believed the press should operate with a "proper respect for propriety in order to best fulfill its responsibility to society."[19] And while certain individuals were born with the ideal characteristics of a reporter, such as curiosity, a nose for news, imagination, empathy, and a sense of responsibility,[20] they were ultimately made in the classroom—specifically, a college classroom.

The Influence of the "Bleyer Boys" and Campus Print Culture

Born into a prominent Milwaukee newspaper family, Bleyer grew up surrounded by all aspects of newspaper production and by people who "revered journalism."[21] That his father and uncles all found employment in newspapers was somewhat surprising. Henry, the family patriarch, arrived in Milwaukee via Detroit in 1837, when the settlement on the shore of Lake Michigan was a small village of roughly 1,400. An immigrant from Hanover, Germany, Henry was the city's first German resident and an expert cabinetmaker. He enjoyed some level of prominence in the city, due to his reputation as a hard worker and his strong will, and he built his business into a thriving establishment.[22] But none of his six sons followed in the footsteps of their father. Instead, the "Bleyer Boys," as they were known, all found work in various Milwaukee newspapers, following the lead of Henry, the oldest. Henry began newspaper work in 1849 as an apprentice in the office of the *Daily Commercial Advertiser*; he moved to the editorial department of the *Milwaukee Sentinel* in 1862, where he worked as a reporter and editor, and he stayed with the newspaper for nearly five decades. Albert, Willard's father, began work as the foreman of the composing room of the *Evening Wisconsin*, and then spent most of his career in the circulation department of the *Milwaukee Sentinel*.[23] Twin brothers Herman and Julius were staff members of the *Evening Wisconsin*, where Louis Bleyer was the marine editor. Clarence, the youngest, began his newspaper career as a typesetter for the *Evening Wisconsin* and worked as newsroom foreman for its successor, the *Wisconsin News*.[24] The young Willard often tagged along with his father and uncles to the various newsrooms around the city.[25]

Henry had the greatest influence on the young Willard Bleyer, and took Willard under his wing as the "leader of the family." Henry and Albert married sisters, and the four lived together in Milwaukee, where Willard was raised by "two fathers and two mothers," as family members described it.[26] A "bright" and "grand student," Willard earned high marks in a variety of subjects, and excelled both inside of and outside of the classroom.[27] Relatives characterized him as "thorough in everything he did, never superficial,"[28] and he was exposed to a variety of activities and areas of study, apart from journalism. Bleyer was an accomplished pianist, and he was exposed to music, art, and literature in the home.[29] Nevertheless, newspapers remained his primary interest, and when he enrolled as a freshman at the University of Wisconsin he immersed himself in the campus's vibrant print culture. Majoring in English, he helped found the school's independent student newspaper, the *Daily Cardinal*, where he served as a reporter and editor and frequently wrote editorials for the paper's opinion page. He also served as editor-in-chief for both the *Badger Yearbook* as well as the campus literary magazine, the *Aegis*, and earned a bachelor's degree in 1896 and a master's degree in English in 1898.

After graduation, Bleyer returned to Milwaukee, where he worked as an English teacher at East Side High School. There, he sought to integrate journalism into his lesson plans, where his continued interest in the educational potential of the subject was evident. "He had the students clipping news items and keeping them in 'strings,' as a method of analyzing style," recalled a former

student.[30] His students kept newspaper articles in scrapbooks, and Bleyer persuaded his supervisors that the exercise was relevant because it "demonstrated
the English language at work in the American press."[31] By all reports, Bleyer was
well liked by his students for his "kindly, friendly manner as a teacher," despite
his "shy," "dignified," and "reserved" classroom demeanor. It was perhaps his
quite formal classroom conduct that encouraged his students to play tricks on
him. "Did we give him the runaround as a teacher," remembered a student.
She noted how Bleyer wore rain boots to school at the mere hint of rain, and
his students' "favorite pastime" was hiding his galoshes in the such places as
the wastebasket.[32] Needless to say, high school teaching did not have the same
allure as further university study, and, after two years, Bleyer returned to the
University of Wisconsin to pursue a doctoral degree in English. After receiving
his degree in 1904, he joined the faculty and was assigned to teach freshman
English in the 1904–5 academic year.

Bleyer arrived at campus just as the university was emerging as a major hub
for progressive thought. Wisconsin, as well as the University of Chicago and
Columbia University, was an important center of a new type of thinking that
attempted to address the challenges evident at the turn of the century. Progressivism in the early twentieth century reflected what the historian Richard Hofstadter described as "the broader impulse toward criticism and change" prevalent
when the social, economic, and political changes wrought by industrialization,
urbanization, and mass immigration inspired a push for reform.[33] The increasing corporatization of the economy, as well as the rise of a mass society, raised
concerns about whether American democracy could survive in a new environment. Largely, progressivism represented an effort to "restore a type of economic
individualism and political democracy" that was widely believed to have flour-
ished in the smaller communities that characterized American life in the nineteenth century; the goal was to bring back, via reform, "a kind of morality and
civic purity that was also believed to have been lost."[34] The emerging middle
class—a predominantly urban byproduct of the new economic landscape—
led the push for reform, with power placed in the hands of experts and professionals.[35] As lawyers, doctors, economists, teachers, and others sought to elevate their social prestige by introducing professional training programs and
schools, along with exclusive credentials that signaled their elevated positions,
the call for journalists to conduct a similar professionalization effort began to
intensify.

American journalism had evolved dramatically in its two hundred years
of existence, and the newspapers hawked on the nation's urban street corners
and circulated throughout the countryside bore little resemblance to their earlier counterparts. By the 1880s, newspapers transformed from small and slight

weekly publications with clear political affiliations that carried largely promotional local news items into daily publications that shed the party mantle in favor of cultivating the largest circulation possible.[36] The resulting products were filled with snark and sensationalism, written by reporters who received little if any formal training. Sensationalism enjoyed a long history in the American press, but it seemingly began to dominate newspaper content during the New York circulation wars of the 1880s between publishers Joseph Pulitzer and William Randolph Hearst, and the resulting push by other newspapers to fill their pages with more entertaining content to win readers. The emphasis on the sensational and catering to the masses "degraded" the role of journalism in society, in Bleyer's view.[37] He criticized papers for "their inaccuracies, their exploitation of crime and scandal, their triviality."[38] Printing purposely falsified news "for any purpose, good or bad, must be regarded as an indefensible violation of the fundamental purpose of the press."[39] The gravity of the situation was due to the pivotal role the newspaper played in the functioning of American democracy; "The character of our democracy," he said, depended on "the accuracy of the newspapers in matters of news."[40] For Bleyer as well as other observers, the food that fed public opinion, to borrow Woodrow Wilson's words, was being poisoned.

Further, newspapers were not immune to the "profound changes" that worked to reshape American life at the close of the nineteenth century. Newspapers responded to "the speeding up of the tempo of life and the resulting high anxiety and tension, due to machinery, rapid transportation, and the complexities of city life" in ways that threatened their privileged position.[41] Their production was increasingly mechanized, resulting in mass-produced publications that relied heavily on standardized content. More rapid transportation and communication technologies increased the amount of news available and facilitated greater and wider distributions than before. By 1920, newspaper publishing was a "big business enterprise" that began to bear a close resemblance to the chain stores that began to dominate the city and the countryside and that decimated independently owned and operated stores.[42] This emphasis on economic efficiency and view of the newspaper as a revenue-driven entity contributed to the shuttering of newspapers, with the number of titles published declining due to mergers and the rise of publishing chains. In Chicago, the number of morning publications decreased from six to two between 1892 and 1912, and in Cleveland, Milwaukee, St. Louis, New Orleans, and Buffalo, only one morning paper was published. These trends weakened the editorial voices of publishers who had once enjoyed national influence, such as Horace Greeley of the *New York Tribune*, Henry Raymond of the *New York Times*, and James Gordon Bennett of the *New York Herald*, and replaced these more high-minded publishers with business-oriented ones.[43] Although these changes in publishing and in the content of newspapers had gone largely unnoticed by the general public, the call for professional journalism education intensified.

The push for the university training of journalists, then, gained strength as a part of the overall move toward professionalization characteristic of the Progressive Era, as well as an effort to combat the sensationalism that seemingly dominated US newspapers. It paralleled the rise of objectivity as a reporting norm—the belief that facts should be separated from values—as more high-minded journalists sought to distinguish themselves from the reporters of the past.[44] It rested on the assumption that newspapers fulfilled a critical part of American democracy. But whether journalists needed a college education, or should instead follow an apprenticeship training model similar to trades, was a point of extended debate at the turn of the century. And further, if college programs in journalism were to flourish, just exactly what should define the curriculum, as well as how to balance a liberal arts education with practical and hands-on training, further divided journalism education advocates. For some, journalism had no place in the university. E. L. Godkin, editor of *The Nation*, and the journalist Horace White of the *Chicago Tribune* saw the newsroom as the only place to learn reporting.[45] The educational reformer Abraham Flexner argued that journalism had no "legitimate" place in the university, as it lacked intellectual rigor and was akin to home economics courses.[46] Joseph Pulitzer wrote in the *North American Review* and defended the establishment of journalism schools (and his offer to endow the first school of journalism in the world in response to a call from *New York Tribune* publisher Whitelaw Reid).[47] Pulitzer described the initiative's purpose as to "exalt principle, knowledge, culture, . . . to set up ideals, to keep the counting-room in its proper place, and to make the soul of the editor the soul of the paper."[48] He argued that an apprenticeship model would result in poorly (and incompletely) trained reporters, and it was outdated. Both medicine and law had abandoned apprenticeship training in favor of professional schools, so students arrived ready to practice with full knowledge of the theories at work; in journalism, where the newspaper offices were the hospitals, students arrived "knowing nothing of principles or theories."[49] What on-the-job training occurred was incidental and not adequate for what was the "most fascinating of all professions," Pulitzer wrote in the *North American Review*. "Most lawyers, most physicians, most clergymen die in obscurity, but every single day opens new doors for the journalist who holds the confidence of the community and has the capacity to address it."[50]

The idea that journalism was the most fascinating, most important, and most pivotal career path one could follow echoed throughout the mission statements justifying the founding of journalism programs, and it comprised a key theme in Bleyer's writings. Further, the recognition that the nature of journalism—and that of newspapers—was an evolving entity, undergoing constant change in response to the needs of the time and financial, political, and cultural pressures, created a largely optimistic outlook regarding the future of reporting. According to the historian William Sloan, Bleyer largely viewed the history of journalism as "the story of continuing progress and the development of proper professional standards in the betterment of society and democracy."[51] Current discussions about newspapers, he lamented, lacked historical perspective and failed "to regard the newspaper as a product of the social, political, and economic forces that have shaped and are still shaping all our institutions, including the newspaper."[52] Consequently, although Bleyer recognized the challenges facing newspapers and reporting—and was indeed troubled by the trends he observed—he was largely idealistic about the opportunities the future presented. In that sense, he echoed the opinions of other intellectuals, such as the sociologist Robert Park, who viewed journalism and the newspaper as a constantly evolving product that transformed in response to the demands of the public,[53] and philosopher and educator John Dewey, who saw mass communication as key to building the community needed for democracy.[54] For Bleyer, the threats newspapers faced in the early twentieth century created opportunities to produce better reporting that served the public interest. Journalists remained a key part of a functioning democracy; they could regain that position and solidify their standing through college-level training that emphasized a progressive view of the role of the press.

University journalism programs were the key to producing the accurate, responsible, reliable, and informed reporting critical to modern democracy. Bleyer's belief in a "high ideal of the press as an advocate for democracy and reform" fit the progressive mold of a reformer. Not a radical, Bleyer represented a moderate, middle-class professional interested in solving social problems, improving conditions, and enlarging enlightened democracy.[55] Further, his view of the journalist as an expert who guided public opinion through the clear conveyance of facts and information applied the growing belief in the power of expertise to newspapers. This idea of the journalist as expert complemented the mission envisioned for the University of Wisconsin by geologist Charles Van Hise, its president from 1903 to 1918, and it reflected the core tenets of the Wisconsin Idea. While an undergraduate, Bleyer advocated for a journalism course of study at the university, and he wrote several editorials on the topic for the *Daily Cardinal*. But his approach to journalism education did not crystallize until he joined the faculty of the university and began to think how to connect journalism to the established curriculum. In an examination of Bleyer's lesson plans, the media historians Carolyn Bronstein and Stephen Vaughn observed that he often "pondered the difference between scientific and artistic discourse," and in the process developed an understanding of journalism as a form of scientific discourse, the purpose of which was to present useful knowledge in an ordered way to the public.[56] Journalists on the whole were "seeking ways to use what they regarded as a scientific method of reporting" in order to distinguish the work they did from the sensational yellow reporting of years past.[57] This way of thinking about journalism was compatible with the strains of progressivism flowing out of the university. As Bronstein and Vaughn note, "If the shared information in newspapers could tie citizens to one another, maintaining social stability and moral cohesiveness in an urban-industrial mass society, then the university was obligated to train men and women for this type of work."[58]

Examining Bleyer's work within the context of the Wisconsin Idea and focusing on the public outreach component of his educational philosophy illuminates Bleyer's belief in journalism as a public good. He advocated expanded collaboration between universities and journalists, and between journalism programs and the broader community. The university's influence should not be limited to the campus, and collaboration between the journalism department and newspapers would result in better-educated reporters well equipped to handle the challenges of interpreting the day's news for their readers accurately and responsibly. The ultimate extension of the good the university accomplished would be in the number of journalism graduates who found their way to the state's urban dailies and country weeklies, and the high ideals they held as reporters, editors, and newspaper publishers.

The program Bleyer built at the University of Wisconsin differed from other university departments of journalism most notably in its strong insistence on the value of a broad, liberal arts education supplemented with practical training and theoretical courses. Courses in political science, economics, history, social sciences, and languages would account for roughly three-quarters of the courses a journalism student took; newswriting and reporting, copyediting, media law, and other courses specific to the practice of journalism would make up the rest. Other schools, such as the University of Missouri, emphasized the practical and technical training component of its curriculum and stressed that this laboratory approach was the only way to provide the experience necessary for reporters.[59] But for Bleyer and Van Hise, the two leading proponents of the new journalism program at Wisconsin, the result would be reporters who lacked the knowledge necessary to interpret the day's news. "The most essential training which the University can give to a student thinking of journalism is to equip him broadly with the knowledge of the ages and give him such intellectual

power that he will be continually fertile in applying that knowledge to present conditions," noted Van Hise in a speech before the Wisconsin Newspaper
Association discussing journalism coursework. "The fundamental qualifica-
tion for a journalist is to possess wealth of ideas from the best that the world has
thought and said not only in literature, but in all fields of human knowledge."
The journalism student "should combine that high sense of responsibility to
the public" with some technical training in news writing, the result being
better-prepared reporters placed in publications that would lead to a more
well-informed public.[60] "No newspaper or periodical can be any better than
those who make it," Bleyer later observed, noting the importance of reporters
and editors to the final product. "If, lacking adequate preparation for their work,
writers and editors are half-educated, superficial, inaccurate, and unscrupulous,
the newspapers and periodicals that they produce will not exert the wholesome influence that is generally assumed the press should exert on readers as
citizens of the state and as members of society."[61] The *Wisconsin State Journal*,
in an editorial noting the beginning of journalism coursework at the university, echoed these messages: "It is not the intention to give instruction in the
technical details of newspaper writing, but rather to lay a broad foundation
for the work. . . . To learn to adopt the newspaper man's disinterested point of
view, to acquire the ability to state an observed fact simply and clearly, and to
learn to promptly and with fairness and precision form and express judgement
upon important questions arising daily, should be of enormous value in any
profession or calling."[62]

Bleyer's careful stewardship of journalism education at the University of
Wisconsin made it a leader in university training for journalists. As the program grew, Bleyer often reminded university leaders that its performance—
and the work of its graduates—reflected well on the university as a whole. In
a 1909 report on the journalism department to university president Van Hise,
Bleyer commented that a growing journalism program would benefit the University of Wisconsin's national reputation: "The university will gain decided
advantage by taking rank with other institutions providing a department in
this field, and also by adding to the practical character of the training which it
offers."[63] The growing interest in journalism courses necessitated the formation of a separate department of journalism, one housed outside of the English
department with its own dedicated faculty. While managing journalism courses,
Bleyer had not given up his duties as an English professor, and he often had
to juggle his teaching obligations; in addition to newswriting and reporting,
he taught English literature, English philology, and the training of teachers. A
dedicated journalism department would facilitate "more effective instruction"
and would rank the university among a small group of state universities that

housed such departments, including the University of Missouri, the University of Kansas, and the University of Indiana.[64] By 1910, nearly eighty students were enrolled in journalism courses at the University of Wisconsin, up from thirty in 1906.[65] When further increasing enrollments and the need to offer a greater variety of coursework led Bleyer to advocate the establishment of a school of journalism, Bleyer noted in a 1918 letter to limnologist Edward A. Birge, president of the University of Wisconsin from 1918 to 1925, that such an initiative would "elevate and dignify the newspaper profession, as well as give the University a wider renown."[66] By promoting journalism education's relevance to the university and the community, Bleyer hoped to further legitimize it as a course of study, improve the professional standing of journalists, and enhance the sharing of knowledge between the university and the state's residents. Further, by leading universities across the country, Wisconsin could establish educational standards for the new field. "The first 10 years . . . were the most fun, for they were pioneering years and everything we did, every new course, was 'the first in the world,'" remembered the journalism school's second director, Professor Grant Milnor Hyde. "We laid out techniques now used in all the schools."[67]

EXPANDING THE INFLUENCE OF
JOURNALISM EDUCATION BEYOND CAMPUS

One part of the way journalism could contribute to the community would be through advancing a research agenda focused on evaluating the way media impacted society. As Bleyer advocated for a school of journalism, he emphasized the value of research work that would examine "the influence of the newspaper on the ideas and ideals of the citizens of the state."[68] Not to engage in a broader understanding of how journalism shaped public opinion, how readers interpreted the news, and how reporting enhanced—or damaged—civic engagement would be merely to develop and promote a technical, skills-based course of study. "Only when newspaper workers and students of journalism are made to realize the effect of the news 'story,' headline, and editorial that they write upon the thoughts and actions of their readers, do they appreciate the importance of their work in relation to society," Bleyer wrote. "Instruction in journalism should be vitalized by research on the part of members of its faculty just as teaching in other branches is made vital by investigation carried out by instructors in those fields."[69] The program's true goal for Wisconsin was to produce "professionals trained not only in how to write the news, but also in how to understand society."[70] While Bleyer advocated for a research component for journalism education, he also wanted the department's courses to advance thinking beyond the rudimentary practice of producing articles. His course in journalism principles taught students to "consider what influence the newspaper may exert on the opinions, morals, tastes, and standard of living of readers," drawing on what they might have learned in psychology courses.[71] Courses in copywriting emphasized news evaluation, and editorial writing focused less on crafting editorials and more on the "careful, impartial, logical analysis of the latest phases of the social, political and economic problems" studied in other courses.[72] As the journalism department continued to grow, and graduate students began to arrive, Bleyer looked to enhance the collaboration between the research agenda pursued by professors and graduate students and the curriculum undergraduates followed.

Additionally, by placing student journalists at community news organizations, Bleyer and the department hoped to improve their work and win continued support for the journalism program from the state's editors and publishers. While advocating for the program, Bleyer, along with Van Hise, noted the positive feedback received from the state's newspaper editors and publishers, and they sought to anticipate criticisms by providing evidence of the real-world experience its students obtained. When introducing the program to the Wisconsin Press Association in 1905, Van Hise said the training offered by the university was "considered good preparation by editors," as demonstrated by the recent hiring of two students by one of the largest Milwaukee daily papers.[73] Nearly fifteen years later, journalism students gained practical experience by working in the offices of the three Madison daily newspapers: "Through the active cooperation of the editors . . . students in the classes in newspaper reporting and editing are given an opportunity to do actual newspaper work on these papers, while pursuing their university work."[74] Additionally, a number of students served as university reporters and correspondents or contributors for newspapers and periodicals in Chicago, as well as Milwaukee, Madison, and elsewhere in Wisconsin. Their experience was not limited to the major dailies. Eight students took complete charge of Wisconsin's weekly *Prairie du Chien Courier*, with a circulation of two thousand, for two weeks. Bleyer reported that the "demonstration seems to have convinced many of the editors and publishers of Wisconsin weekly newspapers that the instruction which we are giving in journalism prepares students for the country weekly field as well as for the daily press."[75]

Further efforts to minimize criticism of the program—as well as the university as a whole—included extending invitations to visit the campus. Bleyer proposed that the journalism department invite the Wisconsin Press Association to a two- or three-day session and extend the invitation to the Wisconsin Daily Newspaper Association and Progressive Newspaper Association for a one-day meeting during the 1913 National Association of Teachers of Journalism

meeting in Madison. "The benefit to the university of getting these representatives of the press to meet here and see the university as it actually is, would
undoubtedly be very great," he wrote to Van Hise. "It would prevent in the
future much of the criticism, particularly by editors of weekly papers who do
not realize the size of the university or the magnitude of its work." He offered
the example of W. H. Bridgman, editor of the *Stanley Republican* and a critic
of the university, who was invited to speak on campus. "Since he was down
here, he has taken on several occasions a decided stand for the university. . . .
I have no doubt that many other editors, both of daily and weekly papers,
would be as much impressed with the university and its work as Mr. Bridgman
evidently was, if we could arrange to get them here at a time when they could
see the university work and then arrange to show them the university as it
really is."[76] The efforts worked, to some extent. A. F. Ender, president of the
Wisconsin Press Association, applauded the "cordial and helpful spirit" from
the journalism department in making its meeting successful. "As far back as
I can remember there has always been a feeling of mutual goodwill and respect between the editors of the state and the University of Wisconsin," Ender
wrote. "I know the College of Journalism is raising the standards of journalism
in Wisconsin, both from an ethical and business standpoint."[77] And in 1916,
the Wisconsin City Editors Association offered their endorsement of the program, after a short campus tour and a series of meetings with Bleyer and his
fellow journalism professors. Before the tour and meetings, association members
had voiced concerns that journalism students graduated with unrealistic expectations about salaries and career expectations and what they saw as "inadequate"
and unnecessary training.[78] They subsequently concluded that the department
was "doing good work."[79]

The approval from the state's journalists was due to Bleyer's promotion of
the program, as well as to its close association with the *Press Bulletin*, which
publicized the activities of the university to the state and country. The *Bulletin* had become a valuable asset to the university under Bleyer's direction; it
claimed responsibility for communicating the research advances made on campus and their impact on the state's citizens. The result was a tool that helped
improve the University of Wisconsin's standing, and one that attracted accolades from newspaper editors and government agencies alike. Bleyer revived
the *Press Bulletin* in 1904, justifying his investment in it with continual references to his belief in the newspaper as "the only effective means" for distrib-
uting information, in part because of the level of influence these publications
claimed in their communities.[80] Newspapers were the "ideal" platform for
"giving to the citizens of the state the results of the investigations for which
their money has made provision," noted Van Hise in a 1905 speech. "And what

better service can the newspapers render to the state than to give to the millions of readers the results of investigations which will be of direct benefit to these many readers. This may be said to be the true form of university extension."[81] By 1909, the publication was issued weekly and contained short articles that chronicled activities on campus, ranging from sections on courses for farmers, horse breeding, soils, inspection laws, home economics, and city government (this last section included information on studies the university produced that were used in local policymaking). Bleyer was not above including athletic news in the *Bulletin* and reports of the campus's fraternities and sororities, and he often published short pieces that spoke to the growth of his journalism program.

With many articles on applied research useful to farmers and others, the *Bulletin* represented an institutionalization of the Wisconsin Idea—namely, that the university should serve all of the state's citizens. In each issue, Bleyer emphasized the communication of scientific information in a way the general public would understand, and he also advocated for establishing ways to connect readers with researchers. This mission continued under a new leader, Professor Grant Milnor Hyde, who took over the *Bulletin* in 1912 when he joined the journalism department as its second faculty member. Under Hyde's leadership, the *Bulletin* took on a larger form, which allowed for the inclusion of more information, including material of interest to magazines and journals outside the state, and it acted as a "record of the progress of the university in matters that are otherwise not recorded."[82] Each edition averaged twenty articles, with up to one-half of the content regularly devoted to agricultural news. Wisconsin newspapers accounted for the majority of the *Bulletin*'s 1,250 subscribers, but circulation also included agricultural and dairy publications, newspapers outside the state with college news departments, news unions and bureaus, national magazines, trade journals and educational journals interested in university news, all county agricultural agents in the state, and other universities and agricultural experiment stations or extension departments that requested it. With its close attention to providing material of interest to editors, "a more or less careful survey of state and national publications indicates that the *Press Bulletin* material is extensively used."[83] Another study revealed that in Wisconsin, at least one weekly newspaper in every county published news from each issue of the *Press Bulletin*; in some counties, five to ten weeklies published news.[84]

The effectiveness of the *Press Bulletin* was due in part to Bleyer's careful consideration of the needs of the state's editors and publishers, as well as an understanding of what news from campus would be of most interest to readers. Bleyer and his supporter Van Hise did not see these activities as advertising in the conventional sense, in part because the university's greatest obligation was not to itself, but to the citizens of the state. "By carrying to the people the full information as to the university, the press has an opportunity to do very great service to the state," Van Hise said.[85] By publicizing the discoveries made on campus, and transmitting this knowledge to the people, the press was helping the university fulfill its ultimate goal: to be a center of research and analysis done to better the lives of those living in Wisconsin. Van Hise continued: "We feel that the university and the newspapers together will be accomplishing work for the citizens of the whole commonwealth, the value of which cannot be estimated."[86] Bleyer believed the university owed its success to its "continuous and consistent policy of publicity," which avoided the promotion of fabricated fluff in favor of accurate, good news that mattered to the citizens of the state.[87] He had proof that the state's editors appreciated his policy: In addition to studies of the number of *Bulletin*-inspired articles that appeared in newspapers, he also received positive feedback. Wrote A. F. Ender, president of the Wisconsin Press Association: "The editors have been glad to keep the world informed on the very practical service the University has been rendering, and I don't think a week goes by but from one to half a dozen articles regarding the University activities appear in every paper in the state."[88]

By the mid-1920s, the journalism program Bleyer built had produced hundreds of graduates and helped solidify the position of journalism as a course of study within universities. There were nearly two dozen schools and departments of journalism at schools across the country, with Bleyer and the University of Wisconsin largely recognized as one of the field's pioneers and leading advocates. Bleyer's influence continued to extend beyond the campus. He wrote four textbooks that were widely used in college (and in some high school) classrooms throughout the country, and he frequently contributed articles on journalism, its history, and role in society to magazines. While Bleyer continued to observe the trends complicating the production of accurate, responsible reporting, he ultimately viewed improved journalism education as key to combating these challenges. Despite concerns about the increasing corporatization of the news, the declining number of publications, and the encroachment of sensationalized and falsified information on the page, he remained largely optimistic about the potential of college-trained reporters.

Throughout, Bleyer remained a staunch advocate of the intellectual training that only a liberal arts training could provide. While he recognized and to some extent embraced the proliferation of high school journalism courses and high school publications and the value they offered, he was careful to remind students that high school students' training as reporters had only started. Writing for the *English Journal* in 1919, Bleyer stated that "we cannot afford to let high-school boys and girls harbor the mistaken notion that, because they have developed a certain facility in writing for the school paper, they are ready, on

leaving school, to enter the profession of journalism."[89] Bleyer used his platform as a leader in journalism education both to advance high school journalism instruction and advocate for university-level training for reporters. "To
be a good newspaper writer or editor you must know something about everything," Bleyer wrote in the *Scholastic Editor*. "Obviously a four-year college
course is the best means of acquiring this broad knowledge. . . . So too, to be
a well prepared, broadly educated journalist, a high school graduate should
attend a school of journalism."[90]

Bleyer's legacy continues to shape the curriculum at the School of Journalism and Mass Communication at the University of Wisconsin–Madison
today, where aspiring reporters must fulfill broad liberal arts course require-
ments in addition to practical classes in news writing and production. While
the school's classrooms and laboratories have changed since Bleyer's tenure,
with rows of computers replacing typewriters, and cameras and multimedia
equipment replacing the school's printing presses, its intellectual foundation
has not. In an age where publications face historic economic constraints, local
news deserts are growing, and the very validity of the press is often under question, the University of Wisconsin–Madison produces reporters interested in
continuing its legacy of promoting Bleyer's brand of journalism: thoughtful
reporting that accurately and responsibly gives to readers the information they
need, in a way that furthers the mission of the university.

NOTES

1. The Central Interscholastic Press Association (CIPA) was not the only organization that served high school publications in the 1920s. Often, these press associations
were tethered to a university or college program in journalism. The University of
Washington organized a Washington High School Press Association, Michigan State
University was behind the Michigan Interscholastic Press Association, Columbia University introduced the Columbia Scholastic Press Association, and other organizations
popped up in Indiana, Illinois, Texas, California, and elsewhere. In 1926, CIPA was
relocated to the University of Minnesota, where it was renamed the National Scholastic Press Association.

2. "Why the Scholastic Editor?" *Scholastic Editor* 1, no. 1 (1920): n.p.

3. "Raise Echo to Second Class," *Superior Telegram*, December 1, 1924.

4. "High School Editors," *Journal of Education* 99, no. 8 (1924): 201.

5. "Pi Editors to Attend Meet," *Superior Telegram*, November 19, 1924.

6. Bristow Adams, "University Extension in Journalism," *Journalism Bulletin* 3
(1926): 7.

7. Carolyn Bronstein and Stephen L. Vaughn, "Willard G. Bleyer and the Relevance of Journalism Education," *Journalism & Mass Communication Monographs* 166
(1998): 3.

8. Bronstein and Vaughn, "Willard G. Bleyer," 11.

9. Willard G. Bleyer, "What Schools of Journalism Are Trying to Do," *Journalism Quarterly* 8 (March 1931): 35–44.

10. Letter from Willard G. Bleyer to Charles Van Hise, May 3, 1911, series 7/19/9 44H2-3, box 1, Willard G. Bleyer Papers 1902–35, University of Wisconsin Archives, Madison, Wisconsin (material from these papers henceforth abbreviated as Bleyer Papers, box 1, or Bleyer Papers, box 3, as appropriate).

11. William David Sloan, "Willard Bleyer and Propriety," in *Makers of the Media Mind: Journalism Educators and Their Ideas*, ed. William David Sloan (Hillsdale, NJ: L. Earlbaum, 1990), 76.

12. Bleyer's (and the journalism program's) most prominent students included future University of Wisconsin School of Journalism director Ralph O. Nafziger (BA, 1921), future University of Illinois professor Fred Siebert (BA, 1923), and future Stanford University professor Chilton Bush (BA, 1925).

13. Interview with John L. Meyer and wife, 110 E. Gorham St., December 10, 1953, Bleyer Papers, box 1 (henceforth cited as Interview with Meyer and wife).

14. Everett M. Rogers and Steven H. Chaffee, "Communications and Journalism from 'Daddy' Bleyer to Wilbur Schramm: A Palimpsest," *Journalism Monographs* 148 (1994).

15. Willard G. Bleyer, "The American Newspaper of Tomorrow," speech before the Iowa High School Press Association, Grinnell College, November 23, 1928, Bleyer Papers, box 3.

16. Willard Grosvenor Bleyer, "In Behalf of Journalism Schools," *Quill* 19, no. 2 (1931): 4.

17. Quoted in Bronstein and Vaughn, "Willard G. Bleyer," 16.

18. For example, see the manuscript "Journalistic Writing in High School and College," Bleyer Papers, box 3.

19. Sloan, "Willard Bleyer and Propriety," 76–77.

20. Qualifications for a Reporter, Bleyer Papers, box 3.

21. Bronstein and Vaughn, "Willard G. Bleyer," 3.

22. James S. Buck, *Pioneer History of Milwaukee, 1840–1846* (Milwaukee: Swain & Tate, 1881), 323.

23. "Obituary: Albert J. Bleyer," *Editor & Publisher*, March 8, 1910, p. 9.

24. "Milwaukee, Wis.," *Typographical Journal* 44 (1914): 252.

25. Bronstein and Vaughn, "Willard G. Bleyer," 4.

26. Interview with Meyer and wife.

27. Interview with Meyer and wife.

28. Interview with Meyer and wife.

29. Bronstein and Vaughn, "Willard G. Bleyer," 4.

30. Interview with Meyer and wife.

31. Bronstein and Vaughn, "Willard G. Bleyer," 4.

32. Interview with Meyer and wife.

33. Richard Hofstadter, *The Age of Reform* (New York: Vintage Books, 1955), 5.

34. Hofstadter, *Age of Reform*, 6.

35. For more on the rise of the middle class in the late nineteenth century and the corresponding push for professionalization, see Robert Wiebe, *The Search for Order* (New York: Hill and Wang, 1967).

36. Notably, the history of American newspapers is much richer than this lone sentence suggests. For more, see Kevin G. Barnhurst and John Nerone, *The Form of News: A History* (New York: Guilford Press, 2001); David Nord, *Communities of Journalism: A History of American Newspapers and Their Readers* (Urbana: University of Illinois Press, 2001); Michael Schudson, *Discovering the News: A Social History of American Newspapers* (New York: Basic Books, 1979); Paul Starr, *The Creation of the Media: Political Origins of Modern Communications* (New York: Basic Books, 2004).

37. Sloan, "Willard Bleyer and Propriety," 80.

38. Quoted in Bronstein and Vaughn, "Willard G. Bleyer," 12.

39. Quoted in Bronstein and Vaughn, "Willard G. Bleyer," 13.

40. Bronstein and Vaughn, "Willard G. Bleyer," 13.

41. Willard Grosvenor Bleyer, "Changing Newspapers in a Changing World," February 21, 1929, Bleyer Papers, box 3.

42. Bleyer, "Changing Newspapers."

43. Bronstein and Vaughn, "Willard G. Bleyer," 12.

44. Schudson, *Discovering the News.*

45. Bronstein and Vaughn, "Willard G. Bleyer," 14.

46. Bleyer, "Schools of Journalism," 38.

47. Columbia University's president first turned down Pulitzer's $2 million endowment, and it wasn't until after his death that the school that bears his name opened. Pulitzer was widely criticized for offering to start a school of journalism as an effort to clear his conscience from the sensational tactics he engaged in and used to build his fortune in the 1880s and 1890s.

48. Joseph Pulitzer, "The College of Journalism," *North American Review* (May 1904), 655.

49. Pulitzer, "College of Journalism," 648.

50. Pulitzer, "College of Journalism," 650.

51. Sloan, "Willard Bleyer and Propriety," 78.

52. Bleyer, "American Newspaper of Tomorrow."

53. Robert E. Park, "The Natural History of the Newspaper," *American Journal of Sociology* 29, no. 3 (November 1923): 273–89.

54. John Dewey, *The Public and Its Problems* (New York: H. Holt, 1927).

55. Sloan, "Willard Bleyer and Propriety," 80.

56. Bronstein and Vaughn, "Willard G. Bleyer," 5.

57. Yellow journalism refers to the use of shocking and sensationalized news to attract newspaper readers and increase circulation. Wiebe, *Search for Order*, 120.

58. Bronstein and Vaughn, "Willard G. Bleyer," 5.

59. Fred Blevens, "Power, Irony and Contradictions: Education and the News Business," in *Journalism 1908: Birth of a Profession*, ed. Betty Houchin Winfield (Columbia: University of Missouri Press, 2008), 105–27.

60. Charles R. Van Hise and W. G. Bleyer, "The Relations of the University to the Press," paper read before the Wisconsin Press Association, February 14, 1905, Bleyer Papers, box 1.

61. Bleyer, "Schools of Journalism," 36–37.

62. Editorial reprint from the *Wisconsin State Journal*, Bleyer Papers, box 1.

63. Letter from Bleyer to Van Hise, January 9, 1909, Bleyer papers, box 1.

64. Bleyer to Van Hise.

65. Number of Students and Graduates of Schools and Departments of Journalism Report, May 16, 1934, Bleyer Papers, box 1.

66. Report of the Chairman of the Course in Journalism, Bleyer Papers, box 1.

67. Quote from "The Editor's Column Write," *Quill*, March 1971, 5, quoted in Sloan, "Willard Bleyer and Propriety," 76.

68. Report of the Chairman.

69. Report of the Chairman.

70. Rogers and Chaffee, "Communications and Journalism," 13.

71. Bleyer, "Schools of Journalism," 41.

72. Bleyer, "Schools of Journalism," 40.

73. Van Hise and Bleyer, "Relations."

74. University of Wisconsin, *Bulletin* 987 (1919/1920), 9, series 29/00/2 77A4–7, University of Wisconsin Archives, Madison, Wisconsin.

75. Letter from Bleyer to Birge, May 16, 1922, Bleyer Papers, box 1.

76. Bleyer to Birge.

77. Correspondence to Bleyer, February 26, 1913, from *Rice Lake Chronotype, Upper Wisconsin's Big Weekly*, signed A. F. Ender, president, Wisconsin Press Association, Bleyer Papers, box 1.

78. David Atwood of the *Janesville Gazette*, Wisconsin City Editors' Association, 1915–17, Wisconsin Historical Society, MAD 4/14/SC 155.

79. "School of Journalism Is Doing Good Work," *Daily Northwestern*, July 24, 1916, in Wisconsin City Editors' Association, 1915–17, Wisconsin Historical Society, MAD 4/14/SC 155.

80. Van Hise and Bleyer, "Relations."

81. Van Hise and Bleyer, "Relations."

82. Report of the Editor of the Press Bulletin, Letter, November 25, 1918, Bleyer Papers, box 1.

83. Report of the Editor.

84. Report of the Editor of the Press Bulletin, June 30, 1912, Bleyer Papers, box 1.

85. Van Hise and Bleyer, "Relations."

86. Van Hise and Bleyer, "Relations."

87. Letter from Bleyer to V. E. Thorp, June 3, 1913, Bleyer Papers, box 1.

88. Letter from A. F. Ender to Bleyer, February 26, 1913, Bleyer Papers, box 1.

89. Bleyer, "Journalistic Writing," 595.

90. Willard Grosvenor Bleyer, "How to Succeed in Journalism," *Scholastic Editor* 1, no. 2 (1921): n.p.

"No Mute, Inglorious Milton"

The Arts and the Wisconsin Idea

MARYO GARD EWELL

I am, both figuratively and literally, a daughter of the Wisconsin Idea.

My father was Robert E. Gard. He was a theater artist and writer, and his thirty-five years on the University of Wisconsin faculty were completely and even obsessively devoted to public service within the framework of the Wisconsin Idea. In his home office hung a photograph of Robert M. La Follette Sr., Governor "Fighting Bob." I vaguely wondered why the image wasn't of William Shakespeare or perhaps Tennessee Williams, and equally vaguely wondered why my father was so rarely home. I asked him about all this, and he said that he and his colleagues sometimes called themselves "the Knights of the Wisconsin Idea,"[1] and that their mission was to assist people all over Wisconsin to make art and build community arts institutions.[2] I sometimes went along on story-collecting expeditions or helped backstage with original Wisconsin Idea Theater musicals at county fairs, or registered students at the School of the Arts in Rhinelander, Wisconsin. I thought that it was a lot of fun and really interesting, but I did wonder what it all had to do with Robert M. LaFollette Sr., or how it was relevant to a changing America. It was the time of the war in Vietnam, and when I challenged him, he would say, "Now, more than ever, Wisconsin people need to write and paint and dance." It wasn't until after his death in 1992, when I was going through his papers, that I realized that I had been very wrong. That work was more than relevant. It was foundational to the evolution of democracy.

Robert M. LaFollette Sr., governor of Wisconsin from 1901 to 1906, and Charles Van Hise, president of the University of Wisconsin from 1903 to 1918, brought to life the notion that Charles McCarthy, who was appointed to head the department of state documents and created the state's Legislative Reference Library in 1901, named the "Wisconsin Idea." Gwen Drury, a scholar who has written and spoken extensively on the Wisconsin Idea, often asks, Is the Wisconsin Idea simply a brand? No, she says, it is, rather, "a set of values and a

97

Robert Gard in the field, 1955. Photograph courtesy of University Archives and
Records Management, University of Wisconsin–Madison.

way of thinking that all combined into such a potent force that it eventually
emerged as a brand, and made Wisconsin famous."[3]

Those early proponents of the Wisconsin Idea sought to make Wisconsin
the crucible where democracy would come into its own. For this to happen,
the people of Wisconsin needed to be comfortable in the world of ideas and
discussion, the realm of independent, critical, and creative thinking. That was
the long-term end: a vibrant, forward-looking democracy of thinking people.
And there were two intertwined short-term means: first, that the newest ideas
in all fields would directly serve Wisconsin communities; and second, that the
University of Wisconsin would serve all of the state's individuals. In 1901,
Governor La Follette said, "The State will not have discharged its duty to the
University, nor the University fulfilled its mission to the people, until adequate
means have been furnished to every young man and woman to acquire an edu-
cation at home in every department of learning."[4]

Van Hise stated it even more strongly: "The greatest waste in our nation is
not economic, but rather the waste of human talent."[5] In an address made in
1908 to the Merchants and Manufacturers Association of Milwaukee, he said,

"I would have no mute, inglorious Milton in this state; I would have everybody who has a talent have an opportunity to find his way so far as his talent will carry him, and that is only possible through university extension supplementing the schools and colleges."[6] The methods were outreach, service, the presence of university faculty members in every hamlet of the state, and the virtual presence of educators on radio and television.

In *Distinguished Service*, a sesquicentennial publication about the statewide endeavors of the University of Wisconsin, Dean Emeritus Ayse Somersan showcased University of Wisconsin–Extension's work in the arts as the first chapter of the book: "There were others in the state who spent a lifetime helping Wisconsin people lead creative and satisfying lives through involvement in the arts. They were University of Wisconsin professors with vision and energy. They partnered with community leaders and artists around the state and institutionalized the idea that the arts are for everyone. This was the University at its best. It was a shining example of the Wisconsin Idea."[7]

THEATER AND DRAMA

If the arts programs are the "shining example" of the Wisconsin Idea in action, let's take a look at them. In 1910, student play production was not considered valid educational activity at the University of Wisconsin, but Professor Thomas Dickinson of the English Department believed that his students should write and produce plays. They were not allowed to do this on campus, and thus was born the Wisconsin Dramatic Society. Dickinson worked with a woman in Milwaukee, Laura Sherry, whose philosophy with her Wisconsin Players company was the same: the theater should not only be the purview of New York professionals, but should also be the purview of nonprofessionals in their own communities. The Wisconsin Dramatic Society sought plays by Wisconsin writers, and among the people who emerged from this so-called "insurgent theater" movement was Pulitzer Prize–winning playwright Zona Gale of Portage, Wisconsin.

How does this relate to the Wisconsin Idea? Consider the two "means" that define the Wisconsin Idea to me. It certainly developed the latent talents of Wisconsin people. And, by challenging the established notion that theater was "owned" by the New York establishment, Dickinson and his colleagues were bringing a new idea of the theater to Wisconsin communities. Reflecting forty years later on his early work with the Wisconsin Dramatic Society, Dickinson wrote: "There is absolutely no question of the organic association of the spirit of our work with LaFollette progressivism. My chief interest was in the outworking of democracy, of which I considered the theatre the workshop."[8] Gale herself said, "Whatever one may feel about the ultimate effect of democracy on art, democracy, when it comes, is going to have its art. . . . The art of democracy will intensify democracy."[9] And, observing all of this, one of America's prominent playwrights of the early twentieth century, Percy MacKaye, wrote in 1912 that "the Wisconsin Idea involves the full scope of popular self-government; and popular self-government without indigenous art forms is incapable of civilized expression."[10]

At this same time, University Extension's community drama director Ethel Rockwell wrote and directed a pageant in Sauk City, Wisconsin, in 1914, attended by four thousand people who came from miles around, including some who arrived in a special car added to a train from Madison, Wisconsin. The pageant was described by the reporter from *Harper's Weekly* as being "as richly significant as the rifle shot at Concord [Massachusetts in 1775] or the signing of the Declaration of Independence."[11] The script for "A Social Center Pageant" says beneath the title that it "signalized the perception that government is no longer merely the selection of agents for repression, but is the all-inclusive and living fellowship of citizens in a creative process of self-education."[12] The pageant's theme dealt with "the new theory that the business of citizenship and the business of education constitute one process. . . . What Sauk City means to do is to make the schoolhouse the shining centre of all things communal— the headquarters of the people; to restore the old town meeting principle in an effort to get *oneness*; to identify politics and education; to reorganize the machinery for carrying on all activities that promote common interests."[13] At the end of the play, participants removed the community's ballot box from the town hall and led a procession to the local schoolhouse where it was installed so that, as a writer said in 2005, both symbolically and in fact, the school would be the "seat of continual learning and open inquiry."[14] Both the Rural Sociology Department at the University of Wisconsin and University Extension championed this new local drama idea, and the university's Lyceum Bureau and the Bureau of Dramatic Activities loaned scripts and offered help in playwriting, acting, and producing plays, often for county fairs. The university's speech department often provided judges for these shows.

MUSIC

This local art-making idea extended to music as well. The 1914 annual report of the University of Wisconsin Board of Regents stated that people are "happier and better if afforded the opportunity to develop their musical abilities and tastes."[15] Perhaps the best-known figure in Extension music was Professor Edgar Gordon, known as "Pop" Gordon. He had gotten his earliest job at the

Chicago Commons settlement house, a satellite of Jane Addams's famous Hull House, where he discovered the power of the arts as he worked with the city's immigrant poor and disenfranchised. He shared Jane Addams's belief that the arts are "a potent agent for making the universal appeal, and inducing men to forget their differences."[16] He became a music educator in his hometown of Winfield, Kansas, which won an award as the best Kansas community in which to raise a child; the judges cited as one of the elements of this award the degree to which the arts were integrated into the life of the community. University Extension invited Gordon to come to Wisconsin to describe how he had helped achieve that, and as a result he was hired as the director of the Bureau of Community Music.

Meanwhile, Professor Earl Terry of the physics department was working with what became WHA radio, licensed since 1922 to the University of Wisconsin, and he contacted W. H. Lighty of the Extension division to explore how WHA could be of greater service to the people of Wisconsin beyond offering weather and agricultural information. Terry and Lighty asked Pop Gordon to take to the air, which he did in 1921. His weekly broadcasts shared good music, and he explained why the music was considered good. But then he realized that he could actually use radio to teach people to *participate* in music-making, and he pioneered this use of radio, moving it from a passive, one-way medium to a participatory one. On July 4, 1922, he invited his listeners to join in the singing of "America." Imagine: Wisconsin families in perhaps thousands of living rooms all singing together in what Gordon called "a great, unseen chorus!" Ultimately, he offered a program for school children, first called *Let's Sing*, and then *Journeys in Musicland* on WHA from 1931 to 1955, and he devised a method for teaching classroom singing via the radio (indeed, not just classroom singing, for he even conducted a joint Madison-Viroqua chorus via radio). The class was extremely popular with teachers and students: in 1931 there were 793 children enrolled; by 1955, there were 70,000. He had two musical thrusts—the so-called great classics, yes, but also music and song from the ethnic cultural traditions of Wisconsin at that time, from Norway to Mexico, from Germany to Czechoslovakia.

But Gordon remembered his work at the settlement house in Chicago, too, and knew the importance of people singing together in the flesh as well as virtually. (And now, of course, we have data to prove what he knew: that there is, quite literally, a health dividend for people who sing together that singing alone does not achieve.) WHA radio sponsored festivals in which children from all over Wisconsin came to the University of Wisconsin campus in Madison to sing. In 1934, three hundred children came to the university's Music Hall. When the numbers of youths swelled, the festival was moved to the university's Stock

Pavilion, which was originally built in 1909 for statewide livestock shows and provided more seating than any building in Madison until 1930. The festival swelled more and moved to the Field House, which was completed in 1930 and used for basketball and large community gatherings. Finally, even the Field House—the largest venue on campus—proved too small, so they were forced to split the festival into fifteen regional festivals across the state. By its last year, 1956, there were 22,300 children involved.[17]

Gordon crisscrossed Wisconsin by train, helping to form singing societies in person as well. Once again, the aim was sociological as well as aesthetic. "He saw in community music and drama a means of combating juvenile delinquency and family disintegration through a kind of wholesome and uplifting recreation. He desired to see large numbers of folks working together in community programs in which the audiences as well as the casts would feel the cooperative and group nature of the work."[18]

Gordon thought music could be useful in helping a community move toward resolving conflict and create a setting for conversation. In DePere, Wisconsin, which was experiencing religious conflict at the time, he helped form an ecumenical group that sang in a Presbyterian church under the direction of a Catholic priest—perhaps as revolutionary as the work of the Wisconsin Dramatic Society.[19] Gordon was driven to serve the public; indeed, he refused any compensation for his work on the radio. In *Wisconsin: An Experiment in Democracy*, published in 1912, reformer Frederic Howe noted that the service ethic of the university's educators was a key to making it all work: "Wisconsin has bred a spirit of service that is unique. There is nothing like it in America. It suggests the existence of an instinct for public work that we have rarely offered an opportunity to develop."[20]

The Visual Arts and Crafts

The University of Wisconsin College of Agriculture (now the University of Wisconsin–Madison College of Agricultural and Life Sciences) was naturally in a particularly fine position to serve rural Wisconsin. Chris Christensen was dean of the college from 1930 to 1943, and he believed that the Danish folk school movement—blending cultural learning for farmers with agricultural learning—dovetailed nicely with the Wisconsin Idea. The Danish folk school movement went back to Nikolaj Grundtvig, a Danish poet and bishop. In 1832 he appealed to the "common" man and woman to think independently on relevant social, spiritual, and national issues, and he encouraged them to become acquainted with the cultural riches of the Danish heritage in order to live fuller lives. His folk schools—intended for people from all classes—taught home economics, agricultural methods, history, literature, Danish mythology, and more. The teaching method was intended simultaneously to "enlighten students and to encourage them to engage in their own thought and discussions."[21] Through "the Grundtvigian philosophy, they were able to forge a new social and political consciousness and also a rhetoric to express it that could accommodate both the old agrarian virtues as well as their newly found economic power."[22] In a history of the folk school, Irish poet-economist George Russell is quoted: "A nation is cultivated only so far as the average man, not the exceptional person, is cultivated and has knowledge of the thought, imagination, and intellectual history of his nation. . . . Governments do not build up civilizations. That is done by the citizens using the creative imagination about life, trying to make the external correspond to something in the spirit."[23]

Dean Christensen thought that the College of Agriculture could be a Wisconsin folk school. He explicitly felt that education in agricultural colleges must be broad and must include good literature, art, music, history—the cultural side of life—as well as the practical training for better farming. He said: "In emphasizing the social or cultural values arising out of the improved economic conditions, it is well to keep clearly in mind that this will come about only if the economic process operates in some kind of cultural framework. The achievement of wealth itself contains no guarantee that it will become the means to more significant living. . . . As a matter of fact, wealth in careless hands may be a two edged sword wielding destruction to its owner and to society."[24]

Christensen hired John Barton into the university's Department of Rural Sociology, and he and Barton—inspired by art historian Oskar Hagen—devised a plan to bring a visual artist onto the staff of the College of Agriculture. The artist would help people reflect visually, creatively, on their own experience. As Dickinson did with the Wisconsin Dramatic Society, the artist in residence would expand art beyond the purview of established great artists (that insurgent idea again) to include people making art in their own communities. Barton said that there were many elements, economic as well as cultural, to this idea of an artist in residence: "It was a country tavern in Portage County which first gave public recognition to a young Polish painter for a series of native landscape murals, and the tavern keeper said it was good business. If it is good business for the tavern, it could also be 'good business' for the local library, school, or community house. If the work is competent, it would seem more appropriate to recognize native talent than to hang a conventional print of three horses' heads, a blind muse playing a harp, or some other worn-out picture from a bygone age."[25]

The artist-in-residence idea also included civic elements; it was part of a democratic ideal, and in this respect it hearkened back to the basics of the

Wisconsin Idea. As Barton put it: "The rural art movement cannot properly be understood apart from the democratic movement. Two centuries ago, the common people were regarded as rather heavy civic liabilities. . . . Rural people, particularly in England, France, or Germany, were supposed to have neither inclinations nor ability to participate in culture-building or fine arts. It was inevitable that the democratic revolution—still in process through universal education and today, adult education—should call into being, among others, a rural people's art."[26] This would be a powerful idea today—and this was 1936. The country's first visual artist in residence was to be in an agricultural college, not an art department, and linked to democratic participation? Who would be that extraordinary person: an excellent artist, one who understood the rural scene, one who could inspire ordinary people to paint their personal vision, one who could see art as part of a bigger democratic ideal?

Christensen knew American painter Grant Wood, an exponent of Midwestern Regionalism best known for his *American Gothic* (1930), and he visited him in Iowa to voice the idea. Wood liked it and suggested that fellow Regionalist painter John Steuart Curry of Kansas, who was at the time working in Connecticut, would be just the person, given his rural background and populist ideals. The dean caught a train to Connecticut to broach the idea to Curry. He would have no teaching responsibilities; just as researchers worked in their labs to advance knowledge, so would Curry work in his studio to advance creativity.

Glenn Frank, University of Wisconsin president from 1925 to 1937, explicitly believed in the idea of Everyman making art. In 1931, he had said, "The art of the theatre, like the art of literature, has been damned by professionalism. . . . The next great dramatic renaissance in America will come when the theater is recaptured from the producers by the people, when we become active enough in mind and rich enough in spirit to begin the creation of a folk-drama and a folk-theatre in America."[27] Frank was very supportive of the visual artist in residence at the College of Agriculture, saying, "There is poetry as well as production on the farm. Art can help us to preserve the poetry while we are battling with the economics of farming."[28] Frank clearly saw how the arts related to the Wisconsin Idea by empowering local people to think creatively for themselves. In announcing Curry's appointment in 1936 as artist in residence at the University of Wisconsin, Frank said, "In launching this new educational venture, we are undertaking to give emphasis to regional art as a force for rural as well as urban culture in the Middle West area."[29]

Curry started traveling, and everywhere he went, he discovered farmers and members of their families who wanted to make art. He saw art in the hills, the farms, the farmers, the animals, the earth of Wisconsin, and he believed that everyone has the ability to paint what is most alive to him—that it was just a matter of enabling people to do so. He emphasized personal vision over technique. As a result, paintings by farmers who worked with Curry are dramatic and breathtakingly alive. Curry said, "If you feel the significance of the life, the design builds itself. The feeling inherent in the life of the world cannot be ignored or trifled with for the sake of theory."[30] This does not mean that he discounted art theory and the deep learning of technique. But the purpose of theory and technique was to go beyond. "I do not despise the classic and accepted form of our civilization, but it is time that people realized that they have in this day a more magnificent life to use and to view in our creative efforts than that of any other age."[31]

He envisioned a statewide exhibit of art by farm family members, and the first exhibit was held in 1940 at the Memorial Union building on the University of Wisconsin campus with thirty artists from seventeen counties participating. A junior show with youth artists was added later. For the first exhibit, Curry and Barton solicited original work from amateurs and, as described by art historian Lauren Kroiz, explicitly advised against sending such items as wood carvings of chains. Kroiz says: "This explicit ban on carved chains helps clarify Curry and Barton's intentions in the exhibition. They accepted and celebrated figurative sculptures carved from wood, as well as several works outside the boundaries of traditional artistic mediums, such as Earl Sugden's sand paintings created in whiskey bottles. Wooden chains, however, differed from these forms because they required their makers to follow a series of standard, technically difficult steps. . . . In banning carved chains, Curry and Barton opposed the rote memorization of technical directions, demanding that artists engage in a process of decision making, creating art objects and images that expressed their individual experience and in so doing, setting an example that encouraged others to represent themselves and their communities."[32]

As the United States entered World War II, many wondered whether the continuing presence of an artist in residence, and his work with farmers, was not frivolous. Kroiz describes Barton's defense of this program: "In 1940 Barton argued that if fascism was to be defeated, Americans needed not only to defend themselves militarily but also to maintain their 'faith in the creative and vigorous possibilities of democracy.' From his point of view, the amateur cultural pursuits of rural people supported that faith."[33]

By 1946 there were 101 artists exhibiting in the statewide show. Its elements included a meal that prompted fellowship among the artists, lectures, discussions, and critique. Any artist could request an assessment of his or her work by Curry himself. Local art clubs were formed (the Rural Rembrandts of Wautoma, Wisconsin, was the first), and their local shows led to regional shows that funneled work to the state show. This model is replicated today by the independent Wisconsin Regional Artists Association with modest assistance from the University of Wisconsin–Madison Division of Continuing Studies; even the Rural Rembrandts are still active!

For the Wisconsin Centennial in 1948, the University of Wisconsin Department of Rural Sociology produced a book, *Rural Artists of Wisconsin*, edited by Barton, showcasing what the artists working with Curry had produced. Seventy years later, Kroiz assessed Curry's impact: "Curry, providing an alternative to the passive subject engendered by commercialism and fascism, taught amateurs to struggle individually and collectively to represent the self in community and to teach themselves to become the active citizens needed to defend participatory democracy."[34]

The work of James Schwalbach, whose title was initially Extension Specialist in Rural Art, complemented that of painter Aaron Bohrod, Curry's successor as artist in residence. Schwalbach traveled the state constantly, working closely with the local artists, continuing Curry's work with amateur artists. But Schwalbach was also familiar to thousands of other Wisconsin people. Believing in progressive educational ideas, he taught art via WHA radio, broadcasting the *Let's Draw* program to the schools of Wisconsin from 1936 to 1970. In *Wisconsin on the Air*, the public radio journalist and University of Wisconsin–Madison faculty member Jack Mitchell wrote: "Perhaps the most surprising use of radio was the 'Let's Draw' series, which taught visual art without visuals. James Schwalbach . . . tapped into students' imaginations to inspire them to create their own art rather than copying what the teacher showed them. In the spring of 1939, for example, he led a unit on capturing 'feelings' in pictures: the feeling of 'coldness,' for example, and the feeling of 'love' . . . abstract concepts more challenging to convey in pictures than a house or a tree."[35]

By the 1955–56 school year, enrollment in *Let's Draw* was ninety thousand.[36] In a typical class, Schwalbach would discuss a concept, such as perspective, for a few minutes. Then he would invite students to paint or draw, often to music, integrating elements of his mini-lecture. My own elementary school used Schwalbach as our de facto art teacher. We were urged to paint our own ideas, just as Curry had urged his students to do. Indeed, Schwalbach rejected the new medium of television on WHA-TV after briefly trying it out for nine sessions because he "found that the images which were broadcast to the students were reproduced in their art products. He then concluded that radio was a more effective medium for a creative art series."[37]

Schwalbach went to Scandinavia in 1963 to study the home crafts movement there. He returned feeling that such a movement could be undertaken in Wisconsin. His colleague, Thomas Echtner, recalled the formation of the

Wisconsin Association of Crafts. They worked with county Extension agents on a bold program for improving the economic well-being of rural people as well as the beauty of American homes. They would ask the Extension agent to identify unemployed or underemployed people in their county who might be able to design things—from puzzles to salt and pepper shakers. Schwalbach was in contact with firms that manufactured these items and marketplaces nationwide in which to sell them, so for a time they were directly helping rural craftspeople to make a living.[38]

Schwalbach believed that it was essential to eliminate the "archaic" distinction between the so-called fine and amateur arts, "to resolve the unnecessary breach between the amateur and the professional," and to recognize multiple standards.[39] This would not be trifling with standards of excellence, but would be building a new kind of art and would spawn a new kind of artist with a new role in society. He said: "The community needs the artist, but an artist who accepts some responsibility towards the community; an artist who can hold forth a vision of the future that is built on the past."[40]

CREATIVE WRITING AND THE
WISCONSIN IDEA THEATER

And then there was my father, Robert E. Gard. The visual arts idea and the music idea were working well. What of creative writing and theater?

Gard was born on a Kansas dairy farm in 1910. He was proud of his skill at milking cows, and he liked writing poetry and stories in high school. Eventually he went to the University of Kansas, and one of his part-time jobs was as a stagehand in the university theater. He was fascinated.

He went to graduate school at Cornell University and studied with theater professor Alexander Drummond, who was a curiously bifurcated character— he was one of the luminaries of the American theater at the time, but, since Cornell was a land-grant university, he also believed that he had a direct responsibility to the people of upstate New York. Drummond was disgusted with the plays considered suitable for rural production on the play list of the American publishing company Samuel French, seeing them as often trivial, disrespectful, and denigrating to the people, and he felt that the answer lay in plays written by people about their own lives.[41] Gard was intrigued, and together they developed the New York State Plays Project in which rural people were encouraged to conceive, write, and produce their own plays with the help of Cornell University.

Gard brought these ideas with him when he joined the faculty of the University of Wisconsin in 1945. Calling the office that he established that year

A Wisconsin Idea Theater production, "Ice Cream Seven Times a Day" (undated). Photograph courtesy of University Archives and Records Management, University of Wisconsin–Madison.

the Wisconsin Idea Theater, he began to articulate the notion that professional artists, skilled facilitator-teachers, and Everyman could together make the promise of America real and meaningful to everyone. "There must be plays that grow from all the countrysides of America, fabricated by the people themselves, born of their happiness and sorrow, born of toiling hands and free minds, born of music and love and reason."[42]

In 1948, Gard taught a writing workshop for leaders of 4-H, a program administered by the US Department of Agriculture that fosters youth development through instruction in useful skills and community service. He paraphrased one of the participants at the end of this three-day workshop: "If the people of Wisconsin knew that someone would encourage them to express themselves in any way they chose, . . . if they knew that someone would back them and help them when they wanted help, it was her opinion that there would be such a rising of creative expression as is yet unheard of in Wisconsin . . . for the whole expression would be of and about ourselves."[43]

From this moment came his idea for the Wisconsin Rural (later Regional) Writers Association, and thousands of aspiring writers joined at once. Like Curry, Gard offered help to anyone: "I had a hunch that quite a few folks would respond to the Rural Writers idea. I was really quite dismayed, however, to find how loaded our mailboxes were each morning with manuscripts. To the horror of my already overburdened small staff, over one thousand poems were sent in in a few days' time. There were short stories, too, and a few plays. The curious thing was that the material for the most part was quite above average. . . . For a while, until I could get special help, we were all reading innumerable manuscripts every day, at lunch, at dinner, at night, and all of us would usually be walking from this to that task with several rural life poems or stories or plays sticking out of our pockets."[44]

Gard also began to see the arts as a way of morphing hard community conversations from dysfunctional bickering to proactive community building, creating a new kind of art at the same time. He describes a farmers' meeting in 1950 to which he had been invited to speak about forming a community theater. But first on the agenda was the discussion of a law just passed, a law that the farmers hated, requiring them to install concrete floors in their milk houses. Gard related:

This particular meeting turned into a hot one. The chair got into trouble trying to keep order, and the county agricultural agent was almost mobbed because some of the folks blamed him for their plight. This community had also summoned its state assemblyman to be present; he had voted for the milkhouse bill in the legislature. They said violent things to him. The discussion was not getting anywhere. They wrangled for a while and then decided to call it off. They turned the meeting over to me.

I was in an uncomfortable spot, faced by anticlimax and the probable futility of trying to stimulate interesting discussion in this particular atmosphere. . . . It suddenly occurred to me . . . that the previous discussion had aspects of a drama: conflict, character, excellent dialogue. So I set about fabricating . . . a comic situation . . . and before we realized it a kind of group play was in progress, only now it seemed in terms of comedy, exciting but laughable, for I had attempted to exaggerate the purpose on both sides and to enlarge on the innocence of the county agent and to exaggerate the well-meaning, slightly self-pitying attitude of the legislator as well as the anger of several of the more outspoken opponents of the milkhouse bill.

In the informally dramatized version of the affair that we made up there at the moment, the farmer was getting his whacks at the legislator and the county agent was making his excuses but within the framework of a creative situation.[45]

The Wisconsin Idea Theater had tentacles everywhere. Gard collected Wisconsin stories, turned them into radio dramas, and had a standing program—*Wisconsin Is My Doorstep*—on WHA radio and then television. His graduate students studied questions such as why people participate in the arts, and they worked across departments to understand this better. Most visibly in rural places the Wisconsin Idea Theater helped people create and produce their own arts statewide. His graduate student in the mid-1950s Marjorie Harbaugh, a folk singer, was given a state car, a year's salary, and a mandate to perform for every school, every community center, and every church that would have her, so that Wisconsin could understand and value its history.[46] In 1963, Gard met David Peterson of Monona Grove High School, who wanted to write musicals based on Wisconsin history and stories, and he joined Gard's Wisconsin Idea Theater staff, creating shows that toured to county fairs, cities and towns, and state parks for nearly thirty years. In Rhinelander, Wisconsin, his show "Hodag!"—based on a local legend—was premiered complete with a big parade that included the cast and crew (in convertibles, of course!) and even a ferocious Hodag monster.

In 1965, Congress created the National Endowment for the Arts (NEA). Gard, whose program was now called the Office of Community Arts Development in the College of Agriculture, believed that since the NEA was supported by the people's tax dollars, it would surely respond to a proposal to promote arts of, by, and for the people. Gard and his team would choose five towns in Wisconsin, each with fewer than 10,000 people. For the next three years, they would work on three levels in each town. First, they would provide access to touring arts and fine professional arts experiences, as decided upon by local leaders, to people right there at home. (We must remember that rural towns were terribly isolated then; there was no interstate highway system, no Home Box Office, no internet, and very few community arts centers.) Second, the team would facilitate opportunities for people to experience and explore art forms for themselves via classes and workshops in their town. Third and finally, they would help people form a local arts organization to continue this work after the three-year grant period was up.

What is significant is that the decision-making would be in the hands of the people to decide what was right for their town. The proposal was deeply rooted in Wisconsin Idea values, and Gard wrote: "In terms of American democracy, the arts are for everyone. They are not reserved for the wealthy, or for the well-endowed museum, the gallery, or the ever-subsidized regional professional theatre. As America emerges into a different understanding of her strength, it becomes clear that her strength is in the people and in the places where the people live. The people, if shown the way, can create art in and of themselves."[47]

Gard felt that the NEA would respond positively to this ultimately American, democracy-based ideal, but it was not easy. NEA staff member Charles Christopher Mark chronicled the early years of the NEA; he observed that in its first year, the focus had been on major institutions like the American Ballet Theatre or the Metropolitan Opera. The National Council (in effect, the board of the NEA), which included many of the arts luminaries of the time—architect I. M. Pei, choreographer Agnes de Mille, composer and conductor Leonard Bernstein, and others—believed that the fledgling state arts councils would take care of rural America. When the proposal from Wisconsin came before them, wrote the staff member Charles Mark, "the reaction was completely negative. Some of the Council members were amused that we should even propose to spend $58,000 a year for three years on such a project." It was clear that the proposal would be voted down. The discussion was heated, and chairman Roger Stevens called a lunch break to calm people down. Leonard Bernstein had missed the morning session, but arrived during the break. Mark continues: "When I told him the rural arts project had been tabled, he told me that that was one reason why he wanted to come to the meeting. I thought he was another negative vote, but he said he read the full proposal and he thought it important. When the session resumed . . . Bernstein . . . raised his hand to speak. After a dramatic pause he said, 'This project has nothing to do with art, but it has everything to do with why we are sitting here.' . . . In short, this man who represented art in its highest form was an unexpected and effective ally of Bob Gard's concept of developing the inherent need for a creative outlet in all people. When he finished, the attitude of the Council had been reversed and the project was passed unanimously."[48]

The final report to the NEA charts five small communities in Wisconsin that were stirred to action in ways they had never imagined. Project director Michael Warlum recalled, "The story is an exciting one, full of hope, full of action, and full of dreams."[49] As Gard and his team encouraged "the articulate neighborly sharing of excellence in art," local leaders with great visions emerged.[50] The final report, published in 1969, was *The Arts in the Small Community: A National Plan*. Forty thousand copies were distributed nationwide and rural arts councils everywhere sprang up.

ARTS EXTENSION AFTER 1969

In 1973, I worked for a year as a secretary to Emmett Sarig, who was chair of the University of Wisconsin–Extension arts department. The number of artists in all disciplines in this now-merged department had grown to twenty-eight by then, based in Madison, Milwaukee, Green Bay, and Shell Lake. The preface to the 1977–78 Annual Report of Arts Development began: "Perhaps more than any other state, Wisconsin has been concerned with University-citizen relationships in the Arts through University Extension."[51]

In addition to the scores of workshops and one-on-one work with people everywhere in Wisconsin, here are just a few of the programs of the University of Wisconsin–Extension arts department during the 1960s through 1980s to bring the university and the people of the state into closer proximity within the framework of the Wisconsin Idea:

- Helen O'Brien, nearly blind and unable to drive, traveled extensively across Wisconsin by Greyhound bus, working with youth drama programs, especially within 4-H clubs, in seventy-two counties.
- Ed Hugdahl created a program to help rural organists improve their music and performance.
- Marvin Rabin created a program to ensure that Norwegian fiddling was kept alive and flourishing, and he also developed a music program for inner-city Milwaukee youth (here we hearken back to Pop Gordon, Jane Addams, and Hull House!), and this led to the inner-city Heritage Symphony and the Jazz Ensemble.
- Rabin and Richard Wolf built the statewide Youth Symphony, Junior Youth Symphony, Concert Orchestra, and Sinfonietta strings group. Their band camps drew thousands of youth to Madison, and the youth musical theater program was similarly popular; and their music educators conferences included rock-and-roll musicians on the faculty to ensure that music teachers stayed in touch with the popular interests of their students.
- Darrell Aderman, based in Shell Lake, Wisconsin, offered arts classes and experiences for the children of agricultural migrant workers.
- Karen Cowan urged people to dance and create choreography, and there were dance workshops statewide.
- Gard continued to guide the Wisconsin Regional Writers Association.
- Harv Thompson helped raise standards in high school drama, and continuing Gard's tradition, documented direct service to more than a hundred community theaters statewide in a single year.
- David Peterson wrote and directed touring musicals that brought Wisconsin history to life at county fairs or in state parks—as well as in traditional arts venues. Records show that in the late 1960s they performed to more than 50,000 people over a three-year period—as well as producing summer shows on the Camp Randall football field in Madison.
- Ken Kummerlein, Leslee Nelson, and Joe Bradley in Madison, Jim Schinneller and Tom Echtner in Milwaukee, and many more continued John Steuart

Curry's Regional Art Program, facilitating twelve regional art shows that culminated in a state art show; it continues to this day. And, like Schwalbach, they developed art pedagogy tools for elementary art teachers.

- Edward Kamarck's *Arts in Society* magazine addressed contemporary issues in aesthetics and art making.
- Faculty offered arts classes in the university's short course for farmers, and classes on campus during the University of Wisconsin–Extension program College Week for Women, as well as countless workshops in schools, Extension offices, or church basements, from inner-city Milwaukee to tiny unincorporated places.
- Faculty helped build and maintain other institutions: the Council for Wisconsin Writers, the Wisconsin Fellowship of Poets, the Wisconsin Arts Foundation and Council, the Midwest Playwrights Laboratory, and the Wisconsin Dance Council, to name a few. They facilitated the Wisconsin Theatre Association and the statewide Theatre convention.
- Michael Warlum, of Gard's Office of Community Arts Development, was relocated in 1970 to Hurley, Wisconsin, to help people of Finnish descent form Little Finland. Located on US Highway 2, Little Finland is a cultural center that includes a museum celebrating the region's Finnish heritage; the grounds are a venue for festivals featuring Finnish music, dance, and food.
- Faculty and their associates founded and facilitated Yarns of Yesteryear, Arts for the Elderly, the We Were Children Then series of three books, and a special theater program to serve senior citizens.
- Faculty created The Arts and Human Needs program and provided leadership training to persons in many social services arenas.
- Faculty produced Native American music and dance programs and facilitated a Native Voices writers conference.
- Faculty planned a Hispanic Cultural Video Tapes series to address the Mexican immigration experience.
- Gard created the School of the Arts at Rhinelander, Wisconsin, in 1964, offering classes in various art forms to adult learners. His conviction was that everyone deserved access to excellence, no matter how much of a beginner they might be; artists in residence at the School of the Arts included writers like Jesse Stuart, Marc Conelly, Dale Wasserman, and Studs Terkel.
- Gard continued to work in this field even after he retired. He and colleagues created the Robert E. Gard Foundation, which produced an exhibit of art by Southeast Asian refugees—Wisconsin's newest immigrant group. They also commissioned a piece of symphonic music that would "capture the spirit of Wisconsin." The result was Michael Torke's "Verdant Music," premiered by the Milwaukee Symphony in 1986. They commissioned new writing by Wisconsin authors.[52]

And remember: it was all about creativity in the service of building a mature, democratic America. Gard wrote the Creed of the Wisconsin Regional Writers Association, which states, "Let us believe in ourselves and our talents. Let us believe in the worth of the individual and seek to understand him, for from sympathy and understanding will our writings grow. Let us believe [that] the democratic process of government is safest in the hands of a cultured, enlightened people."[53]

Things change, of course. Arts Extension, as a group of always-traveling, omnipresent "Knights of the Wisconsin Idea," is no more, though there are still arts classes within the University of Wisconsin–Madison Division of Continuing Studies. Jeffrey Russell, dean of the Division of Continuing Studies, drew attention to this change in a March 2017 op-ed reflecting on University of Wisconsin–Madison political scientist Katherine J. Cramer's 2016 book, *The Politics of Resentment: Rural Consciousness in Wisconsin and the Rise of Scott Walker*, which addresses the state's urban-rural divide. Cramer had visited many Wisconsin communities to gather her information. Russell wrote: "People thanked Cramer for showing up, showing respect and listening. Most residents could not recall meeting someone else from UW–Madison."[54] The people who experienced *Let's Sing* or *Let's Draw* are in their sixties, seventies, and eighties now. Memories fade quickly, and Cramer's observations are real—and terribly ironic. Few remember that faculty relocated to the city of Hurley for a year, or that Ed Hugdahl visited rural churches to coach their organists, or that the city and village of Adams-Friendship was like a second home to Gard and his staff, or that John Steuart Curry sat with artists in the city of Wautoma, or that Pop Gordon created an ecumenical choir in the city of DePere.

Of course, things change. But I believe that big ideas exemplified by the arts programs of the University of Wisconsin–Extension are constant. Those ideas include:

- a profound respect for each person;
- a conviction that each individual has ideas worth expressing;
- a certainty that people have latent talent that simply needs to be uncovered and nurtured;
- a belief that community life can be made more meaningful through the arts;
- a certainty that all cultures have values and expressions to be savored and shared and understood;
- a passionate love for and belief in Wisconsin, its history, its stories, its quirks, its cultures, its communities, and its many meanings, as well as the "strength . . . in the people and in the places where the people live";[55]

- a passionate belief in rural America, exemplified in Gard's call for the United States to "rediscover, cherish and strengthen its small communities" and assign to them "the important role deserved in the forthcoming renaissance of the arts";[56]
- a commitment to service, which entails the giving of time, coupled with humility and faith;
- and most important, a fundamental certainty that as individuals uncover their personal creativity and share their ideas, Wisconsin's people can indeed become, as art historian Lauren Kroiz has said, "the active citizens needed to defend participatory democracy."

Broad participation in the arts, then, could indeed help fulfill La Follette's and Van Hise's idea that Wisconsin could design, and define, democracy. And that is why Robert E. Gard had a photograph of Robert M. La Follette Sr. over his desk. So as we struggle to articulate the Wisconsin Idea in the twenty-first century, we walk with Governor La Follette and President Van Hise, Pop Gordon and Ethel Rockwell, Robert E. Gard and John Steuart Curry, Jim Schwalbach, Zona Gale, Chris Christensen, John Barton, and so many, many artist-teacher-visionaries who were the Knights of the Wisconsin Idea. What challenges are they posing to us? How can we embrace these challenges, surface their big ideas, use them in the context of the twenty-first century, and pass them on to the next generation?

I close with the words of Robert Gard, who ended *The Arts in the Small Community* thus:

If you try, what may you expect?
First a community
Welded through art to a new consciousness of self:
A new being, perhaps a new appearance—
A people proud
Of achievements which lift them through the creative
Above the ordinary—
A new opportunity for children
To find exciting experiences in art
And to carry this excitement on
Throughout their lives—
A mixing of peoples and backgrounds
Through art; a new view
Of hope for mankind and an elevation

Of man—not degradation.
New values for individual and community
Life, and a sense
That here, in our place
We are contributing to the maturity
Of a great nation.
If you try, you can indeed
Alter the face and the heart
Of America.[57]

NOTES

1. Robert E. Gard, *Grassroots Theater: A Search for Regional Arts in America* (Madison: University of Wisconsin Press, 1955), 103–6.

2. The arts programs went by many names, but for ease of reference the generic term "arts extension" is used here to refer to them.

3. Gwen Drury, email message to the author, November 15, 2018.

4. This quote is typically attributed to Robert M. La Follette Sr., and it is in his Biennial Message to the Joint Session of the Wisconsin Legislature on January 10, 1901. Wisconsin State Assembly, *Journal of Proceedings of the Forty-Fifth Session of the Wisconsin Legislature, for the Year 1901* (Madison: State Printers, 1901), 43. However, these same words were used by George H. Noyes, president of the Board of Regents, in his report to the governor on December 8, 1900. University of Wisconsin Board of Regents, *Biennial Report of the Regents of the University for the Years 1898–99 and 1899–1900* (Madison: State Printers, 1900), 4.

5. Charles R. Van Hise, quoted in Robert E. Gard, "A Six-Year Plan to Study the Arts in Community Life: Based on Research on the Effectiveness of the University of Wisconsin State-Wide Cultural Arts Program" (unpublished manuscript, 1952), record group 1.2, series 200, subseries 200.R: United States—Humanities and Arts, University of Wisconsin—Community Arts, 1949, 1951–52, in Rockefeller Foundation Archives, Sleepy Hollow, New York.

6. Charles R. Van Hise, "What the University Can Do for the Business Man," in *The Bulletin of the Merchants & Manufacturers Association of Milwaukee*, no. 16 (Milwaukee: The Association, May 1908), 15.

7. Ayse Somersan, *Distinguished Service: University of Wisconsin Faculty and Staff Helping to Build Organizations in the State* (Friendship, WI: New Past Press, 1997), 13.

8. Thomas Dickinson, quoted in Gard, *Grassroots Theater*, 86.

9. Zona Gale, quoted in Joshua Wachuta, "Laura Sherry and the Wisconsin Players: Little Theatre in the Badger State," A Tree Left Standing (blog), May 12, 2011, https://www.acceity.org/2011/05/.

10. Percy MacKaye, "The Wisconsin Idea in the Theater," *Wisconsin Stage* 9, no. 2 (Summer 1955): 4.

11. George Creel, "America's Foremost City," *Harper's Weekly*, November 21, 1914, 495. The "rifle shot at Concord," described by Ralph Waldo Emerson as the "shot heard round the world," is associated with the American Revolution.

12. Ethel Rockwell, "A Social Center Pageant," typescript, 1914, Tripp Heritage Museum, Prairie du Sac, Wisconsin.

13. Creel, "America's Foremost City," 495.

14. Sally Konnak, notes dated April 2005, appended to Rockwell's "Social Center Pageant" script.

15. University of Wisconsin Board of Regents, *The University of Wisconsin Biennial Report of the Board of Regents for the Years 1912–13 and 1913–14* (Madison: State Printers, 1914), 194.

16. Jane Addams, quoted in Anthony Barresi, "Edgar B. Gordon: Teacher to a Million," *Transactions of the Wisconsin Academy of Sciences, Arts and Letters* 75 (Madison: The Academy, 1987), 57.

17. The sketch of Pop Gordon is primarily drawn from Barresi, "Edgar B. Gordon." Barresi indicates that he has in turn drawn on WHA Radio, *The First 50 Years of University of Wisconsin Broadcasting, WHA 1919–1969 and a Look Ahead to the Next 50 Years* (Madison: n.p., 1969) for many of his figures. See Jim Feldman, *The Buildings of the University of Wisconsin* (Madison: University Archives, 1997), on Old Music Hall (39–42), the Stock Pavilion (115–16), and the Field House (213–16).

18. Gard, *Grassroots Theater*, 91.

19. Gard, *Grassroots Theater*, 92.

20. Frederic C. Howe, *Wisconsin: An Experiment in Democracy* (New York: Charles Scribner's Sons, 1912), 41.

21. Catherine Hiebert Kerst, "Enlightenment, Fellowship and Celebration at the Danebod Folk Meeting: Danish-American Grundtvigian Cultural Expression in the Spirit of the Old Folk School" (PhD diss., George Washington University, 1989), 239.

22. Kerst, "Enlightenment, Fellowship and Celebration," 241.

23. Olive D. Campbell, *The Danish Folk School* (New York: MacMillan, 1928), 5–6.

24. Chris L. Christensen, foreword to University of Wisconsin College of Agriculture, *An Exhibition of Work by John Steuart Curry* (Washington, DC: The College, 1938), http://digicoll.library.wisc.edu/cgi-bin/WI/WI-idx?id=WI.ExhibCurry.

25. John Rector Barton, *Rural Artists of Wisconsin* (Madison: University of Wisconsin Press, 1948), 6.

26. Barton, *Rural Artists of Wisconsin*, 7.

27. Glenn Frank, quoted in Ethel Rockwell's preface to *Wisconsin Rural Plays* (Chicago: Dramatic Publishing Company, 1931), 4.

28. Glenn Frank, "Toward a People's Theater in Wisconsin," preface to Mrs. Carl Felton, *Goose Money: A One Act Play* (Madison: Extension Service, College of Agriculture, University of Wisconsin, 1928), n.p., University of Wisconsin–Madison Archives, Steenbock Library, RBW7 AB SPC v.1918–29.

29. Gard, *Grassroots Theater*, 99.

30. Lucy Mathiak, "Bringing Life to Canvas: John Steuart Curry and the Rural Art Program," in *The Art of Rural Wisconsin, 1936–60* (Madison: Department of Agricultural

Journalism for the University of Wisconsin–Madison College of Agricultural and Life Sciences, 1985), 6.

31. Laurence E. Schmeckebier, *John Steuart Curry's Pageant of America* (New York: American Artists Group, 1943), 83.

32. Lauren Kroiz, *Cultivating Citizens: The Regional Work of Art in the New Deal Era* (Oakland: University of California Press, 2018), 214–15.

33. Kroiz, *Cultivating Citizens*, 215.

34. Kroiz, *Cultivating Citizens*, 222.

35. Jack W. Mitchell, *Wisconsin on the Air: 100 Years of Public Broadcasting in the State That Invented It* (Madison: Wisconsin Historical Society Press, 2016), 39–40.

36. Mary Louise Kelly, "Lets Draw: James Schwalbach, 1936–70, Broadcasts for Schools" (PhD diss., University of Wisconsin–Madison, 1990).

37. Kelly, "Let's Draw," 122.

38. Thomas Echtner, oral history interview by Maryo Gard Ewell, Harv Thompson, and Anne Pryor, March 23, 2015, interview #1416, University of Wisconsin–Madison Archives and Robert E. Gard Foundation Oral History project, https://minds.wisconsin.edu/handle/1793/72140.

39. James Schwalbach, "Personal Involvement in the Arts," in *The Arts in the Small Community*, Supplementary Volume 1 (Madison: University of Wisconsin Extension Division, 1969), 55.

40. Schwalbach, "Personal Involvement in the Arts," 57.

41. Recollections of Drummond from Robert E. Gard, personal communication to the author.

42. Gard, *Grassroots Theater*, 33.

43. Gard, *Grassroots Theater*, 217.

44. Gard, *Grassroots Theater*, 219.

45. Gard, *Grassroots Theater*, 130–31.

46. Marjorie Harbaugh Bennett, oral history interview by Maryo Gard Ewell, May 15, 2015, interview #1427, University of Wisconsin–Madison Archives and Robert E. Gard Foundation Oral History project, https://minds.wisconsin.edu/handle/1793/73408.

47. Robert E. Gard, Michael Warlum, Ralph Kohlhoff, Ken Friou, and Pauline Temkin, *The Arts in the Small Community* (Madison: University of Wisconsin Extension Printing, 1969), 4. Available at http://gardfoundation.org/projects/arts-in-the-small-community/. All the records of this project can be found in the Robert E. Gard papers, 1910–1980, University of Wisconsin–Madison Archives, Steenbock Library.

48. Charles Christopher Mark, *Reluctant Bureaucrats: The Struggle to Establish the National Endowment for the Arts* (Dubuque, IA: Kendall-Hunt, 1991), 118–19.

49. Michael Warlum, personal communication to the author.

50. Gard et al., *Arts in the Small Community*.

51. University of Wisconsin–Extension Arts Development, Annual Report, 1977–78 (unpublished manuscript in the author's possession), p. 2.

52. This list of programs is not comprehensive and draws upon the author's memory, personal friendships with many of the faculty, various written materials including a

scrapbook from the Robert E. Gard Foundation, and information contained in the Robert E. Gard Foundation Oral History Project at the University of Wisconsin–Madison.

53. "Creed of the Wisconsin Rural Writers' Association," *Creative Wisconsin* 1, no. 1 (January 1954): n.p., University of Wisconsin–Madison Archives, Steenbock Library, series 9/4/00/7 23A5.

54. Jeffrey S. Russell, "Lessons in Listening for UW–Madison," *Capital Times*, March 14, 2017, http://host.madison.com/ct/opinion/column/jeffrey-s-russell-lessons-in-listening-for-uw-madison/article_8b05ae8a-9432-5532-9a34-02846d86fe9e.html.

55. Gard et al., *Arts in the Small Community*, 4.

56. Gard et al., *Arts in the Small Community*, 6.

57. Gard et al., *Arts in the Small Community*, 98.

The Crucible of Conservation

Land, Science, Community, and the Wisconsin Idea

CURT MEINE

Conservation is not a practice, a program, a technical standard, or a plan. . . .
Conservation is a journey.

—PETE NOWAK, Emeritus Professor, UW–Madison (2011)[1]

PICTURING THE WISCONSIN IDEA

"If you had to choose one picture to illustrate the Wisconsin Idea, Andy, what
would it be?"

I posed this question to Andy Kraushaar, longtime curator of Visual Materials at the Wisconsin Historical Society. For thirty years Andy oversaw collections
that include some three million photographs, drawings, posters, films, and
other items. Andy, it is safe to assume, holds more images of Wisconsin places,
culture, and history in his mind than any other person in the state.

We tossed around a few candidates. We agreed that the short list had to
include a 1930 image showing the Ingenues, a popular all-woman jazz band,
squeezed in among the stanchions in the University of Wisconsin's on-campus
dairy barn. The flapperish girls are playing their horns, saxophones, and clarinets
for the bemused Jerseys in an experiment to determine if cows would produce
more milk when exposed to music.[2] A far stretch, it might seem, from more
sober expressions of university instruction, research, and extension. But something in those eyes—of the musicians and the cows—conveys the spirit of creativity that has marked the Wisconsin Idea at its best. (And, after all, generations
of Wisconsin dairy cows and dairy farmers have tuned into the radios in their
milking parlors.)

Andy nominated another image of about the same vintage. A hundred
mostly younger men sit on the ground and in folding chairs, gathered around
a makeshift plywood stage under a canopy of elms. They are participants in
the university's farm short course. On stage an instructor holds forth on what

could have been any of a hundred topics, from crop rotations to veterinary science to farm accounting methods. The short courses date to 1886—the first agricultural courses offered in the state, open to any Wisconsin student over the age of sixteen. Andy's choice made good sense. To this day the short course epitomizes the Wisconsin Idea: providing educational opportunity and access to knowledge for all the citizens of Wisconsin.

My own top choice was a photo I have long used in lectures on conservationist Aldo Leopold. Leopold and one of his graduate students, Ellwood Moore, are visiting a farm near the whistle-stop village of Riley, west of Madison in rural Dane County. It is a hot day in 1935. Leopold has his sleeves rolled up and a cigarette in hand. He is talking with a farmer and his two sons. One of the sons is shirtless. Leopold was two years into his university career, charting new directions in wildlife ecology and land conservation. Since 1931 he had been fostering a collaboration between Riley farmers and a group of sportsmen from Madison.[3] A dominant theme for Leopold in these years was encouraging wildlife management on private lands, involving farmers, other landowners, hunters, and students in the field work and in research.[4]

Why does this image stand out for me? I like the notion of the farmer and the professor working alongside one another. Leopold and his student were no doubt learning as much as they were sharing, the information flowing both directions between citizens and the university campus. In the portrait of their

Aldo Leopold visiting with farmer Reuben Paulson in Riley, Wisconsin, in 1935. Photograph courtesy of the Aldo Leopold Foundation.

conversation I find the essence of the Wisconsin Idea. People from different backgrounds cultivating relationships, sharing experiences, and exploring practical applications of knowledge. Citizens coming together to solve problems and create opportunities—while keeping in mind the land, its plants and animals, its human community, and future generations.

Similarly, if I had to choose just one historic graphic to illustrate the complexity of our conservation challenges today, I would again draw upon Leopold. At the Seventh North American Wildlife Conference, held in Toronto in April 1942, Leopold delivered a short paper entitled "The Role of Wildlife in a Liberal Education."[5] His presentation included a figure labeled "Lines of dependency (food chains) in a community." More than three-quarters of a century later, that figure remains transformative, even revolutionary. Depicting what would have been a typical (if simplified) set of ecological relationships in a Wisconsin landscape, the figure shows chains connecting *rock—soil—ragweed—quail—horned owl*, and *rock—soil—alfalfa—rabbit—red-tailed hawk*. The study of such "lines of dependency" had become increasingly important in Leopold's work, especially after English ecologist Charles Elton, Leopold's friend and colleague, published his landmark book *Animal Ecology* (1927). Elton's volume defined such basic ecological concepts as the *niche, food webs*, and the *pyramid of numbers*.[6]

On this occasion, however, Leopold pushed into territory where few other ecologists ventured. The ecological chain that led from *rock* to *soil* to *alfalfa* to *cow* Leopold extended to connect *farmer* to *grocer* to *lawyer* to *student*; another line linked *farmer* to *implement maker* to *mechanic* to *union secretary*. In his diagram Leopold also highlighted the various academic disciplines required to understand the workings of the entire "land community." He included, as would be expected, geology, soils, botany, mammalogy, and ornithology. But Leopold also included animal husbandry, sociology, and economics. For Leopold, human and natural communities were intimately intermingled. Our social, economic, and political realities did not, and could not, exist in an ecological vacuum. Our conservation challenges did not, and could not, be addressed apart from the social sphere. Today, in the effort to comprehend the full complexity and dynamism of interconnected human-nature relationships, researchers in the social and natural sciences study *linked socio-ecological systems*.[7] Leopold is looked back upon as a pioneer in that approach.[8]

It is especially fitting that Leopold prepared this figure for a talk focused on liberal education. His accompanying text is dense with pedagogical insight:

> Perhaps the most important of [ecology's educational] purposes is to teach the student how to put the sciences together in order to use them. All the sciences

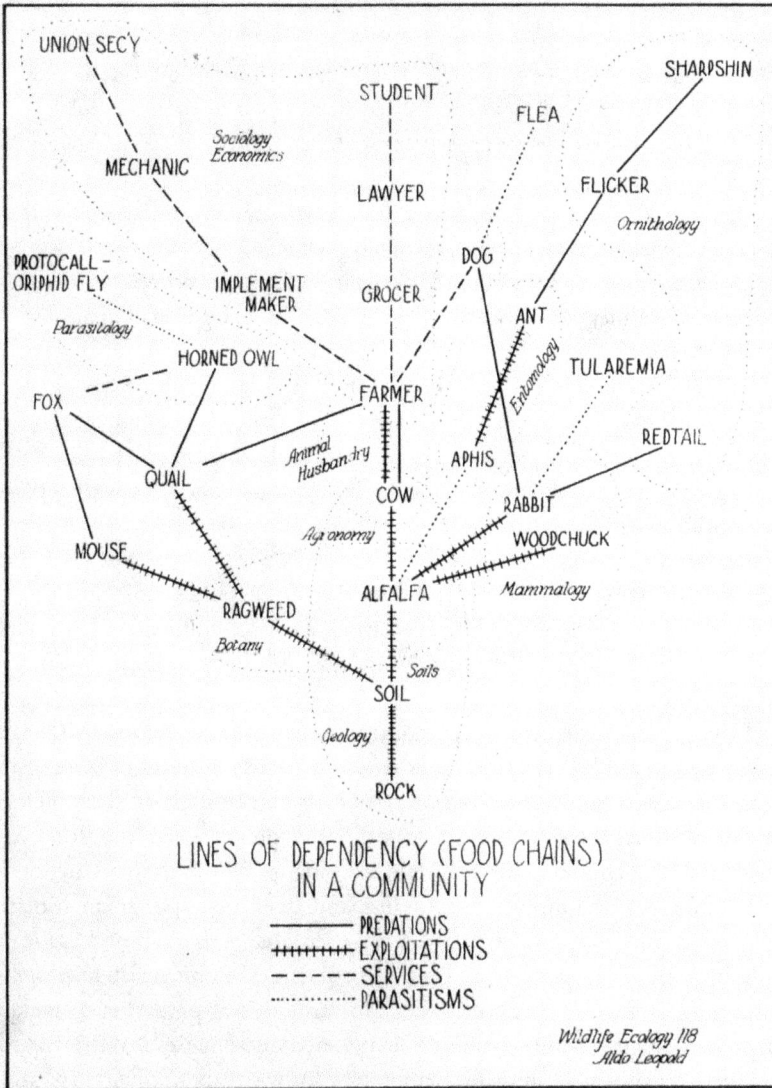

Figure from Aldo Leopold's 1942 article "The Role of Wildlife in a Liberal Education." It illustrates, he wrote "some of the lines of dependency (or food chains, so called) in an ordinary community. These lines are the arteries of a living thing— the land. In them circulates food drawn from the soil, pumped by a million acts of cooperation and competition among animals and plants. That the land lives is implicit in its survival through eons of time. Who is the land? We are, but no less the meanest flower that blows. Land ecology discards at the outset the fallacious notion that the wild community is one thing, the human community another." Figure courtesy of the Aldo Leopold Foundation.

and arts are taught as if they were separate. They are separate only in the classroom. Step out on the campus and they are immediately fused. Land ecology is
putting the sciences and arts together for the purpose of understanding our
environment. . . .

   Land ecology discards at the outset the fallacious notion that the wild community is one thing, the human community another.

   What are the sciences? Only categories for thinking. Sciences can be taught
separately, but they can't be used separately, either for seeing land or doing anything with it. . . .

   There is no need to persuade the student of land ecology that machines to
dominate the land are useful only while there is a healthy land to use them on,
and that land-health is possibly dependent on land-membership, that is, that
a flora and fauna too severely simplified or modified may not tick as well as the
original.[9]

Such statements represented the full flowering of Leopold's ecological understanding. They also reflected the special institutional influence of the University of Wisconsin, with its already impressive history of contributions to
conservation.

   Thirty years earlier, in 1912, political scientist and reformer Charles
McCarthy had published *The Wisconsin Idea*, the classic account of Wisconsin's
leadership role in the Progressive movement—with emphasis on the vital relationship between the state university and public policy. Theodore Roosevelt,
president of the United States from 1901 to 1909, provided an introduction to
the volume. An accomplished naturalist and dedicated sportsman himself,
Roosevelt during his presidency had led the national conservation crusade. In
his post-presidency years he was even more relentless in his insistent progressivism, and as *The Wisconsin Idea* went to print he was preparing to make a
run to reclaim the White House.[10] In his introduction Roosevelt famously
described Wisconsin as "literally a laboratory for wise experimental legislation
aiming to secure the social and political betterment of the people as a whole."[11]

   If Wisconsin was a vital laboratory of democracy, it was more specifically a
crucible for conservation. Beginning in the late 1800s, Wisconsin's landscape of
resource exploitation and ecological devastation would be transformed into one
of restoration and resilience, with the university and the Wisconsin Idea playing
a catalytic role. But conservation has never rested upon a static foundation of
scientific knowledge and concepts. Conservation evolves continuously. Land
changes. New needs and opportunities emerge. New approaches take hold
and new tools are invented. Challenges to democratic governance and equitable policy-making are ever-present. The values that shape our relationship to

land, and to the planet, shift.[12] Over the last century the role of the Wisconsin Idea in conservation has evolved accordingly.

Leopold wrote in 1940 that "conservation, viewed in its entirety, is the slow and laborious unfolding of a new relationship between people and land."[13] That unfolding continues as the critical environmental trends of the twenty-first century press upon us. Science understands the functioning of linked socio-ecological systems better than it has in the past. Yet resistance to scientific expertise, conservation values, and effective environmental policies has also grown stronger in recent years. For much of the last century, Wisconsin was widely regarded as an innovative leader in conservation, its impact extending well beyond the boundaries of the state. That reputation, however, waned with neglect, as opposing political forces asserted their power. Wisconsin can no longer claim the mantle of leadership, at least in the public sector.

Wisconsin, and the Wisconsin Idea, thus stand at a crossroads. Where will Wisconsin go from here? In the face of accelerated social, economic, and environmental change, does the Wisconsin Idea remain relevant to conservation? Can it continue to catalyze conservation? Conversely, can conservation help to reimagine the Wisconsin Idea in this time of rapid transformation? If so, what new and different means—and meanings—must be built into the expression of the Wisconsin Idea? What picture of the Wisconsin Idea will the future bring?

THE WISCONSIN IDEA AND WISCONSIN'S LANDSCAPE

To inform the answers to those questions we may turn to the land and its history, and revisit the origins and development of the Wisconsin Idea. Wisconsin's landscape is itself a "linked socio-ecological system." It of course has people in it, but people in community with its climate, geology, soils, waters, plants, and animals. The Wisconsin Idea is a product of Wisconsin as a particular place, reflecting its unique natural and cultural history, and affecting the character of that place in turn. It has evolved in this landscape, influencing in important ways our human relationships with and within it.

A specific set of environmental, historical, economic, and cultural circumstances prepared the way for the emergence of a robust conservation movement in Wisconsin in the early 1900s. Wisconsin's topography of glaciated and unglaciated lands featured abundant fresh water, varied soils, and a diverse flora and fauna occurring in an array of lake, stream, wetland, prairie, savanna, and forest communities. Native peoples have inhabited the landscape now called Wisconsin for at least twelve postglacial millennia. Earlier waves of human activity on the land had lasting environmental effects: exploitation of the Pleistocene megafauna; development of Native American agroecosystems;

prehistoric mining, burning, hunting, gathering, and fishing; the cross-cultural fur trade beginning in the 1600s. However, these effects were relatively slow, intermittent, or localized compared to the unprecedented rush of resource exploitation that altered the character of Wisconsin's landscape after the confiscation of Native American lands in the early to mid-1800s. That wave accelerated after statehood in 1848 and reached an apogee in the last three decades of the 1800s.[14]

By 1900 migrant settlers from the eastern United States and Europe had largely converted the state's southern prairies and savannas to agriculture. In much of the region, this stage of agriculture involved continuous cropping of wheat and other grains, leading to soil erosion, nutrient depletion, and widespread pest outbreaks. Ditching and draining steadily diminished Wisconsin's ten million acres of wetlands. Many of the state's larger rivers were dammed to facilitate the logging boom that deforested the northern pineries by 1900. The subsequent cutting of northern hardwood forests would be all but complete by 1930, leaving in the aftermath millions of abandoned acres of barren and fire-prone "cutover" land. Wild fish and game populations were depleted, in some cases to the point of local extirpation (as in the case of elk and white-tailed deer) and ultimate extinction (as with the passenger pigeon). In short, the common asset resources of the state were exploited without check, leading to what later generations might term a crisis of sustainability. Fundamentally, the question before the citizens of Wisconsin was whether the mechanisms of democracy could be used in new ways to safeguard the long-term public interest in those natural assets.

Within a generation Wisconsin became a national leader in effective conservation policy and practice. By the mid-1900s, the trends in overexploitation and depletion were, if not halted, significantly slowed and in many cases reversed through restoration and management for sustainable yields. By the 1970s, Wisconsin stood at the forefront of the emerging environmental movement, responding to new threats such as air and water pollution, poor land-use planning, and the indiscriminate use of pesticides and industrial chemicals. The first Earth Day, observed in 1970 and led by Wisconsin's senator Gaylord Nelson, symbolized the state's continuing leadership in conservation and environmental stewardship, playing out now on a global stage.

Across these generations, Wisconsin's conservation and environmental legacy has been characterized by qualities that distinguish it from the legacies of, say, California or Massachusetts. These qualities include:

• a dynamic interplay between conservation and environmental science, ethics, policy, and practice;

- diverse and integrated approaches to conservation, embracing resource protection, sustainable management and stewardship, and ecological restoration;
- conservation efforts on public, private, and tribal lands, and across the landscape from wildlands to rural lands to urban lands;
- a robust tradition of collaborative and community-based approaches to conservation;
- and a strong focus on the role of public awareness and education in forging effective public policy.

But what *accounts for* these qualities and for Wisconsin's unusual record of leadership? Among the factors that conservationists and environmental historians have noted:

- Wisconsin's Native American nations have long played an active role in environmental caretaking.[15]
- Wisconsin's human and natural history can be easily read in the land, affording its citizens constant opportunity to appreciate the dynamic relationship between human and natural communities.
- As a state, Wisconsin grew in response to, and in concert with, the conservation and environmental movement.
- Wisconsin remains a largely rural state, and personal connections to land remain relatively strong.
- Wisconsin's is a "working" landscape of farms, forests, and development, but with wildness in relatively near proximity.
- Wisconsin is a tourism magnet, with a long tradition of hunting, fishing, and other outdoor recreational activities.
- Wisconsin's conservation commitment has, until recently, been carried forward through bipartisan political commitment.

This list draws upon the reflections of University of Wisconsin–Madison environmental historian William Cronon. In his essay "Landscape and Home: Environmental Traditions in Wisconsin," Cronon highlights an additional factor that explained Wisconsin's prominence in environmental affairs: the University of Wisconsin as an institution, and the Wisconsin Idea as its guiding philosophy. Cronon writes:

> [The University of Wisconsin's] combination of liberal arts and agricultural colleges in a single great research institution is not as common as one might think, and has promoted a cross-fertilization of pure and applied environmental scholarship that happens much less often at pure liberal arts institutions like Oxford

or Yale. The famed Wisconsin Idea has encouraged scholars with an interest in land to share their knowledge with the people of the state, and this has had as much effect on the professors as on the citizenry. The UW is in and of Wisconsin in a way that Yale will never be in and of Connecticut.[16]

In short, it is difficult to imagine the state's legacy of environmental leadership apart from the essential role that the university has played in fostering scientific knowledge, public awareness, and innovative policy.

WISCONSIN BEFORE THE CONSERVATION MOVEMENT

That role begins in the consequential year of 1848, when Wisconsin achieved statehood and established a public state university. Although the Wisconsin Idea was not reflected in the university's charter, the core of the Idea—that the state's primary institution of higher learning should serve the citizens of the state and the public good—soon took hold. The "Forty-Eighters," political refugees who fled Europe after the failed reform movements of 1848, brought to Wisconsin a strain of German idealism and a high regard for education, science, and the role of reason in the public arena.[17] Under the federal Morrill Act (1862), the University of Wisconsin became the state's land-grant university. Unlike many other states, Wisconsin did not establish a new university, but supplemented the existing University of Wisconsin, with its existing curriculum in the liberal arts, with new emphases in agriculture and engineering. As Cronon notes, that mixture of academic fields and competencies would ultimately enable the University of Wisconsin to become an incubator of conservation leadership.

In the second half of the 1800s, conservation did not yet exist as a movement, and the term did not carry its modern meaning. However, Wisconsin's Native American communities had developed abiding land-ethic traditions and practices over the centuries and millennia. Their continuing presence on the landscape provided models of resistance and resilience, their tribal cultures keeping traditional knowledge alive even as they adapted to modernity. Frontier Wisconsin was home to key individuals who would contribute importantly to the coalescing of the conservation movement. Carl Schurz was a Forty-Eighter who settled in Watertown, Wisconsin, and later served as a general in the Union army during the US Civil War and as US senator from Missouri (1869–75). As the US secretary of the interior (1877–81), Schurz focused public attention on the need for forest preservation.[18] The geologist and ethnologist John Wesley Powell grew to adulthood in Walworth County, exploring Wisconsin and the rivers of the Mississippi basin, presaging his epic explorations of the

Colorado River and the American West.[19] Both became national figures in reforming federal approaches to land settlement and land use, and in connecting science and policy through the agencies of government.

Other early figures had direct University of Wisconsin connections. The naturalist John Muir's consequential career as a defender of wild nature can be said to have begun with his several years as a student in Madison in the early 1860s, absorbing his first formal lessons in the natural sciences.[20] Increase Lapham, "Wisconsin's first scientist," was a quintessential naturalist of the 1800s, contributing to fields ranging from archaeology and botany to geology and zoology. His 1867 *Report on the Disastrous Effects of the Destruction of Forest Trees, Now Going on So Rapidly in the State of Wisconsin* was the first to sound a warning about the gathering threat of deforestation in the state. Lapham contributed to the founding and growth of many of Wisconsin's primary scientific and educational organizations, including the Wisconsin Geological and Natural History Survey, the Wisconsin Historical Society, and the Wisconsin Academy of Sciences, Arts and Letters. After Lapham's death in 1875, the University of Wisconsin acquired his extensive storehouse of fossils, minerals, plants, and other specimens and artifacts, forming the foundations of its herbarium and museum collections.[21]

Within the young state university, the establishment of agricultural research and education programs on campus marked the beginning of a dialogue at the intersection of agriculture and conservation that continues to this day, and that has distinguished Wisconsin's conservation legacy. The marriage of the liberal arts and agriculture that Cronon notes was somewhat fractious in its origins. As University of Wisconsin president (1874–87), John Bascom defined the vision of an educational institution informed by the Social Gospel and distinguished by its commitment to knowledge in service to society.[22] At first this did not sit easily alongside the mission of training in the agricultural and mechanical arts as mandated by the Morrill Act. However, the university soon became a leader in agricultural reform, led by such key figures as Professor William A. Henry, Professor Franklin H. King, and dairyman William D. Hoard (who served as chair of the university's board of regents and as Wisconsin governor from 1889 to 1891). The University of Wisconsin College of Agriculture spurred the great transition, after the Civil War, from unsustainable continuous grain cropping to more diverse and regenerative dairy farming. Although the rise of dairying would bring its own set of conservation challenges, it served to stabilize rural life, the agricultural economy, and agroecosystems across much of southern Wisconsin.[23]

In this "preconservation" era, few did more to strengthen the academic foundations of the Wisconsin Idea and its relevance to conservation than geologist

Thomas Chrowder (T. C.) Chamberlin, who served as University of Wisconsin president from 1887 to 1892. Chamberlin did not share Bascom's qualms about the mingling of the liberal arts, sciences, and applied fields. As exemplified by the University of Wisconsin's role in the dairy revolution, Chamberlin comprehended the links connecting all the components of the university, and championed the Wisconsin Idea as it gained sharper definition. "Scholarship for the sake of the scholar is simply refined selfishness," he wrote in 1890. "Scholarship for the sake of the state and the people is refined patriotism."[24] In addition to his service as a visionary educational leader, Chamberlin's extensive contributions as a scientist provided foundations for all those who would make the University of Wisconsin a global leader in geology, climatology, and the other earth sciences.[25]

By the 1890s the cutover forestlands of the upper Great Lakes had become a focal point for policy reform and innovation at the national and state level. The imminent exhaustion of northern pine forests was a key factor behind passage of the US Forest Reserve Act of 1891. The act established the first federal forest reserves, later renamed *national forests*, on the public lands of the American West. In Wisconsin the policy challenge involved not forest protection, but the reality of forest depletion. In 1897 the Wisconsin legislature established a State Forestry Commission. That same year, forester Filibert Roth delivered the first lectures in forestry at the university. As with the shift from wheat to dairy, the emergence of professional forestry over the next decade marked the beginning of the effort to put Wisconsin's (and the nation's) frontier economy of unchecked land exploitation on a new and more sustainable basis.[26] The fate of the cutover lands would remain a critical public policy issue for the next three decades.

Disrupted though Wisconsin's ecological landscape was, it held within it the seeds of social and political reform. Land exploitation had, as one its ancillary effects, the channeling of extracted wealth into the accounts of the Midwest's lumber barons, rail bosses, and milling and mining magnates—and from there into the coffers of political parties and campaigns. In Wisconsin and much of the Upper Midwest, the movements for land-use reform and political reform were commingled. Wisconsin's famed historian (and student of T. C. Chamberlin) Frederick Jackson Turner identified the significance of the passing of the Euro-American frontier in 1893. The consequences of that transition for culture, democracy, economics, and the land raised basic questions that Americans had never faced so directly before. Could a self-governing populace overcome the power of concentrated wealth to make government work for the general welfare of all citizens? Could policy changes address the inherent connections between society and the landscape in which it is embedded? In modern terms, could Wisconsin as a *linked socio-ecological system* be placed on a more durable ecological footing? In the first decade of the twentieth century, these questions framed the rationale and political mission of the Progressive Era conservation movement in Wisconsin and nationwide. The University of Wisconsin would play a disproportionate role in defining conservation. Conservation in turn became one of the central public issues that would help to define the Wisconsin Idea.

CONSERVATION, THE PROGRESSIVE MOVEMENT, AND THE WISCONSIN IDEA

In 1910 University of Wisconsin president (1903–18) Charles Van Hise published *The Conservation of Natural Resources in the United States*. Based on a series of university lectures, the book was the first "correlated statement [on conservation] covering the minerals, waters, forests, soils, their relations, and the relations of the subject as a whole to humanity."[27] Van Hise, another of Wisconsin's eminent geologists, stood at the intersection of education, science, and national policy, working alongside Wisconsin governor (1901–6) and US senator from Wisconsin (1906–25) Robert M. La Follette Sr. and the insurgent Wisconsin progressives, as well as the national conservation leadership under Theodore Roosevelt. Van Hise was a central figure at the 1908 White House Conference of Governors, in many ways the high-water mark of the nascent conservation movement.

Van Hise's text provided not only a comprehensive summary of scientific and technical information but a statement of conservation principles. Progressive Era conservation aimed to promote the efficient use and reuse of materials, to ensure "complete utilization" of flowing waters and to renew degraded forests and other organic resources. These principles "require for their practice a sense of social responsibility upon the part of the individual and the corporation." They had, too, to be "embodied in the law and the law enforced by the community."[28] Such legal means had in 1908 been reinforced by the US Supreme Court, which held that the state, "as quasi-sovereign and representative of the interests of the public, has a standing in court to protect the atmosphere, the water, and the forests within its territory, irrespective of the assent or dissent of the private owners immediately concerned."[29] This alignment of scientific expertise, education, economics, policy, and enforcement would be a hallmark of the Progressive Era conservation movement.[30]

But to what end? Van Hise answered that question as well. Conservation, he wrote, "is for man. Its purpose is to keep the resources of the world in sufficient abundance so that man may have a happy, fruitful life, free from suffering—a relatively easy physical existence."[31] It was a philosophy of conservation shared by Van Hise's contemporary and Roosevelt's "chief forester," conservationist Gifford Pinchot: "The first great fact about conservation is that it stands for development. . . . Conservation does mean provision for the future, but it means also and first of all the recognition of the right of the present generation to the fullest necessary use of all the resources with which this country is so abundantly blessed."[32] Pinchot provided the byword for the utilitarian approach to conservation, holding that it was to serve "the greatest good to the greatest number for the longest time."[33] Wisconsin (and the United States) might eventually come to be understood as socio-ecological systems, but the human economic components of those systems would, according to the Progressive Era's concept of conservation, come first and foremost.

Notwithstanding, that is, Wisconsin alum and expatriate John Muir. Having long since decamped for California and sauntered up-elevation into the Sierra Nevada, Muir provided an alternative worldview behind the fight for conservation: "The world, we are told, was made especially for man—a presumption not supported by all the facts. A numerous class of men are painfully astonished whenever they find anything, living or dead, in all God's universe, which they cannot eat or render in some way what they call useful to themselves."[34] The storied schism between utilitarian and preservationist approaches to conservation would play out for decades to come—indeed, it continues in contemporary debates involving priorities in the environmental movement.[35] Wisconsin, and the University of Wisconsin, would remain at the center of that essential debate.

This philosophical divide was not conservation's only persistent tension. Progressive Era conservation policy emphasized top-down administration and rational management of resources by ostensibly neutral scientific experts working in centralized government agencies. This quickened, in turn, the trend toward specialization within the varied fields of resource management (forestry, fisheries management, soil science and agronomy, wildlife management, recreation, etc.). While the role of local citizens and communities in policy and decision-making was largely neglected, the entrenched economic interests behind resource development continued to exert their dominant political influence.

As these fundamentals of conservation—and these fundamental tensions *in* conservation—were coming into focus, so too was the Wisconsin Idea. In 1900 the university's Board of Regents declared in its *Biennial Report* that "the state will not have discharged its duty to the University nor the University fulfilled its mission to the people until adequate means have been furnished to every young man and woman in the state to acquire an education at home in every department of learning."[36] In 1905 Van Hise gave his own classic expression of the Idea: "I shall never be content until the beneficent influence of the university reaches every family of the state."[37]

These statements stand as key points in the development of the university's extension function. Antecedents to the university extension system dated back decades. These efforts accelerated under Van Hise.[38] The regents established the Division of University Extension in 1906. Passage of the federal Smith-Lever Act in 1914 bolstered Extension by providing support through the US Department of Agriculture. University Extension became for many the most tangible expression of the Wisconsin Idea, connecting citizens and the university campus. It also became a primary conduit for the collection and dissemination of conservation information statewide. Given its key role at the interface of the public and the university, Extension could also be seen as a continual testing ground for the Wisconsin Idea. How best could university-based researchers serve the evolving public interest? And how best could the public, via Extension, both shape and benefit from the work and resources of the university?

Three Generations of Conservation and Environmental Leadership

As conservation became an important piece of the university's portfolio and a core area of state policy, it was woven into Wisconsin's lifeways and landscapes. And across the twentieth century, the University of Wisconsin would play a central role in Wisconsin's rise to leadership in conservation and the modern environmental movement. That story is too extensive even to summarize here. However, key themes, individuals, and episodes in that story illustrate how the Wisconsin Idea contributed to the state's prominent role:

- In addressing the vexing problem of restoring the vast northern cutover, Wisconsin became an academic center for innovation in land-use and agricultural economics.[39] Professor Henry C. Taylor established the University of Wisconsin Department of Agricultural Economics within the College of Agriculture in 1909. Together with colleagues Benjamin Hibbard, George Wehrwein, and others, he provided innovative economic tools for reforming land use across Wisconsin. Economist Richard T. Ely founded the university's Institute for Research in Land Economics and Public Utilities in 1920. He and economist John R. Commons made the university home to the field of institutional economics, emphasizing interdisciplinary inquiry and collective action through social institutions, rather than the study of abstract economic laws.[40]

• In the midst of the Great Depression, the University of Wisconsin College of Agriculture enlisted the eminent regionalist painter John Steuart Curry as its artist-in-residence—the first such residency established at any American university. Under Dean Chris Christensen and University of Wisconsin president Glenn Frank, the university emphasized the connection between the arts and sciences on campus. And through the university extension system, the College of Agriculture highlighted the role of the arts in contributing to the quality of rural life.[41]

• Aldo Leopold's *A Sand County Almanac*, published posthumously in 1949, was itself in many ways a product of the spirit of innovative outreach in the College of Agriculture. Leopold's core contribution, in the *Almanac* and elsewhere, was to recognize the revolutionary perspective that the science of ecology brought to the management of natural resources, public policy, education, ethics, and aesthetics. Leopold held that "the citizen conservationist needs an understanding of wildlife ecology not only to enable him to function as a critic of sound policy, but to enable him to derive maximum enjoyment from his contacts with the land."[42] Through his fifteen years as a University of Wisconsin faculty member (1933–48), Leopold devoted a significant portion of his time to sharing—in person and in print, in the lecture hall and over the airwaves—the lessons of ecology and the substance of his "land ethic" philosophy.[43] That philosophy challenged the assumptions of both utilitarianism and preservation, opening conservation to a broader range of values and a reconfigured set of social and ecological goals.[44]

• Wisconsin became (and remains) a global leader in the study of freshwater systems due to the work of generations of university researchers. Edward Birge, Chancey Juday, Arthur Hasler, John Magnuson, Steven Carpenter, and a host of other eminent scientists examined in innovative ways not only the physical, biological, and ecological functions of aquatic ecosystems, but the social interactions that characterize and affect those systems.[45]

Even this tiny sample from its rich history demonstrates why the University of Wisconsin became so important a crucible for conservation. University researchers contributed significantly to virtually every branch of the basic and applied natural sciences, social sciences, and humanities. The breadth of disciplinary expertise available on campus was matched by a commitment to problem-solving that required applied and interdisciplinary approaches. Conservation Wisconsin-style began to outgrow the narrow utilitarianism of its origins and to explore its broader social, economic, and ethical implications. The fusion—or at least the engagement—of the natural and social sciences and the humanities helped carry conservation beyond government chambers, research laboratories, and classrooms, and connected it in concrete ways with Wisconsin's citizens and communities. Conservation was no longer the domain of experts, managers, and policymakers, but increasingly an arena of citizen participation and action.

This participatory approach emerged in 1927 with new laws, guided by the University of Wisconsin land economists and with strong citizen support, to reform forestry and land use in northern Wisconsin. That same year, sportsmen and other citizen-conservationists led the way in enacting another law that established a Wisconsin Conservation Department, overseen by an independent citizen board that would in turn appoint a professionally qualified director. Several years later, in 1934, the Conservation Department established the annual Conservation Congress as a means of encouraging citizen involvement in decision-making.[46]

These institutional innovations were matched on the ground by new programs to promote reforestation, soil conservation, and land restoration. One especially important project was the pioneering watershed conservation efforts at Coon Valley in western Wisconsin. By the early 1930s, watersheds across the Driftless Area of the upper Mississippi River basin were in crisis due to extreme rates of soil erosion and sedimentation. Coon Creek, Wisconsin, became the focus of the nation's first watershed conservation demonstration project. Agency and university experts were closely involved, but the project could and would succeed only through the active participation of the watershed's farmers. More than four hundred signed up. The New Deal's Civilian Conservation Corps supplied additional labor, bringing unemployed urban youth into the Wisconsin countryside. This "adventure in cooperative conservation," as Leopold described it, turned the tables on conservation as undertaken by the earlier Progressive movement.[47] This was conservation literally from the ground up, seeking new ways to integrate and apply multidisciplinary knowledge, to engage the citizens most affected, and, more broadly, to protect the public interest in private land.

Coon Valley was not the only promising example of collaborative conservation arising in the uneasy 1930s. These innovations were soon overwhelmed, however, by national and global events. World War II altered the character of conservation and the role of science *in* conservation—and in society—in basic ways. In particular, the postwar creation of the National Science Foundation (NSF) put into place the modern mechanism for federal funding of science through a national research agency. It was a contentious birth. Several years of congressional debate over the administration of science policy reflected questions directly relevant to the Wisconsin Idea. Should the nation's research agenda be directed primarily by scientists and other experts, or by the wider public through its civil servants? Should funding be channeled toward a few elite institutions or should it be more widely distributed? Should support be provided for basic research or also for the social sciences? By the time the NSF was established in 1950, the proponents of the more centralized, expert-driven model prevailed.[48] The consequences of that outcome continue to echo into our time.

In the meantime, rapid postwar changes in American society, economics, technology, and land use were altering the context of the conservation. The University of Wisconsin was uniquely poised to play a leading role in the emergence of the modern environmental movement. The university's culture of conservation had passed on to a new generation of academic leaders in Madison and throughout the statewide system of university campuses. Wisconsin's array of university researchers continued to forge new directions in ecology and other natural sciences, the applied fields of resource management, and policy-relevant social science. As Wisconsin governor (1959–63), Gaylord Nelson—native of Clear Lake and graduate of the University of Wisconsin Law School—actively enlisted university faculty in new planning initiatives that addressed intensifying demands on Wisconsin's lands, waters, and wildlife. As US senator from Wisconsin (1963–81), Nelson became nationally recognized as a prominent advocate of environmental reform, especially through his role in organizing the first Earth Day.[49] That same year the University of Wisconsin–Madison established what is now the Nelson Institute for Environmental Studies to promote interdisciplinary research, instruction, and outreach.

Nelson's leadership represented in many ways an expansion of the Wisconsin Idea, and its catalytic role in conservation, from the state to the national and global stage. Nelson inherited a tradition of conservation policy, citizen advocacy, and land ethics that made this seem a natural next phase in the evolution of the movement. As US senator, Nelson was explicit in his goal of putting conservation on the national political map, at a time when few elected officials gave it attention, much less priority. But he also recognized the need to engage academic expertise *and* foster grassroots public engagement. Nelson was accustomed to calling upon university experts in public policy-making, and university campuses around the nation served as hubs for Earth Day organization and action. Finally, Nelson framed his aims in both social and ecological terms. "Our goal," he stated on Earth Day, "is not just an environment of clean air and water and scenic beauty. The objective is an environment of decency, quality, and mutual respect for all other human beings and all other living creatures."[50]

The rather astonishing success of the American environmental movement in quickly establishing itself as a political force can be attributed to many causes and influences, emanating from many centers of social and political change around the nation.[51] Wisconsin's special contribution reflected its deep and distinctive conservation roots and the essential role of the Wisconsin Idea in shaping environmental science, policy, and ethics.

DIVIDE AND CONQUER

Sometimes overlooked in the light of Nelson's transformative career was the broad political base that allowed for innovative conservation and environmental policies to take hold in Wisconsin in the 1960s and 1970s.[52] The institutional foundations of conservation in the university, the state government, the political parties, and civil society were robust enough to weather—in fact, to lead—the transition from the older conservation movement to the modern environmental movement. That transition involved basic shifts in Wisconsin and national political culture. In general, conservation had its primary base in rural communities and landscapes; environmentalism's core constituency resided in the cities and suburbs. Issues of land use and the stewardship of natural resources now competed with concerns over environmental contamination and pollution control. In addressing these issues, emphasis shifted away from education and cultural change and toward legislative and regulatory measures. As ecology and related environmental sciences grew increasingly sophisticated, they began to identify and address complex new problems (e.g., toxicology, anthropogenic climate change, biodiversity loss). As the purview of conservation and environmental policy *expanded* to embrace national and global issues, it *deepened* to consider the structural causes and economic drivers of environmental degradation.[53]

Until the 1990s Wisconsin's tradition of shared conservation values and bipartisan consensus tempered the tensions arising from these shifts. The university remained a bulwark and a trusted source of information and instruction. The commitment to environmental education and scientific information as the basis of sound policy withstood the gathering forces of ideological polarization. But Wisconsin was not immune to those forces. Through the 1990s, environmentalism became one of the arenas where lines of partisan loyalty hardened and culture wars broke out. Instead of a space of common values and strategic compromise, environmental policy became another battleground in the standard competition of political philosophies: private interest vs. the public good; local control vs. the centralized state; the reign of the free market vs. the regulatory authority and responsibility of the state; bottom-up, voluntary stewardship vs. top-down, "command and control" management.

At the national level, an environmental backlash gained traction during the presidency of Ronald Reagan (1981–89), leading the Republican Party as a whole to move away from its own long-standing conservation tradition. Meanwhile, as the Democratic Party's political base became increasingly urban, it neglected the trends that were hollowing out the communities and economies of rural America (especially those that came with the postwar industrialization of agriculture). While generally supportive of strong environmental policies, Democrats found themselves vulnerable to the driving of political wedges along the increasingly evident urban-rural divide.[54]

One might choose any of a number of issues to illustrate these trends, but the most obvious one is also the most consequential: climate change. Although the basic science behind climate change dated back well into the 1800s—and University of Wisconsin researchers had contributed importantly to that body of science—it was not a matter that the older conservation movement had to confront. Until the late 1980s, climate change was not a particularly divisive or partisan topic. Both political parties had advocates for forward-looking policy—and neither gave it necessary urgency, or fully recognized it as an unprecedented social and political challenge.[55] Instead, as evidence mounted and the political power of the fossil fuel industries exerted itself, climate change as an issue was driven into deep ideological ruts. It became what it remains today: an extreme example of the limitations of scientific knowledge—and the power of special interests to deflect that knowledge—in shaping effective public policy.

In Wisconsin these trends fundamentally challenged and changed Wisconsin's conservation tradition, and eventually brought into question the resilience of the Wisconsin Idea at the core of that tradition. Tommy Thompson, the Republican governor of Wisconsin from 1987 to 2001, recognized the importance of the University of Wisconsin to the state and advocated policies that reflected the Republican Party's traditional support for conservation. Yet in other ways Thompson undermined that tradition—by, for example, turning the state's independent Department of Natural Resources secretary into a governor-appointed position. Wisconsin governor James Doyle (2003–11), a Democrat, oversaw modest conservation gains, but in general did not place a high priority on strengthening environmental policies. When presented with the opportunity to sign legislation restoring the independence of the Department of Natural Resources secretary, he declined to do so.

The stage was then set for the rise of Scott Walker, the Republican governor of Wisconsin from 2011 to 2019. It was a signal of things to come when Walker, on his first day in office, in his first executive order, called upon the state legislature to meet in special session to (among other items) weaken wetland

protections.[56] Over the next eight years, the Walker administration systematically undermined many of the basic institutional foundations of Wisconsin's
conservation tradition.[57] Most pertinent with regard to the Wisconsin Idea,
Walker and his allies in the state legislature instituted substantial funding cuts
to the University of Wisconsin campuses, reduced the capacity of the University
of Wisconsin–Extension system, removed University of Wisconsin scientific
experts from state advisory committees, gutted the scientific bureau within the
state's Department of Natural Resources, and reduced state-mandated environmental education efforts. Opponents thwarted other proposals, including
Walker's effort in 2015 to eliminate the Wisconsin Idea itself as the guiding
philosophy of the state university system.[58]

For many in Wisconsin, it came as a shock that the state's conservation legacy,
so fundamental to its identity, could be so easily and swiftly dismantled. But
the winds had been shifting for decades. The tools of "divide and conquer"
politics had long since been sharpened and were well-funded. However justified or not, the denigration of science and suspicion of higher education had
been growing for decades, as had frustration with bureaucratic procedures
and top-down environmental policies. The ever-increasing power of money in
electoral politics, the rise of the hyper-partisan media, the politicization of the
judiciary, and the disruption of the Great Recession from December 2007 to
June 2009—all served to erode the foundation of shared conservation values.
The rural-urban divide widened in Wisconsin as elsewhere, with few seeking
to understand the cultural, economic, and demographic changes that exacer-
bated the divide (even as others exploited those changes for political gain).
Many modern heirs to the conservation tradition had failed to read these
signals or were otherwise unable to adapt and respond to these trends. And for
younger generations, much of Wisconsin's special conservation history was
simply unfamiliar to them.

The response to climate change again demonstrated all too well the consequences of these developments. With some of the nation's leading climate
scientists on hand in Madison and at other University of Wisconsin system
campuses, the state was well positioned to be a leader in charting a course into
the uncertain future. Scientists in the Wisconsin Department of Natural
Resources and at the University of Wisconsin–Madison came together in 2007
to form the Wisconsin Initiative on Climate Change Impacts (WICCI). The
effort soon expanded to include representatives from other state and federal
agencies, the University of Wisconsin System, Wisconsin's tribal communities,
businesses, and nonprofit organizations. WICCI released its first report in 2011
as Scott Walker came into office.[59] Although university scientists were able to

continue their research, and the WICCI partnership ostensibly survived, the Department of Natural Resources no longer provided leadership. Indeed, administrators directed the state agency to scrub information about climate change from its website, and instructed its personnel to avoid mentioning the topic. In one episode that made national headlines, Tia Nelson, executive secretary of the Wisconsin Board of Commissioners of Public Lands (and daughter of Gaylord Nelson), was forbidden to discuss the topic or to undertake any work related to climate change.[60] Even as the impacts of anthropogenic climate change took an increasing toll within Wisconsin and beyond, the state government had actively abandoned its leadership role.

By the time Scott Walker left office in January 2019, Wisconsin's conservation legacy, and the Wisconsin Idea with it, had been severely tested. As rather bluntly reported in the *Milwaukee Journal Sentinel*, the largest newspaper in Wisconsin, "Walker's tenure was controversial and consequential, a dramatic break from Wisconsin's traditions."[61] The conservation ethic that was for so long a hallmark of Wisconsin's civic culture bore the scars of that break. As did Wisconsin's land. The people of Wisconsin were indeed well *divided*. Fifty years after the first Earth Day, the question remains: Has conservation as an expression of the public interest been *conquered*?[62]

A LEGACY RECLAIMED?

To answer that question, the hard reality must be faced directly. The conservation and environmental values that made Wisconsin a leader and that were thought to be a rock-solid and distinguishing part of our character have languished. The shared commitment to conservation has faded—has in fact been directly and effectively attacked. Conservation in Wisconsin and nationally is now caught in the bind of our political culture's hard ideological dualism. Is there a way forward?

In 1952 US political leader and diplomat Adlai Stevenson hailed the Wisconsin Idea by stating, "The Wisconsin tradition meant more than a simple belief in the people. It also meant a faith in the application of intelligence and reason to the problems of society. It meant a deep conviction that the role of government was not to stumble along like a drunkard in the dark, but to light its way by the best torches of knowledge and understanding it could find."[63] Amid a postwar atmosphere of technological optimism, economic expansion, and Cold War anxiety, Stevenson affirmed that the Wisconsin Idea, born to address an older set of circumstances, could continue to provide guidance in a rapidly changing world. But he also provided a subtle hint that the Wisconsin Idea had to evolve. *Knowledge* was necessary, but insufficient, to address problems;

understanding was also needed. Science, in and of itself, does not and cannot determine policy. Science provides essential information about how the world works, but it cannot prescribe how society uses that information. Understanding, informed by values and ethics, guides society's application of knowledge.

It is precisely because values, ethics, and competing priorities shape policymaking that conservation can become so divisive—but can also bridge divides. What we mean today by *conservation* is very different from what it meant a century ago. It remains a contested term and an evolving idea. Meanwhile, Charles Van Hise and "Fighting Bob" La Follette and Aldo Leopold would not recognize the term *environment* as now used. But the fundamental aim of conservation remains sound: to promote thriving human and natural communities within healthy landscapes. And that requires knowledge, moral leadership, engaged citizens, and creative institutions dedicated to the long-term public interest. We will need these things even more than our ancestors did as we confront the synergistic challenges involving climate change, water, food, energy, biological diversity, health, justice, equity, and economic resilience.

What might such a reinvigorated commitment to conservation under the Wisconsin Idea look like? The way forward might well begin by facing directly the same gaps and tensions that have allowed that commitment to wane. Instead of pursuing research in isolation from its cultural context, scientists would explicitly explore the ethical assumptions and socioeconomic implications of their research. Instead of ignoring or downplaying the indigenous knowledge of Wisconsin's Native American communities, institutions would value and draw upon traditional wisdom within the context of an ever-evolving land ethic. Instead of exploiting differences between our urban and rural communities, elected officials would focus on the continuity and connections between them. Instead of weighing success by narrow quantitative measures of productivity and efficiency, agriculture would again consider how profoundly our food systems shape our health and the quality of rural life, communities, and landscapes. Instead of scientific research fragmented into disciplines and detached from the realities of the entire land community, universities would look again to the land and ask hard questions involving long-term resilience. Instead of turning away from the sobering reality of anthropogenic climate change, skeptics and agnostics would turn toward it with full acknowledgment of the responsibilities we bear and the epic changes we must undertake. Instead of depending on and expecting leadership on these matters to come from above, citizens would collectively realize that they must first grow from the soil, the grassroots, and our communities.

It is hard to envision making progress on these points in the harshly divided political landscape we now inhabit. If Wisconsin's conservation legacy is to be

reclaimed, new approaches to political dialogue must take hold and new opportunities for consensus must be created. As conservation biologist David
Ehrenfeld has written, "Clear and ominous portents warn us to change course,
to use the wisdom we have accumulated and select from the conservative and
liberal traditions the timeless, disaster-defying elements best suited for life in
the different and difficult world ahead."[64] Jim Kurth of the US Fish and Wildlife Service has spoken to this same need to draw upon the best aspects of our
competing political philosophies: "There is nothing more conservative than
the conservative use of natural resources. There is nothing more progressive
than building a sustainable future for our nation and our planet. They are, of
course, the same thing."[65] As goes our political culture, so goes the Wisconsin
Idea. As goes the Wisconsin Idea, so goes conservation in Wisconsin.

In his 1995 article "The Wisconsin Idea: The University's Service to the
State," lawyer and former English professor Jack Stark noted that the fate of
the Wisconsin Idea is not assured. "A major determinant of the Wisconsin
Idea's future is desire, the desire of state government's policymakers and University administrators and faculty members. If they resolutely decide that the
Idea will die, it will die. If they resolutely decide that the Idea will become
stronger, it will become stronger."[66] Yet history as well as recent events have
shown that the destiny of the Wisconsin Idea reflects the desire not only of
those in government and academia, but of citizens throughout the state. Historically, the citizens of Wisconsin made and maintained the Wisconsin Idea
as a living reality. And when in 2015 the Wisconsin Idea was attacked, Wisconsin citizens showed that they cared enough to sustain it in the face of powerful
political opposition.

In a similar manner, neither the state government nor the University of
Wisconsin can *conserve* Wisconsin, or the world. In the long run, only citizens
and communities can do that. But conservation will always require that citizens have access to teaching and training, research and knowledge. It will need
institutions to nurture the next generation of conservation leaders, teachers,
scientists, and practitioners. It will need government officials dedicated to the
long-term public good, receptive to scientific information, and able to inspire
community action. And it will entail a retooled Wisconsin Idea that can link
knowledge to *understanding* to *policy*.

The journey of conservation continues, in Wisconsin and the world. That
journey has always been marked by advances and retreats, dead ends and new
directions. And the Wisconsin Idea has evolved with it. What will the picture
of the Wisconsin Idea look like in the future? Perhaps it will show students
at a workshop on urban gardening in Milwaukee, or Ojibwe elders working
alongside researchers in the *manoomin* (wild rice) beds of a northern lake, or

perhaps even musicians returning to the stanchions of an organic dairy. In a thousand different ways, we may imagine how in Wisconsin we can still—can again—"put the sciences and arts together for the purpose of understanding our environment."

Notes

1. Pete Nowak, "The Conservation Journey," *Journal of Soil and Water Conservation* 66, no. 3 (2011): 61A–64A, quotation from p. 61A.

2. This image is available at https://www.wisconsinhistory.org/Records/Image/ IM2115.

3. See Aldo Leopold and Reuben Paulson, "Helping Ourselves: Being the Adventures of a Farmer and a Sportsman Who Produced Their Own Shooting Ground," *Field and Stream* 39, no. 4 (August 1934): 32–33; Aldo Leopold, "History of the Riley Game Cooperative, 1931–1939," *Journal of Wildlife Management* 4, no. 3 (1940): 291–302; Bob Silbernagel and Janet Silbernagel, "Tracking Aldo Leopold through Riley's Farmland: Remembering the Riley Game Cooperative," *Wisconsin Magazine of History* 86, no. 4 (2003): 34–45.

4. See especially Aldo Leopold, *Aldo Leopold, for the Health of the Land: Previously Unpublished Essays and Other Writings*, ed. J. Baird Callicott and Eric T. Freyfogle (Washington, DC: Island Press, 2001).

5. Aldo Leopold, "The Role of Wildlife in a Liberal Education," *Transactions of the 7th North American Wildlife Conference* (April 8–10, 1942): 485–89; reprinted in several collections, including *The River of the Mother of God and Other Essays by Aldo Leopold*, ed. Susan L. Flader and J. Baird Callicott (Madison: University of Wisconsin Press, 1991), 301–5.

6. Charles S. Elton, *Animal Ecology* (London: Sidgwick & Jackson, 1927).

7. See Fikret Berkes, Carl Folke, and Johan Colding, eds., *Linking Social and Ecological Systems: Management Practices and Social Mechanisms for Building Resilience* (New York: Cambridge University Press, 2000); Michael Schoon and Sander Van der Leeuw, "The Shift toward Social-Ecological Systems Perspectives: Insights into the Human-Nature Relationship," *Natures Sciences Sociétés* 23, no. 2 (2015): 166–74.

8. Fikret Berkes, Nancy C. Doubleday, and Graeme S. Cumming, "Aldo Leopold's Land Health from a Resilience Point of View: Self-Renewal Capacity of Social-Ecological Systems," *EcoHealth* 9, no. 3 (2012): 278–87.

9. Leopold, "Role of Wildlife."

10. Edmund Morris, *Colonel Roosevelt* (New York: Random House, 2010).

11. Theodore Roosevelt, in Charles McCarthy, *The Wisconsin Idea* (New York: Macmillan, 1912), vii.

12. Curt Meine, "Aldo Leopold: Connecting Conservation Science, Ethics, Policy, and Practice," in *Linking Ecology and Ethics for a Changing World: Values, Philosophy, and Action*, ed. Ricardo Rozzi, Steward T. A. Pickett, Clare Palmer, Juan J. Armesto, and J. Baird Callicott (New York: Springer, 2014), 173–84.

13. Aldo Leopold, "Wisconsin Wildlife Chronology," *Wisconsin Conservation Bulletin* 5, no. 11 (November 1940): 8–20.

14. Among other key sources, see William Cronon, *Nature's Metropolis: Chicago and the Great West* (New York: W. W. Norton, 1992); Robert C. Ostergren and Thomas R. Vale, eds., *Wisconsin Land and Life* (Madison: University of Wisconsin Press, 1997); James L. Theler and Robert F. Boszhardt, *Twelve Millennia: Archaeology of the Upper Mississippi River Valley*, vol. 1 (Iowa City: University of Iowa Press, 2005); Donald M. Waller and Thomas P. Rooney, ed., *The Vanishing Present: Wisconsin's Changing Lands, Waters, and Wildlife* (Chicago: University of Chicago Press, 2009).

15. Patty Loew, *Seventh Generation Earth Ethics: Native Voices of Wisconsin* (Madison: Wisconsin Historical Society Press, 2014).

16. William Cronon, "Landscape and Home: Environmental Traditions in Wisconsin," *Wisconsin Magazine of History* 74, no. 2 (1990): 83–105, quotation from p. 105.

17. Charlotte L. Brancaforte, *The German Forty-Eighters in the United States* (New York: Peter Lang, 1989).

18. Donald J. Pisani, "Forests and Conservation, 1865–1890," *Journal of American History* 72, no. 2 (1985): 340–59.

19. Donald Worster, *A River Running West: The Life of John Wesley Powell* (New York: Oxford University Press, 2002).

20. Donald Worster, *A Passion for Nature: The Life of John Muir* (New York: Oxford University Press, 2008).

21. Martha Bergland and Paul G. Hayes, *Studying Wisconsin: The Life of Increase Lapham, Early Chronicler of Plants, Rocks, Rivers, Mounds and All Things Wisconsin* (Madison: Wisconsin Historical Society Press, 2014).

22. J. David Hoeveler, *John Bascom and the Origins of the Wisconsin Idea* (Madison: University of Wisconsin Press, 2016).

23. Edward Janus, *Creating Dairyland: How Caring for Cows Saved Our Soil, Created Our Landscape, Brought Prosperity to Our State, and Still Shapes Our Way of Life in Wisconsin* (Madison: Wisconsin Historical Society Press, 2011).

24. Thomas C. Chamberlin, *The Coming of Age of the State Universities: A Charter-Day Address Delivered on the Twenty-First Anniversary of the University of Nebraska, February 15, 1890* (n.p.: 1890), 9. A copy is in the Cutter Collection of the University of Wisconsin–Madison Memorial Library. Chamberlin is also quoted in John O. (Jack) Stark, *The Wisconsin Idea: The University's Service to the State* (Madison: Legislative Reference Bureau, 1995), 114. Reprinted from the *State of Wisconsin 1995–1996 Blue Book*, ed. Lawrence S. Barish (Madison: Wisconsin Legislative Reference Bureau, 1995), http://digital.library.wisc.edu/1711.dl/WI.WIBlueBk1995. See also Vernon Carstensen, "The Origin and Early Development of the Wisconsin Idea," *Wisconsin Magazine of History* 39, no. 3 (1956): 181–88.

25. Robert H. Dott Jr., "Rock Stars: Thomas Chrowder Chamberlin (1843–1928)," *GSA Today* 16, no. 10 (2006): 30–31.

26. Robert F. Fries, *Empire in Pine: The Story of Lumbering in Wisconsin* (Madison: State Historical Society of Wisconsin, 1951); James Willard Hurst, *Law and Economic Growth: The Legal History of the Lumber Industry in Wisconsin, 1836–1915* (Madison:

University of Wisconsin Press, 1964); Michael Williams, *Americans and Their Forests: A Historical Geography* (New York: Cambridge University Press, 1989).

27. Charles Van Hise, *The Conservation of Natural Resources in the United States* (New York: Macmillan, 1910), quoted from p. v.

28. Van Hise, *Conservation*, 359–63.

29. Van Hise, *Conservation*, 363. The key US Supreme Court decision was *Hudson County Water Co. v. McCarter*, 209 U.S. 349 (1908).

30. The classic account of the Progressive Era conservation movement is Samuel P. Hays, *Conservation and the Gospel of Efficiency: The Progressive Conservation Movement, 1890–1920* (Cambridge, MA: Harvard University Press, 1959).

31. Van Hise, *Conservation*, 363. Modern critics of the Progressive movement and the Wisconsin Idea are quick to point out the repellant component of racism that tainted the early conservation movement, and in particular the support for eugenics that some conservationists professed. See, for example, Thomas C. Leonard, *Illiberal Reformers: Race, Eugenics, and American Economics in the Progressive Era* (Princeton, NJ: Princeton University Press, 2016). Van Hise does indeed include a paragraph on eugenics, in which he argues that "human defectives should no longer be allowed to propagate the race." This line of criticism is not new; conservationists themselves have long recognized this unflattering original sin. Neither does it recount the opposing tradition of linkages between social and environmental justice. Despite the presentism of contemporary critics, the topic deserves further exploration. Rather than a discomforting and exploitable Achilles heel, it demonstrates the inadequacy of the Progressive Era's "gospel of efficiency." It provides a clear example of the co-evolution of value frames, ethical guidelines, scientific information, and policy in conservation and within society at large.

32. Gifford Pinchot, *The Fight for Conservation* (New York: Doubleday, Page, 1910), quotation from p. 42.

33. Pinchot, *Fight for Conservation*, 48.

34. John Muir, *A Thousand-Mile Walk to the Gulf* (Boston: Houghton Mifflin, 1916), 136.

35. See, for example, J. Baird Callicott and Michael P. Nelson, eds., *The Great New Wilderness Debate* (Athens: University of Georgia Press, 1998); Ben A. Minteer and Stephen J. Pyne, eds., *After Preservation: Saving American Nature in the Age of Humans* (Chicago: University of Chicago Press, 2015).

36. University of Wisconsin Board of Regents, *Biennial Report of the Regents of the University for the Years 1898–99 and 1899–1900* (Madison: State Printers, 1900), 4. These words are usually attributed to Robert M. La Follette Sr. from his first address to the state legislature.

37. Charles Van Hise, "Speech to the Wisconsin Press Association," February 15, 1905; see Merle Curti and Vernon Carstensen, *The University of Wisconsin: A History,* vol. 2, *1848–1925* (Madison: University of Wisconsin Press, 1949), 88.

38. University of Wisconsin–Extension Chancellor's Office, "Highlight History of Extension in Wisconsin, 1862 to 1999," https://archive.li/MSIFo#selection-385.0-385.56 (last updated on March 29, 2007). Carstensen, "Wisconsin Idea." Jerry Apps, *The People*

Came First: A History of Wisconsin Cooperative Extension (Madison: Wisconsin Epsilon Sigma Phi Alpha Sigma Chapter, 2002).

39. Robert J. Gough, *Farming the Cutover: A Social History of Northern Wisconsin, 1900–1940* (Lawrence: University Press of Kansas, 1997).

40. Malcolm Rutherford, "Wisconsin Institutionalism: John R. Commons and His Students," *Labor History* 47, no. 2 (2006): 161–88; Marvin Arnold Schaars, *The Story of the Department of Agricultural Economics, 1909–1972* (Madison: University of Wisconsin, 1972), http://www.horwitzfam.org/histories/Wehrwein%20Univ%20Wisconsin.pdf.

41. See Maryo Gard Ewell's essay in this volume. See also Jennifer A. Smith, "The Culture of Ag: CALS' Unique Legacy of Celebrating the Arts and Humanities in Agriculture," *CALS News*, August 20, 2012, https://news.cals.wisc.edu/2012/08/20/the-culture-of-ag-cals-has-a-unique-legacy-of-celebrating-the-arts-and-humanities-in-agriculture/.

42. Aldo Leopold, "Teaching Wildlife Conservation in Public Schools," *Transactions of the Wisconsin Academy of Sciences, Arts and Letters* 30 (1937): 77–86; quotation from p. 80. Available online at http://digicoll.library.wisc.edu/cgi-bin/WI/WI-idx?id=WI.WT1937.

43. See Susan Flader, "Building Conservation on the Land: Aldo Leopold and the Tensions of Professionalism and Citizenship," in *Reconstructing Conservation: Finding Common Ground*, ed. Ben A. Minteer and Robert E. Manning (Washington: Island Press, 2003), 115–32.

44. See Curt Meine, "The Utility of Preservation and the Preservation of Utility: Leopold's Fine Line," in *The Wilderness Condition: Essays on Environment and Civilization*, ed. Max Oelschlaeger (San Francisco: Sierra Club Books, 1992), 131–72; Minteer and Pyne, *After Preservation*; Gavin Van Horn and John Hausdoerffer, eds., *Wildness: Relations of People and Place* (Chicago: University of Chicago Press, 2017).

45. Annamarie L. Beckel and Frank Egerton, "Breaking New Waters: A Century of Limnology at the University of Wisconsin," *Transactions of the Wisconsin Academy of Sciences, Arts and Letters*, Special Issue (Madison: The Academy, 1987), http://digicoll.library.wisc.edu/cgi-bin/WI/WI-idx?id=WI.WTBreakWaters; John J. Magnuson, "Three Generations of Limnology at the University of Wisconsin–Madison," *Internationale Vereinigung für theoretische und angewandte Limnologie: Verhandlungen* 28, no. 2 (2002): 856–60.

46. Christine L. Thomas, "One Hundred Twenty Years of Citizen Involvement with the Wisconsin Natural Resources Board," *Environmental History Review* 15, no. 1 (1991): 61–81.

47. Aldo Leopold, "Coon Valley: An Adventure in Cooperative Conservation," *American Forests* 41, no. 5 (1935): 205–8; Rena Anderson, "Coon Valley Days: A Short History of the Coon Creek Watershed," *Wisconsin Academy Review* 48, no. 2 (2002): 42–48; Curt Meine and Gary P. Nabhan, "Historic Precedents to Collaborative Conservation in Working Landscapes: The Coon Valley 'Cooperative Conservation' Initiative, 1934," in *Stitching the West Back Together: Conservation of Working Landscapes*, ed. Susan Charnley, Tom E. Sheridan, and Gary P. Nabhan (Chicago: University of Chicago Press, 2014), 77–80.

48. Daniel Kevles, "The National Science Foundation and the Debate over Postwar Research Policy, 1942–1945," *Isis* 68 (1977): 4–26.

49. Bill Christofferson, *The Man from Clear Lake: Earth Day Founder Senator Gaylord Nelson* (Madison: University of Wisconsin Press, 2004).

50. "Partial Text for Senator Gaylord Nelson, Denver, Colo., April 22," http://www.nelsonearthday.net/docs/nelson_26-18_ED_denver_speech_notes.pdf.

51. Adam Rome, *The Genius of Earth Day: How a 1970 Teach-In Unexpectedly Made the First Free Generation* (New York: Macmillan, 2013).

52. Thomas R. Huffman, *Protectors of the Land and Water: Environmentalism in Wisconsin, 1961–1968* (Chapel Hill: University of North Carolina Press, 1994).

53. Curt Meine, "Conservation and the Progressive Movement: Growing from the Radical Center," in *Reconstructing Conservation: Finding Common Ground*, ed. Ben A. Minteer and Robert E. Manning (Washington: Island Press, 2003), 165–84.

54. See Curt Meine, "Crossing the Great Divide," *Quivira Coalition Journal* 30 (2007): 3–11; Katherine J. Cramer, *The Politics of Resentment: Rural Consciousness in Wisconsin and the Rise of Scott Walker* (Chicago: University of Chicago Press, 2016).

55. See Nathaniel Rich, "Losing Earth: The Decade We Almost Stopped Climate Change," *New York Times Magazine*, August 1, 2018, https://www.nytimes.com/interactive/2018/08/01/magazine/climate-change-losing-earth.html. Among the many responses and critiques, see Rebecca Kaplan, "'Losing Earth' Sparks Broad Debate—on Climate Change, Blame, and Gender," *Pulitzer Center Update*, August 2018, https://pulitzercenter.org/blog/losing-earth-sparks-broad-debate-climate-change-blame-and-gender.

56. State of Wisconsin Office of the Governor, Executive Order #1 Relating to a Special Session of the Legislature, https://docs.legis.wisconsin.gov/code/executive_orders/2011_scott_walker/2011-1.pdf.

57. Siri Carpenter, "How Scott Walker Dismantled Wisconsin's Environmental Legacy," *Scientific American*, June 17, 2015, https://www.scientificamerican.com/article/how-scott-walker-dismantled-wisconsin-s-environmental-legacy/.

58. Valerie Strauss, "How Gov. Walker Tried to Quietly Change the Mission of the University of Wisconsin," *Washington Post*, February 5, 2015, https://www.washingtonpost.com/news/answer-sheet/wp/2015/02/05/how-gov-walker-tried-to-quietly-change-the-mission-of-the-university-of-wisconsin/?utm_term=.d6f7bcef95d3. For similar reports, see also Alia Wong, "The Governor Who (Maybe) Tried to Kill Liberal-Arts Education," *Atlantic*, February 11, 2015, https://www.theatlantic.com/education/archive/2015/02/the-governor-who-maybe-tried-to-kill-liberal-arts-education/385366/; Patrick Marley and Jason Stein, "Records: Scott Walker Wanted Wisconsin Idea Changes," *Milwaukee Journal Sentinel*, May 27, 2016, http://archive.jsonline.com/news/statepolitics/judge-orders-scott-walker-to-release-emails-on-wisconsin-idea-b99733921z1-381151041.html/.

59. WICCI (Wisconsin Initiative on Climate Change Impacts), *Wisconsin's Changing Climate: Impacts and Adaptation* (Madison: University of Wisconsin Board of Regents, 2011), https://www.wicci.wisc.edu/report/2011_WICCI-Report.pdf.

60. Steve Verburg, "Months after Climate Change Gag, Earth Day Founder's Daughter Moves On," *Wisconsin State Journal*, July 21, 2015, https://madison.com/wsj/news/

local/environment/months-after-climate-change-gag-earth-day-founder-s-daughter/
article_040be7eb-3a91-502c-8834-90840b9c1a93.html.

61. Bill Glauber and Patrick Marley, "Scott Walker's Eight Years as Governor Ush-
ered in Profound Change in Wisconsin," *Milwaukee Journal Sentinel*, January 4, 2019,
https://www.jsonline.com/story/news/politics/2019/01/04/scott-walkers-eight-years
-wisconsin-governor-were-consequential/2473616002/.

62. On April 22, 2019, the forty-ninth anniversary of the first Earth Day, Wisconsin's former governor Tommy Thompson and former US senator Russ Feingold wrote:
"As a conservative Republican and a progressive Democrat, we don't agree on many
things, but we both believe that Americans need to be good stewards of the natural
resources upon which our environment, economy and public health are dependent.
We need to put partisanship aside and focus on finding commonsense solutions that
will make this world more prosperous for this and future generations." Russ Feingold
and Tommy Thompson, "On Earth Day, Let's Restore Bipartisanship on the Environment," *USA Today*, April 22, 2019, https://www.usatoday.com/story/opinion/2019/04/
22/earth-day-find-bipartisan-common-ground-conserve-environment-column/35089
91002/.

63. Stark, *Wisconsin Idea*, quotation from p. 101.

64. David Ehrenfeld, *Becoming Good Ancestors: How We Balance Nature, Community, and Technology* (New York: Oxford University Press, 2009), quotation from p. 241.

65. National Wildlife Refuge System chief Jim Kurth (commencement remarks,
University of Wisconsin–Stevens Point, May 19, 2012), https://www.fws.gov/refuges/
Kurth_Commencement_Speech/.

66. Stark, *Wisconsin Idea*, 172.

Wisconsin Academics Outing LGBT Policies

R. RICHARD WAGNER

University of Wisconsin president Charles Van Hise's 1905 wish that "the bene-ficent influence of the university reaches every family in the state" could hardly knowingly have included any lesbian, gay, bisexual, or transsexual (LGBT) citizens in that embrace. At that time, almost no one acknowledged that they even existed, or if they did admit to their presence, they were in the crime statistics as arrests and prison inmates. Indeed, much later during the fight for better legislation in the 1970s, the University of Wisconsin–Madison Gay Law Students Association would accurately represent themselves as "the only orga-nized criminals" on campus.[1]

The story of how Wisconsin left the group of states that sought to suppress all manifestations of nonnormative sexual orientation or gender expression to become the first gay-rights state is one that was shaped, in part, by the state's academics. While in 1905 the geographic boundaries of the state were clear, the same clarity erroneously was presumed for its social boundaries. The univer-sity short courses trained the farmers, the home economics programs sought to improve domesticity, and traveling libraries aided rural education, all within the acceptable social boundaries.

Studying homosexuals and gender-nonconforming persons would not have been a presumed part of the university mission. Informing fellow citizens about LGBT lives as accepted behaviors was not desired by any social norms of the early twentieth century. Yet Wisconsin academics of the mid-century refused to be limited by the supposed boundaries on who were the people of the state. They would reveal the lives of gay, lesbian, and even perhaps transsexual per-sons who did indeed exist in Wisconsin. Their subjects would range from prison inmates to military personnel, from Native Americans to University of Wisconsin–Madison students. Not only these individuals' existence, but the dimensions of their social networks and their own voices would also come through these academic endeavors. While academics placing their subjects in

criminal systems, medical contexts, and disapproved social status would reflect
the negative policies of their day, the studies also at least suggested alternative
possibilities about how to think of these LGBT individuals. By the second half
of the century, faculty and staff advocates for change took up the matter of
LGBT rights and influenced the actual changes from the traditional policies
of repression.

CRIMINALS ALL

Police reports showed the existence of homosexuals—at least the ones who got
caught. For the early decades of the twentieth century, Madison police reports
would list each sodomy case on the department's important crimes list with
murders and major thefts. In Milwaukee for the decade 1910–20, there was an
average of eight sodomy arrests a year, with seventeen in 1919. Those males
arrested were overwhelmingly white and native-born. In the 1930s Milwaukee
averaged ten sodomy arrests a year, with nineteen in 1931. Most such "criminals" had bench trials before a judge only, with no legal representation for the
defense.[2]

It wasn't just male homosexuals who were swept up. In 1914 Milwaukee had
the sensational case of a woman who dressed as a man and who claimed an
African American father and a Potawatomi mother. Using the name Ralph
Kerwino, proclaiming that "my heart and soul are more those of a man than
a woman," he had married another woman. His wife then was upset that
he carried on with another woman and complained about him. Whether this
might have been an instance of a transsexual is not discernible at this distance. Madison also had a case of lesbianism in 1939 when two women "homosexuals" were arrested. One was sent to a sanatorium, and the other to her
home city.[3]

The courts supported this criminal status for nonnormative sexual behavior.
In a 1905 ruling the Wisconsin Supreme Court noted "this vile, abominable
crime." The defense had argued fellatio was outside the sodomy statute. The
court claimed, "There is sufficient authority to sustain a conviction in such a
case, and if there were none, we would feel no hesitancy in placing an authority upon the books." In a 1928 case the Wisconsin Supreme Court noted, "The
crime itself is so repulsive and detestable." In a 1935 case it was claimed that in
Waukesha County there existed a "school of sodomists" corrupting youth where
"unnatural perverted lust" was satisfied. The court upheld this conviction.[4]

Some later Wisconsin studies would show most homosexual behavior did
not actually result in arrest and incarceration, but those cases appearing in the
records did reinforce negative attitudes. Thus, for traditional moralists there

was little doubt that nonnormative heterosexual activity and gender expression were outside the legal and social boundaries of society.

PROGRESSIVE ERA SUPPRESSION

At the turn of the twentieth century, rapid urbanization was posing challenges for guardians of traditional morality that would in part renew a focus on homosexuals. Antivice crusades and the social purity movement attacked some of the most visible evils. In Wisconsin, Milwaukee's mayor David Rose was in office from 1898 to 1906 and from 1908 to 1910. Known as All the Time Rosy or Anything Goes Rose, as mayor he ran a wide-open town where heterosexual prostitution was tolerated in a red-light district. In the same spirit of the city ignoring the state vice laws, a European writing in 1908 would list Milwaukee as one of the eight "homosexual capitals" of America. La Crosse, a river town with many transient males, also had a well-known red-light vice district down by the Mississippi River. Superior, with its plentiful lumberjacks and miners who often lived in male-only camps, was another active vice spot. Hysteria over women forced into the prostitution trade nationally resulted in the federal Mann Act of 1910, targeting "white slavers" who abducted women across state lines for immoral purposes.[5]

In 1913, the Wisconsin legislature got into the act and created a legislative committee "to Investigate the White Slave Traffic and Kindred Subjects." It was known as the Teasdale Committee after its chairman, Wisconsin state senator Howard Teasdale of Sparta. He was a progressive Republican and was associated with the senior Robert M. La Follette. Senator Teasdale also supported Prohibition, thought by some at the time to be another Progressive reform, though not entirely popular with the Germans and Irish of Wisconsin. Committee investigators were sent into the field, and hearings were held in thirteen Wisconsin cities. A survey of district attorneys' enforcement practices was conducted. This technique will resurface in our tale. The Teasdale Report, largely written by the senator himself, was issued in 1914 and focused on the connection between commercialized sex workers and saloons. Several investigation reports among the kindred subjects did allude to homosexuality, birth control, and abortion, but these concerns did not make it into the report, though the report did reprint the state's statutes against sodomy and improper liberties.[6]

University of Wisconsin sociologist Edward Alsworth Ross was a star witness for Teasdale, and the senator placed in the report ten pages of Ross's testimony, almost 5 percent of the report, because it "so fully covers the problem with which we are directed to deal with that we feel justified in publishing it in full." Ross, a native of Illinois, like many scholars at the end of the nineteenth century did graduate study in Germany. He was awarded a doctorate by Johns Hopkins University in 1891 and came to the University of Wisconsin in 1906. He taught sociology until he retired in 1937. He visited Russia and embraced the revolution.[7]

Ross began by admitting to Teasdale that he had been an uncritical advocate of permitting segregated prostitution as in red-light districts. Ross spoke of why he had changed: "I realized, then, that we were not dealing with what you might call the old Adam in man, the ungovernable desire, which if denied gratification in one direction would be certain to seek it in some other." He continued, "As soon as I saw that this demand is multiplied by some hundreds of per cent in order to sell more wares, on the part of those who handle the business of sexual intercourse, then I began to change my position entirely, so that my present position is to hit the thing entirely wherever you see it." Ross was a student of social control; in fact, that was the title of his 1901 book. Ross in the Progressive Era also supported Prohibition, though he would move to more liberal positions and became for the decade of the 1940s national chairman of the American Civil Liberties Union.[8]

Ross's testimony before Senator Teasdale emphasized traditional norms: "I came thus to a realizing sense that the most deadly foe of the home and the family and of normal fecundity is prostitution." Ross argued in 1913 that if nonnormative sexual behavior was accepted it would "rot the foundations of society." He argued that of the women sex workers, "possibly 50% of them are subnormal in intelligence." He added that it was not because of lack of education, but because they were "congenitally subnormal." His further comments were, "I think that immorality springs either from subnormality in the individual or from something wrong in the home." Both Ross and Teasdale felt social principles overrode any pleasure-seeking impulse, even though half the women in the investigative reports expressed little interest to leave the business.[9]

Ross's stance against vice was largely supported by socialist Victor Berger. Berger, editor of Milwaukee's socialist newspaper, had been elected to the US Congress in 1910 in a Milwaukee Socialist sweep that also saw Mayor Emil Sidel elected mayor. Socialist mayor Sidel had proceeded to end Milwaukee's red-light district. Berger, claiming sexual diseases were unknown to the old Germanic tribes, found them particularly prevalent in modern American cities. As a good class warrior, Berger saw that "the mainspring of prostitution is poverty." He decried that it is "the woman alone who is punished." Perhaps alluding to Rose, he said that when the man is caught, "He is usually let go with a smile— or perhaps they run him for mayor later on." Riffing on the economic and moral structure of marriage law, he declared, "Wealth is the only consideration.

We are more careful how we mate our horses and dogs, and cattle, and even our swine, than we are in the mating of our boys and girls." Berger believed he had the solution to vice: "If we want a different world we must emancipate men and women economically, politically and socially." While Berger wished to end vice, "It is impossible to abolish prostitution under the present capitalist system."[10]

The attacks on vice in the Progressive Era showed a general agreement on supporting social norms of traditional morality rather than accepting sexualized human behavior outside of marriage, much less outside of normal heterosexuality. Despite the reality of sexual variation they saw occurring, it was all to be deplored for one reason or another—lack of social control or capitalist degeneracy.

SODOMITES IN THE CELLS

Born in Iowa, John Gillin had bachelor's degrees from Upper Iowa University and Grinnell College, where he studied under Ross. Gillin's 1906 doctorate in sociology from Columbia University was paralleled by a third bachelor's degree in divinity from Union Theological Seminary of New York. Gillin also was an ordained minister in the Church of the Brethren. He came to the University of Wisconsin in 1912 and taught sociology until retirement in 1942. In the 1930s Professor Gillin would take up the study of sexual minorities. Results were published in *The Wisconsin Prisoner: Studies in Crimogenesis.* On the occasion of his death in 1958, university president Conrad Elvehjem would laud him as an "eminent criminologist." He served as president of the American Sociological Society from 1926 to 1927 and was also a frequent contributor to criminology journals. His public service included the Madison Fire and Police Commission and the Wisconsin Parole Board appointed by Progressive governor Philip La Follette.[11]

Gillin examined three classes of Wisconsin prisoners: murderers, property offenders, and sex offenders. Statistical tables and case histories of each group were presented in his book. In Gillin's view, "These three groups were reclassified on the sociological basis of the act rather than on the legal basis." Of the 128 sex offenders in the system at this period, twenty-nine were convicted of sodomy. One was a case of bestiality, so twenty-eight were presumed homosexuals. Throughout the book, while all were discussed in the criminal context, Gillin wavered back and forth between calling them sodomites and homosexuals. Sodomy was their particular legal "crime against nature," versus homosexual, which was their identity or status as part of a social group. Of the sodomy cases nine (or 31 percent) were at Central State Hospital in Waupun, showing a growing presumed medical framework for homosexuals. For other sex offend-ers, only 7 percent were at Central State.[12]

Gillin would break ground by treating the "criminal" homosexuals differ-ently in presenting them as a group about which scientists had recently created a body of literature. His book has a four-page essay on theories of homosexual-ity. Murderers and property offenders are given no such literature to reference their behavior, which might have ascribed a collective identity as with homo-sexuals. For the chapter "How Murderers Are Made," the observation was that they were "not always a result of a given kind of background or a given type of personality." Regarding the literature on rape sex offenders, Gillin dismis-sively observed, "On this subject the psychologists are as silent as the tomb." Incest was "almost neglected."[13]

The literature review on homosexuality begins with Sigmund Freud, for according to Gillin, he and his "colleagues and disciples [had] produced most of the writing on homosexuality." In reviewing this writing, he brings in bisexu-ality. "Some homosexuals are absolutely inverted; for others the sexual object may be someone of either sex; still others are only occasionally inverted." Gil-lin quoted Austrian psychoanalyst Wilhelm Stekel: "Homosexuality arises out of bi-sexuality." An opposite view to the predominant mental sickness model listed was German sexologist Iwan Bloch, who held that "the largest section of original homosexuals, are perfectly healthy, physically normal persons." Beyond the psychoanalytical school, he profiled the ideas of another German sexolo-gist, Magnus Hirschfeld, who held social views that "their heredity predisposes them strongly toward homosexuality." Gillin mentions endocrine theories of homosexuality. Thus he presented to the reader social, biological, and psycho-logical explanations for homosexuality as an identity.[14]

Speaking of the different grounds about same sex attraction from his own research, Gillin wrote, "These selected case histories show that numerous fac-tors go to produce homosexuality." Gillin begins to suggest that homosexual-ity is a status, not a criminal choice: "Some of the prisoners seem almost to have been destined by physical constitution and early conditioning to become homosexuals." Pushing theories later more fully enunciated by the American student of human sexual behavior Alfred Kinsey, Gillin writes, "In some, which strengthen the contentions of Freud and Stekel that everyone is poten-tially bi-sexual, the individual was capable of both heterosexual and homo-sexual relationships." Gillin did not push the concept of bisexuality, but this assumption of sexual fluidity was certainly not normative for the day. In one of the case histories, he described the prisoner as "the bi-sexual type of homo-sexual." Yet he maintained that of the sodomites, some "had a decided pref-erence for their own sex." Among causes Gillin tended to Freud's idea: "The evidence indicates that the basic cause is emotional distortion of some sort during development." Gillin found according to his data that "the prisoners who distinctly preferred homosexual love relations, were fond of female pursuits, and had the physical characteristics of the female." He does not appear to question that these types of individual may have been the ones to come to the attention of the police and thus processed through the criminal justice system. But it was encouraging he could view attachments as "love relations" and not just carnal actions. In another case history he would describe that the subject occupied the "inferior position" in the "love relationships."[15]

Gillin also observed among his subjects the rampant homophobia of the day that the homosexuals tended to internalize. He wrote, "Though there is widespread tolerance of extra-legal heterosexual relations, most people are so antagonistic to homosexuality that only the very rationalistic can enjoy such a relationship without a feeling of degradation." Compared to other sex offenders, the homosexuals were "more likely to have an average or high I.Q . . . [and] more likely to have been steadily employed." An observation that there existed a gay subculture glimmers in the remark, "Almost all had demoralized associates, and many had deadened by excessive drinking whatever inhibitions they may once have had."[16]

One of the case histories presented (S-2) may have been a transsexual, though Gillin would not have had this term for the individual. The case was described as "so effeminate a person that he had been dubbed 'Lipstick Bill.'" Further, "the prisoner had been a fastidious dresser and even used cosmetics," plus he "always sought the friendship of young boys or adult women."[17]

Gillin's work was important in revealing a possible scientific framework for homosexuality as expressed by a growing body of scholars. He also hinted at more complicated concepts of sexual fluidity than might be generally presumed, including changed gender expression. A glimmer that same-sex love existed was also presented. This University of Wisconsin research work was well beyond standard criminology and normative ideas.

Is the Answer in Endocrinology?

In 1947 Dr. E. L. Severinghaus of the University of Wisconsin Medical School, in collaboration with Major John Chornyak, published the article "A Study of Homosexual Adult Males" in the *Journal of Nervous and Mental Disease*. A native of Indiana, Severinghaus was awarded his BA in 1916 from the University of Wisconsin and an MD from Harvard University in 1921. He returned to Madison and was a professor of medicine associated with Wisconsin General Hospital. In the 1930s he served as editor of the endocrinology section of the *Yearbook of Neurology, Psychiatry, and Endocrinology*. His co-investigator Major Chornyak was also a doctor in the medical corps of the US Army Air Force stationed at Truax Field at the end of World War II. Chornyak had been active with the Philadelphia Psychiatric Society and had commented on a previous paper on homosexuality and larger testes.[18]

The article began claiming a "widespread opinion that homosexual behavior is related to an abnormality in sex hormones," and it referred to a bibliography of research on homosexual behavior. The specific theory was an increase in female estrogen levels in male homosexuals. Judgmental attitudes still prevailed in choosing "abnormality" rather than a more neutral term like variation about the hormones. Nevertheless, this placed homosexuality squarely in the 1940s medicalization of the condition. The authors did note that the hormone idea had been challenged by Kinsey in a 1941 publication, though Kinsey would note the Severinghaus and Chornyak study in his own groundbreaking *Sexual Behavior in the Human Male*. Severinghaus and Chornyak's framing of the article was significant in indicating that sexual orientation should be viewed not primarily as the carnal acts or crime of sodomy but an inherent characteristic of a group. This academic insight again was beyond normal ideas.[19]

The medicalization of homosexuality had been boosted in the recent world war with American medical screening that sought to prevent homosexuals from being in the military. Much later research has shown how miserably such screening failed, but the 1947 Severinghaus and Chornyak article would be early evidence that homosexual soldiers did indeed exist. The article focused on twenty-one soldiers who had self-admitted their sexual orientation at the Truax military field in Madison during 1945 and "who were under observation" in the hospital for their diagnosis. Multiple urine samples were taken that inconclusively demonstrated any theory of hormone levels. The result: "We are at a loss to offer an explanation" for the absence of hormone differences. And "our data do not lead to any explanation of homosexual behavior."[20]

The subject soldiers were "asked to write their own stories concerning their sexual habits." From reviewing the stories, the authors concluded these persons at Truax would probably be termed "overt homosexuals" according the cited standard work on bisexuality and homosexuality. The authors wrote, "Our subjects were all definitely aggressive in their homosexual activities." It was noted, "They had participated apparently without conflict in a wide variety of homosexual practices."[21]

That these homosexual soldiers had rejected the sickness theme of the medical model ascribed to them was clear. "In none of these cases was there a true neurotic type of conflict over the homosexuality as such." Further, "the cases would be extremely questionable from the standpoint of profiting from any therapy; in fact, therapy was not requested or desired by any of them."[22]

Yet this group of gay soldiers were realistic about understanding the homophobia surrounding them. "They expressed a realistic anxiety that their homosexuality would lead to court martial." The authors detected that gay soldiers had found identity through mutual support as a group, for "homosexual stories were remarkably similar." And they continued, "In fact four of them were known to be members of an organized group."[23]

The study led by Severinghaus had shown that homosexuals could be patriotic citizens, serving in the armed forces even when the welcome mat was not out. It also framed the discussion of homosexuals in the medical context, leaving out entirely the criminal frame with which Gillin had gone back and forth. The clear gay rejection of the medical model was surprising for its day.

THERAPEUTIC DISCIPLINE

After World War II, the number of student discipline cases involving homosexuals on the University of Wisconsin campus ballooned. Correspondence with other campuses indicated like increases. Dean C. R. Reuisili came across a paper titled "Knitting at the Guillotine: An Approach to the Therapeutic Handling of Discipline." The paper argued for a modern concept "that discipline is an educative process, corrective not punitive." The idea was "Careful therapeutic discipline can help the individual." He transmitted the paper to Professor Howard Jackson, head of the Student Conduct Committee, and this approach would infuse the University of Wisconsin campus weighing of homosexual cases.[24]

Dr. Annette Washburne was among those on the medical staff at Student Health who would be asked to implement this approach. Her opinion, however, was that "this kind of medicine is very slow." The campus reached an agreement with the Dane County district attorney and local judges that morals cases would require each student to report to Dr. Washburne, "not for further penalization, but for guidance and advice." In a paper outlining "therapeutic discipline," Washburne wrote, "Clinical psychologist and professional counselors must be available in making proper diagnosis and in carrying out appropriate remedial programs." Dr. Washburne had been involved with several students who participated in Haresfoot, a cross-dressing theatrical group on campus. She observed "dressing and clothing of the opposite sex tends to accentuate the problem of homosexuality."[25]

Some of the doctors at Student Health felt a student "will benefit rather well and rapidly from psychiatric help." Another felt a student was "amenable to psychiatric help." The Student Conduct Committee would most often refer these students to Student Health with the indication, "You were to receive psychiatric treatment indicating that you had been cured of your tendencies." Many were suspended from enrolling unless they successfully completed such treatment.[26]

As the decades progressed, the psychiatrists at Student Health changed their views. In 1962 a campus purge of homosexuals derived from investigations encouraged by Dean Ted Zillman caused a crisis. The minutes of the April 12, 1962, meeting of the Student Conduct and Appeals Committee confronted the problem. Most cases involving homosexuality had been handled by a smaller administrative group working with psychiatric reports from Student Health. Now this full committee meeting chaired by Law School professor Frank Remington was told that Dr. Herman Gladstone of Student Health "refused to remain a party to normal committee-department procedures apparently because of objections to the investigation and his staff's conviction that effective evaluation under stress circumstances was not possible." A result of this functioning of campus faculty governance was an understanding "that the University in the exercise of its disciplinary authority, should not be concerned with the homosexual orientation of a student, per se, any more than it is concerned with another student's heterosexual orientation."[27]

Thus therapeutic discipline had gone full circle from supposedly sympathetic psychiatric treatment to change individuals due to their so-called medical condition to a campus policy of equality about sexual orientation. Admittedly, attitudes changed slowly, but such a policy could encourage an acceptance of the status of homosexuality as a variant sexuality.

STUDENTS AS HOMOSEXUALS

In May 1951, Dr. Benjamin Glover published "Observations on Homosexuality among University Students" in the *Journal of Nervous and Mental Disease*. The 1954 book *The Homosexuals: As Seen by Themselves and Thirty Authorities* republished his article, giving it a broader circulation. A Chicago native, Glover studied at Northwestern, earning an MD in 1944. After serving in the US Navy from 1944 to 1946 he joined University of Wisconsin Student Health and became part of the psychiatry department and was thus involved with therapeutic discipline.[28]

Glover began by alerting readers, "Since the war there has been a noticeable increase in cases of homosexuality . . . among the general type of psychiatric problems seen in the University of Wisconsin Student Health Department.

A great majority of the cases have been veterans." Clearly he was presenting homosexuality in the medicalized psychiatric context. He also reinforced Sev- eringhaus's unveilings both that the military medical screening had failed and that homosexuals had been patriotic participants in the war. Five of the six veterans were homosexually active in the military though none "were intro- duced to homosexuality via the service."[29]

As a doctor, he held the theory that "fear, of course, is the basic mechanism which drives patients to doctors." Regarding those homosexuals voluntarily coming to Student Health, he wrote, "In the case of these individuals, who are usually first seen in a homosexual panic, there is intense fear of being caught, of being noticeably different." Thus he acknowledged without naming it that these gay men that he saw were suffering from the homophobia of society. Glover mentions such panics "were often times with publication of some local news item concerning exhibitionism or discovery of a group of consorting indi- viduals." Madison and the university had experienced just such an uncovering of a homosexual ring of consorting gay men in 1948 where at least a dozen individuals were in the press for morals charges and several students swept up were expelled. The same year also saw a quieter campus investigation into the presence of homosexuals among the cross-dressing theater group Haresfoot.[30]

When the campus police filed reports on alleged homosexual incidents, the procedure was to refer them to Student Health for psychiatric evaluation. Many of these cases involved men's restrooms where individuals were caught masturbating and peeking through partitions. Glover was one of the doctors who often handled these cases. In many instances, after a consultation, he gave the deans a standard reply—almost a rubber stamp since it was used repeat- edly. "Psychiatric opinion: Not psychotic, not homosexual, not a danger to themselves or to others, able to differentiate between right and wrong, and to act according to accepted social standards." For Glover, these would have fallen into his previously mentioned reference about increased exhibitionism rather than homosexuality. Student discipline also faced a number of peep- ing toms outside women's dorms. Both the peeping toms and the "not homo- sexuals" might face probation but were not up for expulsion. Diagnosed real homosexuals were often suspended until successfully completing approved psychiatric therapy. Thus there was a belief they might be adjusted or cured of a medical condition.[31]

This distinction about "true homosexuals" was in the Glover article as he used the term to describe the twelve student cases he chose to report. His qualifiers were that they could be called "overt performers of deviant sex prac- tices with their own sex by reason of personal choice, without coercion, with enjoyment—who frequently sought the haunts and company and engaged in the activities of other homosexuals." Glover also revealed a gay underworld that appeared to exist in the state. Glover excluded, besides the exhibitionist, and masturbators in semiprivate places, another seventeen cases of latent homosexuals "since they were without overt experience or were limited to a few trial episodes." As a number of students in the overall discipline cases for all these incidents were married, they might have been considered bisexuals.[32]

Glover gave credence to the concept that homosexual identity was inherent: "All . . . noticed they were different from others of their age group in childhood, and definitely in a different social category after puberty." A further observation: "Socially, these patients attained a fairly significant status." Glover wrote, "None expressed religious or racial prejudice." Further he observed, "two members consorted regularly with Negroes. One attempted to room with a Negro but owing to private and public reaction was prevented from doing so." Thus, the homosexual world could itself be integrated but a double animus could bear down on such integrated couples.[33]

In taking case histories, Glover was able to describe the homosexual world. "The city square at night is often a favorite place for picking up companions." And "taverns and bars were most often centers of congregation." Further, "movie theatre back seats are used as rendezvous." Glover, like Gillin, also observed, "Love is a commonplace word." Thus homosexuality might be seen as more than just carnal acts. Further, he noted, "each homosexual among the 12 felt that his present amour was a permanent one." And "they are devoted to their loves with an expressed passion."[34]

However, Glover wished to accept none of this world of homosexuals despite his touting of the supposed "non-judgmental" attitude of Student Health. "These people represent a parody and a paradox in emotions; in a sense they burlesque love as a heterosexual knows it and yet they are a continual tragedy of failure." He wrote that homosexuals had "a narcissistic selfishness." And despite the veterans of military service, he put forth that they had "no nationalistic or patriotic feeling." Glover clearly believed in the predominant norms faulting homosexuals for a lack of "ability to change actively to more socially acceptable sexual performance." Glover believed their "well-known instability and suicidal ideas indicate a large schizoid element in their personality." In places he describes them as possessing "deviant sex practices."[35]

Unfortunately for him, Glover had to report "poor psychotherapeutic results." His study, despite the negative attitudes, continued the placement of homosexuality in a medical rather than the criminal framework. Glover's research finding that homosexuality was not subject to easy change pointed to considering it an inherent condition.

Gender-Nonconforming Native Americans

In December 1953, Nancy Oestreich Lurie published an article on the "Winnebago Berdache" in the *American Anthropologist*. Both of the title terms are dated today, as the First Nation is now known as the Ho Chunk Tribe, and the word berdache is shunned in favor of the term "two-spirited." Lurie, a Milwaukee native, received her bachelor's degree from the University of Wisconsin and her doctorate from Northwestern University in 1952. She taught at the University of Wisconsin–Milwaukee (created in 1956) and was head of anthropology at the Milwaukee Public Museum. She served as an expert witness for tribal petitioners in the federal courts and was on the editorial board of *Handbook of North American Indians*.[36]

In her research Lurie claimed the two-spirit role was "still evident in Winnebago culture until close to the turn of the century." She put forth that this gender tradition showed a connection between Woodland and Plains Siouan groups. In 1953, she wrote that the last berdache had died fifty years before. She noted that the berdache "dressed as a woman, performed women's tasks better than any normal woman could perform them, and had the ability to foretell future events." The person was "a man who had taken on this role because he had been directed to do so by the moon, a female spirit at the time of his vision quest." One informant "mentioned that berdaches sometimes married other men, but no data were obtained concerning the attitude of the society toward the husband of a berdache." There was evidence of a two-spirited person acting as a foster mother. Changing attitudes were expressed. "Most informants felt that the berdache was at one time a highly honored and respected person, but that the Winnebago had become ashamed of the custom because the white people thought it amusing or evil." This borrowed antagonism was reflected in a comment. "By the time the last known berdache attempted to fulfill the role, his brothers threatened to kill him if he 'put on the skirt.'"[37]

In her article, Lurie alternated between the title term berdache and the Ho Chunk term *siange*. From the descriptions of her Native American informants, it was clear the vision quest was the determining factor in the First Nations. In her writing there was a real tension between this spirit-directed role and the ascription of the term berdache. The term berdache derived from French explorers who came in contact with the phenomenon and sought to name it from their own cultural context. The French word implied a male prostitute or catamite, and thus was dominated by a sexual meaning rather than a gender meaning. The Ho Chunk usage as reported by Lurie does not seem dominated by the European sense of sexuality or our modern notion of transsexuals. Certainly, however, most Wisconsinites would see her description of the two-spirited as a nonnormative identity.[38]

PSYCHIATRY PUBLISHES A FORUM ON HOMOSEXUALITY

In early 1973, Lorna Benjamin, editor of *Forum*, explained why in the period following the 1969 Stonewall uprising the Wisconsin Psychiatric Institute at the University of Wisconsin–Madison devoted a whole issue of their magazine *Forum* to a "Symposium on Homosexuality." She observed, "Homosexuals are regularly coming through our intake clinics, and wondered what kind of treatment they were getting." She recalled that an assumption of the day had been "homosexuality itself being regarded as sufficient reason for entering psychotherapy." She admitted to recently being involved with a case of lesbianism and had been impressed "by the apparent tenderness between these two women—their caring and lovingness surpasses that of many so-called 'normal' heterosexual relationships." Benjamin claimed the magazine issue presented "a wide variety of facts and opinions about homosexuality." One illustration in sync with post-Stonewall concepts showed an empty closet with an open door.[39]

The issue gave voice to several Madison gay and lesbian activists. Dale Hillerman, coordinator of the Gay Center in Madison, wrote "A Personal Perspective of the Gay Movement." He argued that the basic premise of gay activism was "coming out" and "realizing that there are common human bonds to be built between oneself and the other gay people." Prior to the present, the small homophile organizations "were, for the most part, unknown to gay people." Demand for openness and an end to oppression forced homosexuals "to discuss issues of our sexual identity." Judy Greenspan and two women who all worked at the Madison Women's Center contributed "An Overview of the Lesbian Movement." They correctly noted the danger in presuming male authority, commenting that the majority of the issue's authors were men. They explained the need for a separate lesbian group in the city because the gay men exhibited "the same sexist attitude . . . we received from the rest of society." They saw gay men sizing "up other men in the same way that men have been objectifying women for centuries." They felt gay men could learn from the feminist movement about collective consciousness raising. Recognizing that "lesbian" has been the worst label thrown at women, they felt feminist examinations of love and power relationships could make fundamental changes. For them, "the women's liberation movement has opened up possibilities of women responding to other women as whole persons."[40]

Other lesbian and gay perspectives were also presented. Sara Hummel, a student at the University of Wisconsin–Madison, discussed how lesbianism was an "uncomfortable subject for most people." She attacked the myth of lesbianism's nonexistence. While she admitted to having played straight through high school, "It was a bad game to play." At age nineteen she expressed her love for a woman. Meeting with other lesbians led to acceptance. Speaking to the psychiatric purposes of the issue, she wrote, "I don't need a cure, nor do I need a therapist implying, with psychological jargon, that I really should be cured."[41]

Steven Lubin, following a troubled upbringing in New York, came to Madison in 1970 to work on his doctorate. He found a Free University course on gay studies and then joined the gay liberation meetings and spoke to other classes. His lover was accepted by straight roommates. After moving to the University of Kentucky to teach human development, he realized he had lost all the advantages that Madison gays had achieved in creating counseling services and support organizations. He pleaded, "We must come to the realization that different is not necessarily the same as wrong." One other contributor listed as Anonymous proceeded to describe his sexual fluidity.[42]

Constitutional Rights Possible?

In August 1973 University of Wisconsin–Madison political science professor David Adamany, an expert in constitutional law, picked up the legal challenge for gay rights in Wisconsin. This was the landmark *Safransky* case. Adamany did his undergraduate work at Harvard and earned a JD there in 1961. Then he attended the University of Wisconsin–Madison for a PhD in Political Science in 1967 while teaching at the University of Wisconsin–Whitewater. After teaching at Wesleyan University, he was tenured as a professor of political science from 1972 to 1975 at the University of Wisconsin–Madison. He served Wisconsin governor Patrick Lucey (1971–77) as a close advisor and as the secretary of the Wisconsin Department of Revenue. Before taking up the *Safransky* case about employment discrimination he came out to Lucey as a gay man.[43]

Paul Safransky, a house parent for the mildly developmentally disabled at the state's Southern Colony near Racine, was fired in 1972 for being a homosexual. The State Personnel Board and a Dane County circuit court judge upheld the firing. The Personnel Board's finding that homosexuality was contrary to "Generally Acceptable Standards of Morality" was also upheld by the circuit court. Safransky was a self-affirming member of the Milwaukee Gay People's Union. Adamany joined the case on a pro bono basis on appeal to the Wisconsin Supreme Court.

The brief filed for Safransky emphasized several constitutional issues including those of due process under the Ninth and Fourteenth Amendments to the US Constitution. The due process claim was that self-avowed homosexuality was not a just cause for discharge. Dismissal required a job-performance reason, not mere status because of sexual orientation, and the firing and appeal process did not consider Safransky's job performance. To deprive someone of a job because of a status like race, religion, or sexual preference was "to deprive that person of life, liberty or property without due process of law." The brief cited a case (*Acanfora v. Montgomery Board of Education*) recently decided on May 31, 1973, in Maryland. That decision stated that "the time has now come for private, consenting, adult homosexuality to enter the sphere of constitutionally protected interests."[44]

One issue raised was that terminating someone's employment because of a self-avowal of homosexuality denied that individual's First Amendment right of free speech. As the brief noted, "He is not required to lie about his life, nor become a recluse, nor conceal pertinent facts." The brief noted that heterosexual employees discussed matters pertaining to their "personal lives and activities relating to sexual preference." Case law, Adamany argued, showed that "no restrictions can be imposed upon appellant's discussion of his personal beliefs and lifestyle if similar restrictions are not applied to other state employees." The argument was that "protecting co-workers from unpleasant subject matter" was not a state interest.[45]

Another First Amendment issue raised was that dismissal for Safransky's off-duty association with other homosexuals violated his constitutionally guaranteed freedom of association. Adamany cited several cases indicating that freedom of association extended even to homosexuals. Again, it was argued that no state interests were violated by having homosexual roommates, going to gay bars, or even in one instance being an unsalaried go-go dancer.[46]

Adamany successfully challenged the Personnel Board's finding that "Homosexual Activity is Contrary to Generally Acceptable Standards of Morality." His argument was that the Personnel Board had no judicially cognizable expertise in this field. Further, they had established no evidentiary record to support such a finding even if they had the capability. The brief then discussed "changing community attitudes toward homosexuals," citing mass media such as the movies *Sunday, Bloody Sunday* and *That Certain Summer,* as well as a *Marcus Welby, M.D.* television episode and the Public Broadcasting Service television series *The American Family.* Adamany noted homosexual magazines and newspapers circulated freely and cited a Wisconsin case where the Milwaukee police chief had tried and failed to suppress newspaper coverage of homosexuality.[47]

Adamany put forth that "in Wisconsin, homosexuality is not a crime." In an attempt to educate the judges, he pointed out, "Nor are certain homosexual sex acts, such as mutual masturbation of adults in private. Members of the same sex may embrace or kiss privately without running afoul of our law." This argument was significant because sodomy or sexual perversion was a criminal act during the 1970s with a five-year penalty, but its definition was explicit. Law enforcement was not the most enlightened on this point, as many police interrogatories in Madison of the 1950s and 1960s had asked, "Did you commit the homosexual act?" Gays had more imagination about acts than the cops, as the legal argument sought to establish.[48]

While the Wisconsin Supreme Court set aside the sweeping finding about homosexuals, it nevertheless found Safransky did not present a sufficient male image to be a houseparent. Basically, Adamany had brought out that the homosexual world and homosexual issues were much more complex than generally assumed. Most importantly, the premise of his argument was that homosexuals were citizens and thus had constitutionally protected rights just like everyone else. The Wisconsin Supreme Court was not ready to accept the argument.

BOTH CRIMINALIZATION AND SOME NEGATIVITY OVERTHROWN

In the 1970s and the early 1980s, the gay and lesbian community led the effort in Wisconsin to pass a consenting adults bill. It would decriminalize homosexual and other sexual acts committed in private by consenting adults. While the state's sexual perversion law forbade both oral sex and sodomy for heterosexuals and homosexuals, rulings by the Wisconsin Supreme Court made it clear in most heterosexual cases it would not be enforced. Cohabitation was another practice prohibited by state morality laws with occasional prosecutions in the press. During those years, the gay community created and led various sexual privacy coalitions to lobby for the law. Quietly gay Wisconsin State Assembly representatives David Clarenbach, Dick Flintrop, and Steve Gunderson all permitted their names to be used by at least one such coalition. These efforts had been preceded in the 1960s by the Wisconsin Young Democrats, a group that adopted a sex plank in 1966 urging such a consenting adults law. Milwaukee's African American state assemblyman Lloyd Barbee had introduced such bills each session since 1967. Barbee was a sexual reformer, especially on gay issues. In 1971, he introduced a gay rights law on nondiscrimination and what may have been the nation's first bill for same-sex marriage. One pushback to the consenting adults proposals was that while these were outdated laws they were not seriously being enforced anymore. So why waste political capital on reform? Here, Wisconsin academics came forward to prove this argument erroneous.[49]

Recall that Wisconsin state senator Howard Teasdale in 1913 had surveyed district attorneys in 1913. In 1979 Professor Martha Fineman of the University of Wisconsin–Madison Law School took up the survey instrument to district attorneys on cohabitation. Fifty-seven district attorneys, or 80 percent, responded to the query. She found forty-five counties had no prosecutions since 1973, but the twelve counties reporting had some ninety prosecutions. Twenty of these responding prosecutors indicated they wished to keep the law on the books, so at least eight who had not used the law still wanted it as a tool. Nearly half of the district attorneys had a policy of nonprosecution of cohabitation cases. Another fact revealed by the Fineman survey was that over one-third of the respondents felt that even if prosecution was only a remote occurrence, having the law "insures that people who cohabit will do so discreetly." Over one-fourth of the respondents felt the frequency of cohabitation would increase if the cohabitation law was repealed. Thus, Fineman revealed a substantial number of district attorneys still used and wished to keep morality laws. Her study would be cited several times during the legislative debates on the need for changed laws.[50]

The cohabitation issue was given another twist by Stephen J. Tordella of the Applied Population Laboratory connected with the Department of Rural Sociology at the University of Wisconsin–Madison. In 1980 he authored a paper based on census data, titled "'Living Together' in Wisconsin and the United States." To the legislature, he reported, "Approximately 22,000 Wisconsin households contained unrelated persons of opposite sexes who could be classified as 'living together.'" He cited national studies showing over one million such households, which "confirms these findings for Wisconsin." For the likelihood that sexual activity might take place, Tordella noted 60 percent of the women and 43 percent of the men were under age thirty in such opposite-sexed households. He concluded that "living together" was a "phenomenon affecting a significant proportion of the population."[51]

Louie Crew, a professor of English at the University of Wisconsin–Stevens Point, also did a survey of district attorneys on sex offenses and the prosecutions of homosexuals. Before coming to Wisconsin in 1973, Crew had been the editor of the groundbreaking book *The Gay Academic*. His survey of fifty-one district attorneys was released in 1981 as "Homosexuals and the Wisconsin Law." The largest counties in the state, including Milwaukee, Dane, Brown, and Outagamie, did not provide any statistical data. The Milwaukee district attorney was thought to be particularly antagonistic as evidenced by his remarks that included this: "At least several of the homicides in our county are believed to have been occasioned by homosexual motivation." Crew released statistical data for the three-year period from 1977 to 1979 for the responding counties, which represented only 32 percent of the state's population. He found eighty-three arrests with eighty-one prosecutions and seventy convictions. The most-reported activity had occurred in the counties of Eau Claire (thirty-three) and Waukesha (twenty-four). Thus, likely hundreds of gay men regularly were caught up in prosecutions across the state. So much for non-use of the so-called archaic laws.[52]

Crew believed all counties "have their usual quota of lesbians and gay men, and presumably they are not all celibate. The effect of the law, even when it is not enforced, is to legitimize the stigma against them, often to force them into an involuntary kind of self-oppression, making them live in constant fear of exposure and reprisals." Crew's work was touted in gay and lesbian media in the state but was not reported in the debates like Fineman's work.[53]

In 1983 the legislature did pass a consenting adults bill. The academic work had shown the sexual privacy rights of many Wisconsin citizens were actually attacked by such outdated laws and policies. That there was a presumed right to sexual privacy was also a groundbreaking change. The energy for consenting adults legislation was harnessed in 1982 to pass the nation's first state gay rights law outlawing discrimination on the basis of sexual orientation in employment, housing, and public accommodations.[54]

Decriminalization was just one part of the success in the decade of the 1980s, with a whole raft of legislation favorable to the LGBT community. The gay rights bill was followed by a law assuring that school services would be provided to students on a nondiscriminatory basis with regard to sexual orientation. A hate crimes penalty enhancement passed in the 1980s also included sexual orientation. Human immunodeficiency virus (HIV) testing confidentiality, a measure required as acquired immune deficiency syndrome (AIDS) made its presence known, was the fifth major piece of pro-gay legislation in this one decade. By uncovering data on the state's homosexuals and putting forth analyses that suggested something beyond criminal behavior, University of Wisconsin academic exploration paved the way to expand the social boundaries of who Wisconsinites were.

CONCLUSION

University of Wisconsin academics studied and explained a homosexual world that existed throughout Wisconsin during the twentieth century. At first this was an underworld clearly connected to criminality. The framing of homosexual acts and their social realities shifted from the Wisconsin criminologist and sociologist to the medical doctors and the psychologists as the century progressed. Academic discourse moved the focus on homosexuals from the carnal acts described in criminal law to an identity or inherent qualities of a social type based on orientation. While this framing often remained predominantly negative, it did offer new options about how to conceive of relationships among LGBT individuals and how to change ideas about them.

Following the 1969 Stonewall uprising, the positive voices of LGBT individuals entered the discussion. Claiming social status, citizenship, and the rights of citizens, they demanded changes in the laws. They used knowledge of their own lives to discuss the dimensions of identity and their commonality in shared human experience. Wisconsin responded positively, moving the state forward. If the Wisconsin Idea could be renewed as shown in this case to expand the social boundaries of the state to include LGBT folks, who knows what other rethinking may be possible? Unlike geographic boundaries, these social boundaries can be constantly expanded. Following the 1980s, other Wisconsin academics would go on to generate further exploration of LGBT issues, continuing to expand both knowledge and social boundaries.

NOTES

1. President Van Hise's comments are memorialized on the University of Wisconsin–Madison campus with a plaque donated by the class of 2012.

2. A review of the series of Madison police reports (incomplete) held at the City of Madison Police Department, Madison, Wisconsin, undertaken by the author. The Milwaukee reports (incomplete) are available at the Milwaukee Public Library, Milwaukee, Wisconsin.

3. Matthew J. Prigee, "The 'Girl-Man' of Milwaukee," *Wisconsin Magazine of History* 96, no. 3 (Spring 2013): 12–27; City of Madison Police Annual Reports.

4. Brief of Plaintiff in Error, Brief of Defendant in Error: Cases and Briefs, vol. 796, Means v. State, 125 Wis. 650; Verhaalen v. State, *Wisconsin Reports*, 195 Wis. 345; Gutenkunst v. State, 218 Wis. 53-126. All in Wisconsin State Law Library, Madison, Wisconsin.

5. David J. Pivar, *Purity Crusade: Sexual Morality and Social Control, 1868–1900* (Westport, CT: Greenwood Press, 1974). Milwaukee was included in the "homosexual capitals" by Xaxier Mayne (pseudonym), *The Intersexes: A History of Similisexualism as a Problem in Social Life* (n.p.: privately printed, [1908?]), quoted in John Lauritsen and David Thorstad, *The Early Homosexual Rights Movement (1864–1935)* (New York: Times Change Press, 1974), 36. Scott Herring, *Queering the Underworld: Slumming, Literature, and the Undoing of Lesbian and Gay History* (Chicago: University of Chicago Press, 2007).

6. Paul Hass, "Sin in Wisconsin: The Teasdale Vice Committee of 1913," *Wisconsin Magazine of History* 49, no. 2 (Winter 1965–66): 138–51. The report was published as *Report and Recommendations of the Wisconsin Legislative Committee to Investigate the White Slave Traffic and Kindred Subjects* (Madison: The Committee, 1914), hereafter cited as *Wisconsin Vice Report*, http://content.wisconsinhistory.org/cdm/ref/collection/tp/id/26592.

7. "Statement of E. A. Ross, Professor of Sociology at the University of Wisconsin," *Wisconsin Vice Report*, 185–94.

8. "Statement of E. A. Ross," Edward Alsworth Ross Papers, 1859–1969, Wisconsin Historical Society Archives, Madison, Wisconsin.

9. "Statement of E. A. Ross."

10. Victor Berger testimony, *Wisconsin Vice Report*.

11. John L. Gillin Papers, 1890–1958, University of Wisconsin–Madison Archives, Steenbock Library, series 7/33/4 45D9-E6; John L. Gillin, *The Wisconsin Prisoner: Studies in Crimogenesis* (Madison: University of Wisconsin Press, 1946). Philip La Follette was elected governor of Wisconsin as a member of the Republican Party in 1930 and then as a member of the Progressive Party in 1934.

12. Gillin, *Wisconsin Prisoner*.

13. Gillin, *Wisconsin Prisoner*, 38–87, 90–96.

14. Gillin, *Wisconsin Prisoner*, 90–94.

15. Gillin, *Wisconsin Prisoner*, 90–94.

16. Gillin, *Wisconsin Prisoner*, 90–94.

17. Gillin, *Wisconsin Prisoner*, 90–94, 97–98.

18. Elmer L. Severinghaus, 1894–1980: An Autobiographical and Biographical Collection, Wisconsin Historical Society State Archives, Madison, Wisconsin; E. L. Severinghaus and John Chornyak, "A Study of Homosexual Males," *Psychosomatic Medicine* 7 (September 1945): 302–5, reprinted in *Journal of Nervous and Mental Disease* 105, no. 5 (May 1947). Chornyak appears in "Society Transactions: Philadelphia Psychiatric Society," *Archives of Neurology and Psychiatry* (March 13, 1936): 193.

19. Severinghaus and Chornyak, "Study of Homosexual Males."

20. Severinghaus and Chornyak, "Study of Homosexual Males"; Allan Berube, *Coming Out under Fire: The History of Gay Men and Women in World War Two* (New York: Free Press, 1990).

21. Severinghaus and Chornyak, "Study of Homosexual Males."

22. Severinghaus and Chornyak, "Study of Homosexual Males."

23. Severinghaus and Chornyak, "Study of Homosexual Males."

24. Letter from C. H. Ruedisili to Professor Howard C. Jackson, April 19, 1948, with enclosure, University of Wisconsin–Madison Archives, Student Affairs Discipline Records, series 19/5/1. These files are loosely organized, sometimes by committee actions and also by named students; confidentiality concerns mean no student names are used here.

25. Annette Clarke Washburne Scrapbook and Publications, University of Wisconsin–Madison Archives, Steenbock Library, Accession 2006/146 54D8.

26. University of Wisconsin–Madison Archives, Student Conduct Files, Student Affairs Discipline Records, series 19/5/1. These files are loosely organized chronologically, with individual student-named files and various committee minutes. Due to confidentiality, student-named files are not here identified.

27. Ron McCrea, interview on "Madison Gay Purge," first appeared in *Renaissance Newsletter*, Madison Gay Center, reprinted in *Midwest Gay Academic Journal* 1, no. 3

(1978): 25–30, University of Wisconsin–Madison Archives, Student Conduct Files, Student Affairs Discipline Records, series 19/5/1.

28. Benjamin Glover, "Observations on Homosexuality among University Students," in *The Homosexuals: As Seen by Themselves and Thirty Authorities*, ed. A. M. Krich (New York: Citadel, 1954).

29. Glover, "Observations on Homosexuality."

30. Glover, "Observations on Homosexuality."

31. Glover, "Observations on Homosexuality."

32. Glover, "Observations on Homosexuality."

33. Glover, "Observations on Homosexuality."

34. Glover, "Observations on Homosexuality."

35. Glover, "Observations on Homosexuality."

36. Wisconsin Academy of Sciences, Arts and Letters, "Nancy O. Lurie," https://www.wisconsinacademy.org/contributor/nancy-o-lurie; Wikipedia, "Nancy Oestreich Lurie," https://en.wikipedia.org/wiki/Nancy_Oestreich_Lurie.

37. Nancy Oestreich Lurie, "Winnebago Berdache," *American Anthropologist* 55, no. 5, pt. 1 (December 1953): 708–12.

38. Lurie, "Winnebago Berdache."

39. "Symposium on Homosexuality," *Forum*, Wisconsin Psychiatric Institute, University of Wisconsin–Madison, November 1973, in Rich Fleutching Papers, University of Wisconsin–Madison Archives, LGBT Collection (hereafter cited as *Forum*).

40. Dale Hillerman, "A Personal Perspective of the Gay Movement," *Forum*, 9–10; Judy Greenspan, "An Overview of the Lesbian Movement," *Forum*, 11–12.

41. Sara Hummel, *Forum*, 33–34.

42. Steven Lubinin, *Forum*, 35–36.

43. David Adamany Papers, 1936–1998, Wisconsin Historical Society Archives, Madison, Wisconsin. David Adamany, personal communication to the author.

44. "Appellants Brief and Appendix," Paul R. Safransky v. State Personnel Board, Wisconsin Supreme Court, August Term 1973, No. 349, submitted by Todd J. Mitchell and David Adamany, Attorneys for Appellant, 1 to 40, Wisconsin State Law Library, Madison, Wisconsin.

45. "Appellants Brief and Appendix," Paul R. Safransky v. State Personnel Board.

46. "Appellants Brief and Appendix," Paul R. Safransky v. State Personnel Board.

47. "Appellants Brief and Appendix," Paul R. Safransky v. State Personnel Board.

48. "Appellants Brief and Appendix," Paul R. Safransky v. State Personnel Board; University of Wisconsin–Madison Archives, Student Affairs Discipline Records, series 19/5/1.

49. Andrea Rottmann, "Passing Gay Rights in Wisconsin, 1967–1983" (PhD diss., Freie Universität Berlin, 2010), see section 3.4, "1978."

50. Martha Fineman memorandum and attachment from Lynn Sarko of University of Wisconsin–Madison Law School to Criminal Justice and Public Safety Committee members, dated August 15, 1979, in David E. Clarenbach Papers, 1974–1992, Wisconsin Historical Society Archives, Madison, Wisconsin.

51. Stephen J. Tordella to David Clarenbach, copy of memorandum dated March 4, 1980, in David E. Clarenbach Papers, 1974–1992, Box 2/3, Wisconsin Historical Society Archives, Madison, Wisconsin.

52. Louie Crew, "Homosexuals and Wisconsin Law," *Our Horizons*, December 9, 1981.

53. Crew, "Homosexuals and Wisconsin Law."

54. Rottmann, "Passing Gay Rights"; R. Richard Wagner, *We've Been Here All Along: Wisconsin's Early Gay History* (Madison: Wisconsin Historical Society Press, 2019).

Then and Now

Taking the Wisconsin Idea to the State Capitol

KAREN BOGENSCHNEIDER

The precise origin of the Wisconsin Idea, as with many innovative concepts, is hard to pinpoint. Despite its obscure origins over a century ago, it took root in the fertile soil of Wisconsin and has grown into an enduring and esteemed tradition. This idea of university outreach and service to the state—widely known as making the boundaries of the university the boundaries of the state—has become a source of pride among policymakers and the people of Wisconsin. The most prominent early manifestations of the Wisconsin Idea appear to be several cooperative connections between the university campus and the state capitol.[1] The focus of this chapter is whether the Wisconsin Idea continues to inspire efforts to connect the University of Wisconsin–Madison, one of the largest research organizations in the United States, to the Wisconsin legislature, a preeminent policy institution in the state. To examine whether these political roots still exist, this paper compares the effectiveness of an earlier example of the Wisconsin Idea (the 1911 Wisconsin legislature) and a contemporary effort that has operated in Wisconsin over the last quarter century (the Family Impact Seminars). Researcher and policymaker perspectives are presented—both then and now—on the commitment to the Wisconsin Idea, as well as the rationale and approach for bringing together these two great institutions.

I argue that the Wisconsin Idea continues to this day, but with less surety and success. A full examination of the reasons that the Wisconsin Idea today has lost luster from its legendary roots is beyond the scope of this chapter. However, some insights may emerge from my personal musings of what it is like to be a faculty member in the arena central to the Wisconsin Idea—where one professorial foot is entrenched in the research community and the other firmly planted in the policy community. This chapter describes my experience working as a knowledge broker in the no-man's-land between the hallowed walls of the university and the harried halls of the state capitol. The chapter explores the joys and challenges of working at close quarters with policymakers and

the ways in which the university encourages and discourages efforts to keep
the policy connections of the Wisconsin Idea alive and thriving. This analysis
concludes with what actions it might take to restore the Wisconsin Idea to its
original political prominence.

EARLY EFFORTS TO OPERATIONALIZE THE WISCONSIN IDEA:
THE 1911 WISCONSIN LEGISLATURE

In the political arena, one remarkable early example of the Wisconsin Idea
was the 1911 legislature.[2] Civil servant Charles McCarthy, an early champion
of the Wisconsin Idea introduced in previous chapters of this volume, alleged
that the 1911 session of the Wisconsin legislature may have been the most
remarkable ever held in a state. To support this audacious claim, McCarthy
referenced both the processes and products of policymaking—"the daring
manner in which great questions were handled" and the landmark laws that
were enacted.[3]

In his 1912 book, *The Wisconsin Idea*, McCarthy observed firsthand how
the legislative and executive branches of government worked closely with the
university on legislation to tackle tough issues of the times. The 1911 legislature
enacted the nation's first workable income tax and workers' compensation
laws and introduced the nation's first minimum-wage bill that subsequently
passed in 1913. Other accomplishments included laws that (a) limited working
hours of women and children; (b) developed standards to make workplaces
safer; (c) established conservation practices for state forest lands; and (d) created
a state life insurance program to guard against sickness, death, accident, and
incapacity. Working with Wisconsin policymakers, university labor economists
also drafted legislation on collective bargaining, industrial regulation, income
maintenance, unemployment insurance, and health insurance. The debate over
these bills extended to the Ohio and New York legislatures and directly shaped
the New Deal social legislation enacted almost three decades later.[4]

The 1911 legislature also was notable for passing laws that served to improve
the policy process itself. Since 1901, the nonpartisan service agency, the Legislative Reference Library (later Bureau), had been tasked with wresting control
over the writing of state laws from corporate interests. In 1912, McCarthy, the
bureau's chief, clearly stated the rationale for investing in the policy process:
"If business interests have excellent lawyers to look after their legislation, the
people should secure the same kind of men to help their representatives. If the
business interests secure statisticians, engineers and scientific men, the public
should do likewise."[5] The 1911 legislature passed strict rules to avoid corruption
in the drafting, processing, and publication of bills. For example, a revision

committee was created to check each bill at every stage of the policy process, and dishonest clerks were prevented from changing the bill at the behest of interested parties. To help ensure that lawmaking was not shrouded in secrecy, committee hearings were scheduled in advance, the exact status of every bill was published in a weekly bulletin, and the votes of each member were recorded.[6]

The Early Twentieth-Century Commitment to the Wisconsin Idea

This remarkable legislative session occurred during a period in history when the issues policymakers confronted were thought to call for expert knowledge. As observed by the influential historian Frederick J. Turner, who began his career at the University of Wisconsin: "The industrial conditions which shape society are too complex, problems of labor, finance, [and] social reform too difficult to be dealt with intelligently and wisely without the leadership of highly educated men familiar with the legislation and literature on social questions in other states and nations."[7] The 1911 Wisconsin legislature convened at a time when the political and intellectual climate in Wisconsin was conducive to collaboration and communication between its state university and its state government. The complexity of state problems together with a receptivity to reform fostered a mutual commitment to the Wisconsin Idea.

The Commitment of the University of Wisconsin to the Wisconsin Idea

The academic climate for the Wisconsin Idea was shaped by university leadership.[8] University president Charles Van Hise (1903–18), in particular, had a solid grasp of its theoretical roots: "It is not enough for knowledge to exist in books to be obtained by men under favorable circumstances; the knowledge must be carried out to the people."[9] University president Thomas C. Chamberlin (1887–92) had a firm command of its practical significance as he set forth at Van Hise's inauguration in 1904: "I hold that it is a legitimate function of the state to train boys to be farmers, yet I believe it to be a much higher and truer function . . . to increase the intellectual activity of every farmer, to improve the agricultural art on every farm, and by such improved art, to furnish better and safer food to every citizen."[10]

During his tenure, Van Hise became known for his insight in transforming the theory of the Wisconsin Idea into practice.[11] For instance, Van Hise strongly advocated for applied research on state problems, vigorously supported the university's Extension Division, and routinely encouraged faculty members and university administrators to serve in state government. Jack Stark, the author of a 1995 essay on the Wisconsin Idea that is discussed in the introductory chapter of this volume, detailed a litany of roles that professors played in 1906 in service to the government as selectively illustrated here:

The professor of bacteriology is a member of the state Live Stock Sanitary Board. The professor of railway engineering has been an aid to the Tax Commission and the Railroad Commission. . . . A professor of political science is chairman of the Civil Service Commission. A professor in the department of political economy has been carrying on investigations for the Tax Commission. . . . The president of the University is president of the Geological Survey Commission, president of the Forestry Commission, and a member of the Free Library Commission.[12]

The contributions that the university made to the state—conducting applied research to solve practical problems, training teachers and public leaders, and graduating an enlightened citizenry—were considered a "safeguard" to democracy. At the time, the university's mission was to serve the whole of society rather than the sole interests of individuals. According to McCarthy, this responsiveness of universities to serving the needs of the state also served the needs of the university:

Certainly the teacher of political science or political economy who is worthy of consultation upon governmental matters can give the students a better idea of those great subjects than some mossback whose theoretical learning was acquired by carefully keeping away from the only laboratory which could be of any service to him. . . . Why then have a professor of political economy [or] political science teach classes in governmental matters when he has never worked at the practical solution of any of the great economic or political questions of the day?[13]

The Commitment of Wisconsin Policymakers to the Wisconsin Idea

The potential of applying the Wisconsin Idea to public policy was apparent from its earliest days. As observed by historian Frederick J. Turner: "The best hope of intelligent and principled progress in economic and social legislation and administration lies in the increasing influence of American universities."[14] In 1911, under the leadership of a Republican governor and a Republican-controlled legislature, the climate at the state capitol was receptive to research. Perhaps this receptivity was best evidenced by the 1910 platform of the Republican Party: "We are proud of the high eminence attained by our state university. . . . We commend its research work. . . . We regard the university as the people's servant, carrying knowledge and assistance to the homes and farms and workplaces."[15] This public acclaim for a university that was committed to using research for the benefit of the people and the good of the state extended well beyond Wisconsin. Theodore Roosevelt, the twenty-sixth president (1901–9) of the United States, was quoted as saying in 1911: "In no other state in the union has any university done the same work for the community that has been done in Wisconsin by the University of Wisconsin."[16]

In firsthand accounts, observers were moved by how receptive the 1911 legislature was to research. In the words of Selig Perlman, a University of Wisconsin economist and labor historian: "That was the most remarkable thing, the faith in education. . . . They were so friendly to the university experts. . . . It really was a most inspiring thing."[17] In fact, the contributions of the university were so substantial that the reformer Frederic C. Howe, author of a book on Wisconsin politics in 1912, characterized the university as "the fourth department of the state."[18]

The Early Twentieth-Century Rationale and Approach for Operationalizing the Wisconsin Idea

In 1912, universities that received public funding were perceived as having a duty to provide expert help on the complex problems facing society in labor, finance, and social reform.[19] The hope was that through research on the issues of the day, legislation could be "made better and be placed upon a more scientific basis."[20] For research-based policy to be realized, McCarthy recognized that busy policymakers would need access to condensed and reliable research on policy responses to the problems of the day:

> Everything which will help him to grasp and understand the great economic problems of the day in their fullest significance, the legislative remedies which can be applied and the legislative limitations which exist is brought to his attention. The legislator is a busy man; he has no time to read. . . . He is obliged to hold conferences with his friends upon political matters; he is besieged by office-seekers and lobbyists and he has no time for study. If he does not investigate for himself, he often is deceived by those who are seeking the accomplishment of their own selfish ends. Therefore, we can be of the greatest service to him, if we index, digest and make as clear as possible all kinds of information.[21]

The approach that was used to provide information to legislators was described by McCarthy, who was both an instructor at the University of Wisconsin (1905–17) and the chief of the nonpartisan Legislative Reference Bureau: "We are not trying to influence our legislators in any way, we are not upon one side or another of any question nor are we for or against anybody or anything. . . . Question after question asked of us by the legislature is investigated in as scientific a manner as time and means permit."[22] McCarthy observed that members of the legislature were pleased to consult with professors on questions ranging from tuberculosis to the regulation of monopolies. Never in his experience did he recall hearing a criticism of the advice of professors, even when they were engaged by private corporations.

CONTEMPORARY EFFORTS TO OPERATIONALIZE THE WISCONSIN IDEA: THE FAMILY IMPACT SEMINARS

The political tradition of the Wisconsin Idea was exemplified and extended by a contemporary effort to connect the research produced at universities to policy decisions made in state legislatures: the Family Impact Seminars. The seminars began in Wisconsin in 1992 and were directly inspired by the Wisconsin Idea. I came to play a leading role in this effort after I was hired in a joint appointment as an assistant professor in Human Development and Family Studies at the University of Wisconsin–Madison and as an Extension Family Policy Specialist for the University of Wisconsin–Extension. The expectation from the university was that I would study, teach, and do family policy in ways that would fulfill the academic standards of my tenure home at the University of Wisconsin–Madison.

The seminars were the brainchild of policy analyst Theodora Ooms, the first director of the Family Impact Seminar. In the 1970s, she began an ongoing series of presentations, discussion sessions, and briefing reports in the nation's capital to communicate high-quality and nonpartisan research to policymakers on timely topics. I decided to explore extending this model, originally developed for the US Congress, to a state legislature. In 1992, the University of Wisconsin–Extension lobbyist at the time, Mark Lederer, was at a meeting at the Wisconsin state capitol with several legislative leaders when one lamented, "Whatever happened to the Wisconsin Idea?" This experienced lobbyist set up appointments for this inexperienced assistant professor with six legislators in key positions such as the Majority Leader of the Wisconsin State Senate, chair of the Higher Education Committee, chair of the Children and Families Committee, and so forth. The lobbyist began each conversation by reminding the legislator of the recent reminiscing over the waning of the Wisconsin Idea. We explained that the Family Impact Seminars could be a political reincarnation of that century-long tradition. The response from legislators was so enthusiastic that they entreated us to expeditiously convene the first seminar and, to a person, each one agreed to serve on an advisory committee to guide the planning. The Wisconsin Family Impact Seminars was born. In short order, the first seminar was held in Wisconsin in 1993.

The methodology of the Family Impact Seminars includes a two-hour convening held at the state capitol that features three presentations by a panel of premier researchers with about one-fourth of the time allocated to policymakers'

questions. The seminar is accompanied by a thirty- to fifty-page briefing report with chapters from each of the speakers summarizing relevant research and
its policy implications. Discussion sessions follow, some that are targeted to
state legislators, some to high-ranking state agency officials, and some to governors or first ladies.[23]

As detailed in a recent article, the Family Impact Seminars are a complex
innovation. A passionate leader is required who is willing to make a long-term
commitment to building relationships with policymakers. This manualized
program distinguishes itself from other interest groups as summarized here:

- providing research on what policymakers are thinking about (not what seminar
  organizers wish they were thinking about);
- using an educational, nonadvocacy approach (in an otherwise influence-driven
  culture);
- establishing a neutral, nonpartisan environment for dialogue across party lines
  (without the presence of lobbyists and the press who quickly politicize policy
  debate);
- translating research in the accessible, nonpartisan style that policymakers prefer
  (rather than spinning the results for a particular political purpose); and
- analyzing policy and practice through the lens of an underrepresented population with the potential for fostering common ground (families, particularly the
  vulnerable).[24]

Track Record of the Wisconsin Family Impact Seminars

To date, thirty-eight seminars have been held in Wisconsin on family issues,
broadly defined to include economic issues (e.g., growing the state economy,
jobs, evidence-based budgeting, youth workforce development), health care
(e.g., covering the uninsured, improving health care quality, long-term care),
and big-ticket items (corrections, education). The seminars have addressed
controversial issues (e.g., Medicaid, tax policy) and often focus on vulnerable
children, youth, and families (e.g., foster care, prisoner re-entry). Since its
inception, seminar evaluations have produced convincing evidence of instrumental, conceptual, and institutional impacts, each discussed in turn below.

Instrumental Impacts of the Family Impact Seminars

Only an inexperienced observer would think that a complex, multiply determined policy decision is a result of a single input, such as the seminars. Yet it
also would be naïve to ignore the instances when seminar research was likely
factored into policy decisions. For example, Wisconsin's senior prescription

drug law that passed in 2001, shortly after two seminars on the topic, included four features of other states' prescription drug programs discussed at the seminar. A legislator explained how seminar information improved his understanding of this timely issue:

> We didn't have a prescription drug plan in the state, so this was a timely seminar because we were in the process of making decisions on what it should be. . . . [The seminars] had experts come in and talk to us and tell us what other states were doing, [and told us] "If you're going to do it, you have to spend enough money to make it worthwhile. Otherwise, don't do it," [because] it's going to cost a heck of a lot more in a couple years than you ever dreamed. . . . They were right.[25]

Seminar research was also valuable to executive agency officials who ultimately would bear responsibility for administering the program, which in 2019 enrolled 87,000 Wisconsin seniors. A follow-up discussion session was attended by eleven officials from the highest echelons of the Wisconsin Department of Health and Family Services. The meeting began with pointed questions by the state secretary, who had read the entire briefing report. Each participant rated the discussion session a perfect five on a score of one (poor) to five (excellent) (with a 50 percent response rate).

Other examples of instrumental impacts include a 2010 jobs law that included five provisions that were discussed extensively at a seminar. The seminars also contributed to laws on advanced manufacturing-skills training, alternative diplomas for disengaged students, home visiting, long-term care insurance, youth tobacco use, workforce training for low-income workers, and so forth. Seminar impact also included legislation that failed to become law, particularly bills that research evidence suggests may be ineffective, such as employer purchasing pools and criminalization of substance use during pregnancy.

The conceptual and institutional impacts discussed below are drawn from an evaluation of a seminar held in January 2014 at the state capitol. This seminar, *The Science of Early Brain Development: A Foundation for the Success of Our Children and the State Economy*, attracted ninety-eight participants, including twenty-six legislators (about half Republican and half Democratic), twenty legislative aides, Wisconsin's first lady, ten staff of the nonpartisan legislative service agencies, twenty-two executive agency leaders and staff, six members of the court system, and five university or extension faculty. The data presented here are taken from the follow-up phone evaluations conducted three to five months after the seminar with eighteen legislators who participated in the seminar (with a 69 percent response rate).

Conceptual Impacts of the Family Impact Seminars

The seminars demonstrated a conceptual impact on a critical challenge facing the United States: the drift toward hyper-partisan and interest-driven politics. One component of the seminar methodology is convening an invitation-only luncheon discussion for legislators in a nonpartisan, off-the-record setting to discuss the research presented at the seminar; in evaluations, these discussions foster the building of relationships with colleagues and the finding of common ground. In the follow-up evaluation, 50 percent of legislators reported that, because of the seminars, they were "quite a bit" more likely to get to know their colleagues on the other side of the aisle. Such informal opportunities to build relationships are rare, which is surprising given that connections with colleagues are essential for being effective in the relationship-based policy culture.[26] As put by a state legislator: "the Family Impact Seminars are very valuable in pulling legislators together from both houses and both parties. I was really surprised by how many legislators were there . . . who were interested in the topic. There will be a lot more opportunity to get policy on this issue that is truly bipartisan."[27]

The follow-up evaluations also indicated that the seminars changed attitudes about research and researchers. Because of the seminars, 83 percent of legislators reported being "quite a bit" more likely to see the practical value of research, and 72 percent reported being "quite a bit" more likely to see researchers as approachable. A legislative aide reported using seminar research to draft seven different bills soon after the program, whereas a legislator mentioned more long-term effects on legislation: "Poverty, education, and health issues are all linked through early brain development. Poverty affects brain development which, in turn, affects health which, in turn, affects school which, in turn, affects poverty. I want to work toward legislation that connects those dots." Another legislator mentioned the added value when relevant research comes from a reliable source: "Bringing in world-renowned experts really impressed me with the research." These attitudinal shifts about research and researchers are important because they transcend any single seminar or any specific topic and dispel stereotypes about arrogant academics who are out of touch with society's pressing problems.

Institutional Impacts of the Family Impact Seminars

According to a former state senator, it is difficult to fix the policy issues that citizens care about without fixing government itself.[28] In evaluations, the seminars have improved not only the products of policymaking but also the policy process. For example, the seminars have yielded a track record of providing research that has fostered more productive policy debate and discourse.

One legislator explained the value of having ready access to research whenever an occasion arises to discuss policy alternatives: "I carry around the [seminar] report on the economic development programs that states can do. It has useful information on the most effective tools. Tax incentives are not effective. When I need research to back up a point, I rely on the Family Impact Seminars."[29]

In Wisconsin, the seminars have moved beyond being only a source of fact-based information to being seen as an institutional mechanism for improving communication and collaboration across partisan and ideological lines. A Democratic state senator explained how critically important this is in the policy culture:

> I've also come to realize that we tend not to make decisions either as voters or as legislators based on facts. We tend to make them based on emotion. Emotion tends to override reason. So we need to find ways of delivering facts, information, and research in a way that breaks down those barriers, that opens our minds to what the research tells us. . . . How do you break down the ideological and the partisan barriers that prevent us from communicating effectively? I think that institutional frameworks such as the Family Impact Seminars are extraordinarily beneficial in making that happen . . . in creating that institutional framework by which we can have a discussion across the partisan and ideological divides that often separate us, unnecessarily. Because what I find . . . is that we have more commonality than differences. But our differences are what keep us from coming to effective solutions.

The capacity of the seminars to engender civility and mutual respect have not gone unnoticed outside the legislature. Bill Kraus, a former co-chair of Common Cause, a nonpartisan organization that promotes good government, wrote about the seminars in an unsolicited blog:

> Through the decades the participants in Karen's seminars have found that ideologies and personalities recede in the process and the atmosphere that Karen's seminars create. The goal becomes finding solutions rather than seeking political advantage. One of the most noticeable and welcome side effects of these sessions is that they dispel the notions that anti-intellectualism is rampant on one end of State Street [the legislature] and unintelligent intellectualism dominates on the other end [the university]. Because the seminars are only about solutions, they somehow engender civility and mutual respect as well. They are also a latter day re-creation of the once famous Wisconsin Idea where the contributions of the academy were welcome in the halls of power.[30]

The seminars also have influenced the formation of other institutional mechanisms for overcoming partisan barriers, such as the legislature's bipartisan
study committees that bring legislators and experts together to discuss issues
and draft legislation. According to a press release issued by two state legislators, the early brain science seminar was credited as "one of the major reasons"
for forming a legislative council committee on supporting healthy early brain
development.[31] Similarly, the impetus for a legislative study committee on
jobs was attributed to the interest created by a Family Impact Seminar on the
topic.[32]

This chapter presents policy impacts in Wisconsin, but the Family Impact
Seminars are an example of a program inspired by the Wisconsin Idea that
reached well beyond the boundaries of the state. In 1999, I was invited to assume
leadership of the national Family Impact Seminar and its mission of building capacity for research-based family policy. I redirected its focus from the
US Congress to state legislatures and began recruiting and training faculty/
extension leaders for state seminar sites across the country. The seminars have
proven to be similarly effective in a couple of dozen states that vary widely in
institutional configuration, political ideation, and partisan polarization.[33]

The Twenty-First-Century Commitment
to the Wisconsin Idea

The following discussion of university and policymaker commitment to the
Wisconsin Idea is viewed through the lens of the Family Impact Seminars.
Granted, this lens is narrow, but it is nonetheless informative.

Commitment of the University of Wisconsin
to the Family Impact Seminars

University administrators recognized the value of the seminars for building better relationships at the state capitol. For example, Peyton Smith, former assistant
vice chancellor and coordinator of the Wisconsin Idea Project at the University
of Wisconsin–Madison, heard about the seminars from legislators: "I have been
told by both Republicans and Democrats about the good work of [the] Family
Impact Seminars. In fact, [four Wisconsin legislators] specifically mentioned we
should do more along the lines of Professor Bogenschneider's Family Impact
Seminars . . . when I asked them how UW–Madison could improve its relationships with the state. Those testimonials are not easy to come by."[34] Other
campus administrators saw the potential of the seminars for building better
public policy. In the words of Thomas Corbett, former acting director of the
Institute for Research on Poverty at the University of Wisconsin–Madison:
"The Wisconsin Family Impact Seminars have been superbly administered

and creatively managed. They consistently attract large numbers of legislators and other policymakers and get high marks for relevance and objectivity.
I can think of no other activity done at the University that affects social policy
in Wisconsin as much as the Family Impact Seminars."[35]

Over time, administrative support for the Family Impact Seminars has been
uneven. For example, in 1992, University of Wisconsin–Extension and the
University of Wisconsin–Madison School of Human Ecology supported my
faculty position as a Family Policy Specialist. While some financial support
for the operation of the seminars has come from university departments and
institutes, most was raised from foundations: Annie E. Casey, A. L. Mailman,
Helen Bader, Lynde and Harry Bradley, W. K. Kellogg, and William T. Grant.
Most recently, the operational costs of the seminars have come from a $531,000
endowment provided by a private philanthropist and one of my former University of Wisconsin–Extension Family Living colleagues, the late Phyllis M.
Northway, and her husband Donald Northway.

Upon my retirement in 2017, university priorities had changed, and the position description for my position was refocused from family policy to family
diversity; without support from Extension or the School of Human Ecology,
this change virtually eliminated faculty leadership for the state and national
seminar programs. Powerful state legislators began inquiring about the future
of the Wisconsin Family Impact Seminars, and the University of Wisconsin–
Madison chancellor's office provided financial support for an academic staff
person at the university's Robert M. La Follette School of Public Affairs to lead
the program. Purdue University and Purdue Extension stepped up to provide
leadership for the national seminar effort.

Commitment of State Policymakers to the Family Impact Seminars

Perhaps the most convincing evidence of policymakers' interest in the seminars
is what is colloquially referred to as "voting with their feet." In the 2015–16
biennium (when I transferred leadership for the seminars), eighty of 132 Wisconsin legislators participated in seminar activities, and thirteen of those not
participating sent an aide. In other words, the seminars engaged 70 percent of
legislative offices. This high level of participation may reflect the consistently
high exit evaluations over the years. On a scale of one (poor) to five (excellent),
the average objectivity rating of the seminars was 4.3; notably, this high rating
for objectivity did not come at the expense of relevance to policymakers' needs
and interests (4.4) or usefulness in their current role (4.2).

In follow-up evaluations from the early brain science seminar, policymakers described several specific contributions of seminar research to their job as a
policymaker. Almost eight of ten legislators reported incorporating the research

into their speeches and presentations (i.e., the researchers' ideas became their ideas), over seven in ten shared information with colleagues, almost four in ten used seminar research to evaluate pending legislation, and almost three in ten used the research to draft new legislation. Legislators also described the larger contribution of seminar research to policy decisions: "It will help in the future to produce policy that's the best in the field, using the available evidence." Legislators also offered unsolicited comments on the role that the Family Impact Seminars play as an honest broker of research. According to one legislator, "[I am] really thrilled that this already exist[s]. If it didn't, I'd make it an initiative on my own!" Without prompting, another legislator relayed: "I think the seminars are very important and I want to make sure that we maintain them."[36]

The Twenty-First-Century Rationale and Approach for Operationalizing the Wisconsin Family Impact Seminars

From the perspective of academics, the rationale for the Family Impact Seminars is how satisfying and gratifying it is for scholars when studies make their way out of the pages of scholarly journals and into the hands of those who can bring them to bear on policy decisions.[37] For policymakers, one of many stated values of the seminars is having ready access to rigorous research. According to a Republican state senator: "The state capitol is loaded with politics. It's not loaded with scientific research or people who have studied these issues from across the country. So, what happens is we hear from a number of well-respected folks who know the issue inside and out, and we get information that we never, ever get an opportunity to hear otherwise."[38]

One trademark of the Family Impact Seminars is its strict adherence to a nonadvocacy educational approach. Instead of making policy recommendations, the seminars encourage speakers to provide a range of policy options and research evidence on the consequences of each. One legislative aide, in the follow-up evaluation of the early brain science seminar, described the contribution this nonpartisan, deliberately dispassionate approach was able to make in their influence-driven environment: "Early Childhood Education, in terms of funding and scale, in our world, is usually viewed through a partisan lens, but this was so nonpartisan and helpful/refreshing to have. I feel like I can use this in conversation with other offices who we are approaching to draft legislation."

ANALYSIS OF EARLY AND CONTEMPORARY EFFORTS TO TAKE THE WISCONSIN IDEA TO THE STATE CAPITOL

Are the connections advanced by the Wisconsin Idea between the state's flagship university and the state capitol still needed today? Since the turn of the twentieth century, the university has changed, and its culture has adapted to contemporary conditions. The legislature and its culture have not remained static. Is the need for connections between the research being produced at the university and the policies being passed at the state capitol as important now as then? I argue that the complex economic, social, and political challenges Wisconsin faces have changed, but the need for research to inform public policy decisions still remains.

Is the Wisconsin Idea as strong today as it was during the turn of the twentieth century? The consensus among faculty, nonpartisan analysts, and policymakers appears to be that the Wisconsin Idea has strayed in recent years from its original mission. In 1992, a faculty member and highly-placed administrator at the University of Wisconsin–Madison, Bryant Kearl, gave a speech that he provocatively called, "Who Killed the Wisconsin Idea?"[39] He contended that the Idea had faded with the 1962 restructuring of Extension during a time when faculty were experiencing too many demands on their time and the public was making too few requests for assistance. Similarly, in a definitive 1995 essay on the history of the Wisconsin Idea, the nonpartisan legislative analyst Jack Stark concluded that "the Idea was stronger in some earlier eras than it is now."[40] In 2012, a state legislator described the Wisconsin Idea as "the greatest discovery ever," yet bemoaned the fact that these two institutions geographically located "only a mile apart" now seem culturally "like they're 1,000 miles apart."[41] This chapter reaches a similar conclusion. Political manifestations of the Wisconsin Idea will not automatically happen without institutional structures designed to overcome the cultural barriers that erode communication and trust between researchers and policymakers.[42]

In today's hyperpartisan political environment, the record of one such institutional structure, the Family Impact Seminars, could be characterized as remarkable in its record of communicating research to policymakers and influencing the processes and products of policymaking. Yet few would claim that the laws influenced by the Family Impact Seminars are as groundbreaking as the landmark legislation enacted by the 1911 legislature that subsequently became models across the nation. I doubt that any recent US president would echo the words of Theodore Roosevelt in commending the University of Wisconsin–Madison for doing more work for the community than any other state university in the Union. It seems incredulous that any professor today would claim that the Wisconsin legislature's faith in education and friendliness to the university are "a most inspiring thing," as Selig Perlman did in 1911.

Why has the Wisconsin Idea lost some of its original political luster, despite remaining a household term among policymakers and the public? Although not intended to be an exhaustive analysis, I will lay bare in this section some of the joys and discouragements that I experienced in working at close quarters with policymakers and the ways in which the culture of the university encourages and discourages policy outreach. Policymaker perspectives in this section and throughout the rest of the chapter derive from a recent study of all state legislators in Wisconsin in the 2015–17 biennium and half of Indiana's 150-member legislature. In Round One, we conducted 123 face-to-face, semi-structured interviews of legislators inquiring about their research use, relationships with colleagues, and partisan polarization, with a 60 percent response rate. In Round Two, we interviewed eighty-nine legislators nominated by their colleagues in Round One as exemplary research users, relationship builders, or youth or family champions, with an 84 percent response rate.[43]

The Joys and Challenges of Working with Policymakers

In twenty-four years of working on the seminars, I experienced more joys than discouragements from being "in the arena" conceived by the Wisconsin Idea. Of course, it is discouraging that the seminars do not work for all policy questions and that research cannot solve all political disputes. I am disappointed when a seminar provides relevant research on a topic of bipartisan interest and still does not move the policy needle. Yet I find myself ecstatic when, on occasion, the seminars have contributed to policy decisions that have changed conditions for hundreds or thousands of citizens across the state. Nothing is more satisfying than being a small part of making such a large difference in people's lives. I also take satisfaction in knowing that the seminars have changed policymakers' attitudes about research and researchers, and also have provided a venue for researchers to build productive working relationships with policymakers. My investment of time and resources was well worth the discouragements I encountered: the immutability of timing, the inability to move policy issues forward, the crowded schedules of busy policymakers, and the polarization of politics.

The Immutability of Timing

One of the biggest challenges of working with policymakers is being on the right topic at the right time with the right research. Based on the political scientist John W. Kingdon's theory of open policy windows, we have developed a systematic planning process with three main steps: (1) individual interviews of twelve legislators and one gubernatorial staffer, (2) a face-to-face meeting of a dozen or more university and high-ranking executive agency officials who specialize in the issue, and (3) follow-up contacts with legislators to determine political and economic feasibility.[44] The data from this environmental scan is used to design the seminar and to coach the speakers on tailoring their presentations to the questions raised by state policymakers. Despite this painstaking care in developing each seminar, the politics can change quickly in the fluid, fast-paced policy world. For example, in 2006, we spent six months planning a seminar on long-term care. A couple of weeks before the scheduled event, Wisconsin's governor scaled back the reach of his long-term care initiative from a statewide effort to a pilot project in a couple of counties. In 2010, two weeks before a recipient of the Nobel Peace Prize spoke about jobs for a clean energy economy, green jobs became so highly politicized that all parties agreed no legislation would move forward on this topic that year.

The Inability to Move Policy Issues Forward

A second challenge of policy outreach is wondering why issues do not move forward even when a seminar does focus on the right topic at the right time with the right research. For instance, in response to policymakers' expressed interest in youth job preparation, a 2013 seminar featured a dynamic presentation by the principal investigator for Career Academies, a strongly evaluated and highly successful model for helping youth transition into work and family life. The Career Academy program was attractive to liberals because it was an evidence-based approach for improving the labor market outcomes of high-risk young men. It was attractive to conservatives because it appeared to build personal responsibility among male graduates, who were more likely to be married, custodial parents, and living independently with their children. The research presentation was supplemented with remarks from a school-based career and technical education coordinator, who explained its benefits to high-risk students in Milwaukee. A representative from the Harley-Davidson Motor Company explained the benefits to business of preparing local youth for employment. Yet despite rigorous research evidence and the support of the public and private sectors, no legislation moved forward to more broadly implement Career Academies beyond its four sites in Wisconsin. Perhaps the timing was not quite right. Perhaps it was not a priority of the Wisconsin Department of Public Instruction. Perhaps teachers were uncomfortable with the scheduling changes the program entailed. Or, as one legislator proposed recently in our study, perhaps the policy ran counter to political interests or to the prevailing philosophy of government:

> The majority party [Democrat or Republican] seems to be more willing to override local control . . . in recent years, it seems to me, you don't want to have any examples of a successful program at the local level that runs contrary to your ideology or to some sort of a base that you support. . . . I think there's also a philosophy of government which is . . . what is the role of government? . . . And

if you feel like there's a limited role in government to provide for the welfare
of people, and people are responsible for their own welfare, then some of these
programs . . . even though they're very successful, they run contrary to your
philosophy. . . . There's also special interests that want to . . . nip something in
the bud because if it's successful locally, then it could . . . migrate up to being a
state or national policy.[45]

The Crowded Schedules of Busy Policymakers

Another challenge of the Family Impact Seminars is the diligent efforts it takes
to attract policymakers to a research seminar, even one in the state capitol
designed specifically for them. To attract a busy legislator takes intensive marketing, typically about four contacts with each legislative office.[46] Personally,
I have attributed legislators' lack of participation less to lack of interest in
research and more to the fluidity and pace of a legislator's life. Their schedules
are crowded. For example, a senator relayed in our recent study that, in one day,
he testified in three different committees on seven different bills. And he quickly
added that hardly an evening went by that he didn't have five different meetings with constituents in five different locations. In this regard, the lives of
legislators in the early 1900s seem similar to the busy lives of legislators today.[47]

To revitalize the Wisconsin Idea, policymakers would need to make research
opportunities a priority. Just as researchers need to extend respect and an open
mind to policymakers, policymakers could avoid stereotyping researchers as
all being cut from the same liberal cloth. In the face of complex issues, policymakers need to exhibit curiosity and stay open to the findings of research (as
many already do), even when they diverge from their preexisting positions. The
age-old divide of government versus personal responsibility needs to be treated
with some skepticism, given that it may be an outdated straw man that fails
to hold up to the complex and multiply determined nature of contemporary
problems. Many of the most vexing policy issues may involve government and
personal responsibility, and entail a both/and political response, as acknowledged by contemporary outreach scholars.[48]

The Polarization of Politics

A final challenge of working closely with policymakers is that research, no
matter how rigorous, may not carry the day because of the polarized environment in which policymakers operate. In a study based on data from the mid-
1990s to 2009, Wisconsin was ranked in statistical modelling as the sixth most
politically polarized state in the nation.[49] Despite the seminars' meticulous
contact with policymakers to select topics of bipartisan interest, power politics

can end up trumping any influence of research. In the words of a legislator in our recent study: "In that situation, no amount of research, no amount of facts will change their mind. Because they were not to be persuaded."[50]

In this era of unprecedented polarization, policymakers may need to take steps to reduce partisan gridlock. Wisconsin state senator Mark Miller (D-Monona) recently proposed an innovative idea that has not been tried in any state in the nation: establishing a legislative institution designed to serve as a catalyst for enhancing trust among legislators of different parties.[51] The institution could create a safe venue for discussion among researchers and policymakers that would help legislators identify potential allies who are sincere in seeking a policy solution. The institution's leadership would need to be rigorously nonpartisan, trusted, and responsive to legislators' needs rather than outside agendas. Based on experience with the seminars, universities may be one of the few institutions that could serve as an honest broker to help foster more trust within legislative bodies and to minimize partisan gridlock.[52]

The Ways the University Encourages and Discourages Outreach to Policymakers

First, I want to acknowledge the university and university Extension for providing the fertile ground over the last quarter century that fostered the development of the Wisconsin Family Impact Seminars and that facilitated its dissemination to a couple of dozen states across the country. The university has encouraged policy outreach in many ways. Unfortunately, it discourages such efforts in other ways, which I discuss here. I am cognizant that the question—the commitment of the university to the Wisconsin Idea—does not have a monolithic answer. In general, I have found university administrators tend to be more interested than deans or faculty members in building research-policy connections. Some schools and faculty are more interested and supportive than others are. Because interest is uneven, I raise several questions that university administrators, schools, institutes, departments, and faculty can use to assess commitment to the political connections inspired by the Wisconsin Idea. These four questions will undoubtedly raise heterogeneous responses across the university regarding the relevance of research, the establishment of policy outreach as a science, the positioning of and reward structures for policy outreach, and the approach used to engage policymakers.

Could More Be Done to Conduct Research Relevant to the World of Policy?

This question raises a conundrum. When asked, most faculty believe that their research contributes to important societal issues. Yet foundation presidents, policy analysts, and policymakers often complain to me that university research does not address society's most pressing challenges. For example, Duncan Watts, who has worked in the professoriate and now at Microsoft, claims that "the vast majority of academic social science research continues to be conducted in isolation of its potential applications in business, government, and policy."[53] Knowledge brokers like Thomas Corbett have criticized researchers for looking through the rearview window at research that has been conducted in the past, rather than focusing on what is coming down the road right in front of them.[54] Similarly, a policymaker in our recent study challenged researchers to be less "insular": "It cannot be that the point of academia is just to talk to other academics about cool, neat stuff that we're learning."[55]

One big mistake that researchers make, according to the most effective seminar speakers in one of our studies, is getting the question wrong.[56] Researchers could ask themselves whether they have taken deliberate steps to identify the questions percolating up from the real world. For example, are researchers speaking with policymakers or with knowledge brokers to determine which questions are on the horizon? Are researchers reaching beyond their own disciplinary silos and methodological boxes to form the tightly coordinated, multidisciplinary teams that the business sector uses to solve problems?[57] Are today's researchers following in the footsteps of those in the early 1900s by seeking out service on committees and boards in the legislature, in executive agencies, and in the nonprofit sector to bring them face-to-face with those on the front lines confronting real-world problems?

Could More Be Done to Produce Research and Theory around the Communication and Use of Science in Policymaking?

The pediatrician and Harvard University professor Jack Shonkoff has called for the academy to capitalize on its comparative advantage as knowledge producers to make the communication and use of research a science unto itself.[58] Yet the scientific evidence on whether research is used in policymaking is thin, which "reflects more an absence of evidence rather than an evidence of absence."[59] Little theoretical and empirical knowledge exists to evaluate the effectiveness of knowledge brokering and to improve future outreach efforts.

Research and theory also remain sparse on three main theoretical dimensions of research utilization in policymaking—the inhabitants, institutions, and cultures of policymaking.[60] Regarding the inhabitants of policymaking, learning about the target audience is not a new concept. In education circles, knowing one's audience is a general principle of good teaching, and social work practice has long pointed to beginning where the client is. Yet on-site studies of policymakers are rare, often referring to the political scientist Richard Fenno's study of members of the US Congress that dates back to the 1960s.[61] Similarly, few studies exist on the policymaking institution itself, specifically what protocols and practices shape decision-making in an elected body and how decisions are affected by institutional structures such as the influence of leadership and the functioning of committees. Little is known about how decisions are made in the relationship-based culture of policymaking, a venue ripe for studies of information flow by epistemologists, relationship scientists, and cognitive psychologists.

Where Are the Functions of Policy Outreach Positioned in the University and What Is the Reward Structure?

The rewards in academic culture are heavily slanted toward publication in peer-reviewed journals targeted to discipline-specific colleagues.[62] The criteria for tenure include gaining an international reputation, according to a professor at the University of Wisconsin–Madison. She emphasized how hard it is to become internationally recognized if your studies focus on Wisconsin—a very white and very midwestern state that has little to do with the rest of the nation and the world: "It's hard to get famous doing that. . . . We're going to have to find other incentives to try to ensure that the faculty and students do focus on the issues of the state."[63] Another disincentive to research on state issues is the decline in public dollars for university and university Extension; shrinking public support forces researchers to seek outside funding that often demands basic research on issues that have implications beyond a single state.

The standard metrics of university rank and rewards can be used to assess the value placed on policy outreach in the university culture. For example, is policy outreach a function valued enough to be performed by faculty or is it assigned to academic staff? Is policy outreach a shared responsibility among faculty and staff or assigned to a single individual to manage for the entire unit?[64] In the faculty merit system, is there a ready way to reward research when it is published as reports targeted to policymakers rather than articles aimed at academic colleagues? Is outreach teaching that takes the form of research seminars convened for policymakers given comparable credit to classroom teaching conducted for students?

Another standard metric of commitment to the Wisconsin Idea is assessing how the university allocates human resources. For example, do administrators allocate staff to lobbyist positions to advance university interests or to policy educators to respond to policymaker interests? Are teaching assistants assigned to outreach efforts like the seminars to prepare the next generation of policy-minded scholars? Are publication editors and press offices tasked to collaborate with researchers to write accessible research reports for policymakers? Are event coordinators made available to assist with the logistical arrangements for organizing research seminars for policymakers? And the list goes on.

Which Approach Do Researchers Use to Engage Policymakers?

In an era of unprecedented partisan polarization, it is important to ask whether researchers approach policymakers as nonpartisan educators or as advocates. Are faculty able to resist moving beyond the confines of their data to advocate for a particular position in line with their personal political predilections? In our recent study, a Democratic legislator described a trend away from the nonpartisan stances that traditionally have differentiated the university from other interest groups: "I think not unique to Wisconsin but certainly taking shape in Wisconsin is a sense that the academy has picked a side as far as the political fight has gone and that, I think, has made it difficult to sort of remove what many see as a bias. . . . But that isn't always the case."[65] If this policymaker is right, this trend toward partisan engagement is a clear departure from the nonpartisan approach university faculty used at the turn of the century.

SUMMARY

The Wisconsin Idea has long captured the public imagination of what it means for universities to be engaged institutions that both generate research and disseminate it beyond the boundaries of the campus to help address the economic, social, and political challenges of the state.[66] Many administrators remain convinced that researchers have an obligation to connect with policymakers, particularly those situated in land-grant universities like the University of Wisconsin–Madison. According to Dave Riley, a former associate dean of outreach in the university's School of Human Ecology: "Simply put, if a gap exists between scholars and public policymakers, then much of the promise of the land-grant mission is lost. Through her research, Prof. Bogenschneider is beginning to build a bridge across that gap, not just for herself, but for every scientist and scholar whose work deserves a hearing in the halls of power. . . . [This serves to] invigorate the promise of the land-grant mission."[67]

Policymakers also remain enthusiastic about the promise of the Wisconsin Idea. In recent interviews for our study, one legislator called the Wisconsin Idea a "serious part of the Wisconsin tradition" and another considered it central to the university mission: "The University of Wisconsin started with the Wisconsin Idea. And if you want to quickly tear down the University . . .

you pull that one block out and it will come tumbling down." Another legislator reported that the Wisconsin Idea, for him, "really inspired my view of good public policy" through its "storied history of using the investment that we're making in the university to help inform good policy solutions with that expertise." He speculated about what he could do to rekindle and renew the political prominence of the Wisconsin Idea:

> I've even thought about [whether there] is something I could propose as a legislator to reinvigorate the Wisconsin Idea. . . . The problem is when the state university was founded in the nineteenth century it was a state institution. . . . But now the people are worried about research, you've got all these international students, it's different. You couldn't sort of do what Charles McCarthy did in 1911 the same way today, right? And so [it is not clear] even how to reinvigorate it and make the Wisconsin Idea more robust and try to get more contributions of evidence-based research into public policy. . . . I don't have any definitive answers, but I will have some questions about how to do it.[68]

From this cursory examination of two prominent political examples (out of many) in Wisconsin history when the Wisconsin Idea worked as its founders envisioned, several themes emerged about what it would take to move beyond isolated examples to establish the institutional structures that can make cross-cultural communication between researchers and policymakers a way of life. For example, universities could take steps to more systematically elevate and reward policy outreach with the same reverence and resources accorded to research. Researchers could consider more seriously the policy relevance of their studies and could assume responsibility for reaching out to policymakers with openness, curiosity, and an offer of assistance. Instead of asking policymakers to support the interests of the university, researchers could ask policymakers how the university could support their interests in building better public policy for the people of the state. Policymakers, too, could reach out beyond the legislature to researchers with an openness and curiosity about what contributions research could make to their decisions. Policymakers also may need to work within the legislature to address the partisan gridlock that threatens the influence of research and the capacity to find common ground.

Revitalizing the political tradition of the Wisconsin Idea, however, will take more than research-minded policymakers and policy-minded researchers, because the legislature and the university (to a lesser degree) are responsive to public perceptions of these two great institutions. If the public called for the legislature and the university to work together to build research-based public policy in the tradition of the Wisconsin Idea, I believe that researchers and policymakers would respond.

But the public, like the university and the legislature, is caught in the tight grip of stereotypes both of its elected officials and public university faculty. These stereotypes cannot be dispelled with minimal or superficial exposure but will take one-on-one citizen engagement with the state's public servants at the legislature and at the university.[69] The readers of this volume each have a role to play in getting to know a legislator or two and a couple of faculty members. In my close work with policymakers over the last quarter century, I have come to know many dedicated, hardworking legislators who are committed to doing the right thing and to making research-based decisions to improve the lives of citizens in the state. In my work on the Family Impact Seminars, I have come to know amazing researchers who have spent their careers tackling tough issues such as improving the attachment of babies to their mothers in vulnerable families, changing the odds that foster children will experience economic success and fulfilling lives, and reforming the juvenile justice system by incorporating the science of how adolescents make decisions.

The Wisconsin Idea has endured for well over a century as one of those generative ideas that has inspired numerous political partnerships. The enthusiasm of policymakers about the Wisconsin Idea gives me hope that it may be restored to its original luster. Yet the onus for preserving the Wisconsin Idea may well lie at the feet of university researchers. Just as the political tradition illustrated by the 1911 legislature inspired today's Family Impact Seminars, researchers may be inspired by an age-old analogy of the university's plant pathology department that still rings true today. Like any ancient piece of lore, this analogy was preserved in the department's history, published in 1885 under the title of *One Foot in the Furrow*. This may be a metaphor for the Wisconsin Idea. Some of our best and brightest faculty should keep one foot in the furrow—the real world where problems can be found—and the other foot in the laboratory—the science world where solutions can be found.[70]

Even as policymaking has become more cynical and partisan, I remain hopeful that we can continue the tradition of taking the Wisconsin Idea to the state capitol. When one takes a historical look at policymaking, as I did in this chapter, one thing is certain: policymaking is fickle. Policy issues rise and fall on the political agenda, policymakers are sworn in and voted out, and the prevailing political winds can shift direction at the voters' discretion in every election.[71] I take heart that today's contentious political times too shall pass. We must continue to nurture that great tradition of the Wisconsin Idea, so the legend of research-based policy of the past remains a guiding light for the future.

NOTES

1. John O. (Jack) Stark, *The Wisconsin Idea: The University's Service to the State* (Madison: Legislative Reference Bureau, 1995). Reprinted from the *State of Wisconsin 1995–1996 Blue Book*, ed. Lawrence S. Barish (Madison: Wisconsin Legislative Reference Bureau, 1995), http://digital.library.wisc.edu/1711.dl/WI.WIBlueBk1995.

2. Stark, *Wisconsin Idea.*

3. Charles McCarthy, *The Wisconsin Idea* (New York: Macmillan, 1912), 273.

4. Harold L. Wilensky, "Social Science and the Public Agenda: Reflections on the Relation of Knowledge to Policy in the United States and Abroad," *Journal of Health Politics, Policy and Law* 22, no. 5 (1997): 1241–65.

5. McCarthy, *Wisconsin Idea*, 224.

6. McCarthy, *Wisconsin Idea.*

7. Quotation from McCarthy, *Wisconsin Idea*, 139.

8. Stark, *Wisconsin Idea.*

9. Quotation from Stark, *Wisconsin Idea*, 146.

10. Quotation from Stark, *Wisconsin Idea*, 114.

11. Stark, *Wisconsin Idea.*

12. Stark, *Wisconsin Idea*, 142.

13. McCarthy, *Wisconsin Idea*, 138.

14. Quotation from McCarthy, *Wisconsin Idea*, 140.

15. Stark, *Wisconsin Idea*, 111.

16. Stark, *Wisconsin Idea*, 1.

17. Quotation from Stark, *Wisconsin Idea*, 111.

18. Quotation from Stark, *Wisconsin Idea*, 4.

19. McCarthy, *Wisconsin Idea.*

20. McCarthy, *Wisconsin Idea*, 224.

21. McCarthy, *Wisconsin Idea*, 216.

22. McCarthy, *Wisconsin Idea*, 228–29.

23. Karen Bogenschneider, "Positioning Universities as Honest Knowledge Brokers: Best Practices for Communicating Research to Policymakers," *Family Relations* 67 (2018): 1–16, doi: 10.1111/fare.12339.

24. Bogenschneider, "Positioning Universities," 13.

25. Videotaped interview conducted in 2003.

26. Karen Bogenschneider, Thomas J. Corbett, and Emily Parrott, "Realizing the Promise of Research in Policymaking: Theoretical Guidance Grounded in Policymaker Perspectives," *Journal of Family Theory and Review* 11, no. 1 (2019): 127–47; Vivian Tseng, "The Uses of Research in Policy and Practice," *Social Policy Report* 26, no. 2 (2012): 1–16.

27. This and subsequent quotations in this section are taken from the follow-up phone evaluations conducted with eighteen state legislators (response rate = 69 percent) three to five months after the Thirty-Second Family Impact Seminar, *The Science of Early Brain Development: A Foundation for the Success of Our Children and the State Economy*, which was held in January 2014 in Madison, Wisconsin.

28. Tim Cullen (D-Janesville), comments at the celebration of life for William Kraus, Madison, Wisconsin, January 2019.

29. This and subsequent quotations in this section are taken from the follow-up phone evaluations conducted with state legislators after the Thirty-Second Family Impact Seminar. See n. 27.

30. B. Kraus, "Peace through Seminar" (blog post), FightingBob.com, December 22, 2013.

31. *Wheeler Report* (Madison: Wheeler News Service), June 11, 2014.

32. Karen Bogenschneider, Hilary Shager, Olivia Little, and Stephanie Eddy, "Connecting Research and Policy: The Story of a Wisconsin Family Impact Seminar on Jobs," in *Researcher–Policymaker Collaboration: Strategies for Launching and Sustaining Successful Partnerships*, ed. Jenni W. Owen and Anita M. Larson (New York: Routledge / Taylor and Francis Group, 2017), 102–20.

33. Karen Bogenschneider, *Family Policy Matters: How Policymaking Affects Families and What Professionals Can Do*, 3rd ed. (New York: Routledge, Taylor & Francis Group, 2014).

34. Peyton Smith, written nomination for an award to the Board of Human Sciences, National Association of State Universities and Land Grant Colleges, 2008.

35. Thomas J. Corbett, written nomination for an award to the Board of Human Sciences, National Association of State Universities and Land Grant Colleges, 2008.

36. This quotation is taken from the follow-up phone evaluations conducted with state legislators after the Thirty-Second Family Impact Seminar. See n. 27.

37. Thomas Grisso and Laurence Steinberg, "Between a Rock and a Soft Place: Developmental Research and the Child Advocacy Process," *Journal of Clinical Child and Adolescent Psychology* 34 (2005): 619–27.

38. This quotation is taken from the follow-up phone evaluations conducted with state legislators after the Thirty-Second Family Impact Seminar. See n. 27.

39. Stark, *Wisconsin Idea*, 164.

40. Stark, *Wisconsin Idea*, 164.

41. Cory Mason (D-Racine), "What the Wisconsin Idea Should or Could Mean" (panel presentation, University of Wisconsin–Madison, March 2012), https://www.pbs.org/video/university-place-what-wisconsin-idea-should-or-could-mean-ep-707/.

42. Bogenschneider et al., "Promise of Research in Policymaking."

43. Karen Bogenschneider, Elizabeth Day, and Emily Parrott, "Revisiting Theory on Research Use: Turning to Policymakers for Fresh Insights," *American Psychologist* 74, no. 7 (2019): 778–93.

44. John W. Kingdon, *Agendas, Alternatives, and Public Policies*, 2nd ed. (New York: Longman, 2003).

45. Quotation from an interview conducted in 2016 as part of a study of state legislators in Indiana and Wisconsin. For details of the study, see Bogenschneider et al., "Promise of Research in Policymaking."

46. Bogenschneider, "Positioning Universities."

47. From an interview conducted in 2016 as part of a study of state legislators in Indiana and Wisconsin. See n. 45.

48. William J. Doherty, "Influencing Policy through Relationships with Legislators," *Journal of Family Theory and Review* 11, no. 1 (2019): 157–60.

49. Boris Shor and Nolan McCarty, "The Ideological Mapping of American Legislatures," *American Political Science Review* 105, no. 3 (2011): 530–51.

50. Quotation from an interview conducted in 2016 as part of a study of state legislators in Indiana and Wisconsin. See n. 45.

51. Mark Miller, "Commentary on 'Realizing the Promise of Research in Policymaking,'" *Journal of Family Theory and Review* 11, no. 1 (2019): 148–50.

52. Bogenschneider, "Positioning Universities."

53. Duncan J. Watts, "Should Social Science Be More Solution-Oriented?" *Nature Human Behavior* 1, no. 1 (2017): 1–5.

54. Tom Corbett, *Confessions of an Accidental Scholar* (Fort Smith, AR: Hancock Press, 2018).

55. Quotation from an interview conducted in 2016 as part of a study of state legislators in Indiana and Wisconsin. See n. 45.

56. Bettina Friese and Karen Bogenschneider, "The Voice of Experience: How Social Scientists Bring Research to Bear on Family Policymaking," *Family Relations* 58 (2009): 229–43.

57. Watts, "Social Science?"

58. Jack Shonkoff, "Evaluating Early Childhood Services: What's Really Behind the Curtain," *Evaluation Exchange* 10, no. 2 (2004): 3–4.

59. Sandra M. Nutley, Isabel Walter, and Huw T. O. Davies, *Using Evidence: How Research Can Inform Public Services* (Bristol, UK: Policy Press, 2007), 3.

60. Bogenschneider et al., "Promise of Research in Policymaking."

61. David R. Mayhew, "Theorizing about Congress," in *The Oxford Handbook of the American Congress*, ed. George C. Edwards III, Frances E. Lee, and Eric Schickler (New York: Oxford University Press, 2011), 875–93.

62. Watts, "Social Science?"

63. Sara Goldrick-Rab, "What the Wisconsin Idea Should or Could Mean" (panel presentation, University of Wisconsin–Madison, March 2012), https://www.pbs.org/video/university-place-what-wisconsin-idea-should-or-could-mean-ep-707/.

64. A. T. Bednarek, C. Wyborn, C. Cvitanovic, R. Meyer, R. M. Colvin, P. F. E. Addison, S. L. Close, K. Curran, M. Farooque, E. Goldman, D. Hart, H. Mannix, B. McGreavy, A. Parris, S. Posner, C. Robinson, M. Ryan, and P. Leith, "Boundary Spanning at the Science-Policy Interface: The Practitioner's Perspectives," *Sustainability Science* 13 (2018): 1175–83.

65. Quotation from an interview conducted in 2016 as part of a study of state legislators in Indiana and Wisconsin. See n. 45.

66. Kellogg Commission, *Returning to Our Roots: The Engaged Institution* (Washington, DC: National Association of State Universities and Land-Grant Colleges, 1999).

67. Dave Riley, written nomination for an award to the Board of Human Sciences, National Association of State Universities and Land Grant Colleges, 2008.

68. Quotation from an interview conducted in 2016 as part of a study of state legislators in Indiana and Wisconsin. See n. 45.

69. Amy Chua, *Political Tribes: Group Instinct and the Fate of Nations* (New York: Penguin Press, 2018).

70. Stark, *Wisconsin Idea*.

71. Karen Bogenschneider and Thomas J. Corbett, *Evidence-Based Policymaking: Insights from Policy-Minded Researchers and Research-Minded Policymakers* (New York: Taylor & Francis, 2010).

The Power to Change Lives

The UW Odyssey Project

EMILY AUERBACH

"The Odyssey Project helped me unwrap my gifts and rewrite the story of my life," wrote an African American man starting over after incarceration and homelessness. "Transformative education" and "lifelong learning" are not just slogans or catch phrases for the faculty and staff of the University of Wisconsin–Madison Odyssey Project: they capture a reality happening each Wednesday night in a low-income neighborhood in Madison, Wisconsin, as we offer a free, two-semester, six-credit humanities course designed to empower adults at the poverty level to overcome adversity and achieve dreams through higher education. Our hard-won successes over the past seventeen years of the program may offer insights to others around the world seeking to raise retention rates for low-income, first-generation college students from racially diverse backgrounds viewing themselves as "not college material."

Prior to starting the Odyssey Project in 2003, I had already spent two decades as an English professor at the University of Wisconsin–Madison charged with an outreach mission, conducting programs on literature for nontraditional adult students in retirement centers, prisons, Elderhostels (an international non-profit organization that offers older adults short-term, low-cost courses, housing, and meals), public libraries, service clubs, the backs of grocery stores, over the radio, and online. More than in the traditional campus classes I taught, I found that nontraditional students craved instruction that lifted the material off the page and into their own lives.

Knowing of my outreach work, the journalist and radio host Jean Feraca (a Distinguished Senior Broadcaster and colleague of mine at Wisconsin Public Radio) approached me about starting a new program. She had been inspired by a guest on her talk show: Earl Shorris, an award-winning author and revolutionary educational reformer known for having started the Clemente Course in the Humanities, an educational institution founded in 1995 to teach the humanities at the college level to people living in economic distress. Jean was thoroughly intrigued by his account of teaching philosophy, literature, history, and art history to the poor in ways that could bring about a transformation and begin a journey out of poverty. How might we start a Clemente Course in the Humanities in Madison?

What Jean did not know was that my own family's story of escape from poverty through a free liberal arts education would shape my approach to the undertaking. I wanted not just a "great works" class but a four-year free college education for those wanting to break a cycle of generational poverty. My mother had come from Appalachia, born into an impoverished region twelve miles from Knoxville, Tennessee, with no running water. Teachers who saw that she was an avid reader told her about a chance for the poor to receive higher education in neighboring Kentucky at progressive Berea College. Founded in 1855 by the abolitionist John Gregg Fee, Berea College is best known for providing free education to students and for having been the first racially integrated and coeducational college in the South. My mother arrived on campus with a wardrobe consisting of one skirt and two blouses and with no extra spending money. Had someone said, "You must buy an expensive textbook," she would have had to go home. Berea changed her life. After graduating valedictorian, she continued on to advanced degrees from Columbia University and the University of Wisconsin–Madison.

While at Berea, she met my father, Robert Auerbach, who was there as an "other" allowed in for diversity at the Christian school. My father's story of poverty was that of the immigrant. Fleeing Nazi Germany, my father's parents lost everything, including the ability to practice their careers as lawyers. Berea offered a chance to get a liberal arts education to those whose families had little or no money. My father went on after Berea to become an internationally recognized scientist, and in 2017 he received Berea's Distinguished Alumnus award.

When I speak of the Odyssey Project, I mention my parents' stories because they cut through stereotypes that I otherwise encounter when speaking about "the poor" or "low-income students" from "diverse backgrounds." Administrators cautioning me about starting a program here in Madison remarked, "Poor people aren't going to want to study Plato, and you'll have trouble filling a class." Clemente Course directors warned, "You'll be lucky if you end up with half the at-risk students you start with." Although I loved Earl Shorris's revolutionary concept of providing the best works of moral philosophy, literature, history, and art free of charge to those trapped in poverty, I cringed at the title of his book: *Riches for the Poor*.[1] My mother *had* riches inside her when she arrived at Berea College; she just lacked the opportunity (as my Odyssey student later put it) "to unwrap [her] gifts." Furthermore, I would argue that the

over four hundred "poor" students I have encountered in the seventeen years
of doing the Odyssey Project have enriched others through their voices and
visions. The concept of "riches for the poor" makes me picture well-meaning
colonialists arriving with boxes of Plato and Shakespeare for the benighted
poor, and that somehow did not square with my growing recognition of the
eloquence and insight of the diverse adults I was working with each week.
In an effort to make our program more reciprocal and engage adult students
more directly in the material, we add in the arts—creative writing, journalism,
theater, music—and encourage our students to respond in original ways to the
material we read.

We made the decision not to run our program as an official Clemente
Course through New York's Bard College but instead to build it directly into
the University of Wisconsin–Madison. Being a "Clemente-inspired" course
gave us the freedom to vary the curriculum, add in the arts, and grant our
students six credits from the University of Wisconsin–Madison, one of the
top universities in the world. Since its early days, the University of Wisconsin
prided itself on the Wisconsin Idea. As former University of Wisconsin president Charles Van Hise articulated it in 1905, "I shall never be content until the
beneficent influence of the University reaches every family of the state."[2] Why
not find ways to make the treasures of this land-grant institution available to
the citizens whose taxes helped support its existence?

The Odyssey Project epitomizes the Wisconsin Idea in action. On a typical
Wednesday night, an unlikely group of thirty low-income adults of color admitted as "special students" to the University of Wisconsin–Madison discusses
Walt Whitman's "Song of Myself," Plato's account of the trial and death of
Socrates, the Declaration of Independence, the meaning of "onomatopoeia"
and "agoraphobia," the logical arguments in "Letter from Birmingham Jail" by
Martin Luther King Jr., or the difference between Doric, Ionic, and Corin-
thian columns in ancient architecture. Yes, they are earning college credits and
gaining practical skills in writing, reading comprehension, and critical thinking.
But the experience affects them at a much deeper level as well, as they are encouraged to make and remake the material, to transform it into something with
direct meaning in their lives. Plato's allegory of the cave in *The Republic* reminds
one student of the trap of drug addiction; it reminds another of domestic
abuse. One student recasts a scene from Shakespeare's *Macbeth* in Chicago
with Lady Macbeth urging her husband to "be a man" and shoot Duncan
while he has a chance. In the hands of a student who has faced homelessness,
Charles Dickens's Ebenezer Scrooge becomes a heartless Madison landlord.

Those of us who teach the humanities often feel on the defensive, as if justifying the value of material deemed impractical or fanciful. Reading Emily

Dickinson does not pay the rent. Acting out scenes from Shakespeare puts no food in the refrigerator. So how does one justify teaching the humanities to adults battling poverty?

I would argue that in addition to promoting literacy, a key pathway to transformation, exposure to the humanities changes one's sense of self in profoundly important ways. After our students read poems by Whitman, Dickinson, Langston Hughes, and others, we ask them to write their own poems, including creating metaphors about themselves and their lives. "My life is a revolving door," writes one student, "because just when I think I'm starting to get somewhere, my drug-using friends drag me back around to the other side and I'm stuck again." To envision her life that way marks the first step to change. Pride in self emerges as students find their voices and discover that their stories have power. Our student newsletter (*Odyssey Oracle*) provides a chance to showcase students' writings; some students go on to publish their editorials and stories in other places, read them on the radio or on television, or hold exhibits of their art. The diversity of our students—predominantly African American, Hispanic, Native American, and Hmong, along with refugees from African and Middle Eastern nations—makes their contributions especially eye-opening and important.

From the start, our program has offered not only free tuition and textbooks but also free childcare. We began to hear reports that children whose parents were in our program started doing better in school, reading more, and exhibiting more interest in learning. One student said that as he sat at the table to do his homework, his sons would gather around him, all "reading like Dad," including a four-year-old son holding his book upside down. In the past three years, we have added on an "Odyssey Junior" program providing enrichment for children of our students on the same night that parents attend classes. Why not have whole families go home talking about vocabulary, art, literature, and other topics? While adults earn college credits, over fifty of their children and grandchildren simultaneously receive intensive work in the arts and on literacy, including field trips, a "Read to a Dog" program, and an *Odyssey Oracle Junior* newsletter printing their writing and art.

When we began the Odyssey Project in the fall of 2003, we could not have envisioned how much it would grow. In addition to Odyssey Junior, we now have Odyssey Beyond Bars, bringing our course materials into Wisconsin prisons. We also have Onward Odyssey, a series of programs designed for our alumni to help them continue toward degrees and better lives. More than half of our budget goes toward keeping graduates of the program in school, supplementing the financial aid they receive. Essential to our high retention rates and our high rate of students continuing on in school (over two-thirds take more college classes after Odyssey) is the family-like community we have built around the program, including an Odyssey Family Learning Center. Students feel cared about and supported. Also essential, quite frankly, is money. We rely on grants, institutional support, and individual donors to help defray the costs of tuition, textbooks, notebooks, printer charges, application fees, and other expenses that threaten to shut low-income students out of higher education. We also have actively engaged a large group of community and campus partners: advisors who help steer students into their next classes or help them fill out financial aid forms, public libraries that provide space for our programs, campus departments that offer resources and credits, churches and service clubs that bring us meals, school districts that help train our graduates to work as aides, businesses that give us discounts, a whole team of volunteer tutors and mentors, and a part-time social worker to link students to community resources.

When an African American mother of three who was homeless for six months when she came to Madison walks across the stage to get her bachelor's degree and then her master's degree from the University of Wisconsin–Madison, it feels like a triumph—and one that needs to be replicated everywhere. The Odyssey Project serves as a catalyst, a jump start, a launching pad—a way to help adults who have gotten off track or never got on the track to find a way to start their journeys toward college degrees and better lives. Necessary ingredients for starting a program are respect for "the poor" as equal in their humanity and gifts, commitment to find ways of addressing whole families and their lives outside of class, and creative teaching methods that engage adults with the material in empowering ways.

Earl Shorris no longer is alive, but his work with the Clemente Course continues not only in the United States but also abroad. From Austin, Texas, to Harlem, New York, versions of Earl's course are transforming lives. Some courses, like ours, have diverged from the original model in key ways. The Clemente Course website offers a directory of courses still up and running, as well as directors to contact for more ideas. Earl's final book, *The Art of Freedom*, has chapters on different versions of the Clemente course, including a chapter called "From Appalachia to Wisconsin" about our Madison program.[3] Programs can occur in homeless shelters, prisons, community centers, and colleges, offering idealistic educators anywhere a chance to fight for social justice by providing equal access to the liberal arts. Although the Odyssey Project evolved in a particular context here in Madison, Wisconsin, using elements from both the Clemente Course in the Humanities and from Berea College, could our life-changing integration of the arts and humanities embolden educators elsewhere to try creative means of engaging adults from underrepresented minorities?

Directing the Odyssey Project for the past seventeen years has restored my faith in the transformative, enduring power of education. An African American grandmother who climbed out of drug addiction and prostitution writes, "Henry David Thoreau said 'You cannot dream yourself into a character: you must hammer and forge yourself into one.' The Odyssey Project helped me hammer and forge myself into the person I was meant to be." A Native American man overcoming alcoholism and discrimination for both his race and sexual orientation comments, "I don't feel lost now. I have a purpose: to educate myself to break free from the manacles binding my mind. I am a philosopher in training." An African American single father of two rebuilding his life after incarceration calls the program "a life jacket tossed just as I was about to drown in a sea of uncertainty." A refugee from Sudan who received her master's degree in social work from the University of Wisconsin–Madison in May 2017 envisions Odyssey as her "passport to higher education and a better life." Hundreds of similar comments, often sparkling with brilliant metaphors, testify to the power of the humanities to break down barriers and change lives.

Notes

1. Earl Shorris, *Riches for the Poor: The Clemente Course in the Humanities* (New York: W. W. Norton, 2000).

2. Van Hise, quoted in John D. Buenker, *The History of Wisconsin*, vol. 3, *The Progressive Era, 1893–1914* (Madison: State Historical Society of Wisconsin, 1998), 379.

3. Earl Shorris, *The Art of Freedom: Teaching the Humanities to the Poor* (New York: W. W. Norton, 2013).

Preserving the "Public Household"

The Wisconsin Idea and the 2011 Protests

JANE L. COLLINS

At first glance the connection between the Wisconsin Idea and the Wisconsin protests of 2011 may not be obvious. The Wisconsin Idea is a concept that has linked the activities of the state's institutions of higher learning to the well-being of citizens for over a hundred years. The 2011 protests were a public outcry over changes to labor law that are briefly discussed in the introductory chapter of this volume—specifically, a bill that effectively abolished the collective bargaining rights of public-sector workers. This chapter argues that a shared set of public values and a shared vision of the role of the state link these seemingly disparate phenomena. The argument proceeds in three parts. First, it explores some of the unspoken assumptions of the Wisconsin Idea, making explicit the vision of the public sector that lies at its heart. Second, it offers a new interpretation of what was going on in the 2011 protests, suggesting that while at one level they were about labor issues, they were also about defending the public sector. Finally, the paper presents historical evidence that, far from being a point of social consensus, the vision of the public sector's role in the life of the state that is at the heart of the Wisconsin Idea has been extremely controversial over the past 120 years, erupting into heated conflict in the 1930s, the 1970s, and in 2011. Review of these historical episodes offers a new angle of vision on challenges currently facing the Wisconsin Idea.

PART I: THE VISION OF THE "PUBLIC HOUSEHOLD" AT THE HEART OF THE WISCONSIN IDEA

Building on the work of Gwen Drury, a scholar who has written and spoken extensively on the Wisconsin Idea, previous chapters in this volume have provided a vivid description of the fraught political context in which it emerged. A key aspect of this context was the corruption and domination of Wisconsin's economy and political life by the railroads, big monied families in timber, and monopolies for other important resources. Drury describes how a project emerged in this context to wrest control of government from these monied special interests and to make it work for the good of a much larger segment of the population. She defines the Wisconsin Idea as "a distinctive approach, developed in Wisconsin, to use knowledge resources of all kinds to keep governance and economy in the hands of the greatest number of people and not just a small number who could corner the market."[1] Drury's definition draws out two important aspects of the Wisconsin Idea. The first is its origins in a critique of predatory wealth. The second is the emphasis it places on the role of government, drawing on the knowledge resources of the public university, as the counterweight and solution to that problem.

Sources from the time support this definition of the Wisconsin Idea. The Progressive Era Wisconsin political scientist Charles McCarthy, in his book on the Wisconsin Idea published in 1912, wrote that its designers were acting in response to monopoly, trusts, the high cost of living, and predatory wealth. He argued that University of Wisconsin president John Bascom, University of Wisconsin economist Richard Ely, and many others who were involved in creating the Wisconsin Idea, believed "that men deserved the right of opportunity; . . . that it was the duty of the state to preserve to them opportunities; that the state was a necessary good and not a necessary evil; that . . . private property was good, and . . . existed for the public good, but if any particular part of it did not exist for the public good, it should be made to do so."[2] Both Ely and Bascom believed in the principle that the state must invest in the life and happiness of the individual to insure widespread prosperity. According to Arthur Altmeyer, a University of Wisconsin graduate and United States commissioner for Social Security from 1946 to 1953, "The essence of Bascom's teaching and of the Wisconsin Idea was . . . the belief that government had an affirmative obligation to promote the well-being of its citizens, and that the University had an equally affirmative obligation to serve the state in helping to achieve that objective."[3] Similarly, Richard Ely wrote: "We regard the state as an agency whose positive assistance is one of the indispensable preconditions of human progress."[4]

These sources make clear that the Wisconsin Idea was not only envisioned and created in response to the great inequality of the Gilded Age and the way that money bought and dominated the political system of that era, but that its creators specifically saw government as a remedy to that problem. They sought a way of taking government back for citizens and providing for collective well-being. In that project, they saw the knowledge resources of the public university as their most important resource and tool.

Wisconsin's early twentieth-century progressive reformers put those knowledge resources to amazing use. Karen Bogenschneider's chapter in this volume details some of the new programs, policies, and laws coming out of Wisconsin at that time, including the nation's first workers' compensation program, the first state income tax, a Legislative Reference Bureau that became the model for the Congressional Research Service, an activist Industrial Commission, a living-wage law, a host of other protections for labor, and unemployment compensation. As she notes, all of these programs were designed with input from faculty and students at the University of Wisconsin. Institutional economists John Commons and Edwin Witte spearheaded Wisconsin's workers' compensation and unemployment compensation programs. These new frameworks for worker security became models for other state programs, and Commons and Witte were tapped to help design national versions of such worker protections and, later, our nationwide Social Security program. But there were many other less famed but extremely consequential innovations. Witte advised the Wisconsin legislature on new antitrust laws. The university's School of Medicine collaborated with state agencies to solve public health problems, establishing the State Laboratory of Hygiene and a system of sanitoriums for tuberculosis. As previous chapters mention in passing, the College of Agriculture established short courses that helped the state's farmers transition from wheat crops that were depleting the soil to dairy farming. As early as 1912, even before many of these contributions had materialized, reformer Frederic Howe could say that Wisconsin had become "an experiment station in politics, in social and industrial legislation, in the democratization of science and higher education. It is a state-wide laboratory in which popular government is being tested in its reaction on people, on the distribution of wealth, on social well-being."[5]

These Progressive Era projects were successful, to a large degree, because they found a strong base of support in at least part of Wisconsin's business community. Not among the railroad trusts and logger barons and their allies, who formed a part of the Republican Party of the time known as the Stalwarts, but among midsized Wisconsin-based firms, many of which were owned by German immigrants, who clustered in the progressive branch of the Republican Party. These progressive business owners were receptive to elements of welfare capitalism similar to those they had known in the old country. They were sympathetic to institutions like workers' compensation because they had seen it work in Germany and England. They adhered to a version of German free-market ideology called Ordoliberalism that held that the full capacities of markets required them to be embedded in a robust legal and social order. Practically speaking, they saw programs like workers' compensation as making the cost of doing right by workers regular and predictable.[6]

In working on all of these diverse projects, practitioners of the Wisconsin Idea contributed to building what Daniel Bell has called "the public household." As a sociologist, Bell chose that term rather than more well-known labels like "public sector" or "public goods" because it highlights the need to work out, through democratic governance, problems of common living. For him the public household was, in part, the arena for meeting common needs and for providing goods and services that individuals cannot procure for themselves. This is the definition of public goods most frequently cited by economists, encompassing the basic functions of the military, police, and the courts. But beyond that, Bell saw government as having a role to play in managing the economy, in underwriting science and technology, and in supporting citizens by protecting their civil rights and providing a socially agreed upon set of safety-net services.[7] With the term "public household," Bell was referencing the collective institutions, both economic and political, that provide for the well-being of citizens. Just as the private household doesn't always agree about budgets and priorities, members of the public household don't either. But they work through those differences collectively—and hopefully without coming to blows.

Primary sources suggest that the Wisconsin Idea had this vision of government at its heart. It is premised on a concept of the public household as the way people work together to promote collective well-being. This was not a vision in which government *usurped* the roles of business or civil society, but to quote Altmeyer again, it was a way that "people can work together effectively through their government to achieve security in such a way as to promote, at one and the same time, individual incentive and mutual responsibility."[8] At its heart, the Wisconsin Idea contains a prescription for a division of labor among state, market, and civil society that gives the state an important role.

PART II: THE VISION OF THE "PUBLIC HOUSEHOLD" THAT ANIMATED THE 2011 PROTESTS

From February 14 through most of the spring of 2011 the grounds and streets surrounding the Wisconsin state capitol were packed with crowds that on some days reached one hundred thousand people or more. Braving the bitter winter and early spring weather, they carried signs, sang songs, gave (and listened to) speeches, and marched. These crowds were made up of public-sector union members, members of other unions who came out in solidarity, and a vast number of individuals who did not work in the public sector and were not union members. Simultaneously, the University of Wisconsin–Madison Teaching Assistants' Association, American Federation of Teachers Local 3220, organized an occupation of the state capitol building that went on for nearly a month, filling the rotunda with chants and music and sleeping bags and signs. The immediate impetus for these protests was Governor Scott Walker's announcement of Act 10—what he called the "Budget Repair Bill," which virtually eliminated collective bargaining rights for public-sector workers and made it harder for public unions to be certified.

The protests were definitely sparked by this new law. Nevertheless, beneath the surface it was possible to discern a deeper issue. There is much evidence that the protests represented a turning point, or a flash point, in an underlying debate about the role of the public sector in the economy. On one side were those who sided with the Wisconsin Idea and Daniel Bell and who saw the state sector as providing essential goods and services. And on the other were those, like Governor Walker and Republican legislators, who felt that the public sector's growth was detrimental to human liberty and drained resources from the economy.

This underlying debate about the value of the public sector was articulated by then US senator Tom Coburn (R-Okla.) in his comments about the protests: "These government employees [referring to the protestors] . . . produce no net economic benefit to our country. Matter of fact, they produce . . . negative economic benefit."[9] Conservative radio host Rush Limbaugh, perhaps not surprisingly, echoed this view: "Public employees do not produce anything. . . . They're not making widgets."[10] Some media reports that appeared in response to the protests referred to public workers as the new "welfare queens"[11] and denigrated public workers as "tax eaters" who lived off hard-working "tax payers."

A high school teacher standing outside the state capitol in February 2011 responded to these criticisms. "They say I produce nothing," he told a crowd of protestors, "but I produce engineers and doctors, accountants and scientists, nurses and architects." Many of the signs that protestors carried echoed his comments in the support they expressed for public workers: "I [heart] my teacher," "Remember this when you hit a pothole," "Don't Scapegoat Public Workers," "I dislike taxes but I like schools, firefighters, roads, parks, and most police officers."[12]

For many protestors who showed up at the capitol, the state workers who were losing their rights were a symbol of public services. And as the uprising went on into March 2011, people who came initially to protest the loss of collective bargaining rights made common cause with those who showed up to protest Walker's austerity budget, released that month, with its deep cuts to services. These individuals rejected the idea that public goods were a drain on the economy—they saw them instead as investments in the economy.

How did we reach a point where working families would take to the streets to defend public services? Over the course of the twentieth century, public workers came to perform many functions crucial to families and households. With the advent of public schools, mothers and fathers did not have to teach their own children. Cities and counties took over plowing snowy roads and collecting garbage—and then later—transporting the elderly to doctors' appointments and providing after-school care. Beginning in the 1970s, as wages stagnated and families and individuals began to work more hours, public services became even more important. As the economists Robert Pollin and Jeff Thompson have written: "For generations now, state and local governments have been the most important providers . . . of education, health care, public safety, and other vital forms of support for families." These authors called the 2011 battle in Wisconsin "the most dramatic expression of a struggle that is ongoing throughout the country over the future of state and local governments."[13] Thus, in the face of arguments by the Wisconsin governor and legislature that society could no longer afford such services, the protestors reasserted their centrality to peoples' lives.

People who attended the protests cited these trends when they talked about what they thought was at stake in combatting the Budget Repair Bill. One union activist explained: "I think it was clear that people really understood this to be an attack not just on unions—that wasn't even the main thing. It was really an attack on public services, on the community. . . . People responded because they saw this as an attack on their children's teachers—the people they count on every day."[14] A teacher said: "The public sector runs so deep in every community that what happened was people would take this back home at night to the dinner table, they'd take it to church on Sunday, they'd take it to the PTA [Parent-Teacher Association] meetings, and so on." A public worker added: "A lot of people came out in support of schools, in support of snow-plow drivers, in support of the folks who work in municipal offices . . . and basically said, 'no, we respect the services that are provided in our state.'"

These views were not limited to people who showed up at the protests. Though in a somewhat different register, leaders in Wisconsin's business community shared an appreciation of government's role in the economy. Given that Wisconsin Manufacturers and Commerce (WMC) and similar organizations had supported Walker's gubernatorial bid, one might have expected them to justify Act 10 with versions of Walker's claims that "Wisconsin is broke."[15] Instead, many business leaders interviewed about the meaning of the protests and the role of the public sector responded with a list of what business needed from government: not just roads and bridges, but also a stable regulatory environment, support for a high-quality workforce, essential services, a social safety net, and supportive programs for business. One former head of WMC said: "Infrastructure's important. You have to have ports, good railroads, a good highway system. . . . The new tech world needs to get around a lot, and they need good air service, and if you don't have it, you're not going to see a lot of growth."[16] Another mentioned the need for government to provide countercyclical stimulus during economic recessions and spoke approvingly of some aspects of former US president Barack Obama's 2008 stimulus plan and even of China's subsidies for business. The tone of these interviews sounded far more like that of Wisconsin's German-heritage progressive business leaders in the early twentieth century than it did the 2011 rhetoric of Wisconsin's national-stage politicians.

It seems clear that the Wisconsin Idea and the 2011 protests both had a vision of the public household at their center. But connecting these two movements raises a thorny question. How did Wisconsin go from being a leader of the nation in *building* the public household in the early twentieth century to a model for how to *dismantle it* in the early twenty-first century? After all, Walker won the protracted battle on Act 10. He survived the 2012 recall election and widely touted his "Budget Repair Bill" and his response to the protests as a model for the nation—at least twelve other states passed legislation that was modeled on Act 10.

Part III: From Building to Dismantling the Public Household

This question—how Wisconsin went from building to dismantling public-sector institutions—led me to the reading rooms of the Wisconsin Historical Society library. In the summer of 2014, sitting in that beautiful space, flipping through the pages of a 1939 issue of the *Wisconsin Taxpayer*, I came across the following passage:

> Taxpayers, except those who directly benefit from state employees' salaries, are beginning to question the whys and wherefores of the recent increases in public salaries and payrolls. As taxes continue to rise, their questionings will continue to rise . . . to the point of resentment. Public employees, their organizations and the departments that employ them, will rise in defiance. If present rumblings indicate coming events, an open clash may result.[17]

The passage was startling. Reading like an editorial torn from contemporary headlines, it inspired me to search for information about previous episodes of conflict over the public sector in Wisconsin.

The debate over the size and functions of government is a central theme of our democracy and it is always present in our public discourse. It is one instance of an underlying tension between principles of individualism and those of communitarianism—between Horatio Alger stories of self-made individuals and Norman Rockwell paintings of collective barn-raisings. But over the course of the past one hundred years in Wisconsin, collective tempers have flared around the issue three times—in the 1930s, the 1970s, and 2011. The resolution of those tensions was different in each case, with implications for the fate of the Wisconsin Idea.

Wisconsin's first great battle over the role of the state came during the Great Depression. The Depression, in the words of US president Franklin Roosevelt's second inaugural address in 1937, left "one-third of a nation ill-housed, ill-clad, ill-nourished," and it challenged the notion that markets, left to their own devices, would correct themselves.[18] The crisis left leaders at all levels of government casting about for new models for economic policy, including the writings of the British economist John Maynard Keynes. Keynes advocated the use of fiscal and monetary policy to mitigate the effects of economic recessions and depressions, and he encouraged the expansion of a social safety net to bolster aggregate demand. These views found their way into an array of New Deal policies, including the provision of relief and work programs for the unemployed.

The state of Wisconsin became highly polarized around this issue. By 1931, its cities and counties were faltering under the strain of providing relief, and Progressive Party governor Philip La Follette (son of the Wisconsin progressive leader, governor, and US senator Robert M. La Follette Sr.) wanted the state to take a stronger role. He called a special legislative session to consider a bill to raise income taxes to fund relief. The legislative debate drew over three hundred observers to the state capitol and rewarded them with a dramatic showdown between progressives of many stripes and fiscally conservative Republican Stalwarts.[19]

The business community in Wisconsin was split over the issue of relief. The Stalwart wing of the Republican Party argued that the additional taxes that relief required would impinge on the individual freedom of hard-working people, taking money from those who used it wisely and putting it in the pockets of those who would not use it well, while simultaneously driving business from the state.

Speaking in favor of Governor La Follette's bill was an alliance of progressive Republicans, socialists, and Democrats. The mayor of Racine, Wisconsin, and representatives of white- and blue-collar labor unions contested the claim that localities could meet the needs of the unemployed on their own. In fact, union members charged, employers were forcing their workers to contribute to community chests for the unemployed under threat of firing and thus were making "labor pay for the illegitimate child of industry—the problem of unemployment."[20] Dairy farmers expressed support for the relief bill on the logic that more people would be able to buy milk. Small-town officials insisted the bill was needed to respond to economic dislocation. Wisconsin progressives were unusual in this period in linking support for a robust relief system with public workers' rights, perhaps because of progressive Republicans' work on civil service reforms and due to the emergent organizational strength of public-sector workers (who formed the nation's first public-sector union, the American Federation of State, County, and Municipal Employees, in 1932).

Despite this show of support, in December 1931 the Republican Stalwarts won the day, defeating the measure and leaving La Follette and supporters to decry the unwillingness of business "to make any contribution to the suffering people of this state out of their enormous profits." La Follette did not give up, however. He kept legislators working into January 1932, when they passed a compromise bill—the Unemployment Reserves and Compensation Act.[21] During this period, the strong ties of Wisconsin politicians and intellectuals to national policymakers, and their national status as leaders in crafting and enacting new progressive programs, bolstered their ability to strengthen the "public household" in Wisconsin.[22]

In February 1932, in the wake of these events, a group of disgruntled Republican Stalwarts met to form the Wisconsin Taxpayers Alliance (WTA). In their founding documents they declared: "Mounting government expenditures have thrown a staggering burden upon the taxpayer, which with the general reduction in wages and earning power in both industry and agriculture . . . has reached the point of confiscation."[23] By late October 1932, the Alliance had formed seventeen chapters across the state. That same year, WTA members gave seventy-two public addresses and held eighty-five conferences with local groups.[24] In January 1933, they published the first issue of *Wisconsin Taxpayer*, a newsletter whose self-described mission was to "bring the 'old ship of state' back to an even keel."[25]

The emergence of the Taxpayer Alliance in Wisconsin mirrored developments across the country. The Depression sparked a wave of property tax revolts from 1930 to 1933. Historian David Beito reports that well over one thousand local groups formed during this period.[26] Chicago was the scene of one of the largest illegal tax boycotts in US history.[27] At its height, the Chicago movement, led by the Association of Real Estate Taxpayers, counted thirty thousand members and nearly bankrupted the city of Chicago.[28] According to the sociologist Isaac Martin, revolts were motivated by the fact that prior to the Depression people expected that their property values would rise but assessments would not change, reducing their bills in real terms year after year. Yet, during the Depression, taxes remained the same as real property values sank, amounting to a yearly tax increase during a time when incomes plummeted.[29]

In 1932, leaders of the Milwaukee Taxpayers' Advisory Council (MTAC) called for a tax strike patterned after Chicago, but backed off when the state's voters approved tax limits in the November election. While no strike occurred, the MTAC sparked public debate about the size and purpose of the public sector. Milwaukee's Socialist mayor, Daniel Hoan, who referred to taxpayer associations as "tax dodger leagues," told a radio audience: "Much as we dislike to pay our tax bills, the fact is that government . . . has stood like the Rock of Gibraltar during this frightful depression to save us the agonies of complete chaos. While the banks bailed, factories closed, shops went bankrupt, pyramided utilities collapsed, the government was expected to function with more vigor and energy than ever."[30]

Meanwhile, Republican Stalwarts produced editorials and cartoons complaining that government had been hijacked by "vested interests," "pressure groups," and "lobbies." Issues of the *Wisconsin Taxpayer* from this period featured cartoons of bloated government bureaucrats being pulled in carts by skinny taxpayers; of taxpayers as packhorses, as dead horses, and as maple trees tapped by government programs; of government as Santa Claus. The publication criticized proposals for new inheritance and estate taxes in remarkably contemporary terms—referring to them as "death taxes." As the New Deal continued, small-government conservatives in the state expressed skepticism about President Roosevelt's Social Security program, running a cartoon of Mother Hubbard going to the Social Security "cabinet" and finding it bare.

Just as in 2011, public employees became lightning rods in the 1930s debate over the public sector. In response, public-sector defenders called out the "popular tendency to assign to public employees the role of villain in the tragedy of present economic conditions," complaining that it was becoming "generally accepted as fact that public employees are extravagant bureaucrats, time-serving payrollers, and non-productive parasites."[31] They worried that municipal reformers, who had labored for a generation to professionalize government and improve its image, would see new waves of hostility and budget cuts damage the reform edifice. The president of the University of Wisconsin weighed in, warning that the spread of antigovernment ideology would divert individuals from public service.[32]

So how were these tensions resolved in the 1930s? In short, Wisconsin's Republican Stalwarts could not gain traction for their small-government views during the Great Depression. Too many citizens held classical free-market liberalism responsible for the economy's crisis. Too many people perceived the fiscal conservatism of the Stalwarts to be a stale and discredited solution to dire new problems. Of equal importance, after the election of President Franklin Roosevelt, the Wisconsin progressives who for decades had been engaged in creative acts of state-building in their own backyards received substantial new support from national politicians. The New Deal political apparatus in Washington generated and popularized new ways of thinking about the state's role in the economy and provided resources to build institutions and programs around them. This connection to a successful national-level political project bolstered the ability of local progressives to continue building the state's public household.[33]

Between the 1930s and the 1970s, lawmakers and politicians at both state and federal levels worked to build and consolidate public institutions. Roosevelt expanded income-tax collection and parlayed new taxes imposed during the Second World War into permanent support for government programs. With these new resources and popular support, the government put in place labor regulations to govern hours of work and wages and to establish the right to join a union. It introduced business regulations that restructured the banking industry and broke up public utility holding companies. It devised a Social Security program that provided resources for old age and for widows and orphans of workers. It provided state resources for rural electrification, fostered farm ownership, and gave work to the unemployed. The new programs excluded many citizens: most African American farmers did not benefit from the farm bills, and domestic and agricultural workers (largely African American and also disproportionately female) were excluded from the National Labor Relations Act. Nevertheless, Roosevelt and his allies forged a new vision of what government could do to improve the everyday lives of its citizens and unprecedented government institutions designed to make that vision a reality.

As US global hegemony and the Cold War bolstered economic growth through the 1950s, and a growing tax base kept up with demands for state services, debates over the size of government remained muted. Growth, in Daniel Bell's words, acted as a "political solvent,"[34] by providing the means to finance social welfare expenditures and defense without reallocating income. This was true in Wisconsin as well as the nation as a whole. The state's economy blossomed, from manufacturing on the shores of Lake Michigan to the paper mills of the Fox Valley and the dairies and vegetable farms in between.

But during this long economic expansion, what some call the golden age of US capitalism, small-government conservatives continued to hone their views on the issue of the public sector. Scholars at Austria's Mont Pelerin Society and in the University of Chicago economics department worked to systematize a new version of economic liberalism (what we now call neoliberalism) that would present an alternative to Keynesianism and social-democratic principles. Rather than simply opposing big government, they worked to articulate a positive vision and a reform agenda, which they nurtured in a transnational network of university departments and think tanks. These efforts created what the sociologist Verta Taylor has called a movement in "abeyance"—a social movement that manages to sustain and reinvent itself through unreceptive periods in order to mount a challenge in another period.[35] While the ideas brewing in Mont Pelerin and Chicago had little impact on political programs at the high point of the US golden age, these scholars, businessmen, and policy entrepreneurs were developing a radical set of free-market policy prescriptions that would be on hand for future decades.[36]

Beginning in the 1960s, the tone of the debate about the public sector, both nationally and in Wisconsin, began to shift. Even as the War on Poverty expanded the social safety net and social movements advocated further state investments, frameworks brewing in conservative think tanks like the American Economic Foundation and the Liberty Fund and organizations like the John Birch Society began to gain a wider audience.[37] Translating and circulating the concepts of economists like Friedrich A. Hayek and blending them with libertarian themes, these groups reopened the question of whether a strong state was corrosive of the free market and individual liberty, and what its size and scope should be. Ronald Reagan's 1964 Republican National Convention speech—in which he proclaimed that the US welfare state had broken with the nation's founding principles and represented a threat to freedom as significant as Soviet communism—marked this change. In the mid-1960s, faced with deficits from expanding social programs and the Vietnam War, President Lyndon Johnson appealed to Congress for tax increases. Led by the powerful chair of the US House of Representatives Ways and Means Committee Wilbur Mills (D-Ark.), Congress refused more funds until the administration agreed to over $6 billion in spending cuts. This maneuver, which left Johnson with the reputation of having sold out the poor to pay for the war, signified the rising power of advocates of government "austerity" within a broader framework of ascendant neoliberalism.[38]

As small-government conservatism gained strength in the 1960s and 1970s, taxation reemerged as a site for debating the size and role of the state. According to the president of the Wisconsin Taxpayers Alliance, the Baby Boom generation was "building homes, building subdivisions, needing streets, needing sewers, needing schools, and by late '60s—needing universities."[39] This put pressure on local property taxes, which by the early 1970s in Wisconsin reached a historic high.

Unlike the tax strikes of the Great Depression, 1970s tax protests were not driven by property depreciation but by a rapid rise in property values and a modernization of the collection system that made appeal difficult.[40] As in California, where in 1978 antitax activists succeeded in passing the tax-limiting Proposition 13, Wisconsin protests were shaped by suburbanization and "white flight" of the postwar era, facilitated by programs like the Servicemen's Readjustment Act of 1944 (known as the GI Bill), the mortgage-interest tax credit, investment in highways and roads, and racially discriminatory zoning policies and red-lining. As white, middle-class families moved out of cities, urban areas saw their tax base shrink, and white suburban property-owners began to balk at paying taxes to support urban social services that they perceived as benefiting "others." A growing public perception that citizens were "consumers" of government services shaped this emergent discourse about what was fair. As the sociologist Clarence Lo has written about California's anti–property tax activism: "Affluent activists objected that their high property taxes did not pay for amenities that would enhance their own properties but rather went for welfare and other social programs for the poor and recent immigrants."[41]

Antitax activists argued that huge amounts of "waste" could be cut from government budgets without affecting services.[42] This form of antitax militancy had a racial dimension that in the Wisconsin case focused white, middle-class rural and suburban anger on Milwaukee, Racine, and other cities with larger African American and immigrant populations. Businesses demanded tax breaks, and activism against the property tax resurged. In Racine, Wisconsin, a group called SOS (Stop Outlandish Spending) lobbied against a local school bond issue, leading to the closure of at least one school.[43]

These trends set the stage for a major confrontation over the public sector in 1974. In the wake of the 1973 oil crisis, inflation rates that year reached 12 percent, and workers in many sectors struck for raises to compensate for the declining value of their salaries. This included a number of teachers' strikes in Madison. But the decade's most contentious strike took place in the Outagamie County town of Hortonville, Wisconsin, a village of two thousand that was home to several paper mills. After months of stalled labor negotiations, Hortonville's eighty-eight teachers went on strike in March 1974, asking for a double-digit raise to compensate for the inflation rate. Administrators offered 1.2 percent. In response, the teachers walked out and the school district fired them. But the community response made this incident noteworthy. A group of local men calling themselves "the Vigilantes" swore vengeance against the teachers, hanging them in effigy and making death threats. One man walked into the teachers' union hall brandishing a six-shooter.[44]

In the heated debate surrounding the strike, public employees once again became the lightning rod in a debate over the public sector and its cost. Many Hortonville residents were union members themselves, including a large contingent of paper-mill workers, but they saw strikes by public employees as fundamentally different. As one resident wrote to a local paper: "Teachers must remember that their employers are the people of these communities . . . who are obliged to finance education by heavy taxes imposed on them." A broader debate about the public sector's role lay just beneath the surface. The Wisconsin Chamber of Commerce took the Hortonville strike as evidence of the "increasing scope and arrogance of the public employee monopoly."[45] Nevertheless, the end result of Wisconsin's wave of teachers' strikes in the 1970s was not a statewide outcry like that in Hortonville, but a mediation-arbitration law that made binding arbitration of bargaining impasses compulsory for nearly all state and municipal employees. At the time of the skirmish in Hortonville, the small-state worldview developed at Mont Pelerin and the University of Chicago was beginning to regain traction in broader political culture, but it had not yet become the dominant strand in Wisconsin's political culture.

If the 1970s saw small-government conservatism begin to flex its muscles, the 1980s saw it develop its strength. The movement found a charismatic spokesperson in Ronald Reagan, frequently credited with ushering in a new era of neoliberal political practice in the United States. In 1981, President Reagan showed what this new era would mean for labor when he used the 1947 Taft-Hartley Act to fire striking air traffic controllers and break their union. Reagan promoted tax cuts as a move to take money out of the hands of government and give it to average Americans. He then used the threat of deficits to justify cutting safety-net programs and government investments. The era's enthusiasm for small government was reflected in the conservative political activist and strategist Grover Norquist's well-publicized 1985 founding of Americans for Tax Reform, with its mantra about shrinking government until it could be drowned in a bathtub.

During the 1980s, these ideas found a home in Wisconsin. Republican Tommy Thompson, governor of Wisconsin from 1987 to 2001, introduced an array of new initiatives that reconfigured government programs to meet tests of supply and demand, efficiency, and cost, rather than broader political and social aims. Implementing plans developed by conservative think tanks, Thompson initiated state-level welfare reforms that provided a model for President Bill Clinton's 1996 national welfare reform and led to the dismantling of the state's cash welfare program. Milwaukee's Bradley Foundation and the Heritage Foundation provided Thompson with templates for the nation's first school voucher program.

Thompson's experiments continued through the 1990s, and the strong growth of that decade muted some of their social effects. Welfare-to-work policies hurt poor families less when there were jobs to be found and wages were rising. The resources that vouchers siphoned from public schools were less damaging than they would be when the economy ceased expanding. But that changed when the economy sank into recession in the following decade. The 2003 recession hit Wisconsin hard—particularly the southeastern cities. The far worse 2008 downturn was deeper in Wisconsin than nationally and left the state trailing the US average in gross domestic product growth, job growth, and wage growth.

By 2011, Wisconsin was battered by these consecutive downturns, but its fiscal house was still in relatively good order. The budget was in deficit, but it was not the worst shortfall the state had seen.[46] Wisconsin's public employee pension plan was one of a handful in the nation that was fully funded.[47] Republican gubernatorial candidate Scott Walker had campaigned on a platform of moderate reforms. But once elected, he unveiled an agenda that had been forged in conservative think tanks and in the American Legislative Exchange Council (ALEC)[48]—and that challenged both the rights of public-sector workers and the size and scope of government programs.

Walker's 2011 Budget Repair Bill, announced in February of that year, effectively ended collective bargaining rights for public-sector unions—restricting them to bargaining over wages and limiting any raises they negotiated to the rate of inflation. Under the guise of solving a budget shortfall, it prohibited negotiations over benefits, work rules, health and safety issues, work hours, shifts and overtime, grievance procedures, and seniority provisions. The bill also required all unions to gain 51 percent of the votes of all members, not just those voting, in yearly recertification campaigns. It eliminated arbitration rights and prohibited unions from collecting dues through payroll deduction.

In explaining these measures, like his predecessors in the 1930s and 1970s, Walker spoke of the need to improve the state's business climate. He argued that cutting government services would reduce tax burdens while reallocating state spending toward the business sector. The governor used a discourse of dependency that disparaged public workers in terms reminiscent of the 1930s. He claimed public employees were overpaid and dependent on tax dollars paid by private-sector workers. "We can no longer live in a society," he declared, "where the public employees are the haves and the taxpayers who foot the bill are the have-nots."[49] He offered Wisconsinites a "beggar thy neighbor" logic that said, Why should someone else have these benefits if you don't? Why should you pay for public workers to have secure retirements when you don't have that luxury? While these arguments had fallen short in the 1930s and had not gained traction in the 1970s, in 2011 they found a more receptive context. The presence of one hundred thousand people in the state's Capitol Square was not enough to hold back the tide of small-government conservatism. How do we explain this outcome?

SMALL GOVERNMENT CONSERVATISM AND THE PUBLIC HOUSEHOLD ACROSS THE DECADES

There are several possible reasons for such different outcomes for the idea of the public household across the three periods. One possibility is that it has something to do with what the sociologist William Sewell Jr. has called "eventful temporality."[50] As the political scientist Mark Blyth has said: "In understanding the role of ideas in institutional change, sequence is everything."[51] As previously noted, during the Great Depression, New Dealers succeeded in pinning blame for economic crisis on unregulated markets and on the business community. A substantial portion of the citizenry saw the protests of Republican Stalwarts and antitax activists as backward-looking and mired in failed solutions of the past. They wanted something else, and a strong public household was a "new" solution. This created an opening to experiment with and build social welfare institutions. When the US economy faltered in 2008, small-government conservatives were able to promote downsizing the public sector as a "new" approach to economic crisis and to governance.

The second thing that seems to matter to the outcomes of these episodes is the connection of local actors to national-level political movements. Political scientists and sociologists have noted that in understanding changes in governance practices, we need to tie the "eventful nature of local change to larger, often-secular trends that characterize capitalist development as a whole."[52] As we have seen, in the early twentieth century, Wisconsin was a breeding ground for progressive ideas and institutions. Its politicians and intellectuals gained national reputations and developed strong relationships with individuals and institutions in Washington. Power flowed in both directions—Wisconsinites arguably influenced national politicians' visions of what it was possible and desirable for the state to do, but these national-level connections also bolstered the ability of the state's politicians to construct strong programs for regulating the economy and supporting citizens.

In the 1970s, when local groups mounted tax protests and challenged striking public workers, they did not receive the kind of material support from national-level political figures or institutions that allowed them to significantly reconfigure the size and shape of local government. They were voicing opinions that, while growing in popularity, still ran against the dominant tide of public opinion.

By 2011, local actors who sought to "shrink the state" found backing not just in the national Republican Party and the Tea Party (a US political movement that emerged in 2009 to demand lower taxes, fewer government regulations and programs, strict immigration control, and a strong military) but a host of other well-financed national entities. These included ALEC, which offered templates for new legislative initiatives; a densely interconnected web of think tanks including the Bradley Foundation, Heritage Foundation, Manhattan Institute, MacIver Institute, and Cato Institute; and a growing network of extremely wealthy donors freed by the US Supreme Court's 2010 *Citizens United v. Federal Election Commission* decision to fund a shifting set of issue organizations that funded both political campaigns and governance initiatives. Once again Wisconsin political figures—this time those on the side of small government—were well networked on the national political scene. Lawyer Reince Preibus chaired the Republican National Committee from 2011 to 2017, congressman Paul Ryan (R-Wis.) served as Speaker of the US House of Representatives from October 2015 to January 2019 and played a leadership role in the Republican Party, lawyer Michael W. Grebe ran the nationally influential Bradley Foundation, and conservative political activist Eric O'Keefe was a founder of the Tea Party movement. As Scott Walker and state legislators crafted plans to roll back public-sector workers' rights and slash the state budget, they counted on abundant national support—backing that proved crucial, for instance, in allowing Walker to survive the recall campaign mounted in response to his actions.

By 2011, conditions in the state of Wisconsin in many ways resembled those in the early part of the twentieth century. Mirroring trends across the nation, income inequality in Wisconsin was at its highest level since the Great Depression. *Citizens United* had opened the door for the great wealth at the top to be translated into political power. Voter identification laws and gerrymandering weakened the voices of the electorate. Meanwhile the families of great wealth of our generation—the Charles G. and David H. Koch brothers, the family of the hedge-fund tycoon Robert Mercer, the family of Walmart cofounders Bud and Sam Walton—financed projects to hobble unions, cut social services, privatize schools and prisons, defund public universities, and undermine Social Security and Medicare. These trends raise a burning question. The Wisconsin Idea played such an important role in building the public household, both in our state and across the nation. In a context where small-government conservatism has become a dominant theme in statehouses and national government, what role can it play in shaping our response to attempts to dismantle it?

NOTES

This chapter is based, in part, on research supported by the National Science Foundation and the University of Wisconsin–Madison. Some parts of the chapter draw on
or duplicate sections of three earlier works: Jane L. Collins, *The Politics of Value: Three
Movements to Change How We Think about the Economy* (Chicago: University of Chicago Press, 2017); Jane L. Collins and H. Jacob Carlson, "State Phobia, Then and
Now: Three Waves of Conflict over Wisconsin's Public Sector: 1930–2013," *Social Science History* 42, no 1 (Spring 2018): 57–80; and Jane Collins, "Theorizing Wisconsin's
2011 Protests: Community-Based Unionism Confronts Accumulation by Disposses-
sion," *American Ethnologist* 39, no. 1 (February 2012): 6–20.

1. Gwen Drury, "The Wisconsin Idea: How Do We Define the Concept?" (lecture, University of Wisconsin–Madison, September 12, 2017), https://wpt4.org/wpt
-video/university-place/the-wisconsin-idea-how-do-we-define-the-concept-cw3an6/.
See also James K. Conant, *Wisconsin Politics and Government: America's Laboratory of
Democracy* (Lincoln: University of Nebraska Press, 2006).

2. Charles McCarthy, *The Wisconsin Idea* (New York: Macmillan, 1912), 29–30.

3. Arthur J. Altmeyer, "The Wisconsin Idea and Social Security," *Wisconsin Magazine of History* 42, no. 1 (Autumn 1958): 19–25, quotation from p. 19.

4. From the Statement of Principles of the American Economic Association,
quoted in "History of the Founding of the American Economic Association," *Journal
of Economic Issues* 20, no. 2 (June 1986): i.

5. Frederic C. Howe, *Wisconsin: An Experiment in Democracy* (New York: Charles
Scribner's Sons, 1912), vii.

6. Robert Asher, "The 1911 Wisconsin Workmen's Compensation Law: A Study in
Conservative Labor Reform," *Wisconsin Magazine of History* 57, no. 2 (Winter 1973–74):
123–40; Gregory C. Krohm, "Workers' Compensation: Wisconsin Pioneers the Nation's
First Constitutional Workers' Compensation Law," in *Wisconsin Worker's Compensation Centennial 1911–2011* (Madison: Wisconsin Department of Workforce Development, 2011), 77–93, https://dwd.wisconsin.gov/dwd/publications/wc/WKC_17033_P
.pdf; Herbert F. Margulies, *The Decline of the Progressive Movement in Wisconsin, 1890–
1920* (Madison: State Historical Society of Wisconsin, 1968).

7. Daniel Bell, "The Public Household: On Fiscal Sociology and the Liberal Society," *National Affairs* 37 (1974): 29–68.

8. Altmeyer, "Wisconsin Idea and Social Security," 25.

9. Nin-Hai Tsing, "Tom Coburn: Government Employees Are a Drag on the
Economy," *Fortune*, March 7, 2011, https://fortune.com/2011/03/07/tom-coburn-gov
ernment-employees-are-a-drag-on-the-economy/.

10. The Rush Limbaugh Show transcript, "Public Sector Workers Conspire to
Steal Money from their Neighbors," February 23, 2011, https://web.archive.org/web/20
160319224252/http://www.rushlimbaugh.com/daily/2011/02/23/public_sector_work
ers_conspire_to_steal_money_from_their_neighbors.

11. Jonathan Cohn, "Why Public Employees Are the New Welfare Queens," *New
Republic*, August 8, 2010, http://www.newrepublic.com/blog/jonathan-cohn/76884/
why-your-fireman-has-better-pension-you; Paul Krugman, "Schoolteachers Driving

Cadillacs," *New York Times*, August 10, 2010, http://krugman.blogs.nytimes.com/2010/08/09/schoolteachers-driving-cadillacs/.

12. Author's observations, February 2011.

13. Robert Pollin and Jeffrey Thompson, "State and Municipal Alternatives to Austerity," *New Labor Forum* 20, no. 3 (Fall 2011): 22–30, quotation from p. 22.

14. All interviews quoted or cited were conducted as part of the 2013–14 National Science Foundation research project Rethinking Value and are reported in more detail in Jane L. Collins, *The Politics of Value: Three Movements to Change How We Think about the Economy* (Chicago: University of Chicago Press, 2017). This quotation is from p. 118.

15. State of Wisconsin, Office of the Governor, Scott Walker 2011 Budget Address, March 1, 2011, https://walker.wi.gov/speeches/2011-budget-address; "Walker Renews Call for Union Concessions," Channel3000, December 7, 2010, https://www.channel3000.com/walker-renews-calls-for-union-concessions/.

16. James Haney, quoted in Collins, *Politics of Value*, 115.

17. *Wisconsin Taxpayer*, September 1, 1939.

18. Franklin Delano Roosevelt, Second Inaugural Address, January 20, 1937, https://fdrlibrary.org/documents/356632/390886/1937inauguraladdress.pdf/7d61a3fd-9d56-4bb6-989d-0fd269cdb073.

19. Jonathan Kasparek, *Fighting Son: A Biography of Philip La Follette* (Madison: Wisconsin Historical Society Press, 2006).

20. "Clashes Mark 'Big Business' Attack on Jobless Relief Plan," *Capital Times*, December 8, 1931.

21. Kasparek, *Fighting Son*, 122.

22. The list included the La Follettes (Robert Sr., Robert Jr., and Philip), the University of Wisconsin economists who drafted national old-age and unemployment insurance plans (John R. Commons, Edwin Witte, Wilbur Cohen, and others), and Arnold Zander, who led the American Federation of State, County, and Municipal Employees (AFSCME) from its formation in 1932 until 1964.

23. Wisconsin Taxpayer Association, "Activity Report," March 17, 1932.

24. *Wisconsin Taxpayer*, February 1982.

25. *Wisconsin Taxpayer*, January 16, 1933.

26. David T. Beito, *Taxpayers in Revolt: Tax Resistance during the Great Depression* (Auburn, AL: Ludwig von Mises Institute, 2009), 18–20, 61.

27. Isaac William Martin, *The Permanent Tax Revolt: How the Property Tax Transformed American Politics* (Stanford: Stanford University Press, 2008); Beito, *Taxpayers in Revolt*.

28. Linda Upham-Bornstein, "The Taxpayer as Reformer: 'Pocketbook Politics' and the Law, 1860–1940" (PhD diss., University of New Hampshire, 2009), 186.

29. Martin, *Permanent Tax Revolt*, 29.

30. Cited in Upham-Bornstein, "Taxpayer as Reformer," 191.

31. Beito, *Taxpayers in Revolt*.

32. Beito, *Taxpayers in Revolt*, 19–20.

33. See Jane L. Collins and H. Jacob Carlson, "State Phobia, Then and Now: Three Waves of Conflict over Wisconsin's Public Sector, 1930–2013," *Social Science History* 41, no. 1 (Spring 2018): 57–80.

34. Daniel Bell, *The Cultural Contradictions of Capitalism* (New York: Basic Books, 1976), 238.

35. Verta Taylor, "Social Movement Continuity: The Women's Movement in Abeyance," *American Sociological Review* 54, no. 5 (1989): 761–75.

36. Daniel Stedman Jones, *Masters of the Universe: Hayek, Friedman, and the Birth of Neoliberal Politics* (Princeton, NJ: Princeton University Press, 2012); Jamie Peck, *Constructions of Neoliberal Reason* (New York: Oxford University Press, 2010), 160.

37. Jones, *Masters of the Universe.*

38. Julian E. Zelizer, *Taxing America: Wilbur D. Mills, Congress and the State, 1945–75* (New York: Cambridge University Press, 1998).

39. Todd Berry, quoted in Collins and Carlson, "State Phobia," 69.

40. Martin, *Permanent Tax Revolt.*

41. Clarence Lo, *Small Property versus Big Government: Social Origins of the Property Tax Revolt* (Berkeley: University of California Press, 1990), 163.

42. Lo, *Small Property versus Big Government*, 17.

43. Naomi R. Williams, "Workers United: The Labor Movement and the Shifting U.S. Economy, 1950s–1980s" (PhD diss., University of Wisconsin–Madison, 2014), 163.

44. Adam Mertz, "The 1974 Hortonville Teacher Strike and the Public Sector Labor Dilemma," *Wisconsin Magazine of History* 98, no. 3 (Spring 2015): 2–13; Eleni Brelis Schirmer, "When Solidarity Doesn't Quite Strike: The 1974 Hortonville, Wisconsin Teachers' Strike and the Rise of Neoliberalism," *Gender and Education* 29, no. 1 (January 2017): 8–27; Christian Schneider, "The Strike That Changed Wisconsin," *Milwaukee Journal Sentinel*, September 11, 2012, www.jsonline.com/news/opinion/the-strike-that-changed-wisconsin-1f6qgi4-169392356.html.

45. Quoted in Mertz, "The 1974 Hortonville Teacher Strike," 11.

46. Mike Ivey, "We Do Have a Budget Problem, but Not a Crisis," *Capital Times*, February 18, 2011, https://web.archive.org/web/20160319232149/http://host.madison.com/news/local/govt-and-politics/analysis-we-do-have-a-budget-problem-but-not-a/article_90196216-3b66-11e0-a327-001cc4c03286.html.

47. Pew Charitable Trust, *The Widening Gap Update*, June 2012, https://www.pewtrusts.org/~/media/legacy/uploadedfiles/pcs_assets/2012/pewpensionsupdatepdf.pdf.

48. William Cronon, "Who's Really behind Recent Republican Legislation in Wisconsin and Elsewhere," Scholar as Citizen (blog), March 15, 2011, http://scholarcitizen.williamcronon.net/2011/03/15/alec/.

49. "Walker Renews Call."

50. William H. Sewell Jr., "The Temporalities of Capitalism," *Socio-Economic Review* 6, no. 3 (July 2008): 517–37.

51. Mark Blyth, *Great Transformations: Economic Ideas and Institutional Change in the Twentieth Century* (New York: Cambridge University Press, 2002), 44.

52. John Krinsky, "Neoliberal Times: Intersecting Temporalities and the Neoliberalization of New York City's Public-Sector Labor Relations," *Social Science History* 35, no. 3 (Fall 2011): 381–422, quotation from p. 412. See also Sewell, "Temporalities of Capitalism."

Laboratory of Oligarchy

LEWIS A. FRIEDLAND

"It is one of the happy incidents of the federal system that a single courageous State may, if its citizens choose, serve as a laboratory, and try novel social and economic experiments without risk to the country." Making this statement in dissent, US Supreme Court associate justice Louis Brandeis asserted that states were free to experiment with social and economic policies that might benefit all of their citizens. If such policies succeeded, they could spread to other states; if they failed, the risk would be contained.[1]

The most famous and successful such laboratory in the twentieth century was the state of Wisconsin. Wisconsin politics in the late nineteenth and early twentieth centuries was a unique hybrid of Free-Soil Republicanism predating the Civil War, agrarian populism, social-democratic and labor traditions brought by Milwaukee's German immigrants, and the progressivism of Robert M. La Follette Sr., which grew from the battle against the power of timber and railroad money that controlled Wisconsin during the Gilded Age.[2] These streams converged at the University of Wisconsin in the Wisconsin Idea to develop a laboratory of democracy that would address problems affecting the entire state: the city and the country, the worker and the farmer.

Many of the innovative reforms that Wisconsin introduced in those years have been discussed in previous chapters of this volume and need only be briefly mentioned here. They include the creation of the first Legislative Reference Bureau in 1901 to bring the drafting of law out from behind closed doors and into the public domain, the first state-level civil-service reform in 1905 to reduce patronage and cronyism, and introduction of the first independent commissions to regulate the railroads, which set a benchmark for the rest of the nation. In addition, in 1909 Wisconsin became the first state to continuously revise its statues to make them clear and accessible to average citizens. Furthermore, as Karen Bogenschneider and Jane L. Collins point out in their contributions to this volume, Wisconsin became the first state to adopt the corporate and individual income tax in a series of steps from 1905 to 1911, creating a model for the federal government in 1913, and it was a laboratory for the social insurance that still forms the foundation of the social safety net in the United States. In 1921 economist John R. Commons at the University of Wisconsin developed the first unemployment compensation law, which Wisconsin finally adopted in 1934 as the Groves Act. Elizabeth Brandeis Raushenbush, Brandeis's daughter, studied and worked with Commons to pass the act and spent a forty-year career at the University of Wisconsin in the economics department. Arthur Altmeyer and Edwin Witte, both students of Commons (and the latter a University of Wisconsin faculty member from 1933 to 1957), played a major role in drafting the Social Security Act adopted by the United States Congress in 1935. Wilbur Cohen, who studied with Witte, accompanied him to Washington and drafted the federal Medicare legislation passed in 1965.[3]

In 2010, Wisconsin began a new age of experimentation that has been openly dedicated to the systematic dismantling of Progressive Era and New Deal reforms. The state's recent political history, including the election of Governor Scott Walker in 2010 and his rejection in 2018, is widely known. But the dismantling of progressive reform in Wisconsin is not the simple result of a Republican victory and a normal alternation of power. Rather, it is the fruit of decades of planning and organization by ultrawealthy, ultraconservative individuals and organizations both within and outside the state that targeted Wisconsin as a center for this counter-reform movement and a model for the rest of the nation. In short, the state moved from being a laboratory of democracy to a laboratory of oligarchy.

The political scientists Benjamin I. Page and Jeffrey A. Winters argue that a "civil oligarchy" exists in the United States. By definition, an oligarchy requires a highly unequal distribution of income and, therefore, an ultrawealthy stratum whose primary interest is the defense of its wealth through the control of tax and inheritance laws. Lowered taxation and increased welfare are in zero-sum competition, so wealth defense also implies active opposition to many social welfare measures. Page and Winters stress the "normal" political operation of wealth defense in a capitalist democracy. More recently, in contrast, Theda Skocpol and Alexander Hertel-Fernandez have focused attention on the ultraconservative segment of the civil oligarchy that has been actively engaged in a forty-year-plus political offensive to roll back Progressive Era and New Deal reforms. My central argument is that this group has actively focused on Wisconsin as a key site for this political experiment.[4]

Theories of democratic and civic pluralism hold that American life features multiple and competing centers for power that are reflected and organized through our party structure. The parties compete by mobilizing both allied groups and public opinion, and through this competition alternate groups exercise political power and shape policy. This system embodies an asymmetry of resources and political structure that favors Republicans and conservatives, but the fundamental democratic competitive processes have mostly held in the postwar period.[5]

Political competition is predicated on two factors: first, a relative balance of power between the two parties that, in normal periods of politics, allows each to put its views before the public with a fair chance of winning. For the Democrats, the major counterbalance to Republican money advantage in the past seventy years has been the labor movement. But the labor movement has shrunk to a shell of its former self, and its stronghold in the public sector has been under blistering attack at the state level.

This leads to the second factor: democratic pluralism requires that both parties accept the consequences of winning and losing. But as the political scientists Norman Ornstein and Thomas Mann and others have argued, the Republican Party has adopted a stance of permanent opposition to both government *and* governance, including the very idea that problems can be solved through government action.[6] Further, the party's policies largely protect the wealthy, and its policy positions—from privatizing Social Security and schools to tax cuts for the wealthy—are unpopular with substantial majorities. The unpopularity of the Republican Party's policies have led it to shift its basic strategy from party competition to fundamentally changing the rules of elections and government. A critical element of the laboratory of oligarchy is the reduction or dismantling of democratic participation itself.

THE TURN TO THE STATES

The emergence of a coalition of ultraconservative political actors focusing on the states has been, until very recently, one of the most understudied aspects of American politics.[7] Since the 1970s, the founders and funders of this network have understood that the states control much of the most important public policy in the United States: laws about property and taxation, health and welfare, social insurance, transportation, labor, and the environment. The states also control voting rights and redistricting at both the state and federal levels. From the administration of US president Ronald Reagan (1981–89) on, this coalition has engineered a continuous and successful push to accomplish two goals: first, to devolve these policy areas wherever possible from the federal government to the states, and second, to gain control over state-level policymaking through a nationally organized but locally focused movement.

Just as the federal system gives disproportionate power to rural states, the districting of state legislatures within states favors lower-population, rural regions, diluting urban votes and creating a built-in conservative constitutional advantage. This has meant that Republican investment in state-level political control is very efficient: a modest amount of money and organization goes further in media, campaign expenditures, and lobbying. Finally, although state legislatures vary in professionalism, the most targeted states tend to be weaker, with part-time, underinformed representatives who are more subject to outside influence in career building.[8]

Beyond this state-level efficacy, the conservative policy network is federated: it is rooted in state-level organization, but its agenda is set and controlled nationally. At the national level, there is a core of powerful, conservative business organizations with national, state, and often local branches or members. The most important are the Chamber of Commerce, the National Association of Manufacturers, and the National Federation of Independent Business. Each of these organizations has well-funded, state-level members and is joined in the states by associations of generally conservative, powerful, industry-specific business interests including real estate companies, builders and construction companies, bankers, restaurant and tavern owners, trucking and transportation businesses, and others.[9] This conservative business alliance has become intertwined in the Republican Party with the ultraconservative network centered around the billionaire brothers Charles and David Koch of Kansas and the Wisconsin-based Lynde and Harry Bradley Foundation.

The Rise of a Right-Wing "Para-Party"

The Republican Party's rightward movement is not a simple response to a long-term shift in public opinion. The Republican coalition since Ronald Reagan has been a complex amalgam of the corporate and banking classes, the Chamber of Commerce and small business owners, suburban and Northeastern Republicans, libertarians, evangelical Christians, "Reagan Democrat" white workers, and former Democrats in the South. Former Southern Democrats were the foundation of US president Richard Nixon's Southern Strategy of bringing dog-whistle racism into the Republican Party's core messaging. The Tea Party movement that emerged in 2009 radicalized and modernized this racism, adding birtherism and other conspiracy theories, and from 2015 forward, businessman and later US president Donald Trump added explicit white nationalism.[10] This shifting coalition has been critical to the party's electoral success, but increasingly since the mid-1970s, a coalition of libertarians and conservatives have allied with business Republicans in a consistent, organized, and well-funded effort to move the party to the right.

The organizational and ideological reorientation begins with the "Powell Memo," written to the US Chamber of Commerce in 1971 by corporate lawyer Lewis Powell, who later became an associate justice of the US Supreme Court (1972–87). Powell argued that the "American economic system is under broad attack" and urged a new wave of corporate investment in scholars, surveillance of the mass media, the build-up of corporate power, and an increased focus on the courts. Powell's memo stirred a wave of investment in a conservative-rightist idea infrastructure, including think tanks, university chairs, and fellows.[11]

Two major intellectual centers emerged on the right. In 1973, Paul Weyrich, a former newspaper and radio journalist in Wisconsin, solicited funding from right-wing beer magnate Joseph Coors to found the Heritage Foundation with the goal of creating a conservative "counter-intelligentsia."[12] Heritage rapidly became the center of gravity of the conservative thought movement. But perhaps the most radical new intellectual center was the Cato Institute, founded in 1977 with the money and funding of Charles Koch. As Nancy MacLean details in *Democracy in Chains*, Cato was the institutional anchor of a radical libertarian program that had begun in the 1960s. Koch, whose father had co-founded the ultra-right John Birch Society, had inherited his father's wealth and also his ideological predilections. An engineer and thinker trained at the Massachusetts Institute of Technology, Koch was convinced that the modern New Deal state was a form of tyranny. Building on the views of the economist Friedrich Hayek, Koch believed that a new ideological infrastructure was necessary to roll back the state.[13]

The Koch brothers have had the money, the clear ideological vision, the organizational skills, and, not least, the patience to persevere over time and through setbacks in the project of reversing the New Deal. By 2018 Charles and David Koch were tied for eighth place on the Forbes list of richest Americans with a net worth $48.6 billion each, but when their fortunes are combined (as for political purposes they effectively are) their combined net worth of $97.2 billion gives them the largest focused war chest in American politics.[14] This mix of resources best describes parties, and Skocpol has aptly characterized the Koch complex and its political organizing arm Americans for Freedom as a *para-party*, a party-like structure that has operated for some years within the Republican Party with the goal of steering it to obtain the para-party's most important political objectives.

The Koch brothers planned a "three-phase takeover of American politics" as outlined by a key Koch lieutenant in the late 1980s: invest in intellectuals to create ideas, the raw product of change; create think tanks to turn these products into marketable ideas; and subsidize "citizens" groups that would pressure officials to implement their policies. Toward this end, in 1984 they launched "Citizens for a Sound Economy" (CSE), a "private political sales force," in investigative journalist Jane Mayer's words, and the prototype modern astro-turf organization. CSE became an umbrella vehicle for other corporate campaigns.[15]

By 1996 the Kochs had begun to focus on the Republican Party itself. David Koch became the vice-chair of US senator Bob Dole's presidential campaign against Bill Clinton. The brothers merged personal political contributions, made business contributions funneled through political action committees (PACs), and funded nonprofit groups as front groups. As Mayer notes, these three streams were viewed as "one investment aimed at paying huge future dividends to donors."[16]

The Kochs' power and influence continued to expand throughout the 2000s as their network of investments began to take root in the states. In 2003 they convened the first of their twice-a-year donor summits, designed in part to raise funds for their broader antienvironmental and antiregulatory crusade. In 2003, CSE morphed into Americans for Prosperity (AFP), whose 501(c)4 status allowed its barely disguised political activity to be tax deductible. Veterans of the powerful Christian Coalition were brought in to run it. AFP was well situated to both stimulate and take advantage of the "Tea Party" backlash against President Barack Obama's health care plan in 2009. Although the Kochs denied direct links, CSE had originated the Tea Party antitax theme as early as 1991.

Although they failed to oust President Obama in 2012, the recognition of Democratic strength at the presidential level reaffirmed the strategy of concentrating on the states. By 2007 AFP had state-level directors in fifteen states covering half the US population and had effectively built alliances with other conservative networks, most notably the Bradley Foundation.

THE BRADLEY FOUNDATION

The Wisconsin-based Bradley Foundation has been one of the most central actors in both US and Wisconsin politics over the past three decades. Although not as widely recognized as the Koch network, it is a cornerstone of the US political wealth defense network. As of June 2016, the Bradley Foundation had $835 million in assets, more than the three Koch family foundations combined.[17] The foundation has disbursed almost $365 million since 2001, more than the other two major conservative funders, the Koch and Scaife Foundations, combined. (This refers to foundation funding; the Kochs, as noted, have made extensive PAC contributions and dark-money contributions from their personal fortunes.)[18]

The Bradley Foundation was built on the Allen-Bradley fortune. Like Fred Koch, founding brother Harry Bradley was a staunch supporter of the John Birch Society. With the sale of Allen-Bradley to Rockwell International in 1985, the foundation's endowment ballooned to $290 million and the foundation hired a new chief executive, Michael Joyce, who "invented the field of modern conservative philanthropy"[19] and held the position till 2001. During this time the foundation spent $20 million to turn Milwaukee into a laboratory for voucher schools and financed studies that laid the foundation for Wisconsin governor Tommy Thompson's "workfare" initiative. It has been a major promoter of "right to work" legislation, the deregulation of campaign finance laws, and efforts to cut back and even kill public-sector unions.[20]

The foundation expanded its political mission considerably under the leadership of Michael W. Grebe, who became president and CEO in 2002. A Vietnam War veteran who cast his first vote for Republican presidential nominee Barry Goldwater in 1964, he eventually became CEO of Foley and Lardner, a leading Wisconsin law firm, and served as general counsel to the Republican National Committee. While still president of Bradley, Grebe chaired Governor Scott Walker's 2010 campaign, chaired his transition team, and chaired the 2011 fight against his recall, sending out a fundraising letter asking supporters to help Walker combat "the Democrats and Big Government Union Bosses" as they spent millions to "spread lies about Governor Walker's record of positive change."[21]

Bradley's coordinated strategy for the states has been less than an open book. In 2016, the foundation's computers were hacked, revealing hundreds of thousands of documents. In an overview of their contents, investigative journalist Daniel Bice of the *Milwaukee Journal Sentinel* found that the foundation had developed a systematic and coordinated strategy that entailed using Wisconsin as a "petri dish" for a network of conservative groups that "defended and promoted Walker and his agenda, including his attacks on labor unions. From 2011 to 2015, these dozen-plus nonprofits, labeled the Wisconsin Network, received more than $13 million from the conservative foundation."[22]

A $200 million infusion of funds in 2016 allowed Bradley to expand its experiment nationwide, including an effort to defund teachers' unions in Colorado, defund private-sector unions in Washington and Oregon, and create a "comprehensive and disruptive communications infrastructure" in North Carolina, including radio, online content aggregation, mobile apps, and an "AP-style news service for local newspapers."[23]

Bradley has taken a leading role in funding the State Policy Network (SPN), a critical but little-known part of the national conservative state policy apparatus. This coalition of conservative state-based think tanks was founded in 1992 by a South Carolina antiunion magnate, Thomas Roe, but its growth has been primarily funded by the Koch network and Bradley. The State Policy Networks produce coordinated policy papers with state branding, but in fact many of the ideas are centrally disseminated.

In 2009 the SPN added an "investigative news service," partnered with the Franklin Center for Government and Public Integrity, and established "news bureaus" in forty states. Franklin's founder, Jason Stverak, told a conservative conference that the organization planned to fill the growing vacuum in state-level media across the United States by 2011, when the SPN's budget was $83 million. In 2012 there were sixty-four separate SPN think tanks, at least one in every state coordinating with AFP, the Cato Foundation, and the Heritage Foundation, all of which receive Koch funding.[24]

Rob Stein, who heads the liberal Democracy Alliance, the closest analogue to the Koch-led network on the left, has said, "The Bradley Foundation has figured this out. . . . If they control state legislatures and both houses of Congress and the Supreme Court, . . . [regardless of who] is president, they control the country." The primary vehicle for exercising this control has been the American Legislative Exchange Council, better known as ALEC.[25]

THE AMERICAN LEGISLATIVE EXCHANGE COUNCIL

Wisconsin native and Heritage co-founder Paul Weyrich founded ALEC in 1973 with the support of the Scaife and Mellon family trusts.[26] But the Koch brothers were early and continuous financial supporters, and since then ALEC has brought together major US corporations with conservative lawmakers to formulate legislative programs tailored to the states. As of 2014, ALEC's membership included two thousand primarily Republican lawmakers, one-third of *all* state legislators, about two hundred corporations, and a variety of leading conservative foundations, funders, and think tanks. It is a unique meeting ground for legislators, ultraconservative think tanks, funders, and major corporations, including many with a centrist or high-tech public identity such as Amazon.[27]

In annual conferences and other task forces, ALEC members draft "model legislation" that state legislators often introduce (frequently verbatim) as their own, yielding an average of a thousand new bills a year nationally, of which about two hundred become state law. ALEC advertises these meetings as "public policy laboratories" and claims that its members set policy. In reality the organization has developed a clear political agenda set by its corporate and large-money donors.[28] Although bills are drafted in task forces, each one has to be approved by ALEC's corporate-dominated board of directors. The core of the agenda is straightforward: tax cuts, particularly for businesses and the wealthy; environmental deregulation; preempting local control; privatizing public services, with particular emphasis on schools and prisons; and gun rights, including the original "stand your ground" legislation.

ALEC's leaders have long understood that the most important barrier to implementing their program in the states is labor unions, especially public employee and teachers' unions. ALEC (and the Bradley Foundation) have been major supporters of public school privatization through vouchers and the "school reform" movement, which undermines confidence in public schools and teachers' unions by taking funds from public education and passing them to charters and private schools. The elimination of public workers' rights has served as the opening salvo in passing broader "right-to-work" laws, which have been an integral part of the Koch program from the beginning. As of 2018, twenty-seven states had passed right to work laws, including Wisconsin.

Finally, because many ALEC-sponsored policies are unpopular and poll poorly (particularly outside the South), the network has sponsored successful legislation to restrict voting rights. In 2011, after the 2010 wave of Republican victories in legislatures and statehouses, thirty-three states introduced voter identification bills that made it harder for citizens to register and vote. Many were based on a 2009 ALEC model bill.[29]

ALEC has been among the most effective political organizations in the United States since its founding, while largely flying under the public radar until about 2010, when the national success of the Tea Party movement and the lightning-quick adoption of Scott Walker's program in the Wisconsin legislature turned a research spotlight on the organization (largely through the efforts of the Madison-based Center for Media and Democracy and reporter Mary Bottari). Despite the withdrawal of some corporate sponsors, ALEC remains the most effective state-level legislative organization.

The Wisconsin Synthesis

Before the 2010 midterm election, Wisconsin had voted for Democrats for president since 1988 and been represented by two Democratic US senators. But it has been a mixed-government state: starting in 1986 it elected Republican Tommy Thompson as governor three times. Under Thompson, Wisconsin became a leading testing ground for national conservative networks to build a model to turn what we now call purple states red.

Thompson had been a state legislator from 1966 to 1987, and in a keynote address to ALEC in 2002 he reflected on his involvement: "I always loved going to [ALEC] meetings because I always found new ideas. Then I'd take them back to Wisconsin, disguise them a little bit, and declare that 'It's mine.'"[30] In 1996 he proposed and passed a "workfare" program that limited benefits for single mothers and required them to work, which became one template for President Bill Clinton's program to "end welfare as we know it." With the support of the Bradley Foundation, Thompson also created one of the nation's first school-voucher programs in 1989 under the rubric of "school choice," turning Wisconsin into a national laboratory for school privatization. The voucher movement laid the groundwork for what would, under Scott Walker, become a broader attack on public education, teachers, and their unions.

Thompson governed from the center-right, constrained by Democratic control of both houses for most of his tenure. His grandfather had supported La Follette, and Thompson himself intentionally employed progressive values and rhetoric of reform as a "powerful symbol to diffuse [sic] opposition to his policy proposals."[31] Thompson was genuinely popular throughout the state and worked with the Democratic opposition to pass his bills, often compromising along the way. He strongly supported the state's education system and the University of Wisconsin–Madison in particular, and he long campaigned for the extension of railroad transportation throughout the state. Thompson's conservatism, combined with his genuine popular appeal and, crucially, his recognition that bipartisan governance was necessary to build his vision of progressive conservatism, serves as a stark contrast to the governance regime of Scott Walker.

RISE OF SCOTT WALKER

Scott Walker was elected to the Wisconsin legislature from the Milwaukee County suburb of Wauwatosa in 1993. As a back-bencher in the legislature he regularly attended ALEC conferences, and one of his earliest causes was an ALEC bill that would clamp down on union political campaign contributions. He was mostly known for his appearances on popular conservative talk radio host Charlie Sykes's show and Sunday morning television. His star rose precipitously in 2002 with his improbable election to county executive in solidly Democratic Milwaukee County in the wake of a pension scandal and recall. He ran as a "change agent" and received small donations from the antitax recall movement. But his support for private schools also won him maximum donations from Walmart heir John Walton. One Republican strategist said that funders "saw Scott as an investment in where they were going."[32]

Walker's term as county executive was marked by ongoing struggles with county worker unions, particularly the American Federation of State, County, and Municipal Employees (AFSCME). He did gain a reputation as a good manager and diplomat and even won limited praise from union leaders. But eventually his honeymoon with labor soured. His two terms in office brought layoffs, service cuts, and the highest bus fares in the United States.

His sights were on higher office.[33] Inspired in part by Republican governors such as Mitch Daniels of Indiana, who had unilaterally wiped out collective bargaining with an executive order in 2005 (which Walker later labeled "a beautiful thing"), Walker ran for governor in 2006, heavily criticizing unions. After stepping down under pressure from the state GOP (and sensing that it was going to be a strong year for Democrats, as Governor Jim Doyle swept to reelection victory), Walker began his next run in 2010.

In 2008, Democrats had won unified control of the statehouse. They passed a budget-repair bill that raised taxes and fees on business and opened twenty thousand campus jobs to union representation. In 2010, Walker ran directly against state workers, saying that they should contribute more to their health benefits and pensions or face layoffs. He also criticized federal support for Medicaid and a high-speed rail line as burdens on "taxpayers." Facing Milwaukee mayor and Democratic gubernatorial candidate Tom Barrett, Walker claimed that he would seek givebacks through tough bargaining with unions, but said he would negotiate; he never publicly mentioned his plans to "drop the bomb" on state labor in Act 10 (discussed below).

The Koch brothers' support was essential to Walker's rise. They had significant interests in the state in lumber, coal, and pipelines. The second largest donation to Walker's $8 million campaign fund came from Koch Industries PAC. John Menard Jr., the richest man in Wisconsin, was a $1 million donor to the Koch network in 2011 and a $1.5 million donor to the Wisconsin Club for Growth, the state's dark-money hub. The Kochs also contributed heavily to the Republican Governors Association, which funneled money back to Walker (violating campaign reporting requirements), as well as to sixteen candidates for the Wisconsin legislature, all of whom won, leading to unified Republican control of the state.[34]

Americans for Prosperity had established a Wisconsin chapter in 2006 organizing against Democratic governor Jim Doyle. AFP's Wisconsin director allied with Walker during his battles with unions as Milwaukee county executive, and Walker was introduced to AFP national director Tim Phillips, who characterized Walker as "getting serious . . . [about] trying to take on the unions on spending and pension issues." By 2010 the chapter had grown to 100,000 nominal members and was a major organizer of Tea Party rallies in the state. AFP was focused on organizing for the Wisconsin 2010 legislative races.[35]

The Bradley Foundation and Michael W. Grebe were Walker's other key base of support. Many of Walker's programmatic proposals came straight from the foundation. Walker's first major meeting after his election was with the Bradley Foundation Board at an expensive Milwaukee restaurant. In 2009 Bradley had given more than $1 million to the Wisconsin Policy Research Institute (WPRI, renamed the Badger Institute in 2017) to develop conservative policy ideas on unions, pensions, and health care and had provided one-third of the State Policy Network affiliate MacIver Institute's budget. Walker's views were regularly promoted on Charlie Sykes's radio program, which was carried statewide. Sykes also edited WPRI's magazine, *Wisconsin Interest*.[36]

During the campaign, Walker regularly framed public workers as an "elite," speaking of the "haves and have nots," and stoking resentment of both state workers and state government, particularly among rural and smaller city residents. He never campaigned on the issue of ending collective bargaining. Nevertheless, he beat Democratic Milwaukee mayor Tom Barrett in Wisconsin's 2010 gubernatorial election (52.29 to 46.52 percent), which also saw both the State Assembly and the State Senate flip to Republican control.

ACT 10 AND THE GUBERNATORIAL RECALL

On February 20, 2011, after only one month in office, Walker detailed plans for a "budget-repair" bill to Republican legislators. Such bills were common in Wisconsin, as budgets moved in and out of balance, and the Doyle administration had left a significant shortfall of $1.5 to $3.1 billion (the numbers were disputed).[37] The plan became known as Act 10, a bill to cut the pension and health benefits of state workers (by significantly raising their contributions) and, more controversially, to eliminate the long-standing collective bargaining rights of more than two hundred thousand state workers as well as "fair share" dues payments by nonmembers to unions. Essentially, this was a move to decertify public unions and cut off their funding, a long-standing dream of the radical libertarian right. Even some Republican senators were shocked.[38]

Walker's intentions were made clear in a January 2011 conversation with Diane Hendricks, a building supplies magnate, the richest woman in the state, and a major Walker donor. A documentary filmmaker caught the conversation, in which Hendricks pressed Walker on turning Wisconsin into a "completely red" "right-to-work" state. Believing the conversation was confidential, Hendricks asked whether there was "any chance we'll ever get to be a completely red state . . . and become a right to work [state]?" Walker responded that he would start in a few weeks with the "budget-adjustment bill." He explained that the first step was to "deal with collective bargaining for all public employee unions, because you use divide and conquer"—implying that full right-to-work legislation was the next step, although he publicly denied this.[39]

In a now-famous prank phone call on February 22, 2011, a blogger named Ian Murphy called Walker posing as David Koch. Believing he was talking with Koch, Walker said that in two days he would lay off six thousand state workers. When "Koch" suggested he "bring a baseball bat," Walker replied that he had "a [Louisville] Slugger with my name on it." After bragging that he talked with Republican governors in Ohio and Florida daily, Walker asked "Koch," first, to mobilize AFP for more people to call lawmakers and, second, to spend money to get the message out "over and over again." Walker divulged that he had discussed the plan with his cabinet at a January Super Bowl party before "we dropped the bomb," adding that while his breaking Wisconsin unions may not have quite the implications of Ronald Reagan's firing of air traffic controllers in 1981, "This is our moment, this is our time to change the course of history."[40]

The plan was carried out with devastating effect. Over the objections of Democrats in both houses, and after Senate Democrats had left the state to block action, Act 10 was passed on March 7 with only one Republican no vote. As Jane L. Collins discusses in her contribution to this volume, the legislation spurred massive public protest. A Facebook page for "United Wisconsin" calling for Walker's recall had more than 142,000 signatures by March 11, setting up the next phase of the fight. By April the group had 176,000 pledges. Up to one hundred thousand demonstrators protested, sang, and blocked the capitol throughout the spring and summer, setting up an ongoing skirmish with the administration, which sought to enact and enforce new restrictions on the public's right to assemble. A "John Doe" investigation into Walker's aides and associates moved forward, uncovering illegal campaign donations and campaign activity on public time before the investigation was eventually suppressed by a Republican-dominated Wisconsin Supreme Court.[41] The entire state seemed to be dividing up into warring camps.

The recall movement went forward with ambivalent support from the Democratic Party and union leaders, but these same groups pressured United Wisconsin to file papers that would force an election earlier than November 2012, when President Obama would be on the ballot and Democratic turnout would be at its peak. This was a fatal decision, and the recall was scheduled for June 2012, a summer election, when students would be away and the pro-Walker vote would be at its highest. Further, many Wisconsinites who disliked

Walker's actions opposed the recall as an undemocratic attempt to annul an election.

Republican observers say that the recall gave Walker new life, allowed him to raise huge amounts of money, and effectively launched his presidential bid. In the end, Republicans spent almost $81 million on the recall with heavy support from billionaires in the Koch network, and Democrats spent $22 million. When the election came on June 5, 2012, Walker cruised to victory over his previous opponent Tom Barrett by a seven-point margin, 1 percent better than his 2010 election. Almost all the Republicans in the Senate and Assembly who had been recalled also withstood the challenge. Underscoring the recall movement's tactical error, in November 2012 President Obama handily beat Republican presidential nominee Mitt Romney, and Democrat Tammy Baldwin beat the popular Tommy Thompson to win a US Senate seat.

Walker won office again easily in 2014, beating Democrat Mary Burke by 52 to 46 percent, numbers almost identical to his 2010 victory over Barrett. This win reinforced Republicans' complete control of Wisconsin and set the stage for Walker's unsuccessful 2016 presidential run.

REPUBLICAN GOVERNANCE IN THE AFTERMATH OF ACT 10

After the 2012 Walker recall victory, the Republican hold on state government was stronger than ever. The Democratic Party had been dealt a major blow, and much of the opposition retreated into gestures of protest, outrage, or despair. The Walker administration lost no time in pressing its advantage; Koch-Bradley policies were implemented with no effective opposition in the legislature. The average time it took to pass a bill dropped 25 percent, and one in four, including the most controversial bills, passed in less than two months.[42] Republicans transformed policy in the areas of labor law, taxation, school funding, higher education, the environment, and business development, among many others.

Act 10, the beginning of a complete transformation of labor relations in Wisconsin, had been passed in just twenty-four days. The immediate effect was an effective median pay cut of 8.2 percent and a two-year wage freeze for all state workers except police and firefighters. More importantly, it was a critical step toward the ultraconservative alliance's long-time goal of destroying public-sector unions, the last major stronghold of unionism in the United States, and then the remaining private-sector unions ("divide and conquer"). Earlier, Walker had denied interest in right-to-work legislation, calling it a "distraction," but in 2015 a right-to-work law was passed in only fourteen days. Senate Majority Leader Scott Fitzgerald denied that any "outside groups" were involved, but he had floated right-to-work as early as 2010. He later admitted that the bill was based on Michigan's 2013 law, which in turn had originated as an ALEC bill that was later published as a State Policy Network toolkit touting Michigan's success.[43]

The antilabor policy has been a success. Since 2011, no state has lost more of its labor-union identity than Wisconsin, according to a *Milwaukee Journal Sentinel* analysis. Union members made up 14.2 percent of Wisconsin workers before Act 10 but just 8.3 percent in 2015.[44] Wisconsin lost 132,000 union members, which placed the state in the bottom third in union membership, joined by mostly southern and western states.[45] With public labor broken and the Democratic Party defeated, Walker and the Republican legislature were free to implement the rest of the ultraconservative program in the state without opposition. Briefly outlined in the introductory chapter of this volume, it is described more fully here.

Tax cuts for the wealthy and business have been at the core of the Republican agenda. The tax strategy was two pronged: cut income and business taxes at the state level and freeze property taxes at the local level to create a crisis in school spending. In the first wave of legislation after achieving unified government control, Wisconsin Republicans passed a large package of tax cuts and tax credits that would primarily benefit businesses and upper-income residents. The Manufacturing and Agricultural Tax Credit, passed in the 2011–13 budget, cut taxes for farmers and manufacturers. Sold as a job-creating bill, three-quarters of the almost $300 million reduction went to people earning more than one million dollars a year in 2017; $21 million went to eleven people earning $35 million or more annually. The legislature also passed dozens of smaller tax credits and cuts benefiting the same upper-income groups, while job creation in the state lagged.[46]

During the same session, Republicans cut the Earned Income Tax Credit and Homestead Credit, which primarily benefited lower-income residents. During 2011–14 Wisconsin Republicans cut taxes totaling approximately $2 billion. Half of these cuts went to the richest 20 percent of the state's residents, and another quarter went to the next quintile. The lowest 20 percent received a benefit of $48 a year.[47] The tax cuts severely reduced income available for education, health care, social services, and roads.

The cuts from income taxes were partly made up through a broad range of regressive taxes and fees, including fee hikes to enter Wisconsin state parks. In 2011 only four Wisconsin communities had vehicle registration fees or "wheel taxes," but the number rose to twenty-seven by the end of 2017, and total revenues rose to almost $21 million.[48]

Walker and the legislature implemented a state-level version of conservative antitax leader Grover Norquist's strategy of "drowning" the government through a relentless cycle of cutting taxes, creating an artificial fiscal crisis, and using this to cut services. When Wisconsin did achieve budget surpluses, as in fiscal year 2015 with a surplus of over $750 million, Governor Walker initiated a new round of tax cuts, resulting in a $2 billion deficit for the 2015–17 budget cycle.[49]

Walker and the legislature slashed $900 million in state aid to local schools, cuts which were partly offset by the effective pay cut for most state workers and teachers (the "savings" from Act 10). But this wasn't sufficient to maintain educational funding, which comes from a combination of local property taxes, state aid, and federal funds. While slashing state funding, the Republicans also limited local school districts' ability to raise property-tax funding, effectively cutting K-12 education budgets across the state in rural and urban districts alike. Wisconsin cut spending per student by 14.6 percent from 2008 to 2015, the fifth largest cuts in the nation. As discussed in the introduction to this volume, higher education was also affected: funding was cut deeply, Walker tried to erase the Wisconsin Idea from the university's enabling legislation, and tenure protections were scaled back. Public discontent with the school cuts was a major issue in the 2018 gubernatorial election, leading Walker to dub himself the "education governor" despite seven years of K-12 cuts. A record number of school bond referenda were passed in 2018, and Walker's Democratic opponent, State Superintendent of Public Instruction Tony Evers, won in part on the strength of the school funding issue, as seventy-seven local referenda raising school funding $1.3 billion were passed across the state.[50]

While the Republicans were cutting taxes for the wealthy and slashing funds for education, they were also trying to consolidate their control over government. A 2014 Legislative Reference Bureau report identified sixty-four measures since 2011 in which the legislature preempted local government, including in the areas of public health, land use, transportation, telecommunication, and wage regulation. Many of these measures came from ALEC model bills. In December 2015, the legislature passed a new civil service law that would replace exams with resumes in state hiring, opening the door to both political abuse and other forms of employment discrimination. The bill also lengthened the time of probation for new employees, during which they can be fired at will, and centralized hiring in the now politicized Department of Administration. In 2017 the legislature passed Act 57, sponsored by Wisconsin Manufacturers and Commerce and supported by AFP, preventing any state agency from promulgating regulations costing more than $10 million without legislative approval, based directly on a 2012 ALEC model bill.[51]

Many of these cuts made it harder for local cities and counties to enforce environmental regulations. Beginning in 2011, there were large cuts to Wisconsin's Department of Natural Resources (DNR), which is responsible for monitoring and enforcing the state's environmental compliance, and DNR experts were prevented from testifying at public hearings. Legislation was passed to ease the enforcement of pollution standards and groundwater protection and sell off public lands. The DNR is also responsible for monitoring chronic wasting disease in deer, a major problem in a deer-hunting state. The disease rose steadily during the Walker years after funding was slashed: between 2012 and 2018, the DNR's budget averaged $1.14 million, a quarter of the 2004–7 average.[52]

Of particular concern to the many Wisconsinites who hunt and fish were cutbacks on habitat protection and wetlands protection. A 2018 bill stripped protection from more than ten thousand acres of wetlands with the support of builders, real estate interests, waste haulers, and farmers, as well as both Wisconsin Manufacturers and Commerce and Americans for Prosperity, which spent $100,000 in a 2018 special election to support a GOP environmental opponent. All told, GOP candidates have received $41 million from interests supporting the wetlands legislation.[53]

A central plank of the Walker administration was the assertion that environmental rollbacks would create jobs and do no harm to the environment. But the number of lakes and streams listed as polluted by the DNR has risen annually. Nitrates now permeate drinking water in many rural Wisconsin counties, and high-volume wells created for the rapid expansion of frack sand mining in Wisconsin have dried up some water bodies altogether. A number of acts have reduced regulation of large industrial farms and concentrated animal feeding operations (CAFOs) that draw heavily on local resources and return large amounts of animal waste, which increases nitrates in the water table and degrades trout streams.

In 2011 Republicans introduced a proposal to construct a massive iron mine in the Penokee Hills in northern Wisconsin on behalf of Gogebic Taconite (GTac), owned by a billionaire coal magnate from Florida. The mine was fiercely opposed by the Bad River Band of the Ojibwe Nation and environmentalists and supported by some northern residents (who saw a promise of some seven hundred jobs) and most large, private-sector trade unions. The mine was defeated with one moderate Republican vote in 2012. But a long-standing mining moratorium (passed under Governor Thompson) that required a company to prove that a sulfide mine can operate for ten years and be closed for another ten without polluting ground or surface water was revoked in 2017, raising hopes for resurrecting GTac in some new form.[54]

When Walker was running for governor in 2010, he pledged to create 250,000 new jobs by the end of his first term, but by 2014 only 147,000 jobs had been created. In pursuit of his pledge, Walker and the legislature in 2011 created the Wisconsin Economic Development Corporation (WEDC), a private agency headed by Walker himself. During the 2011–12 fiscal year alone, the WEDC controlled $519 million in bonds, loans, grants, and tax credits. By 2012, the agency was already under a cloud. It lost $12 million in loans because it never asked the receiving businesses for repayment, and it spent $10 million in federal funds without authorization. A 2013 report by the nonpartisan Legislative Audit Bureau found that the WEDC did not have sufficient policies and had made awards to "ineligible recipients, for ineligible projects, and for amounts that exceeded specified limits." In addition, it had failed to perform oversight duties, including monitoring recipients' performance and job creation. The audit further found that the WEDC had lent $500,000 to Walker campaign contributors.[55]

Despite the WEDC record (which Walker had to publicly renounce), the agency was the spearhead for bringing Foxconn, the Taiwanese manufacturer of Apple iPhones and other higher-tech LED screens, to Wisconsin. Foxconn became notorious in 2011 when so many workers at its Shenzen, China, factory attempted to commit suicide by jumping that it had to place nets around the plant to catch them. Founder Terry Guo also likened workers to animals and brought in a zoo director for management advice. Nonetheless, Governor Walker put together a package of $3 billion in state funds with a promise of thirteen thousand jobs—the largest foreign subsidy and the fourth largest corporate subsidy in US history. The package included an estimated additional $1.5 billion in subsidies by state and local governments, pushing the cost for each $30,000 annual salary job to $300,000.[56]

The highest estimate if the original plant is built is that it will become a $9 to $10 billion complex, but Foxconn was already altering its plans in 2018 (even before construction began), as it prepared to assemble smaller screens and TVs from imported components. Outside experts have said that only two thousand (or 15 percent) of the promised jobs will likely be delivered *if* the original high-tech LCD plant is built. By 2019 Foxconn had reneged on its original promise to build a manufacturing plant, although it hastily backtracked under pressure from President Trump. A University of Georgia economist has said that the payback period for a $100,000 per job deal is somewhere "between hundreds of years and never. At $230,000 [or more] per job, there is no hope of recapturing the state funds spent from taxes on the company and its workers."[57]

Further, all taxes have been waived for Foxconn, and it was given a unique right to appeal directly to the conservative Wisconsin Supreme Court in the event of any disputes, an alteration of the constitution for one corporation. The 4.5-square-mile complex, a quarter of the size of the city of Racine, will draw twenty million gallons of water per day from the Great Lakes, which provide 21 percent of the world's fresh water supply. Walker staked his reelection on Foxconn, but reception in Wisconsin was so highly critical that midway through his 2018 campaign, he stopped mentioning the Foxconn deal, although his opponent Tony Evers made criticism of it a prominent part of his campaign. Walker was defeated in 2018.

Minority Rule

The discussion to this point has focused on, first, the origins of the ultraconservative network within the Republican Party, both nationally and in Wisconsin; and second, the measures that the Republican Party took after it achieved a narrow victory in 2010 to cripple its democratic opposition, beginning with labor. The Republicans achieved unparalleled success, turning Wisconsin into a successful laboratory for the defeat of unions, the privatization of education, control over universities and the restriction of higher education, the rollback of virtually all environmental rules and regulations, the repeal of civil service reform, the expansion of cronyism, and one of the largest corporate giveaways in US history (to Foxconn).

This leaves us with two critical questions: Why was this effort successful? And did it reflect popular will?

The answers are not simple, but among the most important is that after narrowly winning the Tea Party election of 2010, the Republican Party changed the rules of the game. The first and central blow was the crippling of public unions and thereby the Democratic Party. Taking advantage of the new *Citizens United v. Federal Election Commission* (2010) US Supreme Court ruling, Republicans built new sluices, legal and sub-rosa, for the flood of money into politics; eroded government transparency; gerrymandered state elections; packed the Wisconsin Supreme Court; and implemented new rules to suppress the votes of minorities and young people.

It is worth reiterating that the primary purpose of Act 10 was broader than crippling public unions. In the remarkably candid words of Senate Majority Leader Scott Fitzgerald in 2011 before the act was passed: "If we win this battle and the money is not there under the auspices of the unions . . . President Obama is going to have a much more difficult time getting elected and winning the state of Wisconsin." The destruction of public unions was not only a long-sought conservative goal, but also a key step toward the explicit goal of crippling a democratic opposition.[58]

To achieve this goal, the Republican network worked tirelessly to open the sluices of dark money flowing into Wisconsin and to keep this activity hidden. The Koch network spent heavily in 2010 to elect Walker and the Republican legislature. During the 2011–12 recall, Walker asked AFP to put money into the Wisconsin Club for Growth (WCG). Evidence leaked to the *Guardian* newspaper shows Walker directly asking billionaire John Menard to contribute $1 million; out-of-state contributors included casino billionaire Sheldon Adelson and Donald Trump. The three-year John Doe investigation found that Walker's campaign manager, R. J. Johnson, was the media buyer for WCG and had coordinated the dark-money group and the campaign illegally.[59]

The John Doe investigation was shut down by the Wisconsin Supreme Court after two judges who had also received WCG funding refused to recuse themselves. Five months later, in September 2015, Walker and the Wisconsin legislature completely rewrote Wisconsin's campaign finance laws through two bills. The first dismantled the Government Accountability Board that had originally launched the probe into the illegal coordination. The second doubled the amount wealthy individuals could give to candidates and also allowed candidates to coordinate with outside issue ad groups, the same activity that had originally launched the probe. Only three organizations lobbied for the bill: Wisconsin Manufacturers and Commerce, the Wisconsin Club for Growth, and Americans for Prosperity.[60]

The second critical step to consolidating minority control was the gerrymandering of Wisconsin. The state had been targeted in 2009 by the national GOP Redistricting Majority Project, or REDMAP, which sought to take advantage of *Citizens United* to target state legislatures that could be flipped from Democratic to Republican control, particularly the lower houses in Ohio, Wisconsin, Indiana, and Pennsylvania.

Unified Republican control of government in 2010 allowed the party to draw the maps for both federal and state legislative districts. Republican lawmakers huddled in secret with lawyers from the firm Michael Best and Friedrich to use computerized geographic information system (GIS) technology to redraw the lines. Each Republican legislator was brought into a closed room to approve his or her map. By 2012, the new map let Republicans flip the Wisconsin State Assembly from a 50–45 deficit (in 2008) to a 60–38 advantage and the Wisconsin State Senate from an 18–15 to a 19–14 Republican majority. Republicans won 74 percent of all seats with only 52 percent of the vote; this was despite a seven-point victory by President Obama and the election of Democratic senator Tammy Baldwin.[61]

Finally, Walker and the Republican legislature set out to systematically restrict the right to vote. The origins of modern voter suppression go back to Paul Weyrich, founder of the Heritage Foundation. In a 1980 speech to a gathering of evangelical Christians, he said, "I don't want everybody to vote. Elections are not won by a majority of people . . . Our leverage in the elections quite candidly goes up as the voting populace goes down."[62] This has since become a central element of conservative Republican doctrine and strategy. In both public and private comments, Wisconsin Republican Party actors and supporters have made clear that the primary goals of voter ID laws are to, first, ensure the election of Republican candidates in state and federal elections by suppressing Democratic votes and, second, allow close or losing elections to be called into question.

A trove of documents leaked to the *Guardian* in 2016 discuss the strategy with unusual candor. In the 2011 race for the Wisconsin Supreme Court, a race that was widely seen as a proxy for the legitimacy of Walker's Act 10, conservative leaders speculated about what would happen if their preferred candidate, David Prosser, was defeated. A senior member of the Metropolitan Milwaukee Chamber of Commerce asked in an email to conservative strategists, "Do we need to start messaging 'widespread reports of election fraud' so we are positively set up for the recount regardless of the final number?" and added, "I obviously think we should." Within minutes Scott Jensen, a former Republican Speaker of the Assembly (convicted of felony misuse of state workers and funds in election activity, later reversed) responded, "Yes. Anything fishy should be highlighted. . . . Stories should be solicited by talk radio hosts."[63]

A month later, the legislature passed Act 23, one of the most restrictive voter ID laws in the country, ostensibly passed to combat in-person "voter fraud," which according to election law expert Richard Hasen of University of California-Irvine is a "shameful falsehood, given the extremely low rates of voter fraud in the U.S., especially the kind of fraud targeted by Republican voter ID laws. . . . It undermines faith in the fairness of the electoral process, which is the bedrock of all functioning democracies."[64]

Republican legislative staffer Todd Allbaugh, who was present inside the Republican Caucus during the formation of Act 23 in 2011, quit his job and the party in 2015, saying, "A handful of the GOP Senators were giddy about the ramifications and literally singled out the prospects of suppressing minority and college voters. Think about that for a minute. Elected officials planning and happy to help deny a fellow American's constitutional right to vote in order to increase their own chances to hang onto power."[65] Only Texas had a law which experts judged more restrictive. After a series of challenges,[66] in October 2014 the US Supreme Court ruled that voter ID could not go into effect so close to the 2014 election.

After a round of appeals, the bill was finally allowed to go into effect in the 2016 election. After the Republican primary, US Representative Glenn Grothman told a Milwaukee television station that the Democratic presidential nominee Hillary Clinton was a weak candidate and "now we have photo ID. I think photo ID is going to make a little bit of a difference as well."[67] While many factors determined Hillary Clinton's 2016 loss in Wisconsin, voter suppression was undoubtedly significant. On September 22, in the run-up to the election, Republican Attorney General Brad Schimmel certified in court that all Division of Motor Vehicles employees were trained to make sure that citizens could get IDs easily, but a *Nation* investigation found that in ten different DMV sites citizens received answers "all over the board." When the Republican presidential nominee Donald Trump carried the state in 2016 by 23,000 votes, almost 41,000 fewer people voted in Milwaukee than in 2012. Afterwards, many African Americans in the city complained of difficulty in obtaining the free voter ID. In April 2017, Schimmel told a reporter that President Trump would not have won and Republican Ron Johnson would not have been reelected to the US Senate without voter ID laws.[68]

From 2011 on, changing the rules of elections became a tool for attempting to ensure minority rule in the state. Professor Barry Burden, who directs the Elections Research Center at the University of Wisconsin–Madison, commented, "When competition filters into making the rules themselves, it's a recipe for disaster."[69]

Democratic Dénouement: Changing the Rules 2018

The midterm elections of 2018 brought sweeping change to the upper level of Wisconsin government. Democrats carried the statewide offices of governor, lieutenant governor, attorney general, and treasurer and reelected Tammy Baldwin to the US Senate. These victories occurred in the aftermath of Act 10 and the decimation of labor, the spending of $100 million by Republicans on the governor's race alone, and continuing voter suppression, suggesting a counterargument: perhaps changing the rules didn't work in the end.

In the normal workings of a democracy, Republicans would have admitted defeat at the executive levels and moved forward into loyal opposition to the new governor. But in an ultimate act of changing the rules to suit one party, the leaders of the legislature held a lame-duck session (directed by Walker behind the scenes), passing a raft of bills that restricted Governor-Elect Tony Evers's executive power over the Wisconsin Economic Development Authority and limiting his ability to enact administrative rules using the same authority that Republicans had given Walker for the past eight years. Evers was blocked from withdrawing from a national lawsuit challenging the federal Affordable Care Act, a central promise of his campaign. (One bill did fail, however, that would have protected preexisting conditions if that suit succeeded.)[70]

New restrictions were placed on the power of the attorney general, and the legislature gave itself parallel powers to intervene in court. Both legislative leaders and Walker blamed his defeat on high voter turnout and so restricted early voting across the state to two weeks in the name of "uniformity."

The Democratic victories in statewide races were relatively narrow, about a percentage point. And while gerrymandering cannot prevent statewide victories for opposing parties (since all voters in the state vote for a single office), the Republican gerrymandering held in the Wisconsin Assembly and Senate. Democrats won 53 percent of all assembly votes cast, yet Republicans carried sixty-three of the state's ninety-nine assembly districts. An analysis by Craig Gilbert of the *Milwaukee Journal Sentinel* shows that the Republicans now have a "built in 64–35 advantage in the partisan makeup" of the ninety-nine districts. Although Evers's election makes it somewhat more likely that the next map will be less partisan, it will be difficult to bring the state's districting back into balance without sweeping nonpartisan redistricting reform now that the US Supreme Court has barred challenges to partisan redistricting.[71]

The template for radically constricting an opposition victory had been tested in 2016 in North Carolina when its Republican legislature stripped the incoming Democratic governor of powers over the judiciary. In 2018 these techniques were applied in Wisconsin, extending its status as a laboratory for the national ultraconservative movement and those Republicans who refused to acknowledge the legitimate alternation of power. As the political scientists Steven Ziblatt and Daniel Levitsky observe in *How Democracies Die*, "Many government efforts to subvert democracy are 'legal' in the sense that they are approved by the legislature or accepted by the courts. They may even be portrayed as efforts to *improve* democracy."[72]

In 2010 Wisconsin became a laboratory for an unelected, ultrawealthy, ultraconservative network to roll back the achievements of one hundred years of progressive, civil government. In 2018 the people of Wisconsin chose to change course. This new Wisconsin story will shape whether civil government and democratic legitimacy is restored to Wisconsin, and, by extension, the United States.

Notes

1. Justice Louis Brandeis dissent in New State Ice v. Liebman (1932), cited in Jeffrey Rosen, *Louis D. Brandeis: American Prophet* (New Haven, CT: Yale University Press, 2016), 109.

2. James K. Conant, *Wisconsin Politics and Government: America's Laboratory of Democracy* (Lincoln: University of Nebraska Press, 2006), 294–98.

3. Abe Bortz, "Unemployment Insurance: Early History," Social Welfare History Project, Virginia Commonwealth University, https://socialwelfare.library.vcu.edu/programs/unemployment-insurance-early-history/.

4. The explication of this theory and analytical application to the Wisconsin case is beyond the scope of this chapter. For the theory of civil oligarchy, see Jeffrey A. Winters and Benjamin I. Page, "Oligarchy in the United States?" *Perspectives on Politics* 7, no. 4 (2009): 731–51; Jeffrey A. Winters, *Oligarchy* (Cambridge: Cambridge University Press, 2011). For the right-wing network in the United States and its political activities, see Alexander Hertel-Fernandez and Theda Skocpol, "Asymmetric Interest Group Mobilization and Party Coalitions in US Tax Politics," *Studies in American Political Development* 29, no. 2 (2015): 235–49; Alexander Hertel-Fernandez and Theda Skocpol, "Why US Conservatives Shape Legislation across the Fifty States Much More Effectively than Liberals," in *SSN Key Findings* (Cambridge: Scholars Strategy Network, 2015); Alexander Hertel-Fernandez, Theda Skocpol, and Daniel Lynch, "Business Associations, Conservative Networks, and the Ongoing Republican War over Medicaid Expansion," *Journal of Health Politics, Policy and Law* 41, no. 2 (2016): 239–86; Theda Skocpol and Alexander Hertel-Fernandez, "The Koch Network and Republican Party Extremism," *Perspectives on Politics* 14, no. 3 (2016): 681–99; Alexander Hertel-Fernandez, Theda Skocpol, and Jason Sclar, "When Political Mega-Donors Join Forces: How the Koch Network and the Democracy Alliance Influence Organized U.S. Politics on the Right and Left," *Studies in American Political Development* 32, no. 2 (2018): 127–65; James Feigenbaum, Alexander Hertel-Fernandez, and Vanessa Williamson, "From the Bargaining Table to the Ballot Box: Political Effects of Right to Work Laws" (working paper 24259, January 2018), https://hdl.handle.net/2144/27524. For work comparing networks on the left and right, see Hertel-Fernandez, Skocpol, and Sclar, "When Political Mega-Donors Join Forces." For a definitive overview, see Alexander Hertel-Fernandez, *State Capture: How Conservative Activists, Big Businesses, and Wealthy Donors Reshaped the American States—and the Nation* (Oxford: Oxford University Press, 2019).

5. This asymmetry is embedded in the constitutional structure of representation in the US Senate by state, a legacy of compromise over slavery, which disproportionately benefits rural and conservative interests. This structure is reproduced to some degree in every state. See Jonathan Rodden, *Why Cities Lose: The Deep Roots of the Urban-Rural Political Divide* (New York: Basic Books, 2019).

6. Thomas E. Mann and Norman J. Ornstein, *It's Even Worse Than It Looks: How the American Constitutional System Collided with the New Politics of Extremism* (New York: Basic Books, 2016).

7. The most important scholarship has been conducted by Skocpol and her students, particularly Hertel-Fernandez. See n. 4.

8. Alexander Hertel-Fernandez, "Who Passes Business's 'Model Bills'? Policy Capacity and Corporate Influence in U.S. State Politics," *Perspectives on Politics* 12, no. 3 (2014): 582–602.

9. Gordon Lafer, *The One Percent Solution: How Corporations Are Remaking America One State at a Time* (Ithaca, NY: Cornell University Press, 2017), 12.

10. For the shift in the party, see Geoffrey Kabaservice, *Rule and Ruin: The Downfall of Moderation and the Destruction of the Republican Party, from Eisenhower to the Tea Party* (Oxford: Oxford University Press, 2013). For the Tea Party and the rightward shift, see Theda Skocpol and Vanessa Williamson, *The Tea Party and the Remaking of Republican Conservatism* (Oxford: Oxford University Press, 2012); Robert B. Horwitz, *America's Right: Anti-establishment Conservatism from Goldwater to the Tea Party* (Cambridge, MA: Polity Press, 2013). Birtherism encouraged doubts or denied that President Barack Obama (2009–17) was a natural-born US citizen, thereby implying that he was ineligible to be president of the United States.

11. Quoted in Nancy MacLean, *Democracy in Chains: The Deep History of the Radical Right's Stealth Plan for America* (New York: Viking, 2017), 125. For a historical account, see Kim Phillips-Fein, *Invisible Hands: The Businessmen's Crusade against the New Deal* (New York: W. W. Norton, 2010), 156–65.

12. Thomas Medvetz, *Think Tanks in America* (Chicago: University of Chicago Press, 2014), 101–5. Medvetz argues that the rise of right-wing think tanks was largely a response to the liberal-technocratic expertise of groups like the Brookings Institution, which formulated policy within a broadly Keynesian consensus that provided the rationale and policy for the Great Society.

13. In a great irony, Koch was exposed to Leninist ideas through Cato cofounder Murray Rothbard, who offered a guide to overthrowing a state through the development of a disciplined party and cadre organization. MacLean, *Democracy in Chains*, 138–41. These claims seem incredible on their face, but MacLean's meticulous scholarship documents each of them in the words and writings of the principal actors themselves.

14. This combined amount would place them second, behind only Amazon's Jeff Bezos. Five of the other top ten are in high technology, rounded out by Warren Buffett and Rob Walton of the Walmart fortune. Alex Langone, "The 10 Richest People in America," *Money*, January 16, 2018, http://time.com/money/5095574/the-10-richest-people-in-america/. Walton was one of the largest contributors to Scott Walker's election as Milwaukee County Executive (see below).

15. Jane Mayer, *Dark Money: The Hidden History of the Billionaires behind the Rise of the Radical Right* (New York: Doubleday, 2016), Citizens for a Sound Economy quotation from p. 160. This is the most important documentary source on the right-wing para-party.

16. Mayer, *Dark Money*, 145.

17. Mary Bottari, "Weaponized Philanthropy: Document Trove Details Bradley Foundation's Efforts to Build Right-Wing 'Infrastructure' Nationwide," *Capital Times*, May 9, 2017, https://madison.com/ct/opinion/column/mary-bottari-weaponized-philanthropy-document-trove-details-bradley-foundation-s/article_e219c36e-2fc4-542d-bd39-e79e05f7d09b.html. Mary Bottari of the Center for Media and Democracy has been one of two journalists (along with Jane Mayer) most responsible for uncovering and documenting the history of the Koch network, and Bottari has led in documenting the work of the Bradley Foundation and ALEC.

18. Daniel Bice, Bill Glauber, and Ben Poston, "From Local Roots, Bradley Foundation Builds Conservative Empire," *Milwaukee Journal Sentinel*, November 19, 2011, http:
//archive.jsonline.com/news/milwaukee/from-local-roots-bradley-foundation-builds
-conservative-empire-k7337pb-134187368.html/. Dark money refers to money contributed to nonprofit organizations that is then used to fund political campaigns without
having to disclose the donors' identities.

19. Mayer, *Dark Money*, 113–19.

20. Bice, Glauber, and Poston, "From Local Roots."

21. Bice, Glauber, and Poston, "From Local Roots."

22. For an overview of this content, see Daniel Bice, "Hacked Records Show Bradley Foundation Taking Its Conservative Wisconsin Model National," *Milwaukee Journal
Sentinel*, May 5, 2017, http://www.jsonline.com/story/news/special-reports/2017/05/05/
comment-hacked-records-show-bradley-foundation-taking-its-conservative-wiscon
sin-model-national/101334754/.

23. Bice, "Hacked Records."

24. Jesse Holcomb, Tom Rosenstiel, Amy Mitchell, Kevin Caldwell, Tricia Sartor,
and Nancy Vogt, *Non-Profit News: Assessing a New Landscape in Journalism*, Pew Research
Center, July 18, 2011, http://www.journalism.org/2011/07/18/non-profit-news/.

25. Bice, "Hacked Records."

26. Medvetz, *Think Tanks in America*, 101–5.

27. Hertel-Fernandez, "'Model Bills,'" 584. ALEC has been steadily losing corporate support as its role has become more and more public, in large part due to the
efforts of the Center for Media and Democracy.

28. Lafer, *One Percent*, 12–16.

29. Brendan Fischer, "ALEC Exposed, Wisconsin: The Hijacking of a State," Center for Media and Democracy, 2012, p. 3, https://www.alecexposed.org/w/images/c/cd/
ALEC_Exposed_in_Wisconsin.pdf.

30. Fischer, "ALEC Exposed."

31. Conant, *Wisconsin Politics*, 5–6. For background on Thompson, see Tommy G.
Thompson and Doug Moe, *Tommy: My Journey of a Lifetime* (Madison: University of
Wisconsin Press, 2018).

32. This account of Walker's rise is primarily drawn from Dave Umhoefer, "From
Milwaukee County to Madison, Scott Walker's Rise Marked by Union Battles," *Milwaukee Journal Sentinel*, November 27, 2016, http://www.jsonline.com/story/news/
special-reports/2016/11/29/comment-milwaukee-county-madison-scott-walkers-rise
-marked-union-battles/94646336/.

33. He immediately began holding national fundraisers, including one sponsored
by a Bear Stearns executive after the bank had won a $100-million county refinancing
deal. Bear Stearns officials discussed their picks for the county Pension Board with
Walker staffers. (Walker officials later said they had "lost or destroyed" all notes from
the deal after a local criminal investigation began.) Umhoefer, "From Milwaukee
County to Madison."

34. Mayer, *Dark Money*, 307–12. Much of the account in this paragraph and the
next several is drawn from Mayer. Information on Menard and his long-standing

hatred of unions, including a ban on hiring anyone who had ever belonged to a union, is on pp. 309–10. His animus toward Wisconsin's Department of Natural Resources stems, in part, from being forced to pay $1.7 million in fines for hazardous waste disposal. (Menards once reportedly labeled arsenic-tainted mulch as "ideal for playgrounds.")

35. Patrick Healy and Monica Davey, "Behind Scott Walker, a Longstanding Conservative Alliance against Unions," *New York Times*, June 8, 2015, https://www.nytimes.com/2015/06/08/us/politics/behind-scott-walker-a-longstanding-conservative-alliance-against-unions.html.

36. Healy and Davey, "Behind Scott Walker."

37. Jason Stein, "Report on Wisconsin's Budget Deficit Contains Hidden Costs," *Milwaukee Journal Sentinel*, November 19, 2010, http://www.jsonline.com/news/state politics/109275069.html; Dave Umhoefer, "Gov. Jim Doyle Says Wisconsin's Projected Budget Shortfall Is $1.5 Billion, Much Lower than Previously Projected," *Milwaukee Journal Sentinel*, November 29, 2010, https://www.politifact.com/wisconsin/state ments/2010/nov/29/jim-doyle/gov-jim-doyle-says-wisconsins-projected-budget-sho/.

38. Jason Stein and Patrick Marley, *More Than They Bargained For: Scott Walker, Unions, and the Fight for Wisconsin* (Madison: University of Wisconsin Press, 2013), 9–11. This remains the definitive history of the Walker election and recall.

39. Stein and Marley, *More Than They Bargained For*, 46–48. Even conservative lawmakers had refrained from introducing right-to-work legislation, knowing how deeply unpopular it was (although Walker had cosponsored an ALEC right-to-work bill in 1993). The comments did not become public for a year because the filmmaker kept to his pledge of confidentiality. Shortly after, Hendricks contributed another $10,000 to Walker, the maximum then allowed for a four-year election cycle, and her company ABC Supply donated $25,000 to the Republican Governors Association, which funneled it back to the Walker campaign.

40. The entire phone call as recounted in Stein and Marley, *More Than They Bargained For*, is worth reading (150–57).

41. The John Doe investigations demonstrate a clear and critical linkage among Koch political organizations, the Bradley Foundation, Walker, and the Republican Party. For reasons of length they cannot be fully explored here. For a digested running account see Daniel Bice, "John Doe Investigations," *Milwaukee Journal Sentinel*, n.d., http://archive.jsonline.com/news/statepolitics/wisconsin-john-doe-investigations-271412751.html. For a full account of the investigation and the flow of dark money to the Republican Party in Wisconsin, see Ed Pilkington and the *Guardian* US Interactive Team, "Scott Walker, the John Doe Files and How Corporate Cash Influences American Politics," *Guardian*, September 14, 2016, http://www.theguardian.com/us-news/ng-in teractive/2016/sep/14/john-doe-files-scott-walker-corporate-cash-american-politics.

42. Teodor Teofilov, "After Gov. Scott Walker Took Office, Bills Moved Faster through the Wisconsin Legislature," *Wisconsin Center for Investigative Journalism*, August 19, 2018, https://www.wisconsinwatch.org/2018/08/after-gov-scott-walker-took-office -bills-moved-faster-through-the-wisconsin-legislature/.

43. Dan Kaufman, *The Fall of Wisconsin: The Conservative Conquest of a Progressive Bastion and the Future of American Politics* (New York: W. W. Norton, 2018), 123–24.

Kaufman outlines the important role that Wisconsin State Assembly member Chris Taylor (D-Madison) played in exposing the extent of ALEC involvement in Wisconsin.

44. Dave Umhoefer, "For Unions in Wisconsin, a Fast and Hard Fall since Act 10," *Milwaukee Journal Sentinel*, November 27, 2016, https://projects.jsonline.com/news/2016/11/27/for-unions-in-wisconsin-fast-and-hard-fall-since-act-10.html; see also Kaufman, *Fall of Wisconsin*, 165.

45. Umhoefer, "For Unions in Wisconsin."

46. Jesse Opoien, "Transforming Taxes: Republican Lawmakers Want to Change the Way Wisconsin Taxes Its Residents," *Capital Times*, July 5, 2017, https://madison.com/ct/news/local/govt-and-politics/election-matters/transforming-taxes-republican-lawmakers-want-to-change-the-way-wisconsin/article_6672c344-d61d-5c05-b990-b763969a13f0.html.

47. Lafer, *One Percent*, 53–54; Wisconsin Legislative Fiscal Bureau, "Tax Law Changes since 2011" (memo), April 30, 2014.

48. Patrick Marley, "Wheel Taxes Have Popped Up around Wisconsin since 2011, Resulting in a Seven-Fold Increase," *Milwaukee Journal Sentinel*, May 23, 2018, https://www.jsonline.com/story/news/politics/2018/05/23/wheel-taxes-have-popped-up-around-wisconsin-since-2011/634841002/.

49. Lafer, *One Percent*, 73.

50. Annysa Johnson, "Wisconsin School Referendums Break Records in 'Landslide for Public Education,'" *Milwaukee Journal Sentinel*, November 8, 2018, https://www.jsonline.com/story/news/politics/elections/2018/11/08/wisconsin-election-school-referendums-break-records/1920426002/; Lafer, *One Percent*, 71; Michael Leachman and Chris Mai, "Most States Still Funding Schools Less than before the Recession," Center on Budget and Policy Priorities, October 16, 2014, https://www.cbpp.org/research/most-states-still-funding-schools-less-than-before-the-recession.

51. Wisconsin Legislative Fiscal Bureau, memo to Wisconsin State Assembly Rep. Peter Barca, "Unfunded Mandates and Items That Would Restrict Local Control," June 10, 2014; Wisconsin Democracy Campaign, "Walker Approves WMC, Koch-Backed Anti-Regulation Bill" (press release), August 10, 2017, https://www.wisdc.org/news/press-releases/78-press-release-2017/5864-walker-approves-wmc-koch-backed-anti-regulation-bill.

52. Steven Verburg, "Unease Growing in Wisconsin GOP Base over Environmental Rollbacks," *Wisconsin State Journal*, March 4, 2018, https://madison.com/wsj/news/local/govt-and-politics/unease-growing-in-wisconsin-gop-base-over-environmental-rollbacks/article_133614cd-6f17-5bfe-be9c-f6b8bed68f5d.html; Patrick Durkin, "Patrick Durkin: Scott's Plan? Gut Wisconsin's Wildlife, Environment," *Wisconsin State Journal*, October 21, 2018, https://madison.com/sports/recreation/outdoors/patrick-durkin-scott-s-plan-gut-wisconsin-s-wildlife-environment/article_e5f87d7d-4800-56e6-8415-53004ed8264d.html.

53. Verburg, "Unease Growing."

54. Kaufman, *Fall of Wisconsin*, 246.

55. Jim Nelson, "Gov. Scott Walker's Promise to Create 250,000 Jobs in Wisconsin Remains Elusive," *Milwaukee Journal Sentinel*, March 12, 2017, https://www.jsonline

.com/story/news/politics/2017/03/12/gov-scott-walkers-promise-create-250000-jobs -wisconsin-remains-elusive/99001742/. Job creation by Wisconsin Economic Development Corporation in Matthew DeFour, "WEDC Awards Increase as Job Creation Numbers Fall," *Wisconsin State Journal*, September 23, 2015, https://madison.com/news/ local/govt-and-politics/wedc-awards-increase-as-job-creation-numbers-fall/article_ba 28699d-a600-5a74-a90a-710149e6acac.html. For a complete account of the WEDC through 2016, see the series by Matthew DeFour, "WEDC under Fire," *Wisconsin State Journal*, January 25, 2016, https://madison.com/wsj/wedc-under-fire/collection_7f59d9 ad-6b0c-59a4-8cc1-3ec42de9bca5.html.

56. Patrick Marley, "Foxconn CEO Compared Workers to Animals, Had Zoo Director Give Management Tips," *Milwaukee Journal Sentinel*, August 17, 2017, https://www .jsonline.com/story/news/2017/08/03/foxconn-ceo-compared-workers-animals-had -zoo-director-give-management-tips/536866001/.

57. Lawrence Tabak, "The Con in Foxconn Wisconsin," *American Prospect*, September 21, 2018, http://prospect.org/article/con-foxconn-wisconsin. For Foxconn's shift in original plans, see Todd Richmond, "A Look at Key Moments in Foxconn's Plan for Wisconsin Plant," Associated Press, February 1, 2019, https://www.apnews.com/87833 f1640fa4168a844db9c682fo6b1.

58. Lafer, *One Percent*, 12.

59. Justin Miller, "Scott Walker Leaks Could Force Supreme Court to Confront Dark Money," *American Prospect*, September 16, 2016, https://prospect.org/article/scott -walker-leaks-could-force-supreme-court-confront-dark-money.

60. Cady Zuvich, "Conservative Groups Helped Gut Wisconsin Election Laws," Center for Public Integrity, December 16, 2015, https://publicintegrity.org/2015/12/16/19 056/conservative-groups-helped-gut-wisconsin-election-laws.

61. For a definitive account of REDMAP nationally and in Wisconsin, see David Daley, *Ratf**ked: The True Story behind the Secret Plan to Steal America's Democracy* (New York: Liveright, 2016). For Wisconsin gerrymandering, see Kaufman, *Fall of Wisconsin*, 145–48, 213–18.

62. Cited in Ari Berman, *Give Us the Ballot: The Modern Struggle for Voting Rights in America* (New York: Picador, 2016), 263.

63. Michael Wines, "Some Republicans Acknowledge Leveraging Voter ID Laws for Political Gain," *New York Times*, September 16, 2016, https://www.nytimes.com/2016/ 09/17/us/some-republicans-acknowledge-leveraging-voter-id-laws-for-political-gain .html. For the full *Guardian* story, see Pilkington et al., "Scott Walker." The original documents are available at http://www.documentcloud.org/documents/3105957-Prosser .html#document/p6/a317546.

64. For a comprehensive review of the 2016 election, see Sami Edge, "A Review of Key States with Voter ID Laws Found No Voter Impersonation Fraud," Center for Public Integrity, August 21, 2016, https://publicintegrity.org/accountability/a-review-of -key-states-with-voter-id-laws-found-no-voter-impersonation-fraud/. The review finds that of some 146 million votes cast between 2000 and 2012 there were only ten documented cases of voter impersonation. For Hasen comments, see Wines, "Some Republicans." The original act banned using student IDs, tribal IDs, and passports for voter

identification, and it gave voters only twenty-four hours to present an ID if they had forgotten one after voting on election day, although passports and tribal IDs were later allowed. Student IDs were also later allowed, although most Wisconsin campuses did not issue IDs meeting state guidelines. As in other states, no statistically meaningful evidence was offered of actual voter fraud; the single case found in Wisconsin was of a Republican voting twice in Waukesha County.

65. Wines, "Some Republicans."

66. The law was challenged in December 2013 by the American Civil Liberties Union, and in April 2014 a federal judge ruled that the law violated the federal Voting Rights Act. In July 2014, the Wisconsin Supreme Court rejected a challenge. State Attorney General Brad Schimmel appealed to the Seventh Circuit of the US Appellate Court, which split on the lower court decision, effectively overturning it.

67. Bridget Shanahan, "Congressman's Voter ID Comment Goes Viral," WTMJ-TV Milwaukee, April 6, 2016, https://www.tmj4.com/news/local-news/twitter-reacts-to-congressman-glenn-grothmans-controversial-comments-about-voter-id.

68. For failure to adequately provide voter ID at Wisconsin's Division of Motor Vehicles, see Ari Berman, "Wisconsin Is Systematically Failing to Provide the Photo IDs Required to Vote in November," *Nation*, September 29, 2016, https://www.the nation.com/article/wisconsin-is-systematically-failing-to-provide-the-photo-ids-requ ired-to-vote-in-november/; Patrick Marley, "DMV Gives Wrong Information on Voter ID," *Milwaukee Journal Sentinel*, September 29, 2016, https://www.jsonline.com/ story/news/politics/elections/2016/09/29/dmv-gives-wrong-information-voter-id/912 83462/. For African American voter suppression, see Ari Berman, "Rigged: How Voter Suppression Threw Wisconsin to Trump," *Mother Jones*, November/December 2017, https://www.motherjones.com/politics/2017/10/voter-suppression-wisconsin-election -2016/. For Schimel's comments, see Todd Richmond, "Wisconsin AG Brad Schimel Suggests Voter ID Helped Donald Trump Win the State," *Wisconsin State Journal*, April 14, 2018, https://madison.com/wsj/news/local/govt-and-politics/wisconsin-ag-brad -schimel-suggests-voter-id-helped-donald-trump/article_f686670a-6760-5faa-9746-1c 7ee033ad14.html.

69. Michael Wines, "As ID Laws Fall, Voters See New Barriers Rise," *New York Times*, December 21, 2017, https://www.nytimes.com/2016/10/26/us/elections/voter-id-laws .html.

70. Mitch Smith, John Eligon, and Monica Davey, "Behind the Scenes in Wisconsin: A Republican Power Play, Months in the Making," *New York Times*, December 8, 2018, https://www.nytimes.com/2018/12/07/us/wisconsin-republicans-power.html; Guy Boulton, "What the Pre-Existing Conditions Vote in Wisconsin's Lame Duck Session Means," *Milwaukee Journal Sentinel*, December 5, 2018, https://www.jsonline.com/story/money /business/2018/12/05/what-pre-existing-conditions-vote-means-wisconsin/2215660002/.

71. Craig Gilbert, "GOP Redistricting Leaves Its Stamp on 2012 Election," *Milwaukee Journal Sentinel*, December 10, 2012, http://archive.jsonline.com/blogs/ news/182754381.html; Rucho v. Common Cause, No. 18-422, 588 U.S. 2019.

72. Steven Levitsky and Daniel Ziblatt, *How Democracies Die* (New York: Crown, 2018), 5.

The Turn Away from Government and the Need to Revive the Civic Purpose of Higher Education

KATHERINE J. CRAMER

> The least commendable purpose of acquiring knowledge . . . is to apply it to one's own advancement—to achieve worldly success. A higher purpose is to fit one to live the intellectual life. . . . A third and the highest purpose of acquiring knowledge is to use it for the benefit of mankind.
>
> —CHARLES VAN HISE, the first person to earn a PhD from the University of Wisconsin–Madison, and its president from 1903 to 1918, in a speech given in Louisiana, 1914[1]

In 1995, the National Association of State Universities and Land-Grant Colleges asked the Kellogg Foundation to fund a national commission of university and college presidents and chancellors that would be charged with studying the future of public higher education. The result was a series of reports, the third of which was called *Returning to Our Roots: The Engaged Institution.*[2]

The Kellogg Commission included the following quote, and highlighted it on page 3: "In the end, the clear evidence is that, with the resources and superbly qualified professors and staff on our campuses, we can organize our institutions to serve both local and national needs in a more coherent and effective way. We can and must do better." In other words, over twenty years ago, the Kellogg Commission warned that the civic mission of higher education was at risk of disappearing.

The warnings have continued unabated. About fifteen years later, the US Department of Education commissioned another study, which warned that a "crucible moment" had arrived. The resulting report, published in 2012, called for yet another renewal of the civic mission of higher education. It warned of a dangerous trend toward a higher-education system driven by the need to prepare people for the workforce rather than the need to prepare people to participate in democracy.[3]

It has not always been the case that the needs of the workforce and the needs of democracy were perceived to be at odds. When land-grant higher-education institutions were first created by the federal government during the Civil War via the Morrill Land Grant Act of 1862, the motivation was that an expanding nation needed to equip its citizens (that is, its white male citizens at the time) with the ability to grow their own food, build their own buildings, and build their own communities. The act gave each state thirty thousand acres of federally owned land per congressional representative to sell in order to fund institutions of public higher education.[4] The policy conveyed an understanding that higher education needed to make sure people had workforce skills as well as skills to serve as democratic citizens. Building new states required both.[5]

Even after World War II, a time of great blossoming of colleges and universities, President Truman's Commission on Higher Education pronounced in 1947 that the future of higher education in the United States should be firmly rooted in democratic values and purposes.[6] Yes, the coming burst in the economy needed workers with skills, but the changes in the world also required citizens who were ready to engage in and protect democracy. The commission noted that the country now needed people with a deeper understanding of social processes and problems, skills necessary for democratic reconciliation in the face of cultural difference, sophisticated knowledge of other countries, and a deep understanding of democracy and its merits.[7]

THE WISCONSIN IDEA

Where I work, the University of Wisconsin–Madison, there is a long and proud tradition of conceiving of this land-grant university as serving the broader public good. Since the early twentieth century, this mission has been called "the Wisconsin Idea." The University of Wisconsin was founded in 1848 and expanded as a land grant in 1866 using the authority of the Morrill Act. Like other land grants, it was intended to equip citizens with a broad variety of competencies. But the people of Wisconsin developed an even deeper meaning of the land-grant mission. By 1911, the state government and the state university were working together to grow the state of Wisconsin and to develop policy such as railroad regulation and workmen's compensation.[8] In other words, many people believed that the university and the state government were public institutions that ought to work together to help create a new society.

Along the way, that sense of connection between the state university system and self-governance has been eroded in Wisconsin. Take, for example, the Wisconsin Idea and its most common current definition: "The boundaries of the university are the boundaries of the state." That is a provocative idea in itself. The notion that there is an imperative that the work we do should serve people well beyond our campus or disciplinary borders goes against the grain of much of the contemporary culture of academia. Our main audiences are located on university campuses, not off of them. We tend to publicize our ideas in specialized journals, not in mass media.

But the original meaning of the Wisconsin Idea was even more provocative. The motivation behind it was not just that university research ought to bene-fit humankind but that it should be directly applied in the process of devel-oping policy. It was also expected that citizens would use this knowledge as one input among others as they exercised their role as participants in the broad project of self-governance.[9]

As the *Crucible Moment* report and the Kellogg Commission have warned, the question of what purpose universities serve with respect to democracy is not the key question driving policy on most campuses. Instead, the question has become what purpose do universities serve with respect to the economy. The recent dominance of this economic question has been shaped by and has reshaped public opinion about universities, with profound consequences for their future.

In the minds of citizens, higher education is often out of step with their needs. In Wisconsin, I have found through my fieldwork with Wisconsinites that although there is a great deal of fondness for the University of Wisconsin–Madison and the entire University of Wisconsin System,[10] many people also feel a great deal of distance from it.[11] This fieldwork involved inviting myself into conversations with thirty-nine groups of people who meet regularly for social reasons across twenty-seven different municipalities in the state. I visited them repeatedly between May 2007 and November 2012.[12] What I observed is not necessarily representative of all people in the state. (My purpose in doing the research was to understand how particular perspectives lay the groundwork for stances on policies and candidates.) However, the perception that the University of Wisconsin–Madison is out of reach in terms of admissions, tuition, and life-style for most Wisconsinites was pervasive, particularly among people living in smaller, more rural communities throughout the state. People who viewed the university through this lens of distance were generally viewing it through an identity as rural folks who were not getting their fair share of resources, power, or respect in their state.[13] In this perspective, the university was like other institutions of authority in their lives—remote and not interested in the lives of people like themselves.

That might sound overly dramatic, but national-sample survey data do not give us much reassurance about the public's attitudes toward higher educa-tion. Such data suggest a widespread view that higher education is driven by something other than a desire to serve the broader public. For example, a December 9–13, 2009, Public Agenda poll of 1,031 US adults found that 60 percent of the public perceives that "colleges today are like most businesses and mainly care about the bottom line," as opposed to "colleges today mainly care about education and making sure students have a good educational experience."[14] That same poll found that 33 percent "agree strongly" and 27 percent "agree somewhat" that "colleges could take a lot more students without lowering quality or raising prices." With respect to public higher-education institutions in particular, the poll found that 49 percent believed that "your state's public college and university system needs to be fundamentally overhauled" came closer to their own view than "your state's public college system should be basically left alone" (39 percent). Across the United States, there is a sense that institutions of higher education are not in tune with the needs of the broader public.

The Civic Mission of Higher Education Is Not Dead, but It Is in Danger

Today, many people are advocating a revival of the civic mission of higher education. Campus Compact is a national organization that was created to promote this civic mission and is now in its thirtieth-anniversary year. As I write this, over 250 college and university presidents have already signed a pledge to rigorously pursue this mission and to create a campus civic action plan by March of 2017. This push exists among research universities, as the Research Universities Civic Engagement Network within Campus Compact promotes community-engaged scholarship among scholars at the top research universities in the United States.

But the context in many of our states is such that promoting the civic mission of higher education is politically risky. Take Wisconsin again, for example. In our last state budget cycle, our governor's administration proposed eliminating the civic mission of our flagship university altogether.[15] Here is the mission statement as it appears in state statute with changes in editing marks, as they appeared in Governor Scott Walker's budget proposed in early 2015:

> the mission of the system is to develop human resources <u>to meet the state's workforce needs</u>, to discover and disseminate knowledge, <s>to extend knowledge and its application beyond the boundaries of its campuses</s> and to <s>serve and stimulate society by developing</s> <u>develop</u> in students heightened intellectual, cultural, and humane sensitivities, scientific, professional and technological expertise, and a sense of purpose. <s>Inherent in this broad mission are methods of instruction,</s>

~~research, extended training and public service designed to educate people and~~
~~improve the human condition. Basic to every purpose of the system is the search~~
~~for truth.~~[16]

These proposed edits suggested fundamental changes to our mission. Had
the revision passed, we would no longer be expected to improve the human
condition. We would be expected to bolster the economy.

The immediate uproar in response to these changes caused the administration to reverse course and restore the original language. We should not discount
that response, which reveals that the civic mission of the university is still
widely valued. But I sense other threats to higher education's ability to contribute to the maintenance, if not improvement, of democracy. One is the very
access that university communities have to participate in democracy. As political scientists, we take it as a basic fact that the fundamental act of citizenship
in a democracy is voting. It follows then that we might, at a minimum, have a
duty to help our students develop the civic competency of voting. But ongoing efforts to expand voter ID legislation present some challenges. In Wisconsin, recent voter ID legislation mandates that voters show a Wisconsin driver's
license or other valid state ID card.[17] Out-of-state students are eligible to vote
in Wisconsin if they have resided in a ward for at least twenty-eight days. But
if they do not have a Wisconsin driver's license or other state ID that is valid for
voting purposes, they must obtain a special ID card. University of Wisconsin–
Madison student IDs are not currently valid because they do not include a
signature and a two-year expiration horizon. University officials have decided
to not change the current student ID so that it would be a valid voter ID, due
to cost and security concerns and the uncertain future of the voter ID given
pending court cases.[18] Even more recently, the state legislature has passed legislation eliminating special registration deputies, citizens trained to register others, who have historically done much of the work of registering students to vote.
These pieces of legislation were not necessarily designed to disenfranchise students. But the problem is that in the current context, in which the reigning
party is Republican, and the student body leans Democratic, encouraging our
students to vote is a delicate issue.

Indeed, encouraging student involvement in democratic processes in general
is risky. The University of Wisconsin–Madison has a campus center devoted
to public service, called the Morgridge Center for Public Service. I currently
serve as the faculty director of that center. Since starting that job in the summer of 2014, I have been struck by the wariness with which we approach the
notion of "public service." As a political scientist, I think of "public service" as
service in government and government-related activities. But our precarious

relationship with the state government in recent years suggests it is not in our interest to get anywhere near government, for fear of appearing partisan. There is a strong sense that behaving in a way that is not consistent with the goals of the party in power (currently, the Republican Party) runs the risk of further erosion to our funding, our mission, and our ability to do our work. At the Morgridge Center, this means we have more ardently pursued connections with nonpartisan organizations than with government agencies, and we avoid working with advocacy organizations.

I agree that public resources should not be used in service of advocating for particular personalities to win office. Universities ought to be places in which the goal is creating knowledge and nurturing broad and informed debate, not using taxpayer resources to win elections or convincing students that one ideological view of the world is better than another. However, our original civic mission includes enabling people to develop the competencies necessary to ensure democracy persists. These competencies include a range of skills and practices, including voting, but also an appreciation for active participation and passionate advocacy for causes.

The University of Wisconsin–Madison does have a variety of important connections with governments of all levels. Our political science department has a thriving internship program for undergraduates in state and federal government. A faculty member in our School of Human Ecology, Karen Bogenschneider, runs a Family Impact Institute, which provides policymakers with research relevant to current policy debates. Individual units on campus consult with government agencies. Our La Follette School of Public Affairs places students in policymaking internships and community-based learning. Next year a UniverCity Year program will marshal the skills of researchers and students in the efforts to solve problems identified by a particular municipality. Our Wisconsin Collaborative for Education Research Network is embedding graduate students in state legislative offices. I could go on. But my personal perception is that we are all treading softly in this work.

There is a strict line in the sand when it comes to using taxpayer dollars for partisan activity, but in reality the line between self-governance and politics is very difficult to distinguish. Providing information about how to register to vote and where to vote seems allowable, but what about registering students to vote? On a predominantly Democratic-leaning campus, in a stridently Democratic city in a state controlled by Republicans, the latter runs the risk of appearing partisan. Playing it safe means avoiding voter registration, and frankly, erring on the side of keeping our distance from government.[19]

On a national scale, we have experienced this chilling effect with respect to federal funding for social science research. In recent years, members of Congress have argued that National Science Foundation funding should only go to re-search that benefits the economy or improves national security, rather than to (perhaps more controversial) topics that pertain to issues in United States democracy more generally.[20]

This is what I mean by the turning away from government. At the same time that democracy seems broken, a set of institutions originally designed to ensure that democracy persists are now hampered in their efforts to revive their original mission and encourage people to participate in their democracy.

Reducing funding for higher education is more palatable to the public when higher education is portrayed as the enemy and not a set of institutions that function in service of the broader public good. Advocates for smaller govern-ment have an easier time pursuing that line of argument when they argue that employees of colleges and universities are elitist and out of step with the rest of the population and are misusing public funds for partisan purposes.

THE POLITICS OF RESENTMENT

I referred earlier to the sense of distance many people in small-town Wiscon-sin feel from the University of Wisconsin–Madison. That perspective is part of a broader view that I have called "rural consciousness," which is an identity as a rural resident combined with a perception that rural communities do not get their fair share of resources, power, or respect.[21] In our current context, politi-cal leaders are capitalizing on that view in an overarching politics of resent-ment.[22] They are making policy arguments and waging election campaigns by emphasizing divides between "us" and "them"—with university faculty, public employees, and urbanites among those cast as "them." Officials have encour-aged citizens reeling from pervasive economic uncertainty to blame particular social groups rather than structural causes.

In Wisconsin, this dynamic has manifested in arguments against accepting federal funding for a high-speed train on the basis that the train would only serve people in the major metro areas, not people in "outstate" Wisconsin.[23] It has also been used to argue against funding for public employees and public higher education, and in favor of legislation that has crippled public employee unions. During my fieldwork, I heard from people in small towns struggling to make ends meet, noticing rising tax bills alongside declining communities and personal situations. At the same time, they perceived that the good jobs, the wealth, and the growth are in the cities. In that view, why would they be willing to pay higher taxes to increase government spending? People with resentment toward the cities had no confidence that paying more into the public coffers would in any way benefit themselves or their community. In this way, the politics of resentment is fertile ground for support for smaller government, including support for cutting back funding for public higher education.

Even if larger government—more government social programs in particular—is not the answer, it is not straightforward that dismantling government and dismantling trust in it is beneficial to democracy in the long run. Even if people believe that "the less government, the better" and "the free market can handle [today's complex economic] problems without the government being involved,"[24] it is in their interests to learn about governance and to gain experience in government itself to be able to advocate for their preferred society. Civic skills are needed by conservatives and liberals alike. The United States needs a nonpartisan civic renewal.[25]

Higher education is caught in a difficult situation. There is a need for a renewed focus on educating people for citizenship, but the forces necessitating that revival are preventing it. At the University of Wisconsin–Madison, the more that the university intentionally encourages engagement in political life, the more it opens itself up to complaints of partisanship. However, the more that we play it safe and keep out of public debates, the more detached and less relevant we seem and the more we further the perception that we are not an institution that exists for the broader public good.[26]

The Treatment of Knowledge and the Threat of Elitism

One of the contributions of the Progressive Era was the notion that democratic self-governance requires a scientific regard for knowledge. The idea was that in order to move forward we need to base legislation on evidence, particularly evidence that is discovered in processes that are not the product of political corruption or favoritism. Many of us perceive that we are creating knowledge free from the taint of partisan bias. But as long as academics are portrayed as people who are out of touch with the lives of ordinary people, the more possible it is for lawmakers to move away from a tradition of evidence-based policymaking and to discount the value of higher education in self-governance.

To combat these trends and restore higher education as a public resource, we need to confront head on the claim that we are elitist. First, we would do well to acknowledge that there is a fair amount of elitism in academia in a socioeconomic sense. To what extent are our lives as academics out of touch from the lives of average Americans? By definition, we have a higher level of education. And those of us in tenure-track jobs also have relatively high salaries, not to mention health care and pensions, compared to many others in the population.

Institutions of higher education are privileged institutions and attending them is a luxury. What must it seem like to people struggling to make ends meet that others in society can afford to pay a large amount of money and not work for four years in order to spend time studying subjects whose connection to job training is not always obvious? What does it sound like to first-generation college students when those of us in academia ridicule the idea that we are in the business of job training? Training for work and training for democracy should not be mutually exclusive things, but we run the risk of feeding the misperception that they are when we deny that we exist in part to enable people to pursue a lifetime of meaningful work.

There is a fair amount of elitism among us in a different manner as well—in what we count as knowledge. Obviously, one of the main things that we have to contribute as academics is knowledge. As the Kellogg Commission put it, "The application of knowledge is a unique contribution our institutions can make to contemporary society."[27] So how do we justify our existence without claiming that the type of knowledge we hold is superior? We are uniquely situated to sift and winnow through evidence. And yet, to the extent that we reinforce the perception that we are the keepers of the only or most valid or valuable knowledge, we fuel public resentment against us.

As academics, we have the luxury of long-term study. We have the luxury of taking the time to learn research methods and existing bodies of knowledge, and the time to collect new information that enables us to extend that knowledge. However, an important input to our understanding of the world ought to be taking the time to learn from "common knowledge" or "folk wisdom" or "experiential knowledge." That is true of scholars of all disciplines—from zoology to art. But it is especially the case for social scientists. We have something to learn from listening to people who are not academics. When we are outsiders to the communities that we study, we ought to take the time to understand the lived experiences and knowledge of the people within those communities, in addition to other forms of knowledge and rigorous scientific analysis.[28]

Let me address this with respect to political knowledge in particular. It has become part of our conventional wisdom as political scientists that ordinary citizens do not have the levels of knowledge necessary for healthy democracy.[29] Even the *Crucible Moment* call to arms to renew our civic mission relied in part on evidence of ignorance of civic facts to make its plea.[30] One of ten pieces of evidence cited to signify "anemic U.S. civic health" was a reference to the results of a civic knowledge test conducted by the conservative Intercollegiate Studies Institute.[31] ISI declared that only 54 percent of graduating college seniors in 2008 could "pass" a sixty-question multiple choice test measuring knowledge of history, international relations, and market economy.

But when we listen to the manner in which citizens make sense of the world, we observe that perhaps our models of civic competence are missing something. Perhaps the main inputs to political preferences are not concrete facts from mass-mediated news, but instead lived experience or social identities.[32] In other words, we assert that what people need to participate in their democracy are facts, but by privileging that type of knowledge over the knowledge people rely on to connect with other people, we are privileging a view of democratic participation that is biased toward our own socioeconomic and occupational perspectives.

We should also consider that when we do interact directly with the public in the course of our research there is a difference between fieldwork and engagement. Fieldwork—immersing ourselves in the lives of people in order to learn about human behavior—is undoubtedly a valuable form of gathering data. But there is something to be said for immersing ourselves in the lives of people beyond our campuses in order to both gather data as well as to contribute to their efforts to improve their lives. In other words, we would do well to revive the notion that we have a duty to engage in service to communities beyond our campuses. I call that combination of learning and service community-engaged scholarship.

One obstacle to doing community-engaged scholarship is entering into it without assuming that what we have to contribute are the answers, or the knowledge, that can fix and solve problems. We need to enter into collaborations with people beyond our campuses with the possibility that our role in these partnerships is something other than providing knowledge and expertise. It just may be the case that these collaborations will teach us something and will expand our knowledge in ways we can not anticipate.

The key differences between engagement and fieldwork are reciprocity and audience. First, with respect to reciprocity, if we spend time with people in order to collect data, we are taking. If we pursue the additional step of spending time with people to communicate what we have learned from them and share that knowledge so that they can use it (or not) to improve their own lives, that is more akin to reciprocity. This might take the form of writing op-eds, of giving public lectures, of teaching a course for people beyond our own institutions. Ideally, reciprocity is not just the giving back of information. It is an approach to research in which listening and openness to mutual learning are central.

Second, with respect to audience, if we pursue our research with only other political scientists or other academics in mind, and publish our findings in ways and in places that typically only other academics access, that is not scholarship that seeks to contribute to the broader public good. We should not expect public support for our work if we do not think part of its purpose is to contribute to a broader public discussion.

WHAT IS THE PURPOSE OF POLITICAL SCIENCE?

What drives us as individual political scientists, and as a discipline? If we are honest with ourselves, we recognize that disciplinary incentives place a premium on publication in top-tier peer-reviewed journals and in gaining visibility among other political scientists. The Kellogg Commission concluded that from the outside it often looks like academics "are so inflexibly driven by disciplinary needs and concepts of excellence grounded in peer review, that we have lost sight of our institutional mission to address the contemporary multidisciplinary problems of the real world."[33]

Many political scientists spend substantial time trying to communicate knowledge to the broader public. This very journal [*Perspectives on Politics*, where this chapter was originally published] was created for that purpose.[34] The Monkey Cage [a website published by the *Washington Post*] and the Scholars Strategy Network thrive in that spirit, too.[35] The American Political Science Association has sponsored task forces charged with communicating what we know about the problems of our democracy and potential solutions to a broad audience.[36] But what are the rewards within the discipline and within our universities for spending substantial energy producing work whose audience is the broader public, rather than just members of the discipline? By remaining focused inwards, we may be perpetuating the perception that we are elitist and thereby providing fodder for those who see no point in providing public support to our endeavors. We remain focused inward at our own peril. As the Kellogg Commission put it back in 1999, "Research and scholarship obviously mean discovering new knowledge. But we must also find ways to reward the scholar who steps back from her investigation or his contributions to a scholarly audience in his discipline and looks for ways to put that knowledge to work."[37]

Please note, however, that increasing institutional support for publicly engaged work is not a relaxing of standards to suit the political winds. Instead, it is a returning to an important, original mission of many of our institutions—to enable democracy to persist. We can also revive this mission through our teaching. We have a duty to help people understand how government works, and also to provide people with the competencies necessary to participate in democracy: a willingness to listen to the "other," an ability to critically reflect, and an ability to communicate with a wide variety of other people to share what we know in terms that others can understand and relate to. We can help our students learn those lessons by engaging them in the actual experience of doing these things.

We can also revive the civic mission of higher education by engaging in these practices ourselves in our research. Our institutions exist to ensure that democracy persists. We can reinvigorate that mission by the manner in which we do our research, how we communicate our results, and with whom we share our knowledge. We exist for the good of the broader public. It is not sustainable to assume that we are somehow removed or above it.

CONCLUSION

I am concerned about the civic mission of higher education in part because I am a political scientist who studies civic engagement. My work brings me into constant contact with indicators that members of the public are uninterested and often disgusted with government as usual. I am also increasingly aware of the evidence that government is in fact out of step with ordinary citizens.[38]

I care deeply about these things, though, not just because I am a political scientist.

I became a political scientist in the first place because I care passionately about the place of ordinary people in the exercise of power. I became an academic because I come from a family whose members believe that institutions of public education are a public good and were designed to ensure that people govern each other with fair and just procedures. I still believe this, and like thousands of others at my institution, I am in this for the long haul. However, my experience in Wisconsin in recent years makes it clear we have our work cut out for us.

NOTES

1. Gwen Drury, "The Wisconsin Idea: The Vision That Made Wisconsin Famous," University of Wisconsin–Madison, July 22, 2011, http://ls.wisc.edu/assets/misc/documents/wi-idea-history-intro-summary-essay.pdf, p. 23.

2. Kellogg Commission on the Future of State and Land-Grant Universities, *Returning to Our Roots: The Engaged Institution* (Washington, DC: National Association of State Universities and Land-Grant Colleges, 1999).

3. National Task Force on Civic Learning and Democratic Engagement, *A Crucible Moment: College Learning and Democracy's Future* (Washington, DC: Association of American Colleges and Universities, 2012).

4. Subsequent acts expanded the Morrill Act. The Hatch Act of 1887 provided for agriculture experiment stations. The Morrill Act of 1890 allocated money for buildings

on land-grant campuses. These and other federal acts also enabled establishment of Black land-grant colleges in the South. John R. Thelin, *A History of American Higher Education,* 2nd ed. (Baltimore, MD: Johns Hopkins University Press, 2011), 135–37.

5. Kellogg Commission, *Returning to Our Roots,* 27.

6. Campus Compact, *A Praxis Brief: Campus Compact's Response to "A Crucible Moment: College Learning and Democracy's Future"* (Boston: Campus Compact, 2012), 3.

7. President's Commission on Higher Education, *Higher Education for American Democracy* (Washington, DC: US Government Printing Office, 1947), 2.

8. Drury, "Wisconsin Idea"; Charles McCarthy, *The Wisconsin Idea* (New York: Macmillan, 1912), ch. 3, 6.

9. Drury, "Wisconsin Idea," 9.

10. The University of Wisconsin System comprises thirteen four-year universities (including the University of Wisconsin–Madison), thirteen two-year University of Wisconsin Colleges campuses, and University of Wisconsin–Extension. [*Editor's note:* In 2017, following the original publication of this essay, the University of Wisconsin System Board of Regents approved a plan to merge the thirteen two-year campuses with seven four-year colleges. The plan also dissolves the University of Wisconsin–Extension as a separate unit and transfers its functions to the University of Wisconsin–Madison and the central System office.]

11. Katherine Cramer Walsh, "The Distance from Public Institutions of Higher Education: Public Perceptions of UW–Madison" (Madison: Wisconsin Center for the Advancement of Postsecondary Education, 2012); Katherine J. Cramer, *The Politics of Resentment: Rural Consciousness in Wisconsin and the Rise of Scott Walker* (Chicago: University of Chicago Press, 2016), ch. 5.

12. For more details on the study and methods, see Katherine Cramer Walsh, "Putting Inequality in Its Place: Rural Consciousness and the Power of Perspective," *American Political Science Review* 106, no. 3 (2012): 517–32; Cramer, *Politics of Resentment.*

13. Cramer Walsh, "Putting Inequality in Its Place"; Cramer, *Politics of Resentment.*

14. Data obtained from the online database Polling the Nations (Silver Spring, MD: ORS Pub., 1997–), http://poll.orspub.com/.

15. Karen Herzog, "Walker Proposes Changing Wisconsin Idea—Then Backs Away," *Milwaukee Journal Sentinel,* February 4, 2015, http://archive.jsonline.com/news/education/scott-walkers-uw-mission-rewrite-could-end-the-wisconsin-idea-b99439020zi-290797681.html.

16. Pat Schneider, "Scott Walker Removes 'Wisconsin Idea' from UW's Mission in Budget Bill," *Capital Times,* February 4, 2015, https://madison.com/ct/news/local/govt-and-politics/scott-walker-removes-wisconsin-idea-from-uw-s-mission-in/article_75700525-7d2c-5f87-9de9-8309258c0674.html.

17. Specifically, valid voter IDs in Wisconsin include one of the following types of IDs, either unexpired or expired since the last general election: a Wisconsin Department of Transportation (DOT)-issued driver's license, even if driving privileges are revoked or suspended; a Wisconsin DOT-issued identification card; a Wisconsin DOT-issued identification card or driver's license without a photo issued under the religious exemption; a military ID card issued by a US uniformed service; or a US passport. The following

are also valid voter IDs, as long as they are not expired: a certificate of naturalization that was issued not earlier than two years before the date of an election at which it is presented; a driving receipt issued by the Wisconsin DOT (valid for forty-five days); an identification card receipt issued by the Wisconsin DOT (valid for forty-five days); an identification card issued by a federally recognized Indian tribe in Wisconsin; or a photo identification card issued by a Wisconsin accredited university, college, or technical college that contains the date of issuance, the signature of the student, and an expiration date no later than two years after the date of issuance. Also, the university, college, or technical college ID must be accompanied by a separate document that proves enrollment or a citation or notice of intent to revoke or suspend a Wisconsin DOT-issued driver's license that is dated within sixty days of the date of the election. Refer to http://bringit.wisconsin.gov/do-i-have-right-photo-id.

18. See an explanation of Chancellor Rebecca Blank's decision at "Campus Support for Student Voting under New Wisconsin Voter ID Law," Office of the Chancellor, January 29, 2016, https://chancellor.wisc.edu/blog/campus-support-for-student-voting -under-new-wisconsin-voter-id-law/.

19. Cf. the avoidance of government activity among nonprofits documented in Jeffrey M. Berry, A Voice for Nonprofits (Washington, DC: Brookings Institution, 2003). A prominent historian on our campus, William Cronon, experienced what can happen when someone perceives those of us on campus to have crossed the line. In early 2011, Scott Walker became governor of Wisconsin and soon after introduced a controversial budget repair bill that eliminated most collective bargaining rights for most public employees in the state. About a month later, Cronon posted a blog entry about the American Legislative Exchange Council, which he perceived was helping to push this and other legislation in a variety of states. A few days afterward, the New York Times ran an op-ed Cronon had written that argued that Scott Walker was departing from Wisconsin government and state Republican Party norms of civility and good government. William Cronon, "Wisconsin's Radical Break," New York Times, March 21, 2011, https://www.nytimes.com/2011/03/22/opinion/22cronon.html. In response, a representative of the Republican Party requested all of Cronon's incoming and outgoing e-mails that mentioned Scott Walker and other words related to the budget repair bill. See William Cronon, "Abusing Open Records to Attack Academic Freedom," Scholar as Citizen (blog), March 24, 2011, http://scholarcitizen.williamcronon.net/tag/alec/.

20. See, for example, Tracy Jan, "GOP Pushes Funding Cuts for Social Science Work," Boston Globe, April 14, 2014, https://www2.bostonglobe.com/news/nation/2014/ 04/14/gop-pushes-funding-cuts-for-social-science-work/5q4mMRROhWuwHaC 46lW23N/story.html. Thanks to Ben Toff for suggesting this as another case in point.

21. Cramer Walsh, "Putting Inequality in Its Place."

22. Cramer, Politics of Resentment.

23. Cramer, Politics of Resentment, ch. 7.

24. This is standard American National Election Studies wording for items gauging small government views. Available at http://electionstudies.org/project/anes-time-ser ies-cumulative-data-file/.

25. Carmen Sirianni and Lewis Friedland, *Civic Innovation in America: Community Empowerment, Public Policy, and the Movement for Civic Renewal* (Berkeley: University of California Press, 2001).

26. Thank you to Joe Soss for helping to clarify this point.

27. Kellogg Commission, *Returning to Our Roots*, 10.

28. Thank you to Ben Toff for helping to clarify this point.

29. Michael X. Delli Carpini and Scott Keeter, *What Americans Know about Politics and Why It Matters* (New Haven, CT: Yale University Press, 1996); Jennifer L. Hochschild and Katherine Levine Einstein, *Do Facts Matter? Information and Misinformation in American Politics* (Norman: University of Oklahoma Press, 2015). But for criticism of this allegation, see Arthur Lupia, "How Elitism Undermines the Study of Voter Competence," *Critical Review: A Journal of Politics and Society* 18, nos. 1–3 (2006): 217–32.

30. National Task Force, *A Crucible Moment*, 7, 9.

31. "Failing Our Students, Failing America: Holding Colleges Accountable for Teaching America's History and Institutions," http://www.americancivicliteracy.org/2007/summary_summary.html.

32. Katherine J. Cramer and Benjamin Toff, "The Fact of Experience: Rethinking Political Knowledge and Civic Competence," *Perspectives on Politics* 15, no. 3 (September 2017): 754–70; Christopher C. Achen and Larry M. Bartels, *Democracy for Realists: Why Elections Do Not Produce Responsive Government* (Princeton, NJ: Princeton University Press, 2016).

33. Kellogg Commission, *Returning to Our Roots*, 20.

34. Jeffrey Isaac, "For a More Public Political Science," *Perspectives on Politics* 13, no. 2 (2015): 269–83.

35. See Monkey Cage at https://www.washingtonpost.com/news/monkey-cage/ and Scholars Strategy Network at http://www.scholarsstrategynetwork.org/.

36. For example, see Stephen Macedo, Yvette M. Alex-Assensoh, Jeffrey M. Berry, Michael Brintnall, David E. Campbell, Luis Ricardo Fraga, Archon Fung, William A. Galston, Christopher F. Karpowitz, Margaret Levi, Meira Levinson, Keena Lipsitz, Richard G. Niemi, Robert D. Putnam, Wendy M. Rahn, Rob Reich, Robert R. Rodgers, Todd Swanstrom, and Katherine Cramer Walsh, *Democracy at Risk: How Political Choices Have Undermined Citizenship, and What We Can Do About It*, A Report of the American Political Science Association's Standing Committee on Civic Education and Engagement (Washington, DC: Brookings, 2005); Lawrence R. Jacobs and Theda Skocpol, ed., *Inequality and American Democracy: What We Know and What We Need to Learn* (New York: Russell Sage, 2005).

37. Kellogg Commission, *Returning to Our Roots*, 48.

38. Namely, analyses of the correspondence between votes in the US Senate and constituency preferences suggest that legislators are responsive to the wealthiest in society, only moderately responsive to those in the middle ranges of income, and not at all responsive to those at the lowest end of the income scale. Larry M. Bartels, *Unequal Democracy: The Political Economy of the New Gilded Age* (Princeton, NJ: Princeton University Press, 2008); Martin Gilens, "Inequality and Democratic Responsiveness,"

Public Opinion Quarterly 69, no. 5 (2005): 778–96; Martin Gilens, *Affluence and Influence: Economic Inequality and Political Power in America* (New York: Russell Sage Foundation, 2012). Similar evidence has been established at the state level. Elizabeth Rigby and Gerald C. Wright, "Whose Statehouse Democracy: Policy Responsiveness to Poor versus Rich Constituents in Poor versus Rich States," in *Who Gets Represented?* ed. Peter Enns and Christopher Wlezien (New York: Russell Sage, 2011); Patrick Flavin, "Income Inequality and Policy Representation in the American States," *American Politics Research* 40, no. 1 (2012): 29–59.

Afterword

GWEN DRURY

Each author in this wide-ranging collection of essays dives deep into a particular aspect of the Wisconsin Idea. Taken together, these essays begin to sketch the outlines of an epic movement, helping us to understand that we are a part of that movement, and that we have a choice to make. Each author offers his or her own questions about the future, but we all need to decide whether we intend to rise to the challenge of authentically renewing the Wisconsin Idea, or whether we will hasten its demise, with or without that intent.

As someone who has studied the history of the Wisconsin Idea to figure out how and why it emerged over one hundred years ago, I was honored by the invitation to write this afterword. I was excited by the chance to offer historically based comments on the chapters in this volume. However, to my surprise, I was asked to comment about the *future* rather than the history of the Wisconsin Idea. At first, that request seemed like situational irony. Then, I realized that all of the reflection I have done about the history of the Wisconsin Idea actually puts me in a position to point out some surprising and important situational irony at the time of this writing and to point us in a direction that can get us beyond it in the future.

Although the title of this volume sounds simple, straightforward, and direct—*Education for Democracy: Renewing the Wisconsin Idea*—it actually runs directly into a major problem. That is a good thing because this particular problem is exactly what requires our attention first: we need a working definition of the Wisconsin Idea. And here's the rub: this definition cannot be reduced to a suggestive, appealing, but empty tagline. Until we clearly articulate the connection between the Wisconsin Idea and democracy, we cannot begin to renew it.

The definition provided at the time of this writing on the University of Wisconsin–Madison website does not help us with this problem; it is lovely but generic, even as it asserts a specific tie with Wisconsin:

One of the longest and deepest traditions surrounding the University of Wisconsin, the Wisconsin Idea signifies a general principle: that education should influence people's lives beyond the boundaries of the classroom. Synonymous with Wisconsin for more than a century, this "Idea" has become the guiding philosophy of university outreach efforts in Wisconsin and throughout the world.[1]

So, what is this guiding philosophy? That education should influence lives beyond the boundaries of the classroom? That same claim could be made by any school, public or private, whether in a democracy, a monarchy, or a dictatorship. If we use this statement as our working definition, renewal would simply mean influencing peoples' lives more deeply or more often. Even a dictator could love that definition. The "what"—the activity of outreach—is represented. The "why"—building the strongest possible grassroots democracy and economy—is missing.

Even our most iconic and historic taglines become suggestive but ultimately meaningless boilerplate if we do not understand their historical context. In a speech in 1905, University of Wisconsin president Charles Van Hise said, "I shall never be content until the beneficent influence of the university reaches every family in the state."[2] Again, the "why" is missing from this popular sound bite. In the early twentieth century in Wisconsin, the context was understood. Taken out of context, this statement could plausibly have been uttered by any "Dear Leader" in any dictatorship.

In the 1930s, a long-serving director of the University of Wisconsin News Service did some wordsmithing to summarize Van Hise's speeches and design a pithy tagline to grace bulletins, letterhead, reports, brochures, and other publications. "The Boundaries of the University are the Boundaries of the State" appeared on every possible University of Wisconsin publication for decades. During this time period, many faculty and staff as well as state legislators and community leaders served for decades as well, so the context was clearly understood and constantly informally communicated. The fact that, if taken out of context, the actual statement is evocative at best was therefore not a concern. However, this successful "branding" exercise served to shift the "ownership" of the Wisconsin Idea to the university rather than to the people of the state. This statement references democracy only in that it references a politically determined governance boundary.

An effort to renew the Wisconsin Idea based on this literal definition would mean limiting University of Wisconsin activities to state boundaries. Today, people often try to get around this limitation by saying, "The Boundaries of the University are the Boundaries of the State, *and Beyond*." Again, this version is largely meaningless, referencing only the "what"—the process of outreach—

and leaving out the "why"—the reason for outreach. And the "where" no longer even references for whom. Although the people who use this tagline are usually very genuine in their desire to communicate inclusiveness, even they would not be able to renew the Wisconsin Idea from this vague starting point.

Is this a matter of renewing an institutional mission? By the mid-twentieth century, this concept had become the brand of the University of Wisconsin, the state's flagship research and land-grant institution. Seeking efficiencies in the 1970s, the state of Wisconsin decided to combine twenty-seven (later twenty-six) of its public higher-education institutions—including University Extension and Cooperative Extension—under one administrative umbrella and one set of regents, creating the University of Wisconsin System. The original University of Wisconsin was now renamed University of Wisconsin–Madison, to differentiate it within the University of Wisconsin System. The newly created entity adopted the Wisconsin Idea as its guiding principle. This system includes a wide variety of institutions with many different missions, so we know that the Wisconsin Idea is not an institutional mission.

If it is not a particular mission, what *is* the Wisconsin Idea? Is anything done at a public college or university in Wisconsin automatically an example of the Wisconsin Idea? Is outreach the Wisconsin Idea? Is it University Extension? Is it life-changing research? Is it any service that someone from the University of Wisconsin renders to the state? What is it that we seek to renew but that some seek instead to remove?

I submit that the Wisconsin Idea is what we in today's world would call an organizational vision. The term was not yet used this way in the early twentieth century, when the Wisconsin Idea was first coined as a phrase. Vision is related to institutional mission, but it is not the same thing. An organization's mission is why it exists, its purpose. For instance, state universities exist in the United States to make higher education available to the people of the state. A vision is larger and shapes how we see, approach, and execute the mission. On the one hand, different states' universities might share identical missions, but the vision shared within each state will shape different outcomes of those identical missions. On the other hand, the diverse missions of twenty-six schools in Wisconsin can all be guided and shaped by a single, shared vision. Indeed, the governing mission of the state legislature can be guided by the same vision. Communities and individuals throughout the state can share the vision as well.

The Wisconsin Idea is a vision of democracy in which the state, by providing cutting-edge knowledge of all kinds to as many of its people as possible, ensures that they are prepared to keep their own lives, self-governance, opportunity, and economy in their own hands and avoid being overcome by outside or outsized interests who gain power because they can corner a market. The first chapter of Charles McCarthy's 1912 book, *The Wisconsin Idea*, is entitled "The Reason for It." A simple chart in the chapter indicates that the reason for the emergence of the Wisconsin Idea was the threat posed to democracy by the rapidly growing income inequality of the time.

In the pages that follow, I would like to take a look at how conceptualizing the Wisconsin Idea as a vision might inform the essays in this volume. In the volume's introduction, Chad Alan Goldberg lays out four themes that the essays address, so I will follow this outline to add my comments.

The Production of Knowledge and Its Potential to Inform Good Government

J. David Hoeveler makes the case in his essay that the original inspiration for what later emerged as the Wisconsin Idea came from University of Wisconsin president John Bascom, who was an original thinker and unique as a college president in that he was actively engaged in the controversial topics of his day. Hoeveler argues that Bascom's breadth of education and focus on intellectual development were what provided the foundation for the Wisconsin Idea. The breadth of education offered makes a university a "house of intellect." Hoeveler argues for the value of an emphasis on intellect and points out that over many decades people who embraced a conservative political stance were also very keen to preserve and expand intellectual endeavors. He notes that in recent years, however, conservatives have embraced anti-intellectual stances, and that Robin Vos, the Republican Speaker of the Wisconsin State Assembly since 2013, even stated on the assembly floor that University of Wisconsin professors should not waste their time studying "the ancient mating habits of whatever." Hoeveler noted that at the same time University of Wisconsin–Milwaukee professors were pursuing research on the mating habits of perch that had the potential to create millions of dollars of economic benefit for the fishing industry of the state.

Hoeveler begins his essay stating that he worries that an over-focus on the service ideal will corrupt the Wisconsin Idea. As an example of such corruption, he contrasts the benefits of Bascom's educational breadth with the constriction of educational offerings proposed in 2018 by the provost at the University of Wisconsin–Stevens Point. The provost sought to cut many majors entirely while increasing others. The majors that were on the chopping block included history and philosophy, while proposed majors were things like forest ecology. The provost stated that students were not pursuing the humanities majors in great enough numbers to justify keeping them, and he proposed instead that other courses could do things like incorporate a focus on history. He said that "too many general education programs have little purposeful cohesion and little relevance to the majority of students."[3] The provost claimed to be creating a new kind of regional university, focused on solving regional problems, and he pitched the new technical problem-solving mission as representing the best tradition of the Wisconsin Idea. Hoeveler's response is that such a constricted "house of intellect" would not even be teaching the subjects that Bascom used to teach and that informed the Wisconsin Idea. Universities have the obligation to provide students with the opportunity to "exercise their intellects and expand their vision as they do." Hoeveler ends by saying that in renewing the Wisconsin Idea, we should honor the legacy that Bascom bequeathed to us.

Thinking of the Wisconsin Idea as a vision serves as a lens to help us critique both the provost's actions in Stevens Point and Hoeveler's conclusion. The decisions undertaken in Stevens Point do not appear to be guided by the vision of the Wisconsin Idea to support democracy by equipping citizens for authentic self-governance. If the General Education programs had been shaped by that vision in the first place, their cohesion and relevance would have been clearly articulated. The courses would all align with the goal of expanding students' understanding of themselves in the world and the challenges of self-governance. If the courses are not accomplishing that goal, we should note that simply removing them does not accomplish it either. The university's proposed emphasis on regional problem-solving is also not expressly focused on developing problem-solving capacity in our citizens. It seems more like the university is presented as a service bureau designed to do things for people rather than with them.

To Hoeveler, renewing the Wisconsin Idea mainly involves renewing a focus on intellect. Applying the lens of the Wisconsin Idea as a vision for the use of knowledge in building democracy immediately makes it clear that developing intellect for its own sake alone would not be renewing the Wisconsin Idea. Bascom is the person who established the expectation that the university and its graduates owed some service to the people of the state, who made their education and intellectual development possible. The service to the state that Bascom emphasized was intellectual service. College graduates were rare in the late nineteenth century. This was a time in which the concept of high school was a new thing. It seems to me that Hoeveler thinks an over-focus on the *technical* alone is the actual threat to the Wisconsin Idea and that limiting service and education to narrowly technical pursuits is what is corrupting it. If the Wisconsin Idea is a vision of the role that knowledge can play in preparing people to actively participate in democracy, then it becomes clear that constricting the breadth of available knowledge corrupts the Wisconsin Idea.

Karen Bogenschneider's essay is about the Family Impact Seminar, a program that makes the most current research about topics related to children and family issues available to legislators in easily digestible form at the exact time when lawmakers are considering those particular issues. This program was started for the US Congress, but Bogenschneider replicated it for the Wisconsin state legislature. Eventually, she went on to head the program at the national level. When she instituted the program in Wisconsin, she found that many people she encountered thought that it represented the Wisconsin Idea, and that people seemed to feel a sense of loss that this sort of thing no longer happens at the state capitol with regard to other issues as well. She compares the Family Impact Seminar with Wisconsin's 1911 legislative session because that session was the focus of McCarthy's 1912 book, *The Wisconsin Idea.* In both cases, the university served as an "honest broker" of knowledge, presenting it to the legislators in such a way that it was easier for busy legislators to access and consider. In both cases, the legislators were the ones making the decisions. These seminars were designed not to pressure legislators in any direction, but to actually relieve pressure by making research on all sides of an issue readily available for their use. Bogenschneider tells us that the Family Impact Seminars actually produced summary booklets that legislators could keep for future reference. Although it's not clear whether she realizes it, the Legislative Reference Library did the same thing in 1911.

Bogenschneider carefully lays out the mechanics of how to make such a program work, both on the legislature's end and on the campuses' end. In some ways, this may be putting the cart before the horse. I think in this case it might be helpful to think of the Wisconsin Idea as a vision of democracy in which the state makes knowledge available to inform self-governance. If both the state legislature and the university started with that shared vision, the mechanics would be easy to figure out, and the divergent institutional incentives would be easier to reconcile. The state legislature's mission of governing and the university's mission of producing and disseminating knowledge can both be guided by the vision of the Wisconsin Idea.

THE UNIVERSITY'S OUTREACH TO THE STATE AND ITS ROLE IN SOLVING PUBLIC PROBLEMS

Caitlin Cieslik-Miskimen relates the story of Willard Bleyer, who played a number of different professional roles at the University of Wisconsin in the beginning of the twentieth century. Bleyer worked to establish professional standards in journalism, which previously had a reputation for being intentionally partisan and sensationalist. Bleyer educated his students to instead pursue "Accuracy

Always" and stressed the importance of accurate journalism to the ability of citizens to make informed decisions in their democracy. Bleyer and his insistence on professional standards became well known in the field since many of his students went on to lead journalism schools themselves. In addition, Bleyer worked as an early public relations strategist for the university. Due to his knowledge of the newspaper industry, he was able to establish a methodical approach to regularly informing the people of the state about what was happening at their state university. He edited the *Press Bulletin*, which provided content that newspapers could use, and he invited journalists from around the state to come to see what was happening on campus for themselves.

In both of his roles, Bleyer clearly shared the vision of the Wisconsin Idea in which getting cutting-edge, accurate knowledge to the people of the state is crucial for their exercise of democracy and participation in their economy. Although his missions were, on the one hand, to teach journalism and, on the other hand, to disseminate information about the university, both were shaped by the vision of the Wisconsin Idea. He worked to get people the knowledge they could use to make wise, considered decisions.

Curt Meine opens his essay with an epigraph by Peter Nowak, an emeritus professor of environmental studies at the University of Wisconsin–Madison. "Conservation is not a practice, a program, a technical standard, or a plan," Nowak says. "Conservation is a journey." Similarly, the Wisconsin Idea is not a practice, a program, a technical standard, a plan, or a *mission*. The Wisconsin Idea is a vision. Renewing the Wisconsin Idea requires understanding what it is and what it is not.

In his essay, Meine discusses the rise of both the Wisconsin Idea and the conservation movement in Wisconsin at around the same time. The particular place, people, and time were crucial to propelling the development of each of them, and each informed the other. Each reflected developments elsewhere in the country as well, but what was happening in Wisconsin at that time propelled the state into leadership in conservation and higher education. Meine mentions that, early on, many conservation decisions were made in a top-down manner, and later they became far more collaborative and grassroots based. This pattern reflected the rest of society at the time, and the change over time may show the influence of the Wisconsin Idea.

During his fifteen years as president of the University of Wisconsin, Van Hise steadily pushed decision-making and responsibility further down the hierarchy at the university. He established a student government, including a student court. Rather than having a top-down, paternalistic response to student behavior issues, he fostered a peer-based accountability system. For years, the faculty had tried to control annual student activities like "Bag Rush" that had

resulted in severe injuries for several students each year. Once Van Hise dele-
gated the official responsibility for safety to the students themselves, the number and severity of injuries declined dramatically. Similarly, Van Hise worked
to decentralize decision-making by encouraging faculty to take on more self-
governance. When the university's Memorial Union building was constructed
in the 1920s to house the functions of the student union and provide a social
and leisure center for the campus, the organization in charge of it, the Wisconsin Union, adopted a constitution specifying democratic governance, with
students always making up the majority of the decision-making body. The
vision of the Wisconsin Idea created a culture that encouraged distributed
rather than centralized power and agency.

Considered as a vision of democracy in which cutting-edge knowledge is
made available to the people of the state for them to use in their decision-
making and self-governance, the Wisconsin Idea was clearly a guide for the
development of the conservation movement in Wisconsin. Natural resources
were another domain in which the opportunities of the many were not to be
curtailed by the ability of someone to get there first and corner a market. "The
greatest good, for the greatest number, and for the longest time," a saying
now associated with the conservation movement, could actually have been
an underpinning of the Wisconsin Idea vision itself. Ensuring that citizens
make the decisions, and that they have the most accurate information to use
in making them, anchors the conservation movement in the vision of the
Wisconsin Idea.

Meine's essay stresses the social and cultural aspects of the Wisconsin Idea.
These are the things that are shaped by an institution's vision. The Ingenues, the
all-woman jazz band that participated in research in 1930 by playing music for
cows while they were milked, speaks to the creativity and skill of the musicians,
the creativity of the research question (whether cows would produce more
milk when exposed to music), the collaborative culture, and even the shared
sense of humor about what it must look like—and why a photographer should
be present to capture an image to be shared with the people of the state.

Conservationist Aldo Leopold and a farm family standing and conversing
outdoors in 1935 did not exactly present an eye-catching or dramatic compo-
sition for a photographer, but it did capture the collaborative values of the
culture. The fact that the photographer understood the importance of that
interaction and decided to capture the image indicates that it is something
that people in the future (like us) would need to understand: the vision and the
culture of the Wisconsin Idea are about the power of the people and the power
of ideas. Leopold understood that as a professor he could provide new ideas
and research—in his case a "land ethic"—but that democratic, collaborative

processes in which people make their own decisions and contribute their own actions are even more important.

Maryo Gard Ewell's essay helps us understand the vision of the Wisconsin Idea as a focus on building capacity for authentic participatory democracy among the people of the state. Her father, Robert Gard, worked for University Extension for many years, specializing in teaching and coaching people around the state to confidently and authentically express themselves in public through the arts. He established the Wisconsin Idea Theater program and traveled the state to open opportunities for individuals and communities to discover and communicate more about themselves. His program stressed that theater was not just for elite professionals in New York, but that writing and acting and stagecraft produced by people in local communities could be powerful and moving—and empowering.

Gard Ewell tells us how Wisconsin was the first state in the nation to create an artist-in-residence program housed in its state university. It becomes clear that the *vision* of the Wisconsin Idea, not the *mission* of the university's College of Agriculture, is what inspired the dean of the college to create this program. He hired artist John Steuart Curry to travel to farm communities across the state, not to paint the scenes he saw or the people he met, but to paint with and talk with the people of rural Wisconsin. Curry's expertise and presence in their hometowns opened opportunities for residents of rural communities to express themselves in ways they had perhaps never tried. (Some even discovered special talent in painting.) They painted things that were familiar to them and expressed how they felt about those things in public settings.

Teaching music appreciation, group singing, or even drawing over the radio demonstrated a vision that outreach did not simply mean showcasing the cultural riches gathered at the university in the state capital; it was about providing opportunities for the greatest number of people to develop their own capacities and confidence.

Who Should the Wisconsin Idea Serve?

Gard Ewell's essay makes it clear that, early on, the University of Wisconsin developed an exceptionally expansive view of who was included in the vision of the Wisconsin Idea. Emily Auerbach and R. Richard Wagner provide essays that remind us that even groundbreaking efforts at inclusiveness can miss people. By understanding the Wisconsin Idea as a vision, it becomes clear that when the broader society cannot "see" or acknowledge a segment of the population, the people at the university may not see them either. Prejudice blinds people and even blinkers visions.

These two essays explore specific populations that were once either intentionally excluded (homosexuals and gender-nonconforming people) or overshadowed (a low-income neighborhood of people of color, near the University of Wisconsin–Madison campus) in such a way that they were left out of the vision of the Wisconsin Idea. In these cases, these groups have now found new power and confidence for participating in society, in partnership with the University of Wisconsin. We need to keep in mind that many other groups are still waiting to really be seen as part of this vision for democracy. Some we may not even see at all right now. The process of renewing the Wisconsin Idea means renewing this vision, so it allows the university to specifically seek out people it has missed in the past and invite them into partnership.

Auerbach's essay on the UW Odyssey Project explains that it was the result of a combination of ideas from other places: the Clemente Course in the Humanities offered by Bard College in New York, and Berea College, a tuition-free college that her parents had attended in Kentucky. So, how can she claim that it is "the Wisconsin Idea in action"? I agree with this claim, but not because the UW Odyssey Project is about the land-grant mission or about sharing the campuses' riches with the taxpayers of the state. I agree with Auerbach because the Wisconsin Idea is a vision of democracy in which the state provides cutting-edge knowledge of all kinds to as many of its people as possible, ensuring that they are prepared to keep their lives, self-governance, opportunity, and economy in their own hands. Auerbach widened the aperture of that vision and established an authentic partnership with a disadvantaged community. The students have publicly grappled with great thoughts gathered from other places and times, and in the process they have realized that they are capable of publicly grappling, in ways they had not previously discovered, with the thoughts and issues of their times. New knowledge has allowed them to build a new sense of agency and take control of their lives in new ways. That is indeed the Wisconsin Idea in action.

Wagner's essay presents another example of how the vision of the Wisconsin Idea was limited in who it included, as he describes how Wisconsin became the first gay-rights state. The essay is tough to read as he details the many ways, over many years, that fellow citizens and community members who are LGBT (lesbian, gay, bisexual, or transsexual) or gender-nonconforming experienced their humanity being systematically erased from view. He includes in detail ways in which university professors initially went along with and contributed to that erasure. But Wagner also outlines the various ways that University of Wisconsin researchers gradually built up enough data, whether intentionally or not, to allow the LGBT community to successfully make the case for its own rights. Over the many years and eras that Wagner covers, he also chronicles various allies from the university who, in later years, took up the cause and helped to win those rights. In this case, documenting knowledge of many kinds did eventually allow people to assert control over their own lives, democracy, opportunity, and economy, and for that reason, the victory for gay rights can be seen as part of the vision of the Wisconsin Idea.

To be sure, Wagner makes it clear that academics at the University of Wisconsin did not have less prejudiced vision than the society around them. The vision of the Wisconsin Idea seems to have expanded to include LGBT communities almost at exactly the same rate that the larger society did. However, the tradition of sifting and winnowing to find the truth continued at the University of Wisconsin, even if the academics there were as blinded by prejudice as everyone else. So, incrementally, the University of Wisconsin built up knowledge that could widen the vision that guided it. In this case, the university's mission of producing knowledge actually served to reshape the notion of who should be included in the vision of the Wisconsin Idea. Eventually, professors from the University of Wisconsin became active allies in securing gay rights in Wisconsin.

CHALLENGES TO THE WISCONSIN IDEA

Katherine J. Cramer's essay was originally written for her colleagues, political science professors in the United States, and it provides an interesting look inside their professional world. Cramer describes a conundrum faced by many colleges and universities in general and political science departments in particular. Their mission is to help students learn about governance in order to make democracy work and preserve it for the future. But incentives embedded in professional competition, compounded by political polarization in the broader society, have combined to make it much easier for political science professors to stay safely inside an ivory tower and publish mainly in journals that are read only by other political scientists rather than engage with the real world of governance or politics in person. At a time in the nation's history when American democracy is strained, citizens need more education about civics, but the exact opposite is happening. This dynamic is happening across the nation, but Cramer suggests that the case in Wisconsin is worth examining.

As Cramer describes this challenge, she identifies the Wisconsin Idea with the mission of the land-grant university, but she adds that "the people of Wisconsin developed an even deeper meaning of the land-grant mission," which included the expectation that state government and the state university would work together for the benefit of the state. I think the "even deeper meaning" and expectations that Cramer describes as Wisconsin's approach to the land-grant

mission are more helpfully described as the Wisconsin Idea vision. Governor
Scott Walker's attack on the Wisconsin Idea in 2015 shows how maintaining
this distinction is helpful, even crucial.

As Cramer recounts, the governor attempted to alter the legal mission statement of the University of Wisconsin System (the precise changes are described
verbatim in her chapter) and submit these policy changes within a budget proposal. If we do not separate mission and vision, we might mistake this action for
a simple, if awkward, attempt to replace abstract concepts in the mission statement with concrete language focused on jobs. Those of us attuned to the civic
realm, like Cramer, would note that those abstract concepts were the ones that
reference the civic mission of the university. However, while that interpretation
is accurate, it does not explain why those concepts were targeted for elimination.

The targeted concepts have deep roots in Wisconsin's history and are associated with the Progressive movement of a century ago and the Wisconsin Idea.
The deleted words are not merely abstractions but powerful anchors of that
culture and vision. Someone would go to the trouble of removing them only
if he or she was targeting that culture and vision and wanted to remove those
anchors.

Although the governor disregarded the proper distinction between policy and
budget proposal processes, he clearly distinguished vision from mission. That
distinction guided him as he removed—with surgical precision—language expressing the specific vision of the Wisconsin Idea from the generic mission of
public higher education. By embedding these policy changes in a budget document well over a thousand pages long, the governor attempted to redefine
the legal mission statement surreptitiously and circumvent the public's participation or discussion. The proposed changes were nevertheless discovered
and generated public notice—but even then, discussion focused on the governor's sleight of hand, not how or whether the legal mission and vision of the
public system of higher education should be changed.

Because there was no public clarity about the actual target of the proposed
edits, proponents of the Wisconsin Idea and even the press fixated instead on
the secretive process. The governor's explanation of the changes as a "drafting
error" and a subsequent lawsuit revealing that they were in fact intentional
intensified this narrow focus on process.[4] Public discussion of the issue never
became nuanced enough to identify the target; distinguishing vision from
mission, as the governor had, would have helped the public to do so.

When the attempted changes to the University of Wisconsin System mission statement are reexamined carefully and contextualized within the history of
University Extension, it becomes clear that the "drafting error" was a glimpse

of the death warrant that would be enacted two years later, again without public notice, against University Extension. The Wisconsin Idea (a vision of democracy in which the state provides as many of its people as possible with cutting-edge knowledge that they can use to maintain control of their lives, democracy, opportunity, and economy) is the vision that brought University Extension into being. This new and vigorous form of extension took the world by storm when it was introduced by the University of Wisconsin in 1906. At that time, a wealthy lumberman and leading Wisconsin citizen named James Stout went on record as saying that if this new University Extension went into effect, the University of Wisconsin would be "the most democratic school in America."[5] In 1907, this new form of University Extension became the first such program in the nation to get its own budget appropriation from the state legislature (by unanimous votes, in both houses). It was rapidly copied by schools across the United States and in other countries. This innovation was in part what motivated Charles William Eliot, president of Harvard University from 1869 to 1909, to proclaim publicly in 1908 that the University of Wisconsin was "the leading state university." This vision of engagement between the state government, the state university, and the state's people is the vision that made Wisconsin famous around the world. Several years later, in 1914, the federal Smith-Lever Act established the Cooperative Extension program to serve rural populations. The "cooperative" part reflects the funding streams: federal (US Department of Agriculture), state (land-grant university), and local (county government). Eventually, in the mid-1960s, the University of Wisconsin Board of Regents merged University Extension and the state's Cooperative Extension and spun it off under its own chancellor, renaming it the University of Wisconsin–Extension.

Was it coincidence that in 2017, two years after Governor Walker's failed attempt to rewrite the University of Wisconsin System's mission, the system president (Ray Cross) unilaterally proposed to eliminate the University of Wisconsin–Extension as a separate unit? No notice was issued, no public discussion was allowed. University staff and faculty were not informed or allowed to give input or conduct evaluations.[6] The very program that had made Wisconsin famous as the most democratic school in the nation was killed via autocratic fiat and allowed no democratic process whatever. Because it was federally sponsored, the Cooperative Extension program could not be killed simply by autocratic fiat from within the state of Wisconsin. Interestingly, it was instead brought back in 2018 under the auspices of its original home: the land-grant university of the University of Wisconsin System, originally known as the University of Wisconsin, but now known as University of Wisconsin–Madison.

Even more interestingly, Cooperative Extension was rebranded as University of Wisconsin–Madison Extension. University Extension, the form of civic education that made history in Wisconsin, was assassinated, and a tougher-to-kill look-alike was installed in its place. The autocratic fiat that effected this substitution is directly connected to the specific changes in wording regarding vision that Walker sought to make two years earlier in the University of Wisconsin System's legal mission statement.

This is the situational irony I mentioned at the start of this afterword. The fact that political science professors in the United States are right to consider civic engagement risky business is also deeply ironic. And I cannot resist pointing out another bit of situational irony as well. Speaking in 1913 to a group of a hundred people who had traveled to Wisconsin from Philadelphia to learn about this new democratic form of University Extension and the Wisconsin Idea, Van Hise said that "just as the spirit of authority represses or destroys universities, so the spirit of freedom creates and inspires them."[7] Van Hise was contrasting the expanding scope of the University of Wisconsin with the repression of universities by the czar in Russia.

Jane L. Collins's essay discusses attacks on government and the public sector in Wisconsin in the 1930s, the 1970s, and 2011. She says that what these attacks had in common was a dispute over the vision of how to run the "public household," meaning the never-ending negotiations over how common resources are spent for common benefit. Perhaps due to my influence, Collins uses the term vision frequently, which helps to make her argument clearer than it would be if she referred to mission. She illustrates the several waves of attacks against the public sector that happened in Wisconsin over time, and she also describes the historical contexts in which they occurred and that shaped the resolutions each time. Furthermore, she describes a conservative "movement in 'abeyance'—a social movement that manages to sustain and reinvent itself through unreceptive periods in order to mount a challenge in another period." In addition, she notes that the most wealthy people in America have now been given the green light by the US Supreme Court's 2010 *Citizens United v. Federal Election Commission* decision to translate their wealth directly into political power. This point again brings to mind the first chapter of McCarthy's 1912 book *The Wisconsin Idea*, entitled "The Reason for It." The reason that the vision of the Wisconsin Idea developed, it may be recalled, was to counter the effects of massive income inequality and ensure that everyday people had a strong say in their democracy. Collins discusses the role that the Wisconsin Idea played in helping to build the public household and wonders what role it could play in "shaping our response to attempts to dismantle it."

I wonder whether it will make any difference to citizens when they realize why the repeated attacks against the university started first. Why? The university cannot play a role in preventing the dismantling of the public household if the university and its civic vision get dismantled first.

Lewis A. Friedland's essay makes the case that in the United States it is assumed that political controversies are usually decided by two different power centers that are somewhat, but not entirely, evenly matched. The group whose ideas win in a given election takes the driver's seat, and the other group steps back. The groups obey the agreed-upon rules and cede the power position when they have legitimately lost it. Politics in the United States is assumed to be a battle of ideas that will inform self-governance. Friedland spends the rest of his essay making it clear that this assumption is no longer valid and that Wisconsin has been targeted by the money-powers who have been part of that movement in abeyance that Collins mentions. According to Friedland, Wisconsin is being used as the test case—the "laboratory of oligarchy"—to determine how and to what extent wealth can control political power, especially after the *Citizens United* ruling. Friedland provides a wealth of detail about the people, groups, and processes that have been assembling behind the scenes to conduct covert operations—like secretly trying to change the mission of the University of Wisconsin System, launching an unexpected blow against the public sector, and eliminating a one-hundred-year-old institution like University Extension by autocratic decree—that we have seen already. Friedland lays out the outline, names the players, follows the money, and establishes that this is no longer in any way a fair fight in the marketplace of ideas. Massive amounts of money are being directed into politics at every level of government, and Wisconsin has been targeted as the site for testing the limits. As Walker said, "If we can do it in Wisconsin, we can do it anywhere."[8]

Friedland ends by saying that in 2018 the people of Wisconsin chose to change course and voted Walker out of office. Does that mean that they understand and share the vision of the Wisconsin Idea? Paul Ryan—US congressman from Wisconsin from 1999 to 2019, Republican nominee for vice president of the United States in 2012, and Speaker of the US House of Representatives from 2015 to 2019—is banking on a different vision. In 2019, he used the funds left in his campaign coffers to launch a new foundation, which he headquartered in his hometown of Janesville, Wisconsin. (Ryan has since moved with his family to the Washington, DC, suburbs.) Ryan is on record saying that he would like to indict the entire vision of the progressive movement. The Wisconsin politician named his new venture the American Idea Foundation.[9]

Renewing the Wisconsin Idea for the Future

If we want to know how to renew the Wisconsin Idea, we need to understand that renewing its mechanics is not the first step. We need to create a much clearer vision of the Wisconsin Idea and focus again on the people and democracy of this country.

One of the arguments offered for why the Wisconsin legislature removed tenure protection and self-governance from state statutes is that each campus in the University of Wisconsin System should be run more like a business, with power centralized at the top. Is that the way to renew the Wisconsin Idea? Is that even the best way to run a business?

In their book *Built to Last: Successful Habits of Visionary Companies*, James C. Collins and Jerry I. Porras report about a study they did of the very top-performing companies in a variety of sectors and industries.[10] They surveyed seven hundred chief executive officers of top companies to identify the visionary companies they should study. Every company they studied was at least fifty years old, with an average age in the ninety-year range. They figured that no original, visionary founder could still be credited with leading the vision in organizations of this age. They then narrowed their group to eighteen companies that they studied in depth, both at the time of the book's writing and through archival documents that were decades old. Collins and Porras found that while many companies were successful, the ones that rose to the top had the clearest visions, most broadly understood throughout the organization. Some had vision statements; others did not. The clearer the vision, the more creative the employees could be in pursuing it, the clearer the priorities became in any decision point, and the easier it was for employees to avoid conflict since they had a common touchpoint to which to refer.

Two examples will help to illustrate their point. The vision of the Sony Corporation was straightforward. Their mission was to build electronics. They had a bumpy start building electric rice cookers. But their vision was to change the world's reaction to the words "made in Japan." After World War II, those words conjured an image of cheap and shabby construction. Sony's vision was to make "made in Japan" mean the best-made product on earth. Sony's business success was propelled by its vision. The history of Apple Inc. is similarly instructive. In a 2009 book entitled *Start with Why* and a popular presentation based on it, author and motivational speaker Simon Sinek talked about how Apple became the business that it is and what vision had to do with it.[11]

Although organizations in the United States during the early twentieth century did not yet use the terms *mission* and *vision*, the historical record tells us that the vision that came to be known as the Wisconsin Idea is what created the conditions that got Harvard University's president to proclaim that the University of Wisconsin was "the leading state university" in 1908. If Wisconsin wants to renew the Wisconsin Idea, or if any other public university would like to renew its vision or bolster itself against attack, the citizens of each state need to lead the way to restoring their shared vision. The public university is yours. Our democracy is yours. Until it isn't.

NOTES

1. "The Wisconsin Idea," University of Wisconsin–Madison, https://www.wisc .edu/wisconsin-idea/.

2. Charles Van Hise, quoted in John D. Buenker, *The History of Wisconsin*, vol. 4, *The Progressive Era, 1893–1914* (Madison: State Historical Society of Wisconsin, 1998), 379.

3. Greg Summers, "The Liberal Arts and the Meaning of a University," *Inside Higher Ed*, April 2, 2018, https://www.insidehighered.com/views/2018/04/02/why-uni versity-wisconsin-stevens-point-plans-eliminate-certain-traditional-liberal.

4. Molly Beck, "Scott Walker Sought Changes to Wisconsin Idea, Emails Show After Judge Orders Release of Records," *Wisconsin State Journal*, May 28, 2016, https:// madison.com/wsj/news/local/govt-and-politics/scott-walker-sought-changes-to-wis consin-idea-emails-show-after/article_268eb62f-d548-5a2d-a2f0-ca977dac2346.html.

5. Merle Curti and Vernon Carstensen, *The University of Wisconsin: A History*, vol. 2, *1848–1925* (Madison: University of Wisconsin Press, 1949), 556.

6. Rich Kremer, "Regents Poised to Vote on UW System Restructuring Plan," Wisconsin Public Radio, November 8, 2017, https://www.wpr.org/regents-poised-vote -uw-system-restructuring-plan; WPR Staff and the Associated Press, "UW Regents Approve Merging System Campuses," November 9, 2017, https://www.wpr.org/uw -regents-approve-merging-system-campuses; Karen Herzog, "Faculty Groups Slam UW System President Ray Cross for Secretly Planning Sweeping Restructuring," *Milwaukee Journal Sentinel*, February 6, 2018, https://www.jsonline.com/story/news/education/ 2018/02/06/uw-system-president-ray-cross-has-further-damaged-already-damaged-rela tionship/312031002/.

7. Curti and Carstensen, *University of Wisconsin*, 641.

8. Scott Walker with Marc Thiessen, *Unintimidated: A Governor's Story and a Nation's Challenge* (New York: Sentinel, [2013] 2014), 8.

9. Ruth Conniff, "Paul Ryan's New Foundation Keeps Him in the Spotlight," *Wisconsin Examiner*, October 31, 2019, https://wisconsinexaminer.com/2019/10/31/ paul-ryans-new-foundation-keeps-him-in-the-spotlight/.

10. James C. Collins and Jerry I. Porras, *Built to Last: Successful Habits of Visionary Companies* (New York: HarperBusiness, [1994] 2004).

11. Simon Sinek, *Start with Why: How Great Leaders Inspire Everyone to Take Action* (New York: Portfolio/Penguin, [2009] 2011). See also Simon Sinek, "How Great Leaders Inspire Action," TED talk posted in September 2009, https://www.ted.com/talks/ simon_sinek_how_great_leaders_inspire_action.

Contributors

EMILY AUERBACH is a professor of English in the University of Wisconsin–Madison's Division of Continuing Studies, the cohost of *University of the Air* for Wisconsin Public Radio, the author of *Searching for Jane Austen*, and the director of the UW Odyssey Project (www.odyssey.wisc.edu) since its founding in 2003. She has won numerous teaching, broadcasting, and humanitarian awards for her work over the past three decades, including the Robert Gard Wisconsin Idea Award, an Athena Award, a UW System Teaching Award, the Bartell Award in the Arts, a Governor's Humanities Award, and others.

KAREN BOGENSCHNEIDER is Rothermel–Bascom Emeritus Professor of Human Ecology at the University of Wisconsin–Madison. She founded and directed for twenty-four years the Wisconsin Family Impact Seminars—presentations, discussion sessions, and briefing reports that communicate high-quality, nonpartisan research to state policymakers. She directed for fifteen years the Family Impact Institute that provides training and technical assistance to about twenty states that have conducted more than 225 Family Impact Seminars. Professor Bogenschneider has authored several publications for the policy and research communities, including her books *Family Policy Matters: How Policymaking Affects Families and What Professionals Can Do* (in its third edition) and *Evidence-Based Policymaking: Insights from Policy-Minded Researchers and Research-Minded Policymakers* (coauthored with Thomas Corbett, second edition forthcoming). She has received several national and state awards, including a named professorship at her university. In 2017, she was honored by the Wisconsin state legislature for her leadership of the Family Impact Seminars and her service to the state.

PATRICK J. BRENZEL worked as a university services associate in the Department of Sociology at the University of Wisconsin–Madison for more than

fifteen years. He was inspired to take the lead in developing a highly success-
ful outreach course and public lecture series on the Wisconsin Idea in 2016.
For his role in organizing the course, he received a prestigious University Staff
Recognition Award from the university's College of Letters and Science in 2017.

CAITLIN CIESLIK-MISKIMEN is an assistant professor in the School of
Journalism and Mass Media at the University of Idaho. She received her PhD
in Journalism and Mass Communication from the University of Wisconsin–
Madison, where she also received her MA and BA in journalism. While an
undergraduate, Caitlin first became acquainted with the legacy of Willard
Bleyer through her work on the *Daily Cardinal*, the student newspaper that
counted Bleyer as one of its first reporters and editors.

JANE L. COLLINS is Frances Perkins Professor of Community and Environmental Sociology at the University of Wisconsin–Madison. An anthropologist
by training but a sociologist for the past twenty-four years, Collins has made
scholarly contributions in two primary areas: the sociology of labor, where her
research focuses on how globalization is changing work relationships; and the
economic sociology of value determination, where she studies the way society
draws boundaries between market and nonmarket transactions. She has published five ethnographic books, four edited volumes, and many scholarly articles
and book chapters on the impacts of economic globalization on workers and
local communities. Her most recent book is *The Politics of Value: Three Movements to Change How We Think About the Economy*.

KATHERINE J. CRAMER is the Natalie C. Holton Chair of Letters and Science and a professor in the Department of Political Science at the University
of Wisconsin–Madison, where she has worked for her entire academic career,
since 2000. She is known for her innovative approach to the study of public
opinion, in which she uses methods like inviting herself into the conversations
of groups of people to listen to the way they understand public affairs. She is
the author of three books, including *The Politics of Resentment: Rural Consciousness and the Rise of Scott Walker*.

GWEN DRURY has been reading, writing, and periodically giving talks about
the early history of the Wisconsin Idea since about 2003. Her husband's family
has had at least one relative on the faculty at the University of Wisconsin–
Madison from 1911 until very recently, in fields ranging from agronomy to
pathology to breast cancer research. Their personal stories of the university
inspired her curiosity and eventually her research into the beginnings of the

Wisconsin Idea. She is thrilled to see such a wave of interest in learning more about the Wisconsin Idea and is honored to be included in this book.

LEWIS A. FRIEDLAND is the Vilas Distinguished Achievement Professor in the School of Journalism and Mass Communication at the University of Wisconsin–Madison, where he is also affiliated with the departments of sociology and educational psychology. He holds a PhD in sociology and was originally a student of social theory. For the past two decades his work has focused on the changing structure of US civil society and the public sphere and the rise of contentious politics, in particular, through the impact of the rapidly changing communication ecology. He is a principal investigator, with others, of the political communication ecology of Wisconsin since 2010, work supported by a UW2020 grant, as well as the Knight, Hewlett, and other foundations. He is a former award-winning television news and documentary producer.

MARYO GARD EWELL currently works for the Community Foundation of the Gunnison Valley in Colorado after a long career in arts administration in Connecticut, Illinois, and Colorado. Her career began with a summer job in 1967 as a project assistant for the first grant awarded by the National Endowment for the Arts for rural arts development. It went to the University of Wisconsin College of Agriculture's Office of Community Arts Development, directed by her father, Robert E. Gard. Considering the role of the arts in fulfilling the Wisconsin Idea has been a passion ever since. She was awarded an honorary doctorate by Goucher College and the Selina Ottum Award for community arts leadership by Americans for the Arts, and she remains active in her local arts scene in Gunnison, Colorado.

CHAD ALAN GOLDBERG is a professor of sociology affiliated with the Center for German and European Studies, the George L. Mosse / Laurence A. Weinstein Center for Jewish Studies, and the George L. Mosse Program in History at the University of Wisconsin–Madison. He is also a proud member of the American Federation of Teachers and the American Association of University Professors. He is the author of *Citizens and Paupers: Relief, Rights, and Race, from the Freedmen's Bureau to Workfare* and *Modernity and the Jews in Western Social Thought*. He is currently working on a book about American democracy and cultural pluralism.

J. DAVID HOEVELER is Distinguished Professor of History Emeritus at the University of Wisconsin–Milwaukee. He has written books in American intellectual history, including *James McCosh and the Scottish Intellectual Tradition:*

From Glasgow to Princeton, Creating the American Mind: Intellect and Politics in the Colonial Colleges, and most recently *John Bascom and the Origins of the Wisconsin Idea*.

CURT MEINE is a conservation biologist, environmental historian, and writer based in Sauk County, Wisconsin. He serves as senior fellow with the Aldo Leopold Foundation and Center for Humans and Nature, as research associate with the International Crane Foundation, and as adjunct associate professor at the University of Wisconsin–Madison. Meine has authored and edited several books, including *Aldo Leopold: His Life and Work* and *The Driftless Reader*. He served as onscreen guide in the Emmy Award–winning documentary film *Green Fire: Aldo Leopold and a Land Ethic for Our Time*. In 2018 he was elected a fellow of the Wisconsin Academy of Sciences, Arts and Letters. In his home landscape, he is a founding member of the Sauk Prairie Conservation Alliance.

R. RICHARD WAGNER is a community scholar with a PhD in American history from the University of Wisconsin–Madison. After publishing and presenting on LGBT community history for several decades, he is the author of *We've Been Here All Along: Wisconsin's Early Gay History* and *Coming Out, Moving Forward: Wisconsin's Recent Gay History*.

Index

academic freedom, 5–6, 20–21, 24, 25–26, 37n15, 44n92, 52n144, 54; freedom of speech on campus, 60–62, 73n30

Acanfora v. Montgomery Board of Education (1973), 164

Act 57 (Wisconsin, 2017), 240–41

Act 10 (Wisconsin, 2011), 209–11, 235, 236–38, 238–43, 244–45, 246, 268n19. *See also* collective bargaining rights; labor and employment; unions, trade

Act 23 (Wisconsin, 2011), 245

Adamany, David, 163–65

Adams-Friendship, Wisconsin, 114

Addams, Jane, 101

Adelson, Sheldon, 244

Aderman, Darrell, 112

administrative commissions, quasi-independent, 7, 38n27, 39n37

adult learners. *See* continuing education for adults

Aegis (literary magazine), 81

affirmative action, 67

Affordable Care Act (US, 2010), 246–47

African Americans, 14, 22–23, 42n69, 150, 160, 165, 217, 246; affirmative action, 67; black land-grant colleges, 267n4; civil rights movement, 23, 46n112, 66; farmers, 215; Odyssey Project, 199–200, 203–4

age: senior citizens, 113, 142–43, 199, 210. *See also* children and youth; continuing education for adults

agriculture. *See* Extension programs

Albright, Madeleine, 62

Aldo Leopold Foundation, 121

Alger, Horatio, 212

Allen-Bradley Company, 231

Altmeyer, Arthur J., 38n33, 206, 208, 226

American Anthropologist (journal), 161

American Association of University Professors (AAUP), 6, 25–26, 46n115

American Ballet Theatre, 111

American Civil Liberties Union (ACLU), 152, 254n66

American Economic Foundation, 216

The American Family (TV show), 164

American Federation of State, County, and Municipal Employees (AFSCME), 213, 223n22, 235

American Federation of Teachers Local 3220, 208–9

American Gothic (Wood), 104

American Idea Foundation, 285

American Legislative Exchange Council (ALEC), 28, 43n74, 219–20, 232–33, 268n19; oligarchy, laboratory of, 234, 239–40, 249n17, 250n27, 251n39, 252n43

www.ingramcontent.com/pod-product-compliance
Lightning Source LLC
Chambersburg PA
CBHW071957260326
41914CB00004B/839